Oracle APEX 4.2 F

Learn how to build complex reporting solutions
using Oracle APEX

Vishal Pathak

PUBLISHING

BIRMINGHAM - MUMBAI

Oracle APEX 4.2 Reporting

First published: August 2013

Production Reference: 1200813

Published by Packt Publishing Ltd.
Livery Place
35 Livery Street
Birmingham B3 2PB, UK.

ISBN 978-1-84968-498-9

www.packtpub.com

Cover Image by Artie Ng (artherng@yahoo.com.au)

Credits

Author

Vishal Pathak

Reviewers

Dietmar Aust

Dimitri Gielis

Satishbabu Gunukula

Shivani Kadian

Alex Nuijten

Acquisition Editor

Edward Gordon

Lead Technical Editor

Neeshma Ramakrishnan

Technical Editors

Veena Pagare

Krishnaveni Nair

Vivek Pillai

Kapil Hemnani

Project Coordinators

Priyanka Goel

Arshad Sopariwala

Proofreader

Lesley Harrison

Indexers

Hemangini Bari

Priya Subramani

Graphics

Abhinash Sahu

Ronak Dhruv

Disha Haria

Production Coordinator

Manu Joseph

Cover Work

Manu Joseph

About the Author

Vishal Pathak is an IT professional with over six years of experience of working in the BI space. He is specialized in Oracle APEX and integrating technologies on a heterogeneous system. His skills include an array of technologies such as Oracle APEX, Oracle BI Publisher, OBIEE, BPEL, PL/SQL, JEE, Jasper Reports, jQuery, and HTML 5.

He has a degree in Electrical and Electronics Engineering from the Birla Institute of Technology, Mesra.

He has worked with multinational giants such as TCS, Wipro, Capgemini, and CTS. He has led and worked on many huge Business Intelligence implementations across diverse industry sectors. Some of the major clients that he has worked with include British Telecommunications, Uninor, Department of Social Services (LA DPSS), Marriot and Sony DADC.

He is also a Sun Certified Java Programmer and an Oracle Certified Associate and blogs about his technical thoughts at `http://obiee-oracledb.blogspot.com`.

He lives in India and he loves to trek frequently. Sitting in a secluded part of his garden, thinking about the world and its numerous complexities, and appreciating its beauty is one of his favorite activities.

I dedicate this book to my parents for standing by me all the time, believing in my abilities and helping me build the right thought process that enabled me to finish this noble task successfully. I thank them for their love and wish to get the same for the rest of my life.

About the Reviewers

Dietmar Aust has been working as a freelance consultant in Germany, focusing on Oracle Application Express since 2006. He started working with Oracle in 1997, and spent three years as a consultant for Oracle in Germany. Since then, he helped numerous leading companies in Germany to successfully deliver web-based applications based on the Oracle product stack, including the Internet Application Server, Oracle Portal, and Oracle Reports. He is an Oracle ACE and a regular presenter at various Oracle conferences (ODTUG, OOW, DOAG). He conducts training classes on APEX and had co-authored two books: Oracle APEX und Oracle XE in der Praxis as well as Expert Oracle Application Express. In 2012 he co-founded the company, JDD-Software (`http://jdd-software.com`) in order to build commercial software products for the APEX developer.

You can reach him at `http://www.opal-consulting.de`, `http://daust.blogspot.com` and `http://jdd-software.com` or via email: `dietmar.aust@opal-consulting.de`.

Dimitri Gielis was born in 1978. He lives in Leuven, Belgium with his family. At an early age, Dimitri started with computers (Apple II, IBM XT) and soon he knew he would like to work with computers and especially with databases all his life. In 2000, he began his career by working as a Consultant for Oracle Belgium, where he got in touch with almost every Oracle product. His main expertise was in the database area, but at the same time he was exposed to HTMLDB, which was renamed as Oracle Application Express later on. From the very start, he liked the Oracle database and APEX so much that he never stopped working with it. He then switched to another company to create an Oracle team and do presales so that he could create and manage Oracle Business Unit.

In 2007, he co-founded APEX Evangelists (http://www.apex-evangelists.com). APEX Evangelists is a company, which specializes in providing training, development, and consulting specifically for the Oracle Application Express products. On his blog (http://dgielis.blogspot.com), he shares his thoughts and experiences about Oracle, especially Oracle Application Express. He is a frequent presenter at OBUG Connect, IOUG Collaborate, ODTUG Kaleidoscope, UKOUG conference, and Oracle Open World. He likes to share his experience and meet other people. He's also President of the **OBUG (Oracle Benelux User Group)** APEX SIG.

In 2008, he became an Oracle ACE Director. Oracle ACE Directors are known for their strong credentials as Oracle community enthusiasts and advocates. In 2009, he received the "APEX Developer of the year" award by the Oracle Magazine. In 2012, he was a part of the LA OTN Tour, where he presented various APEX topics.

You can contact Dimitri at dimitri.gielis@apex-evangelists.com.

Satishbabu Gunukula has over 13 years of experience in the IT Industry. He has extensive experience in Oracle and SQLServer Database Technologies, and specialized in high availability Solutions such as Oracle RAC, Data Guard, Grid Control, SQLServer Cluster. He has master's degree in Computer Applications. He has been honored with the prestigious Oracle ACE Award. He has experience in a wide range of products such as Essbase, Hyperion, Agile, SAP Basis, MySQL, Linux, Windows, SharePoint and Business Apps admin, and he has implemented many business critical systems for Fortune 500, 1000 companies. He has reviewed articles for SELECT Journal - the publication of IOUG and reviews books for Packt Publishing. He is an active member in IOUG, Oracle RAC SIG, UKOUG, and OOW and has published many articles and presentations. He shares his knowledge on his websites http://www.oracleracexpert.com and http://www.sqlserver-expert.com.

Shivani Kadian has been in the IT Industry from the last 10 years, primarily working in the Business Intelligence and data warehousing field. She is an experienced BI specialist with good exposure to solution architecting and consulting using Oracle BI technologies.

She is currently working for Cognizant Technology solution as a Lead Architect in the Oracle BI Center of Excellence and is responsible for providing OBIEE consulting to various clients to do BI assessment, architecture roadmap, due diligence, solution design and development of best practices and standards.

Alex Nuijten works as a senior consultant for Ordina Oracle Solutions in the Netherlands. Besides his consultancy work, he conducts training classes, mainly in SQL and PL/SQL. Alex has been a speaker at numerous international conferences, such as ODTUG, Oracle Open World, UKOUG, IOUG, OUGF, and OGH and OBUG. He was a part of the Nordic ACE Directors Tour in 2012.

He is also a frequent contributor at the Oracle Technology Network forum for SQL and PL/SQL. He wrote many articles in Oracle-related magazines, and at regular intervals he writes about Oracle Application Express and Oracle database development on his blog "Notes on Oracle" (nuijten.blogspot.com). Alex is a co-author of the book "Oracle APEX Best Practices" (published by Packt Publishing). In August 2010, Alex was awarded the Oracle ACE Director membership.

www.PacktPub.com

Support files, eBooks, discount offers and more

You might want to visit www.PacktPub.com for support files and downloads related to your book.

Did you know that Packt offers eBook versions of every book published, with PDF and ePub files available? You can upgrade to the eBook version at www.PacktPub.com and as a print book customer, you are entitled to a discount on the eBook copy. Get in touch with us at service@packtpub.com for more details.

At www.PacktPub.com, you can also read a collection of free technical articles, sign up for a range of free newsletters and receive exclusive discounts and offers on Packt books and eBooks.

http://PacktLib.PacktPub.com

Do you need instant solutions to your IT questions? PacktLib is Packt's online digital book library. Here, you can access, read and search across Packt's entire library of books.

Why Subscribe?

- Fully searchable across every book published by Packt
- Copy and paste, print and bookmark content
- On demand and accessible via web browser

Free Access for Packt account holders

If you have an account with Packt at www.PacktPub.com, you can use this to access PacktLib today and view nine entirely free books. Simply use your login credentials for immediate access.

Instant Updates on New Packt Books

Get notified! Find out when new books are published by following @PacktEnterprise on Twitter, or the *Packt Enterprise* Facebook page.

Table of Contents

Preface

Oracle APEX, a 4GL rapid application development technology is gaining ground in the application and reports development community. This is because of the simplicity of architecture and the plethora of objectives that can be achieved with minimum effort. So, when Packt contacted me to write a book that presents Oracle APEX as a Business Intelligence and reporting solution, I had no second thoughts.

The book is stuffed with a number of examples that present the use of jQuery, CSS, and APEX templates to solve some of the most vexing presentation problems and is also laden with examples that demonstrate more decorated reports. The book is also loaded with illustrations that showcase exotic queries and functions to use Oracle database for your reporting requirements.

If we plan to use APEX for reporting then we generally have to integrate it with some existing reporting system. Hence, this book extensively talks about some of the most popular reporting solutions and their integration touch points with APEX. The book also informs its readers about the strengths of each of these technologies. This collective information can enable a reader to make an informed decision to pick the tools which can serve as the extensions of APEX.

Writing this book has been a privilege. It made me think about some interesting scenarios in which APEX can be employed. It helped me articulate and organize my thoughts, gave me a new perspective and helped me understand the numerous ways in which technologies can simplify the art of creation. This book is about getting a newer outlook and evolving as a programmer.

While we have a number of other books that talk about Oracle APEX, this one is intended to show a full throttled demonstration of the tool. We dig into the various possibilities with the product as early as *Chapter 2, Conventional Reporting in APEX*, while discussing the all-important architecture and installation in *Chapter 1, Know Your Horse Before You Ride It*. This book addresses most of the reporting requirements using Oracle APEX and presents an application with every chapter so that the reader can see the code in action. Instead of just introducing the features of APEX, it shows the ways to use them for report creation.

While this book uses and occasionally directs you to Oracle documentation from numerous places, it empowers you to do more and fills the gap between understanding and implementation.

I must thank the whole team at Packt for being immensely supportive in the process of writing this book, and for their valuable suggestions to make the content easily comprehensible.

What this book covers

Chapter 1, Know Your Horse Before You Ride It, lays the foundation of understanding the tool. A deep understanding of this chapter is vital to know the framework of APEX. This chapter talks about the anatomy of APEX and enables the reader to set up an environment.

Chapter 2, Conventional Reporting in APEX, is dedicated to ethnic reporting. The reports introduced in this chapter exist as an out of the box feature of most reporting technologies. This chapter presents ways and means to implement these known reporting requirements in APEX.

Chapter 3, In the APEX Mansion – Interactive Reports, covers interactive reports in detail. These reports let a user do a lot more with a report. The possible tasks include highlighting, filtering, coloring, selecting columns, creating aggregates, and so on. The chapter also introduces the visual delights such as Interactive Report Dashboard. It deals with complex APEX issues such as putting multiple Interactive Reports in a single page of APEX. It also talks about some advanced techniques to create dynamic reports in APEX.

Chapter 4, The Fairy Tale Begins – Advanced Reporting, brings a different flavor to reporting, and clients love this flavor. This chapter deals with images and all kinds of animations along with advanced reporting features. This chapter helps you engineer secret drilldown tunnels and magical mystical paths in APEX reports. This chapter is the difference between an average reporting experience and a user friendly, visually soothing, sensually appealing, and smooth reporting experience.

Chapter 5, Flight to Space Station – Advanced APEX, opens a new dimension to conventional reporting. This chapter presents advanced reporting methods and also shows the use the newest features of APEX 4.2 to standardize report development. The world can exist without these, but merely existing is not fun.

Chapter 6, Using PL/SQL Reporting Packages, Jasper, and Eclipse BIRT, introduces us to an array of technologies which can be used with APEX. These technologies include PL/PDF, PL_FPDF, Apache fop, Apache cocoon, Eclipse BIRT, and Jasper Reports.

Chapter 7, Integrating APEX with OBIEE, presents the use of BI Publisher and OBIEE. The chapter not only manifests the requirements which can be easily implemented in these technologies but also talks about the integration of these technologies with APEX. BI Publisher has been the most popular reporting engine and is integrated with most enterprise solutions. It has been everybody's sweetheart because people do not have to shell out a lot of cash for it. It produces pretty reports, the development environment (MS Word can be used for creating templates) is familiar, and Oracle is coupling it with everything else in the Oracle world. OBIEE, on the other hand, is the grand old lady of BI world. It has been facilitating business examination since the beginning of modern analytic culture.

Chapter 8, All About Web Services and Integrations, combines the best of every tool to make an unbeatable machine. I adore this workshop. Some of the highlights of this chapter include BPEL implementations with human workflows and their use in APEX, integration with technologies such as Oracle R and Google API, understanding various ways to create web services in APEX, and converting Oracle forms to APEX.

Chapter 9, Performance Analysis, is focused on understanding various ways to fine tune APEX applications for a good user experience. One can never have enough of this. This chapter talks ways to tune and debug client-side code such as JavaScript. It also talks about a number of pointers that can help in the development of better APEX applications and finally it talks about the database tools that can help us understand and fix performance bottlenecks.

Appendix, contains sections that are are not vital for understanding the concepts of APEX reporting, but can boost your understanding of the way APEX functions. It includes steps to create PACKT_SCHEMA, SQL Injection, and a talk about database and web interaction in DAD and Listener configurations. This chapter also helps you see the entire flow of commands which are responsible for the generation of all pages in APEX.

What you need for this book

The following is a list of software that you will need to use this book. I wish to point out that the book mostly talks about APEX, so in a typical scenario, you might not need all these products. However, if you wish to master the art of using APEX with almost everything that exists under then Sun, then I suggest that you download all the following products:

- Oracle Database 11gR2
- Oracle APEX 4.2
- WebLogic
- Oracle APEX Listener 2.x
- jQuery
- Google Visualization API
- AnyChart (it is embedded in APEX)
- FusionCharts
- PL/PDF (2.7.0)
- PL_FPDF
- Apache FOP
- Apache Cocoon
- Jasper Reports
- Eclipse BIRT
- OBIEE 11.1.1.6
- BI Publisher 11.1.1.6
- JXplorer
- SoapUI
- BPEL
- SAP Crystal Reports
- Google Places API
- Oracle R Enterprise
- Oracle Analytic Workspace Manager
- MS Word (For BI Publisher templates)

Who this book is for

The book is intended for all those who believe that making technologies work in harmony and using their strengths to meet the objectives is a potent challenge. This book is for you if you wish to spring into the action of APEX development from the time you hold this book in your hand. The book is designed for innovative architects and enthusiastic developers.

Conventions

In this book, you will find a number of styles of text that distinguish between different kinds of information. Here are some examples of these styles, and an explanation of their meaning.

Code words in text are shown as follows: "We can include other contexts through the use of the `include` directive."

A block of code is set as follows:

```
SELECT account_status
FROM dba_users
WHERE username = 'XDB';
```

When we wish to draw your attention to a particular part of a code block, the relevant lines or items are set in bold:

```
{
var xmlhttp = new XMLHttpRequest();
xmlhttp.open("POST", "http://localhost:9704/xmlpserver/services/
PublicReportService_v11",true);
xmlhttp.setRequestHeader("Content-Type","text/xml; charset=utf-8");
```

Any command-line input or output is written as follows:

```
C:\ >java -jar <Directory holding apex.war>\apex.war configdir
```

New terms and **important words** are shown in bold. Words that you see on the screen, in menus or dialog boxes for example, appear in the text like this: "clicking on the **Next** button moves you to the next screen".

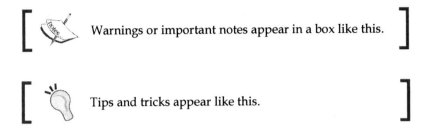

> [Warnings or important notes appear in a box like this.]

> [Tips and tricks appear like this.]

Reader feedback

Feedback from our readers is always welcome. Let us know what you think about this book—what you liked or may have disliked. Reader feedback is important for us to develop titles that you really get the most out of.

To send us general feedback, simply send an e-mail to feedback@packtpub.com, and mention the book title via the subject of your message.

If there is a topic that you have expertise in and you are interested in either writing or contributing to a book, see our author guide on www.packtpub.com/authors.

Customer support

Now that you are the proud owner of a Packt book, we have a number of things to help you to get the most from your purchase.

Downloading the example code

You can download the example code files for all Packt books you have purchased from your account at http://www.packtpub.com. If you purchased this book elsewhere, you can visit http://www.packtpub.com/support and register to have the files e-mailed directly to you.

Errata

Although we have taken every care to ensure the accuracy of our content, mistakes do happen. If you find a mistake in one of our books—maybe a mistake in the text or the code—we would be grateful if you would report this to us. By doing so, you can save other readers from frustration and help us improve subsequent versions of this book. If you find any errata, please report them by visiting http://www.packtpub.com/submit-errata, selecting your book, clicking on the **errata submission form** link, and entering the details of your errata. Once your errata are verified, your submission will be accepted and the errata will be uploaded on our website, or added to any list of existing errata, under the Errata section of that title. Any existing errata can be viewed by selecting your title from http://www.packtpub.com/support.

Piracy

Piracy of copyright material on the Internet is an ongoing problem across all media. At Packt, we take the protection of our copyright and licenses very seriously. If you come across any illegal copies of our works, in any form, on the Internet, please provide us with the location address or website name immediately so that we can pursue a remedy.

Please contact us at copyright@packtpub.com with a link to the suspected pirated material.

We appreciate your help in protecting our authors, and our ability to bring you valuable content.

Questions

You can contact us at questions@packtpub.com if you are having a problem with any aspect of the book, and we will do our best to address it.

1
Know Your Horse Before You Ride It

The book presents **Oracle Application Express (APEX)**, as a reporting solution. Oracle APEX is a 4GL technology based on PL/SQL that helps in rapid application development. It can easily be integrated with a number of reporting technologies and also has extensive reporting functionalities of its own. We will talk about these subjects in this book. In this chapter, we will see the practical details of APEX and try to understand the process by which the APEX engine processes our requests. A clear answer to this question will not only empower you to cook your own recipes in APEX but will also make you more confident in the development process and will cut your debugging time.

 I wish to inform you that the code throughout the book has been tested on Internet Explorer 9.0, so please work with Internet Explorer 9.0.

We will cover the following in this chapter:

- Advantages of APEX
- APEX web server configurations
- Installing APEX Listener on the WebLogic server and creating an APEX workspace
- Understanding the APEX URL and having a brief look at session management, cache management, and debugging
- Understanding APEX page submissions and using DB audit trail to track APEX requests from the backend

- Considering some of the lesser known alternatives of `mod_plsql`
- Zones of caution: The *A pessimist's view of APEX* section describes the subjects about which an APEX developer should be cautious

What is really new in the new avatar of APEX?

APEX (APplication EXpress) is a 4GL RAD tool and is it a true incarnation of its name. Its strength lies in its architecture, which greatly minimizes the number of layers in the enterprise solution and helps a developer to minimize his development efforts by generating the façade and the layouts of the application on its own. It is driven by a metadata repository which stores the necessary objects required for the tool to function. This repository is stored in the database.

Some of the other advantages of APEX are:

- The developer does not have to explicitly code the underlying HTML and CSS, and he can still get a glittering pretty application.
- The wizard-based development approach further simplifies development efforts.
- Inherent grouping of logical elements helps to prevent the code from becoming messy and error-prone.
- The approach of encapsulating the code in applications, pages, regions, and items is intuitive because it is in sync with the final visible output.
- The fact that APEX is shipped along with all versions of the database starting with 10gR2, and the fact that no external environment is required for its development, makes it very cost effective.
- Since APEX sleeps in the database's house, its code is backed up with the regular backup of the DB and there is always a possibility of rollback.
- APEX lets us design the lock for our house. The authentication and authorization schemes can be custom-written, giving the developer all opportunities to protect its brainchild. Integration with **LDAP** and Oracle SSO is much easier in the newer versions. **AJAX** rhymes with APEX and both in word and deed.
- APEX codes the layout for us but we can tinker with it if the need be.
- Entire business logic is written by the developer in PL/SQL so that all the opportunities to code the best solution rest in the hands of the coder.

I could go on and on and I haven't even started on the newest features in APEX 4.x.

Let me briefly pen the reasons for you to go for the newest avatar of APEX:

- **Plugins**: It opens a plethora of opportunities as it lets the development community contribute in adding new features to the tool.
- **Team development**: Get a team and start playing. APEX gives you the interface for the management of your development.
- **Websheets**: Developers, pack your bags. This feature lets the business users design their own pages, and APEX does all the work from creation of DB objects to making frontend reports for them.
- **Dynamic actions**: Why code when working on APEX? Create dynamic actions, and APEX codes the JavaScript for you.
- **RESTful web services**: Rest is the new mantra in APEX. Send the HTTP requests and get web service responses. All modern day web services including those of Google and Yahoo can now be accessed using RESTful web services.
- **APEX now has ears**: APEX Listener is a complete JEE approach of working on APEX applications. It makes direct JDBC connections to the DB.
- **Calendars**: Playboy calendars will get tough competition from the pretty APEX calendars. These are new kinds of reports that both the developers and the end users love.
- **Error Handling**: To err is human, to present a user friendly statement for the error is APEX.

Wait… there is more:

- **Better bricks, better building**: New improved items with features such as auto complete.
- **From papyrus to paper, from JavaScript to jQuery**: Inbuilt jQuery lets you do more with less code.
- **Beauty lies in the eyes of the beholder and in the APEX charts**: The newer version has been fused with **AnyChart 6**—newer types of charts such as **gantt** and **maps** are now available.
- **Improved interactive report**: Our very own **interactive report** from previous versions has been improved.
- **Our workshop gets a makeover**: Application builder has a new glittery feel. Items can be dragged-and-dropped from one place to another. Almost feels like a small computer game.
- **Advanced skin care**: Improved and ameliorated themes and templates are available now.

APEX configurations

Apex needs a web server to fulfill web requests. We will dedicate the next few pages to understanding each one of the possible web server configurations with APEX.

The following diagram shows the various types, and classification of APEX configurations:

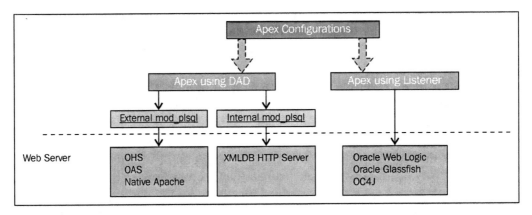

APEX configuration using DAD

Under this section we will check out two configurations (external and internal mod_plsql) of apex DAD.

DAD is Database Access Descriptor. DADs are the means of transporting HTTP requests to the database. DADs have the authority to run under the privileges of a schema configured at the time of their creation. Once authorized, a DAD becomes the king of his fort and can execute any procedure in his kingdom. DADs can be created by using mod_plsql. mod_plsql, formerly known as **Oracle PL/SQL Cartridge** or **Oracle Web Agent (OWA)**, has been the heart of APEX systems. mod_plsql, an extension module of Apache HTTP server, converts the HTTP request to database queries and vice versa. **mod_plsql** has a database connection pool which helps better performance.

 mod_psql is also a part of SQL Developer and is used for the OWA output pane that enables us to see the HTML output in the SQL Worksheet.

The mod_plsql configurations are of two types:

- **Internal mod_plsql** – This configuration is internal to the Oracle database and mod_plsql is a part of **Embedded PLSQL Gateway (EPG)**

- **External mod_plsql** – This configuration of mod_plsql is external to the database and can be done only using Apache-based web servers such as native Apache, OHS, and OAS

The Oracle 11*g* installation, by default, creates a DAD called `apex`. The preinstalled APEX in 11*g* is an internal mod_plsql configuration which uses, out of the box, the embedded PL/SQL gateway and the `ANONYMOUS` schema. This DAD is authorized to execute any procedure on which the `ANONYMOUS` schema has the `execute` privileges.

Internal mod_plsql configuration

Let me talk a little about the flow in this configuration. When a user opens the APEX URL, a HTTP/HTTPS request is sent to the **XML DB HTTP server** which is a part of **XMLDB**. This request then flows through **EPG** to mod_plsql. mod_plsql authorizes the request using the `wwv_flow_epg_include_modules.authorize` procedure. The APEX engine, in combination with the OWA web toolkit and user-defined stored procedures and functions, generates the response HTML. Calls to the user-defined functions and procedures are coded by the developer in the APEX application. Once the response HTML has been generated, mod_plsql gives the response back to the user using XMLDB HTTP server. I have drawn this process flow in the following diagram:

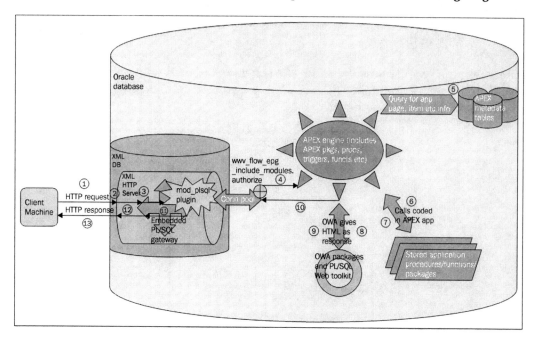

Now let us see the process to configure the XML DB HTTP server (also called XMLDB protocol server), bundled with database, to work on port 8080.

The port on which the inbuilt XML HTTP server operates, can be configured using the DBMS_XDB.sethttpport procedure as shown in the following screenshot:

```
SQL> BEGIN
  2     DBMS_XDB.sethttpport (8080);
  3  END;
  4  /

PL/SQL procedure successfully completed.
```

The account status of the XDB schema should be OPEN. Check this using the following SQL script:

```
SELECT account_status
FROM dba_users
WHERE username = 'XDB';
```

Downloading the example code

You can download the example code files for all Packt books you have purchased from your account at http://www.packtpub.com. If you purchased this book elsewhere, you can visit http://www.packtpub.com/support and register to have the files e-mailed directly to you.

Enter your XDB schema password (the XDB schema is created with database installation) after opening the URL: http://<hostname>:8080. You should be able to see the following page:

Oracle XML DB protocol server maintains a shared pool of sessions, but these connections are to handle the client web requests. Each protocol connection or client request is associated with one session from the pool of the protocol server. After a connection is closed, the session is put back into the shared pool and can be used to serve later connections.

To enable the Oracle XML DB repository to use secure HTTP connections (HTTPS), a DBA must configure the database accordingly. This configuration includes the setting of the `http2-port` and `http2-protocol` parameters, enabling the HTTP Listener to use SSL, and enabling the launching of the **TCPS dispatcher**. After doing this, the DBA must restart the database and the Listener.

Now let us check the DADs configured in the EPG. To do this, we will first have to compile the `Chapter1` package in PACKT_SCHEMA. If you have not already created PACKT_SCHEMA, the user may check the *Steps to create PACKT_SCHEMA* section of the *Appendix* for the steps to do this. Execute the following command from SQLPLUS as SYSDBA to create CHAPTER1 package.. Make sure that you are running SQLPLUS from the directory that holds `4-98-9_01_chapter1.sql`. Put PACKT_SCHEMA in the `Enter the schema in which you want to compile this code:` prompt:

```
SQL> @4-98-9_01_chapter1
```

Now execute the following two statements:

```
SQL> set serveroutput on
SQL> exec packt_schema.chapter1.get_dad_list();
```

The output will list `apex` along with the other DADs configured in the EPG. Run the following statement to find the configured database username for the `apex` DAD:

```
SQL> exec packt_schema.chapter1.chk_apex_dad_usr_nam();
```

You should get the output as shown in the following screenshot:

```
SQL> exec packt_schema.chapter1.chk_apex_dad_usr_nam();
ANONYMOUS

PL/SQL procedure successfully completed.
```

The *Database and web interaction in DAD and Listener configurations* section of the *Appendix* demonstrates the process of creating a DAD and assigning privileges to it. The demonstration also includes the use of this DAD for database and web interaction. Principally, APEX does the exact same thing. The difference is that APEX does it on a bigger scale.

Using the configurations done in the DAD, the EPG determines the database account to be used to fulfill the request, and authenticates the request based on the `request-validation-function` attribute configured for the DAD.

The EPG configuration of any database can be found out by running the following script:

`<OracleHome>\RDBMS\ADMIN\epgstat.sql`

You should get the output after running this script, as shown in the following screenshot:

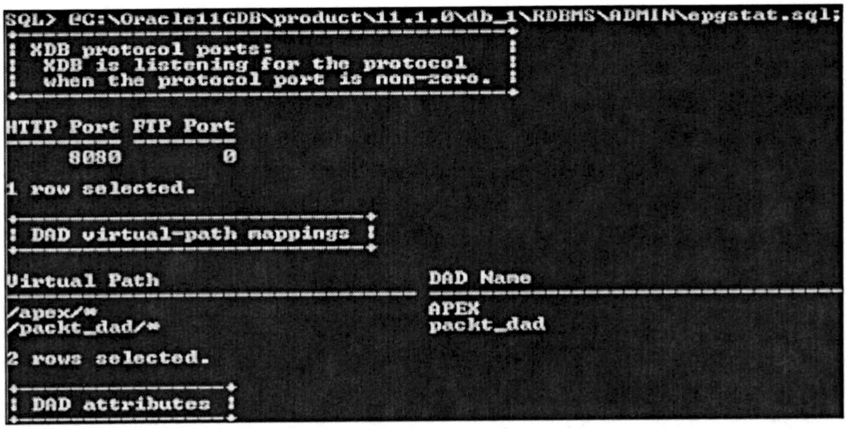

External mod_plsql configuration

Depending on the requirements, we can choose, from a number of possible server combinations for external mod_plsql configuration. The possibilities are: Native Apache, **Oracle HTTP Server (OHS)**, **Oracle Application Server (OAS)**, or OHS + WebLogic Server.

Let me now talk about the flow in this configuration and how it is different from internal mod_plsql configuration. The only difference between external and internal mod_plsql configuration is that the mod_plsql plugin is external in the external configuration. So, if the EPG configuration (internal mod_plsql configuration) is a perfect human, then external configuration is a human with its heart beating outside the body. That may seem like a weird analogy, but that's what it is. Since mod_plsql is a module of Apache HTTP server, and since OHS is based on Apache, and since OHS is a component of OAS, both OHS and OAS can also be used for external mod_plsql configuration. OHS also offers HTTP services in **OFM (Oracle Fusion Middleware)** and can be configured in front of the WebLogic Server. So it is possible to configure OHS + WebLogic and then use the **mod_plsql** in OHS for the DAD configuration.

It is important to point out that WebLogic is certified to host APEX Listener so the Listener configuration can be another way to use WebLogic to access the APEX engine.

The following diagram shows the external mod_plsql configuration:

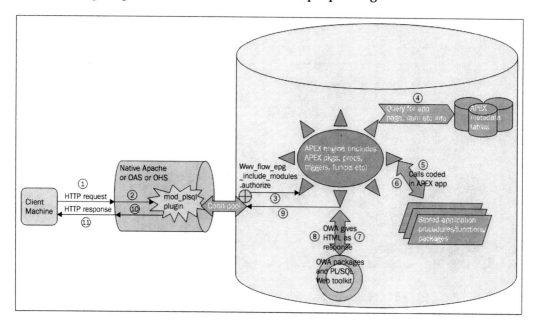

External Apache has configuration files called `httpd.config` and `dads.conf`.

`dads.conf` holds the name of the DAD of APEX. The `dads.conf` file has a virtual path mentioned in the `Location` directive. The URL of external mod_plsql configuration looks like the following:

```
http://<hostname>:<port>/<virtual_path_in_location_directive>/
f?p=app_id:page_no:session_id:Request:Debug:ClearCache:Params:ParamVa
lues:PrinterFriendly
```

The following is a screenshot of a typical `dads.conf` file. Check out the similarities between the `dads.conf` file and the attributes configured for EPG:

```
 1  # =============================================================
 2  #                 mod_plsql DAD Configuration File
 3  # =============================================================
 4  # 1. Please refer to dads.README for a description of this file
 5  # =============================================================
 6  #
 7  # Note: This file should typically be included in your plsql.conf file with
 8  # the "include" directive.
 9
10  # Hint: You can look at some sample DADs in the dads.README file
11
12  # =============================================================
13
14  Alias /i/ "D:\Oracle\product\10.2.0\db1\Apache\Apache\images/"
15  AddType text/xml          xbl
16  AddType text/x-component              htc
17
18  <Location /pls/apex>
19    Order deny,allow
20    PlsqlDocumentPath docs
21    AllowOverride None
22    PlsqlDocumentProcedure        wwv_flow_file_manager.process_download
23    PlsqlDatabaseConnectString    localhost:1521:ORCL
24    PlsqlNLSLanguage              AMERICAN_AMERICA.AL32UTF8
25    PlsqlAuthenticationMode       Basic
26    SetHandler                    pls_handler
27    PlsqlDocumentTablename        wwv_flow_file_objects$
28    PlsqlDatabaseUsername         APEX_PUBLIC_USER
29    PlsqlDefaultPage              apex
30    PlsqlDatabasePassword         APEX_PUBLIC_USER_PASSWORD
31    PlsqlRequestValidationFunction wwv_flow_epg_include_modules.authorize
32    Allow from all
33  </Location>
```

Directives such as `PlsqlRequestValidationFunction` (refer the previous screenshot), which are allowed in the context of the `Location` directive, help us configure the attributes which get configured in EPG using the `dbms_epg` package. Note that the `wwv_flow_epg_include_modules.authorize` procedure is declared as the validation function in the `dads.conf` file. The same function is also configured as the value of the `request-validation-function` attribute of the `apex` DAD, which is created along with the installation of Oracle 11*g*. We can check this out using the following script:

SQL> exec packt_schema.chapter1.chk_apex_req_val_funct();

The `wwv_flow_epg_include_modules.authorize` procedure is called before creating an APEX session. This function in turn calls the `wwv_flow_epg_include_mod_local` function. The Gods of APEX have given you the freedom to invoke our own procedures using the `apex` DAD. All functions on which the ANONYMOUS schema have `execute` privileges, and have been declared in the `wwv_flow_epg_include_mod_local` function, can be invoked using the DAD of `apex`. Let us now have a look at the `wwv_flow_epg_include_mod_local` function:

```
create or replace function wwv_flow_epg_include_mod_local(
    procedure_name in varchar2)
```

```
return boolean
is
begin
    --return false;
    if upper(procedure_name) in (
         '') then
        return TRUE;
    else
        return FALSE;
    end if;
end wwv_flow_epg_include_mod_local;
```

To invoke the procedures from apex DAD, comment the `return false;` statement and mention the procedure name which you want to invoke using the apex DAD in the `in` list of the `if` statement.

If you wish to call your own procedures in Listener configuration, then you can configure the same in the `defaults.xml` file of the Listener. A demonstration of calling a custom procedure in Listener configuration is shown in the *The Listener configuration* section of *Appendix*.

Similarly, we can see that other attributes configured in the EPG DAD are also configured in the external DAD configuration using the `Location` directive of the `dads.conf` file. In the previous screenshot of `dads.conf` file, the directive `<Location>` has `/pls/apex` as the virtual path. So you would have the following URL for your apex DAD with this configuration file:

```
http://<hostname>:<port>/pls/apex/f?p=4550
```

 You can configure more than one DAD in this configuration file by using multiple `<Location>` directives.

`Httpd.conf` is another important character in the story. If `dads.conf` is a super hero, then `httpd.conf` is super hero's brother and has got his own set of powers. It can hide the trademark APEX URL by helping you set virtual hosts. The `RewriteRule` directive in `httpd.conf` takes the concept of concealing the URL to a whole new level. It lets you define patterns of characters and if the URL entered by the user matches the pattern in this directive, then it will redirect to a page which is also defined in the directive. So you can have any URL for APEX, define its pattern in the `RedirectRule` directive, and then have your APEX application's URL as the URL to which the server will redirect.

APEX Listener configuration

We will be using the Listener configuration in all our discussions henceforth. This is because the Listener is the latest fashion and everyone is talking about it. It is in line with the whole architecture of database server and database Listener. The Listener is Oracle's direction for the future.

We have already seen what mod_plsql can do, so let's look at Listener as well.

Listener is a JEE replacement of mod_plsql and performs all the functions of mod_ plsql. These include calling OWA and web toolkit functions to generate the HTML for APEX pages and accepting client requests. Just like mod_plsql was maintaining its connection pool, Listener also maintains a connection pool but it is a JDBC connection pool. Its URL is similar to the EPG URL with the difference that the apex DAD of EPG is replaced by apex web application context. So, it is important to realize that the look of the URL might not have been affected, but the underlying architecture is completely different. DADs are not used here at all. The configuration files and the method of implementation of various features are also completely different. For example, the validation function here is defined in the security. requestValidationFunction parameter of the defaults.xml file. In case of EPG configuration, it is defined in the EPG DAD attribute called request-validation-function. In the case of external mod_plsql configuration, the validation function is in the Location directive of the dads.conf file and the name of the directive holding it is PlsqlRequestValidationFunction. Let's have a look at the architecture now:

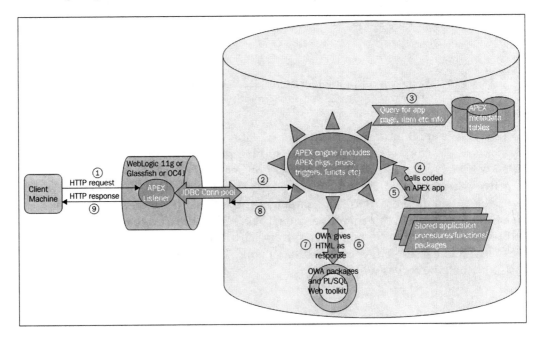

The APEX Listener does not have Apache in any form, so it doesn't have mod_plsql. In fact, APEX Listener is built for letting JEE-based web servers harness the powers of APEX and to increase APEX's acceptability.

Installing APEX engine and Listener

Till now, we have discussed all possible configurations of APEX. This section is dedicated to setting the APEX environment using the APEX Listener configuration on the WebLogic Server. The assumption here is that you have Oracle database 11.1.0.6.0 or higher installed on your machine. If not, then get the installer from `http://www.oracle.com/technetwork/database/enterprise-edition/downloads/index.html`.

We will discuss the following in this section:

- Installing the APEX engine in the database
- Creating a WebLogic domain and starting the servers
- Setting the APEX Listener
- Creating the APEX workspace

Installing the APEX engine in the database

Perform the following steps for installing the APEX engine in the database:

1. Create a tablespace for APEX. Change the path of the data file according to your machine:

   ```
   CREATE TABLESPACE apex_tablespace datafile 'C:\Oracle11GDB\
   oradata\orcl\oracle_apex_datafile.dbf'
   SIZE 500 m
   autoextend ON maxsize 500 m
   ```

2. If you are using an existing tablespace then use the following script to check if sufficient space is available for APEX:

   ```
   SQL> @4-98-9_01_chk_free_space_in_tablespace
   ```

   275 MB of space is required in APEX tablespace and 100 MB of space is required in the SYSTEM tablespace.

   Besides this, 278 MB of space is required on the filesystem if we use the English only download (apex_4.2_en.zip) and 935 MB of memory is required if we use the full download (apex_4.2.zip).

3. Run the following query to get the version of PL/SQL Web Toolkit. This version should be greater than 10.1.2.0.6:

```
SELECT owa_util.get_version
FROM dual;
```

4. Go to the command prompt and silence the Listener. Enter the following command in the command prompt:

```
lsnrctl stop
```

5. Check the Listener status:

```
lsnrctl status
```

You should get the following error messages in the console:

```
TNS-12541: TNS:no listener
 TNS-12560: TNS:protocol adapter error
  TNS-00511: No listener
```

6. Open the command prompt and navigate to the apex directory under the directory in which apex_4.2.1_en.zip is unzipped.

7. Connect to SQLPLUS in this command prompt window as sysdba, and execute the following command:

```
@apexins apex_tablespace apex_tablespace temp /i/
```

8. The previous script installs APEX. You should get the following message after the installation is finished:

```
...Exiting validate 18:09:31
timing for: Validate Installation
Elapsed: 00:01:56.14
timing for: Development Installation
Elapsed: 00:14:58.71
Disconnected from Oracle Database 11g Enterprise Edition Release 11.2.0.1.0 - 64
bit Production
With the Partitioning, OLAP, Data Mining and Real Application Testing options
```

A logfile is created in the directory from which the installation was started (the directory in which we unzipped apex_4.2.1_en.zip). The name format of this log is installYYYY-MM-DD_HH24-MI-SS.log. This file will have the following message:

```
Thank you for installing Oracle Application Express.
Oracle Application Express is installed in the APEX_040200 schema.
```

9. Run the following query to validate the installation after connecting to the database as `sysdba`. The status should be `VALID`:

```
SELECT status
FROM dba_registry
WHERE comp_id = 'APEX';
```

10. Run the following script after logging in as `sysdba` to set the password for the `ADMIN` user. The `ADMIN` user will be used to create the APEX workspace and for other admin activities. This script exists under `<apex_4.1_en_Unzipped_Location>/apex` along with `apexins.sql`.

```
@apxchpwd
```

11. Restart the Listener. This is done in the command prompt and not in the SQL prompt:

```
lsnrctl start
```

12. Unlock `APEX_PUBLIC_USER` and change its password after connecting as `sys`:

```
alter user APEX_PUBLIC_USER account unlock;
alter user APEX_PUBLIC_USER identified by new_password;
```

13. Run the following commands. This is to ensure that the password of `APEX_PUBLIC_USER` does not expire every few days:

```
CREATE PROFILE
    apex_public_user_profile
LIMIT
    PASSWORD_LIFE_TIME UNLIMITED;
ALTER USER apex_public_user PROFILE apex_public_user_profile;
```

Creating a WebLogic domain and starting the servers

WebLogic will hold our APEX Listener. So, all the action will take place inside this. We can create a domain that has an admin server, a node manager, and a managed server, and configure the managed server to hold the APEX Listener. The managed server can be controlled from the admin server using node manager. We will, however, create a domain with just the Admin server. This reduces the memory requirement and suits a desktop class installation. APEX Listener will be deployed on the Admin server.

 The process described here is to install WebLogic—the generic version of 11*g* on Windows 7 OS and it is assumed that the Oracle 11*g* database is already installed on your Windows 7 box.

Perform the following steps for creating a WebLogic domain and starting the servers:

1. Download WebLogic 11*g* from `http://www.oracle.com/technetwork/middleware/ias/downloads/wls-main-097127.html`.

2. Click on the **Install** button. The wizard will help you install WebLogic on your machine.

3. Click on **QuickStart** in the newly installed program group of WebLogic and then click on **Getting started with Weblogic Server**.

4. This will open **Fusion Middleware Configuration Wizard**. Select **Create a new weblogic domain** in it, and click on **Next.**

5. Select **Generate a domain configured automatically to support the following products**. The **Basic weblogic server domain** checkbox will be checked by default. Do not select any other checkbox. Click on **Next**.

6. Give the name and location of the domain which you want to create. This can be any fancy name. I gave `apex_weblogic_domain`. Fill these values and click on **Next**.

7. Give the username and password for the administrator of this domain and click on **Next**. My username is `apex_weblogic_admin`.

8. Select the **Development mode** radio button and select **Sun SDK** as the JDK.

9. Select the **Administration Server** checkbox.

10. If you want your Listener to listen on secured connections using HTTPS, then select the **SSL enabled** checkbox and give the port number on which this managed server will listen to HTTPS requests.

If you do not want your APEX Listener to listen to HTTP requests, then do not give a port number in the **Listener port** textbox. I have not opted for HTTPS. Click on **Next**.

11. All set. Click on the **Create** button to create a domain for your APEX Listener.

To start the Admin server, go to WebLogic program group where you will see your newly created domain. Get in it to find the link to start the Admin server. Alternately, you could navigate to <MiddlewareWeblogicHome>\ user_projects\domains\apex_weblogic_domain\bin in command prompt and execute:

```
startWebLogic
```

apex_weblogic_domain is the name of my domain in the previous path. You should be able to see the following message after starting WebLogic admin server:

```
<Jun 19, 2012 11:04:55 PM IST> <Notice> <WebLogicServer> <BEA-000331> <Started t
he WebLogic Server Administration Server "AdminServer" for domain "APEX_Domain"
running in development mode.>
<Jun 19, 2012 11:04:55 PM IST> <Notice> <WebLogicServer> <BEA-000365> <Server st
ate changed to RUNNING.>
<Jun 19, 2012 11:04:55 PM IST> <Notice> <WebLogicServer> <BEA-000360> <The serve
r started in RUNNING mode.>
```

Setting the APEX Listener

The prerequisites are:

- You should have Java 6 Update 20 JDK or higher. Go to command prompt and write the following to check this:

    ```
    C:\> Java -version
    ```

- You should have Java Servlet Specification 2.3 or higher, and WebLogic 11*g* R1 certainly has it.

APEX Listener can work in standalone mode and can also be hosted on Glassfish or OC4J or WebLogic. It uses Grizzly to build a scalable web server for itself in standalone mode. Running Listener in standalone mode is not supported in a production environment.

More info on Grizzly can be found at:

http://grizzly.java.net/

The HTTP server API of Grizzly can be found at:

https://grizzly.java.net/docs/2.3/apidocs/org/glassfish/grizzly/http/ server/HttpServer.html

Grizzly can be embedded with other applications to provide HTTP services:

`https://blogs.oracle.com/oleksiys/entry/grizzly_2_0_httpserver_api`

Configuring and deploying APEX Listener on the WebLogic domain

1. Go to the `<Weblogic domain root directory>\config` directory and edit the `config.xml` file in it. Add the `<enforce-valid-basic-auth-credentials>false</enforce-valid-basic-auth-credentials>` tag just before the closing the `</security-configuration>` tag. This is important for the Listener to function properly.

2. Execute the following command:

   ```
   C:\> java -jar <path in which you unzipped the listener>\apex_listener.2.0.1.64.14.25\apex.war
   ```

   You will be prompted to enter the location of the configuration directory. Your Listener configuration files will be stored in the directory which you put here. You will also be prompted to put the database details and the credentials of the APEX_PUBLIC_USER schema along with the credentials of schema for RESTful service configuration. The following screenshot shows the configuration when I executed the previous command:

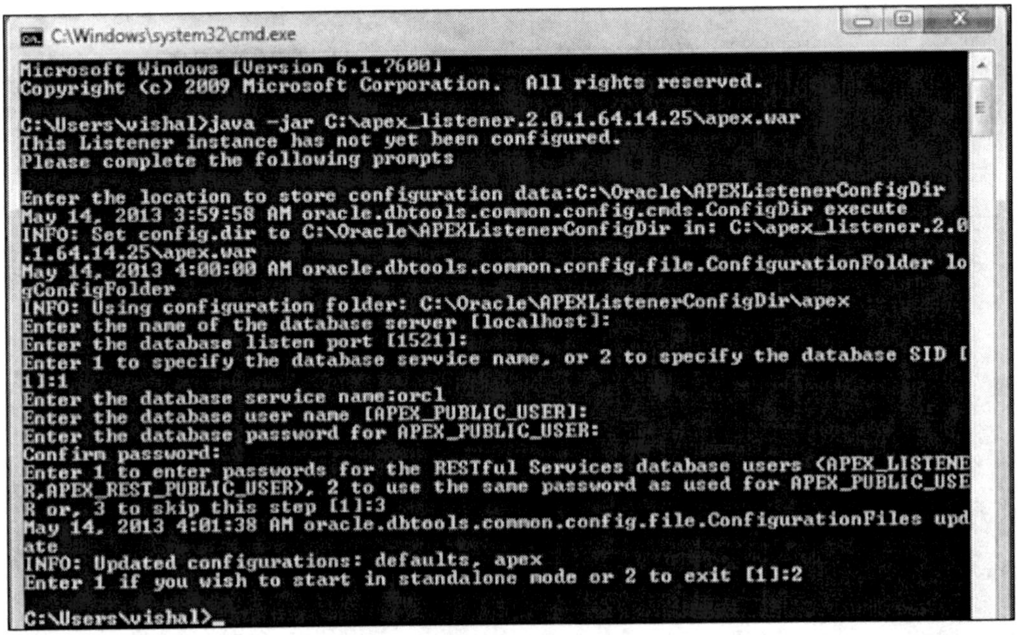

The `jar` command will work only if the `Path` environment variable is set to the `bin` directory of your JDK. An example of bin directory is: `C:\Program Files\Java\jdk1.6.0_26\bin`.

3. Start your WebLogic Admin server and open your WebLogic domain console. The link for this is present in your WebLogic program menu under your domain. It has the following form:

   ```
   http://<hostname>:<port_number_of_admin_server>/console
   ```

4. Enter your WebLogic Admin credentials. You had created these in step 7 of the *Creating a WebLogic domain and starting the servers* section.

5. Click on the **Deployments** link under **Domain Structure** panel on the left-hand side of the console.

6. Click on **Install** and select `apex.war`. We had configured `apex.war` in step 2.

7. Select **Install the deployment as an application** radio button and click on the **Next** button.

8. Install on the Admin server.

9. Select the following security model and click on the **Next** button:

   Custom roles: Use roles that are defined in the administration console; use policies that are defined in the deployment descriptor.

10. Keep the other default settings and click on **Next**, and then click on **Finish.**

11. Click on the **Save** button after everything is done.

12. Open the command prompt and run the following command. This will generate a `.war` file called `i.war` that will help APEX to use static resources such as images, logos, SWF, CSS, and JavaScript files which are necessary for APEX to work.

    ```
    C:\> java -jar <Directory in which listener is unzipped>\apex.war
    static <Directory in which APEX is unzipped>\apex\images
    ```

You should get an output as shown in the following screenshot:

13. The previous command will create `i.war` in the directory from which you executed the command. I executed the command from the `C:\Users\vishal` directory shown in the previous screenshot and got `i.war` in the same directory. Install `i.war` just the way you did `apex.war`.

Creating APEX workspace

Perform the following step for creating APEX workspace:

1. Log in to the admin console using ADMIN as the username and INTERNAL as the workspace. The password of the ADMIN user can be set using `<Directory in which APEX is unzipped>\apex\apxchpwd.sql`. The URL for logging in to the INTERNAL workspace is:

   `http://<host>:<port>/apex_weblogic/f:p=4550`

2. Click on **Manage Workspaces** and create a new workspace. Name it PACKT_WORKSPACE.

3. Select **Yes** in the **Re-use existing schema?** dropdown and put PACKT_SCHEMA in the **Schema Name** text box. If you haven't created PACKT_SCHEMA yet, then go the *Steps to create PACKT_SCHEMA* section in the *Appendix* to find the steps of creating this schema.

4. Put PACKT_ADMIN in the **Administrator Username** textbox, set its password, and put an e-mail address.

5. Click on the **Create Workspace** button to create the workspace.

You can also get a free test drive at `http://apex.oracle.com`. You can register here, and Oracle gives you a workspace of your own.

Understanding the APEX URL

The URL in APEX is related to sessions, debugging, caching, requesting actions, and passing variables. The URL is also closely coupled with the architecture of APEX and is dependent on the server configuration. So let's see it all.

 Colons are a part of the URL and hold special meaning in the URL. Hence, the values passed by the developer cannot contain colons. We will see more on this in the *Passing values and navigation* section.

A typical URL is as follows `http://<hostname>:<port>/dad_name_or_web_context/f?p=app_id:page_no:session_id: Request:Debug:ClearCache:Params:ParamValues:PrinterFriendly`.

Let's dissect this URL in the following sections.

The protocol

Consider the following example:

`**http**://<hostname>:<port>/dad_name_or_web_context/f?p=app_id:page_no:session_id:Request:Debug:ClearCache:Params:ParamValues:PrinterFriendly`

`http` is the protocol here. If the **SSL (Secured Socket Layer)** is enabled, then the protocol will be `https`. The protocol depends on the web server configuration.

The hostname and port number

Consider the following link:

`http://**<hostname>:<port>**/dad_name_or_web_context/f?p=app_id:page_no:session_id:Request:Debug:ClearCache:Params:ParamValues:PrinterFriendly`

`<port>` in the previous URL is the port of your web server. Your web server can be GlassFish, WebLogic, or OC4J if you are using APEX Listener. **XMLBD HTTP Protocol Server** will be used if you are using EPG configuration. Native Apache, OHS, OAS or OHS + WebLogic can be used if you are using external mod_plsql configuration.

The DAD name and web context

Consider the following link:

```
http://<hostname>:<port>/dad_name_or_web_context/f?p=app_id:page_
no:session_id:Request:Debug:ClearCache:Params:ParamValues:PrinterFrie
ndly
```

Previous versions of APEX used DAD, but APEX 4.x can also use APEX Listener. The *Database and web interaction in DAD and Listener configurations* section of the *Appendix* will boost your understanding of this part of the URL.

It contains:

- A discussion on the creation of a DAD and a demonstration of the use of that DAD to do both database and web interaction. The mod_plsql configuration of APEX also does the same thing but it does it on a bigger scale.

- A section on calling a custom function from the URL using the Listener configuration.

The f procedure

Consider the following example:

```
http://<hostname>:<port>/dad_name/f?p=app_id:page_no:session_id:
Request:Debug:ClearCache:Params:ParamValues:PrinterFriendly
```

f in f?p is the name of a stored procedure and p is its argument. We can draw an analogy between f and APPENDIX.DAD_PROC which is defined in the *Database and web interaction in DAD and Listener configurations* section of the *Appendix*. f has a single argument, that is, p while APPENDIX.DAD_PROC has val and redirect_url as its arguments.

The application ID in the URL

Consider the following example:

```
http://<hostname>:<port>/dad_name/f?p=app_id:page_no:session_id:
Request:Debug:ClearCache:Params:ParamValues:PrinterFriendly
```

app_id in the above URL is the application ID of your application. We can hide the application ID by using application alias, but the application ID will be exposed when the user navigates between the pages. This also holds true for page number. Permanent hiding of the app_id and page_id can be controlled only through the web server.

We can, however, use an application alias instead of our `app_id` value in the URL. Our application alias should be unique in a workspace, and if two workspaces have the same alias then the syntax of our URL will be like the following:

```
f?p=common_alias:page_alias_or_page_number:&APP_SESSION.&c=desired_
workspace
```

This makes sense since APEX should have a way to uniquely identify the desired application. If two applications have same alias, then APEX will need the support of our workspace name to find the application which it should present to us.

The page number in the URL

Consider the following example:

```
http://<hostname>:<port>/dad_name/f?p=app_id:page_no:session_id:
Request:Debug:ClearCache:Params:ParamValues:PrinterFriendly
```

`page_no` is the identifier to your APEX page. The name itself explains it all. It's the page number; nothing more, nothing less. This can also be replaced by page alias.

Session management

Consider the following example:

```
http://<hostname>:<port>/dad_name/f?p=app_id:page_no:session_id:
Request:Debug:ClearCache:Params:ParamValues:PrinterFriendly
```

`session_id` is the APEX session ID and is very different from the DB session. Every APEX page request is furnished by an existing or new DB connection. On every page view request, APEX picks a database connection from the pool and then relinquishes it soon after the request is fulfilled. If no connections are free, then a new DB connection is created. The big guys, **mod_plsql/Listener**, take care of this connection pool.

APEX has some views to check the session activity. `Apex_activity_log` logs the activity in APEX applications. `Apex_workspace_activity_log` is a view in the APEX schema that helps us track every activity in APEX. The granularity of the log in this view is page view. So, the setting and resetting of APEX items do not get logged, but every page view does. This logging is done only for the applications which have logging enabled. We can also check the `WWV_FLOW_DATA` table to see the state of our items in some of our previous sessions. `Flow_instance` of this table holds our session ID and `flow_id` holds our application ID.

We can also click on the **Session** button in the developer toolbar of APEX to see session states of various items.

To capture the session values of various items in your application, do one of the following:

- `:MY_ITEM` – It can be used in SQL or PL/SQL. The item name cannot be more than 30 characters long. Use `:"MY_ITEM"` if item name contains special characters.

- You can also reference them as substitution strings, that is, as `&MY_ITEM`. Again, if the name contains special characters, then you can use `&"MY_ITEM"`.

- Substitution strings can be used in page template and region source. Substitution strings are also sometimes referenced as `#MY_ITEM#`.

- If you are coding in PL/SQL, then you have the freedom to use `V('MY_ITEM')` for getting the value of any item or `NV('MY_NUMERIC_ITEM')` for getting the value of numeric items.

We can use the following query to check out the setting and resetting of items in the development environment (`flow_id = 4550`) when we navigate from one page to other to develop our code. This information can also be viewed using public APEX views which expose APEX data for our use:

```
Select flow_instance, item_name, item_value_vc2, flow_id
From apex_040200.wwv_flow_data
Where flow_id = 4550
```

The session ID is created at login time and APEX preserves the sanctity of a user session by continually verifying it against the value in the APEX session cookie and the value of the session in the database.

Execute the following anonymous block from SQL Workshop to get a feel of what the session cookie looks like:

```
BEGIN
  owa_util.print_cgi_env();
END;
```

Search for `Cookie` in the output. You might get something like the following when you search for it:

```
Cookie = WWV_CUSTOM-F_1301809025994046_101=00C1A195B51BDAFDC8B2A3
C3E006DCC2; LOGIN_USERNAME_COOKIE=packt_admin; ORA_WWV_ATTRIBUTE_
PAGE=4495%2C%23COMMENTS; ORA_WWV_REMEMBER_UN=PACKT_ADMIN:PACKT_
WORKSPACE;
```

The highlighted piece of code is the hashed session ID. We can match this hashed session ID with the `session_id_hashed` column of the following query to get the actual APEX session ID from the corresponding value of the `id` column of the following query.

```
SELECT session_id_hashed,
    id,
    created_on
FROM apex_040200.wwv_flow_sessions$
```

For security reasons, APEX hashes the session ID and stores this hashed value in `session_id_hashed`. This value is then passed in the cookie.

Session ID is our passport to know everything about the relation of this cookie to our APEX session. Use `apex_workspace_activity_log` to know more:

```
SELECT *
FROM apex_workspace_activity_log
WHERE apex_session_id = '241352717594401'
```

More snooping can be done using the `APEX_CUSTOM_AUTH.GET_COOKIE_PROPS` and `APEX_CUSTOM_AUTH.GET_SESSION_ID_FROM_COOKIE` procedures of the APEX API. `APEX_CUSTOM_AUTH.GET_SESSION_ID` can help us get the session ID of the session from which it is called. This value will match with the value in the URL.

 There are many more procedures scattered all around the API to set and get various properties of the session. Some examples of these functions are: `APEX_UTIL.SET_SESSION_LANG` and `APEX_UTIL. SET_SESSION_TIME_ZONE`.

The zero session ID

This is a novel step to increase the popularity of APEX among web applications on the Internet. The success of a website hugely depends on its appearance in the relevant search results. Google crawler and other bots do the laborious task of crawling through various links on a website and bookmarking them so that they can be presented to the user when related keywords are searched. Since the session ID of APEX is a part of the URL and since it changes in every session, it is virtually impossible to bookmark an APEX page. We can solve this problem in the following three ways:

- Set a reverse proxy on the web server.

- Create a PL/SQL function, have the redirection to the APEX URL from the function, and call this function by setting the `path-alias` attribute of a DAD. Know more about path aliasing from the following link:

  `http://docs.oracle.com/cd/E23943_01/portal.1111/e12041/concept.htm#i1006110`

- Use the zero session ID.

If an application that does not require authentication is opened with `0` in the session ID place of the URL, APEX will internally generate a session ID, pass it to the browser cookie, and use it to maintain the APEX session, but will show `0` as the session ID in the URL.

You can check this by enabling the audit trail. Follow the steps mentioned in the *Enabling auditing on the APEX_PUBLIC_USER schema* section of the *Appendix* to check the calls made to the web toolkit.

Now open your APEX development console with zero session ID. For example

`http://localhost:7001/apex_weblogic/f?p=4550:1:0:::::`

Now execute the `4-98-9_Appendix_check_calls_by_lsnr_2_web_toolkit` script from SQL Prompt after logging into the database using the `SYSDBA` user. This script can be found in the code pack. You should be able to see `nobody:3011100369646501` in the `client_id` column. The `client_id` column is a combination of user ID and session ID. So, you see that the URL was opened with the `0` session ID but APEX internally is maintaining an actual APEX session ID.

Execute the following script using `SYSDBA` to turn off the auditing:

```
SQL> @4-98-9_Appendix_disable_auditing
```

Request handling

Consider the following link:

```
http://<hostname>:<port>/dad_name/f?p=app_id:page_no:session_id:
Request:Debug:ClearCache:Params:ParamValues:PrinterFriendly
```

Request in the previous URL is to differentiate between the requests going from one page to another page. Let's say we have a report which has links on every row to edit the corresponding row and also to delete the record. Let's say we have another page that handles both these requests. There should be a way to tell the drilldown page that the user has requested to edit the row and not to delete it. `Request` in the URL is a method to achieve this.

Now every button in the application can set the value of `Request` to its own name. So, when the user navigates from one page to another on the click of a button, this part of the URL will hold the name of the clicked button. The value of `Request` can be retrieved using any of the following:

- **Substitution string**: `&REQUEST`
- **PL/SQL**: `V('REQUEST')`
- **Bind variable**: `:REQUEST`

There are many functions in APEX's JavaScript API which set `Request`, for example, `apex.submit(pRequest)` and `apex.confirm(pMessage, pRequest)`. The following function call submits the page, sets the value of `REQUEST` to `NEW`, and sets the value of `P1_ITEM` to `555`:

```
apex.submit({
request:"NEW",
set:{"P1_ITEM":555}});
```

 G_REQUEST is a global variable in the `APEX_APPLICATION` package which holds the most recent value.

Request value is also set when we call an **OnDemand** APEX process. Syntax is `f?p=application_id:page_id:session_id:APPLICATION_PROCESS=process_id`.

The syntax gives a feeling that this is applicable only for application processes but it works well for page OnDemand processes as well.

Debugging

Consider the following link:

```
http://<hostname>:<port>/dad_name/f?p=app_id:page_no:session_id:
Request:Debug:ClearCache:Params:ParamValues:PrinterFriendly
```

Debugging is never fun and can sometimes trouble you more than your mother-in-law. So, it makes sense to learn a few things that will reduce the time you spend with debugging.

DEBUG is actually a flag. You will either see YES or NO in this place of the URL. If the value is set to YES and if you have logged in using developer credentials, then you will be able to see the debug log by clicking on the **View Debug** button in the developer toolbar at the bottom of an APEX page. You can set the value of DEBUG by clicking on the **Debug** button on the developer toolbar or by manually putting YES in this part of the URL, and then loading the page. DEBUG gives you the divine eye which lets you see what you otherwise might not. Use it when nothing makes sense to you. Use it when you think APEX is drunk.

Ways to get the value of this flag:

* **Short substitution string**: &DEBUG
* **PL/SQL**: V('DEBUG')
* **Bind variable**: :DEBUG

But all this fun only happens if you have enabled debugging at the application level if it is not already enabled. To do this, click on the **Edit Definition** link that appears on the right pane under **Shared Components** and then select **Yes** in the **Debugging** dropdown under the **Properties** section.

In APEX 4.2, debugging is enabled by default. The debug feature in APEX 4.x also gives you a pretty cool graph. The debug report tells you about the processing time for each step. You should store these messages in your own table if you want to check the trends in the performance of APEX reports because the messages in APEX log table age out after two weeks. The debugging messages are logged at log level 4 and can be queried by using the APEX_DEBUG_MESSAGES view.

There is a whole package in APEX called APEX_DEBUG_MESSAGE to give you more freedom to use DEBUG. This package lets you log messages at different log levels. A developer can put his messages too. Again, we can query to retrieve messages of a certain log level. The package also has functions to clear the log messages.

We can use this package to capture the flow of control in our APEX application since we can use this for logging messages in stored PL/SQL procedures and functions as well.

The functions of this package are not affected by the application-level debugging setting.

G_DEBUG is a global variable in the APEX_APPLICATION package which tells whether DEBUG is enabled or not. APEX_PLUGIN_UTIL also has some functions such as APEX_PLUGIN_UTIL.DEBUG_DYNAMIC_ACTION which let us debug **Dynamic Actions**, the newest gig in APEX.

Other functions such as APEX_PLUGIN_UTIL.DEBUG_PAGE_ITEM let us debug page items. Now we can obviously check the value of an APEX item by clicking on the session link in the developer toolbar. We also have functions such as APEX_PLUGIN_UTIL.DEBUG_PROCESS, and APEX_PLUGIN_UTIL.DEBUG_REGION. These functions do the job that their name suggests.

 Debugging of JavaScript in your application is possible using tools such as Firebug of Mozilla Firefox and Microsoft Script Debugger. Similarly, debugging of Dynamic Actions is also a little different. When the application debugging is on and the page is rendered in the debug mode, JavaScript debugging tools such as Firebug will show you information about timing of the firing of a Dynamic Action, its name, and the action resulting in its execution.

It is also important to note that AJAX calls are not tracked by APEX's debugging functionality. Since interactive reports make a lot of AJAX calls, most of the actions performed on interactive reports are also not traceable using the debug functionality. We can, however, call the procedures in APEX_DEBUG_MESSAGE to log messages inside the processes called by AJAX calls. Some information about PPR or interactive report AJAX calls can also be seen in browser script debugging tools. Similarly, flash charts also offer very little scope for debugging.

Error handling

We can specify the name of a function in **Error Handling Section** of **Application Definition** or in the **Error Handling** section in page attributes to declare a function which will generate custom error messages. These places also let us specify the display location of error messages.

The implementation of this function must be:

```
function <name of function> (
p_error in apex_error.t_error )
return apex_error.t_error_result
```

Apart from this, we also have the usual error and success display sections in page processes. We also have an error message section in application processes.

The API documentation of APEX_ERROR can be found at http://docs.oracle.com/cd/E37097_01/doc/doc.42/e35127/apex_error.htm. The documentation also shows an example of the error-handling function.

TKPROF

Consider the following link:

```
http://localhost:7003/apex_weblogic/f?p=105:1:416650869240101&p_
trace=YES
```

Add `&p_trace=YES` at the end of a page request to generate the trace for the request. APEX drops the DB connection once a page request is fulfilled and then takes an existing or a fresh connection to furnish a fresh page request. Adding `&p_tracle=YES` turns on 10046 level trace and does it only for the page request with which it is associated.

We can use the following procedure to find the name of the trace file in which 10046 level trace is written:

1. Run the following query to find the location in which all the trace files exist on your database

   ```
   SQL> select value from v$parameter where name    = 'user_dump_
   dest';
   ```

2. Put the following in the same page for which you want to get the trace:

   ```
   select sys_context('userenv','sessionid') from dual;
   ```

Use the output of this in the **Enter the session id from USERENV context in APEX:** prompt while executing the following script to get the trace filename:

```
SQL> @4-98-9_01_get_trace_file_name
```

Cache management

Consider the following link:

```
http://<hostname>:<port>/dad_name/f?p=app_id:page_no:session_id:
Request:Debug:ClearCache:Params:ParamValues:PrinterFriendly
```

We can edit the definitions of regions and pages to enable caches in them. Application items are set and reset multiple times so the cache of these can also be cleared.

The `ClearCache` part of the URL is used to clear the session state of an item, all items on a page, a group of pages, an application, or all applications. The page which makes the request has to put the "right text" in this position in the URL to clear the cache. The data for a cache is fetched directly from the `WWV_FLOW_PAGE_CACHE` table instead of the actual execution of the code for the page. The following are the available options to clear the cache:

- Put the name of an item in this part of the URL if you want to clear the value of a particular item in the requested page.

- Put the page number in this part of the URL if you want to clear the state of all items and any stateful process on a single page.

- Put a comma-separated list of pages in this part of the URL if you want to clear the cache for a set of pages. The comma-separated list can include collection names to be reset.

- Keyword `RP` resets regional pagination on the requested page.

- Keyword `APP` is a tsunami. It clears all pages and application level items of an application.

- Keyword `SESSION` is apocalypse. It clears items associated with all applications which have been used in the current session.

 Please do not confuse this with the `SESSION` which we discussed earlier. These two have different places in the URL and have totally different meanings. If this is chalk, then that is cheese.

We can use a combination of the the previous options to have multiple effects. Let's say that we want to render 10th page, reset its pagination and clear cache for page 11 and 12. Our URL in such a case will look like the following:

```
f?p=101:10:2141754341423301::NO:RP,11,12:::
```

`APEX_UTIL` has tons of functions for clearing cache. Some of the cache related functions in this package are `APEX_UTIL.CLEAR_PAGE_CACHE`, `APEX_UTIL.CLEAR_USER_CACHE`, `APEX_UTIL.CACHE_PURGE_STALE`, `APEX_UTIL.CACHE_PURGE_BY_PAGE`, `APEX_UTIL.CACHE_PURGE_BY_APPLICATION`, `APEX_UTIL.CACHE_GET_DATE_OF_REGION_CACHE`, and `APEX_UTIL.CACHE_GET_DATE_OF_PAGE_CACHE`.

There are many more scattered all across the API to clear certain parts of the application. An example of this can be APEX_COLLECTION.TRUNCATE_COLLECTION, which clears a named collection.

Administrators can clear the cache by following the following steps:

Click on the arrow next to the **Administration** button on the top, select **Manage Services**, select **Application Cache** present in the **Manage Meta Data** list on the right side of the page.

This will take you to a list which will let you clear cache for pages and regions.

If you are still looking for more ways to clear the cache, then you can use the **Session State** process for this. You can also use the **Link** section in **Column Attributes** of either **Classic** or **interactive reports** to clear the cache. Calendar regions also give this option.

Alright, I'm tired of writing about ways to clear cache but I will still keep listing. **Dynamic Actions**, buttons, branches, lists, bread crumbs, and navigation bar entry, can also be used for clearing cache. The **Cache** button on the developer toolbar lets you manage cached regions and pages.

Apart from this, there is a relatively unsecure feature called browser-side cache. You can enable this by going to the **Browser Security** section in **Shared Components | Security Attributes**. Enabling this lets the browser store vital information and can lead to security problems. Enabling this has also been known to create problems with pages which have partial page refresh content. It is important to note the distinction between this cache and the other cache which we have been talking about. Apart from this paragraph, we have been talking about setting and resetting APEX **server-side cache** while this one is **browser-side cache**.

Passing values and navigation

Consider the following link:

```
http://<hostname>:<port>/dad_name/f?p=app_id:page_no:session_id:
Request:Debug:ClearCache:Params:ParamValues:PrinterFriendly
```

This is the developer's playground Params:ParamValues is to let you set the items in the application to certain values. Params is a comma-separated list of item names whose values have to be set and ParamValues is a comma-separated list of values of the corresponding item names.

Colons are a part of the URL and hold special meaning in the URL. Hence the values themselves cannot contain colons. If there is a possibility of item values containing colons, then we should use `translate` or `replace` functions to encrypt the string so that colons are removed from the values. We can then decrypt the encrypted string at the destination page. If a value contains comma, then enclose the value within two backward slashes. For example, `\1,234\`.

Some of the APEX API functions also let us set the session state of an item. One of these functions is `APEX_UTIL.SET_SESSION_STATE`.

Making APEX printer friendly

Consider the following link:

```
http://<hostname>:<port>/dad_name/f?p=app_id:page_no:session_id:
Request:Debug:ClearCache:Params:ParamValues:PrinterFriendly
```

`PrinterFriendly` is a flag which when set to `YES`, renders the page in printer-friendly mode. It tells whether the page is in printer-friendly mode or not. We can get the value of this using `V('PRINTER_FRIENDLY')`.

The `G_PRINTER_FRIENDLY` global variable in the `APEX_APPLICATION` package is a flag, which tells whether the application is running in print view mode or not.

Decoding the APEX page submissions

Now that we understand the URL of APEX and have a broad understanding of the tool, I want to get into the specifics. I want to talk a little about the mechanism used by APEX to submit pages. This section tries to answer the following questions:

- How does APEX submit pages?
- How does a `submit` request flow from the browser to the APEX engine?
- How do HTML requests get converted to PL/SQL processing and how the switching happens?

APEX creates an HTML form for any APEX page created by us. APEX items defined by us become the various elements of the HTML form. The name of the APEX items become the IDs of the HTML elements and these HTML elements are given any name between `p_t01` to `p_t200` inclusive.

For example, if we have an item named P2_REPORT_SEARCH in our APEX page, if this item is a textbox and if this is our first page item, then APEX will generate the following HTML for this APEX item:

```
<input type="text" id="P2_REPORT_SEARCH" name="p_t01" value=""
size="30" maxlength="2000" onkeypress="return submitEnter(this,event)"
class="text_field" />
```

The p_t01 to p_t200 range is reserved for page items excluding shuttles and multiselects. Other APEX objects have other ranges of names. Now the big question is, why couldn't APEX assign the names of items as the names of HTML elements? The answer lies in the way in which APEX submits its pages.

The HTML form created by APEX is submitted using the HTTP POST method. We can check this in the form action code at the bottom of this paragraph. The HTML form generated by APEX has wwv_flow.accept in its action attribute. I am sure that wwv_flow.accept is ringing some bells in your head. This looks like the name of some APEX package and procedure. If you check the packages under the APEX_040200 schema, you will see wwv_flow package and the accept procedure in that package. The body of this package is wrapped but you can still check out its specification. Now, every argument in the signature of wwv_flow.accept is directly fed from the HTML form. The HTML name directly maps to the name of the arguments in this procedure. So APEX has to assign the names of the arguments of this procedure as the names of the elements in the HTML form (an APEX page), otherwise the values submitted on the page cannot pass to the APEX engine. Hence, the names of the APEX items cannot be assigned as the names of the HTML elements generated for the items. The HTML element names have to be the names of the arguments of the wwv_flow.accept procedure. This is the entry point of all foreign values that get passed using forms. Let me show you the beginning of a typical HTML form generated by APEX:

```
<form action="wwv_flow.accept" method="post" name="wwv_flow"
id="wwvFlowForm">
```

You should be able to find a similar string if you right-click on any APEX page and check out the HTML page source.

Now, wwv_flow.accept is invoked, just the way procedure f of f?p is called from the apex DAD/Web context. The Wwv_flow.accept is also a procedure just like f and is called in a similar fashion. Both these functions are called using the apex DAD / web context but in case of f, its argument, that is, p is passed in the URL (passing argument in the URL is called the HTTP GET method) and in case of wwv_flow. accept, the arguments are passed from the form using the HTTP POST method. Arguments passed using the HTTP POST method do not appear in the URL.

Are you wondering that how does a mere mention of the name of a procedure in the action attribute of a form direct the APEX engine to run the procedure and pass values to its arguments? The answer lies in the fact that the action you mention in the action attribute of a form is searched in the calling resource. Let us put this statement to test.

Write the following HTML code in a plain text editor and save it on your desktop as `test.html`:

```
<html> <body>
<form action="dummy_accept" method="post">
  First name: <input type="text" name="p_dummy_item" />
  <input type="submit" value="Submit" />
</form>
</body> </html>
```

Now open `test.html` in your web browser and hit the **Submit** button.

What do you see? A **Cannot display the Webpage** message? This message is generally not a good omen but in our case, this message is fine. We want to see what is going on in the URL.

When you open `test.html`, your URL will be similar to `C:\Users\acer\Desktop\test.html` and after hitting the submit button, `test.html` in the end of the URL will change to `dummy_accept`. The URL will then look like `C:\Users\acer\Desktop\dummy_accept` and you would get a **Cannot display the Webpage** message because `C:\Users\acer\Desktop\dummy_accept` does not exist, that is, nothing called `dummy_accept` exists on `C:\Users\acer\Desktop`. The important point to note here is that the HTML page tried to search for `dummy_accept` (the value of form action) in `C:\Users\acer\Desktop`. Similarly, a typical APEX URL is:

`http://<host_name>:<port>/<dad_or_web_context>/f?p=blah,blah,blah`

When you submit this APEX page, the HTML form in it is submitted and the resource called is:

`http://<host_name>:<port>/<dad_or_web_context>/wwv_flow.accept`

The URL has `wwv_flow.accept` in the end because `wwv_flow` accept is the value of form action in an APEX page.

The process of calling `wwv_flow.accept` from `http://<host_name>:<port>/<dad_or_web_context>/f?p=blah,blah,blah` is similar to the call of `C:\Users\acer\Desktop\dummy_accept` from `C:\Users\acer\Desktop\test.html`.

APEX behind the scenes

Behind the scenes, APEX Listener / DAD calls web toolkit functions. These calls can be seen by enabling the **db audit trail** on user configured in the APEX Listener / DAD. Since the APEX developer environment is also an APEX application, these calls can be seen as soon as you open your console login page to log in to the development environment. A point by point process to enable auditing and then see these calls has been described in the *APEX behind the scenes* section of the *Appendix*.

More information on db audit trail can be found at `http://docs.oracle.com/cd/E11882_01/server.112/e10575/tdpsg_auditing.htm`.

Other web interfaces

There are some less known relatives of mod_plsql, and this section plans to bring these web interfaces to your notice.

Out of these, the most important one is **Thoth Gateway**. Thoth is an open source interface which has been developed for **IIS** and performs almost the same functions which mod_plsql does for the Apache servers. Since it is free, it can easily be extended, whenever required.

DBPrism is a SourceForge's initiative to produce a JEE alternative to mod_plsql. More info on DBPrism can be found at `http://sourceforge.net/projects/dbprism/`.

Mod_owa is functionally similar to mod_plsql but does not share any common code. While serious efforts have been made to use mod_owa for APEX applications, its use is still not completely tested. More information on mod_owa can be found at `https://oss.oracle.com/projects/mod_owa/dist/documentation/modowa.htm`.

A pessimist's view of APEX

Let's check out some of the most valid criticisms in the following sections.

Cap of 200 page items

As discussed in the *Decoding the APEX page submissions* section previously, only 200 page items are possible on an APEX page.

SQL Injection

This works like a charm. The only problem is that the charm does not work in your favor.

SQL Injection is PL/SQL hacking and can be stopped to a large extent if proper coding practices are followed. The attack is easy if your PL/SQL code contains dynamic SQL, and the code is generated by concatenating variables to the dynamic SQL string. Again, if your code assumes some implicit conversions and formats, then an experienced hacker can change those assumed formats and demolish your security like it was a deck of cards.

SQL Injection is of two types. Refer to *SQL Injection* section of the *Appendix* to see a discussion about both of these types with a working example of one of the types of SQL Injection and various ways to combat SQL Injection.

Cross-site scripting

Cross-site scripting is an attack by which hackers can bypass access controls such as **same origin policy** of the target server, and hence access sensitive data using client-side scripting such as JavaScript. Check out the *Cross Site Scripting* section of the *Appendix* to see the same origin policy in action. You will find a piece of code to use client-side scripting to access vital web resources of the same domain. Cross-site scripting also uses similar code but the attack is from a different domain.

Summary

APEX is a sophisticated 4GL RAD development tool and is fun to work with. When you have to do something as boring as *work*, then you better do it with something as interesting as APEX. It lets you code where it makes sense to involve a human brain and takes care of the layouts and themes.

This chapter presented the wiring of APEX and it also presented a step-by-step process to install APEX engine and APEX Listener. The following chapters will build on the concepts introduced in this chapter. The next chapter will talk about using classic reports for all possible reporting requirements known to man. We will blend classic reports with AJAX, jQuery and Dynamic Actions to orchestrate the variety of uses of each one of these. We have a long road ahead and miles to go before we sleep. It's time to have a short break and a glass of water before we dive into the next chapter.

2
Conventional Reporting in APEX

This chapter is dedicated to ethnic reporting. The reports introduced in this chapter exist as an out-of-the-box feature of most reporting technologies.

This chapter will cover the following topics:

- Environment variables and the method to capture them.

- Various methods of implementing group reports in APEX.

- A number of methods to format a classic report. These are spread all across the chapter.

- Methods to implementing matrix reports. These methods involve the use of the `with` clause, the `pivot` operator, and substitution strings.

- Recursive methods to implement hierarchical reports. These are implemented using the `with` clause, traditional hierarchical queries, and also using APEX trees.

- Methods to download files in APEX. These methods include the use of the download mask in APEX, the `wpg_docload` package, the `apex_util` package, and using a combination of `p` procedure and `APEX_FLOW_FILES`. We will also see a system to upload files.

- Slicing and dicing of a classic report using the traditional method and using **Dynamic Actions (DAs)**.

- Implementation of tabular forms and master detail reports.

- Implementing time series reports in APEX. This section demonstrates the use of the query partition clause for data densification, the use of `model` clause, and the use of analytical functions such as `ratio_to_report`, `lead`, and `lag`. The section also talks about the windowing clause.

Creating database objects and installing the reference application

Let us start by creating the database objects and installing a reference application. The reference application has all the implementations discussed in this chapter. Check the *Steps to create PACKT_SCHEMA* section of the *Appendix* for the steps to create PACKT_SCHEMA. Execute the following script to install the supporting objects for the reference application after connecting as sysdba and enter PACKT_SCHEMA in **Enter the schema** prompt:

```
SQL> @4-98-9_02_install_schema
```

Create a fresh SQL Plus session and execute the following from sysdba to create the chapter2 package. This package is used in our reference application.

```
SQL> @4-98-9_02_chapter2
```

Execute the following statement from sysdba to check whether the installation is successful or not. This statement should not return any records.

```
Select * from all_objects where owner='PACKT_SCHEMA' and status =
'INVALID';
```

Import the chapter 2 reference application (4-98-9_02_APEX_app_Chapter2.sql) supplied with this book. The chapter 2 reference application uses external table authentication. Let us understand it now.

> Note that page 8 of the reference application talks about reports based on web services. We will talk about this page in *Chapter 8, All About Web Services and Integrations*, where we will learn about creating web services and then look at the reports (the one on page 8) based on those web services.
> We can use SKING/SKING (in capitals) to log in to the reference application.

Implementing external table authentication

Let us understand the process to implement external table authentication in APEX. We will use the OEHR_EMPLOYEES table to present external table authentication. Ideally, any password stored in the database should be encrypted. We can use the DBMS_CRYPTO package for this. The following is the link to know more about the DBMS_CRYPTO package:

http://docs.oracle.com/cd/E11882_01/appdev.112/e25788/d_crypto.htm

The DBMS_CRYPTO package provides a range of algorithms for encryption. We can also store the hash value of the password instead of storing the password itself. When a user tries to log in, we can get the hash value of the password entered by the user by using the DBMS_CRYPTO.Hash function, and compare it with the with the hash value stored in the database to authenticate the user. Hashing password is more secure, since it is a one-way road. We can get the hash value of a string, but we cannot get the string from the hash value.

The **Custom authentication** scheme under **Authentication Schemes** in **Shared Components** is used for authentication in the reference application. Let us understand this scheme now. This scheme uses the chapter2.authenticate function for authentication, and chapter2.sentry as the sentry function. The sentry function is executed before any request (for example, opening of a page) is made. If the sentry function returns false, then the session is marked as invalid. The chapter2.authenticate function just checks that the values entered in the username and password textboxes of the login page should match with any of the values in the email column of the oehr_employees table. The chapter2.sentry function compares value of v('APP_USER') and the email column of the oehr_employees table. The page is displayed if these comparisons is successful.

Displaying environment properties using the USERENV namespace

In this section, we will try to understand the code of the region that displays information captured using the USERENV namespace. The USERENV namespace helps in capturing a number of interesting properties of the underlying database session of an APEX session. These properties include information such as current user session, current SQL, and SID. A detailed list of attributes can be found at the following link:

http://docs.oracle.com/cd/E11882_01/server.112/e17118/functions184. htm#g1513460

The following is a section of region source query for the **USERENV Parameters** region of page 1 of the reference application. The query uses the sys_context function and the USERENV namespace. Sys_context returns the value associated with the context namespace. The context namespace in this place is USERENV. The values returned by this query help in auditing and debugging. The entire query is available in the reference application as follows:

```
select DBMS_SESSION.UNIQUE_SESSION_ID() UNIQUE_SESSION_ID, sys_
context('USERENV', 'CLIENT_IDENTIFIER') CLIENT_IDENTIFIER,
```

```
sys_context('USERENV', 'SID') SID, sys_context('USERENV',
'STATEMENTID') STATEMENTID, sys_context('userenv','sessionid')
sessionid from dual
```

The output of the **USERENV Parameters** region is shown in the following screenshot:

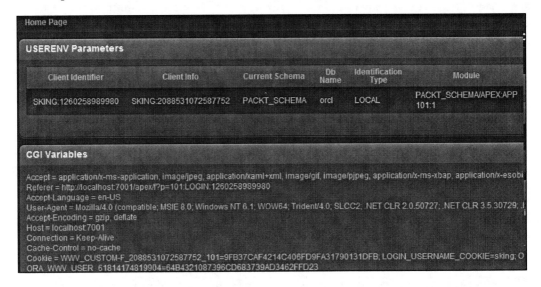

The preceding query also uses the DBMS_SESSION package. The DBMS_SESSION package has functions to clear and set contexts, and also has the UNIQUE_SESSION_ID function, which returns a unique ID for every session connected to the database. A list of subprograms in the DBMS_SESSION package can be found at http://docs. oracle.com/cd/E11882_01/appdev.112/e10577/d_sessio.htm#i996747.

 We can also create our own context namespace using the CREATE CONTEXT statement.

Displaying the CGI environment variables

This section will discuss the code that will help us to capture the CGI environment variables. The **CGI Variables PL/SQL Dynamic Content** region on page 1 of the reference application holds the following anonymous PL/SQL block:

```
begin owa_util.print_cgi_env();end;
```

We can see the output of this code in the preceding screenshot. This anonymous block uses `owa_util.print_cgi_env` to display the CGI environment variables. The list of variables is displayed as name-value pairs. If we feel that one of the variables can be used in our code then we can capture the value of that variable using `owa_util.get_cgi_env('variable_name')`. We can learn more about CGI variables from `http://docs.oracle.com/cd/E23943_01/portal.1111/e12041/concept.htm#i1006126`.

Implementing a classic report search functionality

We will dedicate this section to learn and implement classic report's search functionality. Do the following while while using the classic report wizard:

- Select **Yes** in the **Enable Search** dropdown
- The **Select Columns for Search** shuttle appears, which allows selecting columns that are needed for search. Select the desired columns in it. The **Select Columns for Search** shuttle is highlighted in the screenshot below.

Use the following screenshot for your assistance:

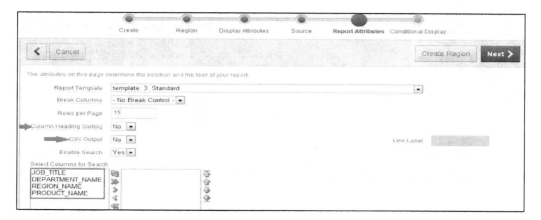

Selecting the columns from the **Select Columns for Search** shuttle creates an encapsulating `select` clause and `where` clause over the original query in the region source. The original query appears in the `from` clause of the encapsulating query. The `where` clause of the encapsulating query helps to filter the records based on our search. The filtering mechanism uses the `instr` function to check the presence of the search string in all the columns which were selected in the **Select Columns for Search** shuttle.

The shuttle has been highlighted in the preceding screenshot. I selected the JOB_TITLE, DEPARTMENT_NAME, REGION_NAME and PRODUCT_NAME columns while creating the **Tabular Report** region on page 2 of the reference application. The following code shows these columns finally appearing in the encapsulating where clause:

```
where (instr(upper("JOB_TITLE"),upper(nvl(:P2_REPORT_SEARCH,"JOB_
TITLE"))) > 0  orinstr(upper("DEPARTMENT_NAME"),upper(nvl(:P2_
REPORT_SEARCH,"DEPARTMENT_NAME"))) > 0  orinstr(upper("REGION_
NAME"),upper(nvl(:P2_REPORT_SEARCH,"REGION_NAME"))) > 0
orinstr(upper("PRODUCT_NAME"),upper(nvl(:P2_REPORT_SEARCH,"PRODUCT_
NAME"))) > 0)
```

Apart from the encapsulating query, a new region called **Search**, a select list, a textbox, and two buttons, a branch to reload the page on submission, a page process to reset pagination, and a page process to clear cache are also created by APEX. P2_REPORT_SEARCH, in the preceding where clause is actually the name of the textbox created by APEX in the **Search** region. This textbox is underlined in the following screenshot. When a user types something in the P2_REPORT_SEARCH textbox and clicks on the **Go** button, the page is reloaded with the data filtered based on the value of P2_REPORT_SEARCH. Note that the filter (where clause shared above) is such that all the rows will be returned, if P2_REPORT_SEARCH does not have any value. The following screenshot is an example of one such search shared for your convenience:

 We will look at a different way of implementing the same functionality when we talk about dynamic reports in the next chapter.

Enabling sorting and CSV download

The first screenshot in the preceding section shows the **Column Heading Sorting** dropdown (highlighted with an arrow). Selecting **Yes** in this dropdown lets a user sort on a column by clicking the heading of the column.

Similarly, the wizard also has the **CSV output** dropdown (highlighted with an arrow in the first screenshot of the preceding section). We can select **Yes** in this dropdown and put a text in the **Link Label** textbox to enable CSV download in an APEX report.

Implementing group reports

In group reports, data is grouped and shown as subtotals, and is then aggregated to show a grand total. These reports can be implemented in APEX in the following ways:

- Using the **Break Formatting** section in classic reports
- Using grouping sets
- Using interactive reports. We will see this method in the next chapter.

Using the Break Formatting section in classic reports

In this section, we will see a report which groups the data based on the PRODUCT_ NAME column and has a grand total of all employees at the end.

In the **Report Attributes** page of any classic report, checking the **Sum** checkbox (highlighted in the following screenshot) of any column of the report which has numeric data and putting **No Breaks** in the **Break Columns** dropdown of the **Break Formatting** section gives an aggregated row at the bottom of the table.

We can use the **Report Sum Label** textbox (highlighted in the second screenshot) to give a label for the aggregated row.

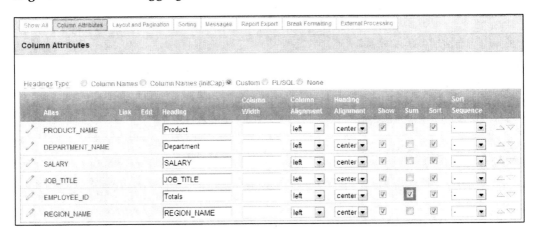

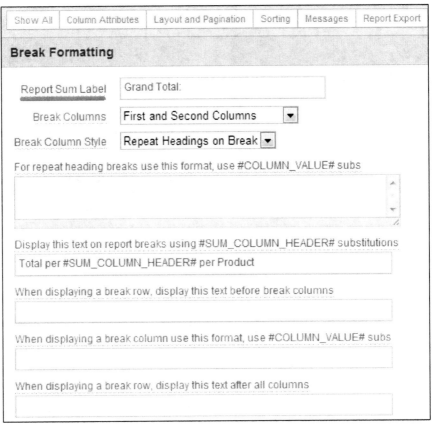

We get additional options if we select anything other than **No Breaks** in the **Break Columns** dropdown. Let me talk a little about these options:

- **No Breaks** in the **Break column** dropdown and **Repeat Headings** in the **Break in Break Column Style** dropdown: Selecting these options result in small sections inside the report and the values of the first column in the **Column Attributes** section in the **Report Attributes** page appear as the headings of these smaller sections. One such value is highlighted in the following screenshot. The rest of the columns are displayed in the table as shown in the following screenshot:

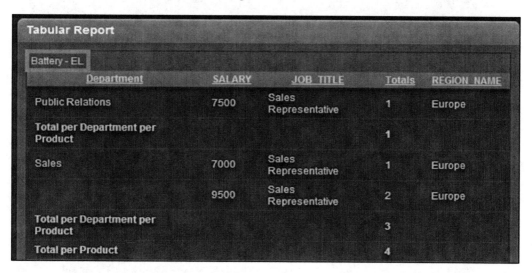

- **First Column** in the **Break column** dropdown and **Repeat Headings** in the **Break in Break Column Style** dropdown: This gives us two levels of aggregations as shown in the following screenshot:

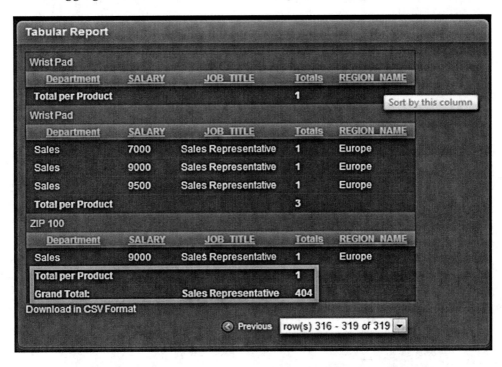

Similarly, we would get three and four levels of aggregations if we select **First and Second Columns** and **First, Second and Third Column** respectively in the **Break Columns** textbox.

- **Default Break Formatting** in the **Break Column Style** dropdown: If we select **Default Break Formatting** then the first column also appears as a column in the table rather than appearing as the heading of the smaller sections.

We can use a combination of other options in the **Break Formatting** region to have a custom display of the text that appears against the aggregated rows.

Using JavaScript to modify a report

We will now see the use of JavaScript to alter a few labels that are displayed with aggregated rows. The method used here can be used to format anything over and above the usual formatting options provided by APEX.

We can format almost any part of our page using this technique; but in order to maintain the simplicity of the code, we should first try the formatting options provided by APEX. Go to the **Region Definition** page of the **Tabular Report** region on second page of the reference application and go to the **Header and Footer** section. You will find the following code there:

```
<script language = "Javascript">
var x=document.getElementsByTagName('td');
for(var i=0; i<x.length; i++)
  {   if(x[i].className == 'data')
      {    if(x[i].innerHTML.indexOf("Total per Product per Product")
!= -1)
          {x[i].innerHTML = '<b>Total per Product</b>';}
      }}
</script>
```

The code first finds all the `td` tags on the page and stores them in variable x. It then loops through these `td` elements and searches for `className data`, and then searches for `Total per Product per Product`. After finding this string, the code is replaced with `<b>Total per Product</b>`. We search for `className data` because our template assigns this class to the data displayed in classic reports. We capture the `td` elements because each value in a HTML table exists in a division called `td`. Divisions exist inside table rows called `tr`, and `tr` exist under the `table` tag. So the entire classic report is actually an HTML table formatted with CSS classes. To see this arrangement, right-click on the HTML page that displays this report and view the HTML source of the page. Search for `Total per Product` and you should be able to see this arrangement.

Using grouping sets and HTML formatting in a query

Our aim here is to create a grouped report using the grouping sets in SQL and to demonstrate a method to format the output by generating the HTML tags in the SQL.

Refer to the region source of **Tabular report using Grouping Sets** region page 2 of the reference application for this section. You will see the following query:

```
SELECT
DECODE (job_title,NULL,DECODE(department_name,NULL,DECODE(product_
name,NULL,'<b>Grand Total:</b>','<b>Total for '
    || product_name || ':</b>'),'<b>Total for '|| product_name
    || ' and '
    || department_name || ':</b>'),product_name) AS "PRODUCT",
```

```
              DECODE (job_title,NULL,'',"OEHR_DEPARTMENTS"."DEPARTMENT_
NAME") AS "DEPARTMENT", "OEHR_EMPLOYEES"."SALARY" AS "SALARY",
'<font color = "red">' || "OEHR_JOBS"."JOB_TITLE" || '</font>' AS
"JOB_TITLE",
COUNT(OEHR_EMPLOYEES.EMPLOYEE_ID) AS Totals, "OEHR_REGIONS"."REGION_
NAME" AS "REGION_NAME"
  FROM OEHR_PRODUCT_INFORMATION, OEHR_ORDER_ITEMS,
OEHR_ORDERS, OEHR_REGIONS, OEHR_COUNTRIES, OEHR_LOCATIONS, OEHR_
EMPLOYEES, OEHR_DEPARTMENTS, OEHR_JOBS
 WHERE OEHR_EMPLOYEES.JOB_ID =OEHR_JOBS.JOB_ID
AND EHR_EMPLOYEES.DEPARTMENT_ID=OEHR_DEPARTMENTS.DEPARTMENT_ID
  AND OEHR_DEPARTMENTS.LOCATION_ID=OEHR_LOCATIONS.LOCATION_ID
  AND OEHR_LOCATIONS.COUNTRY_ID=OEHR_COUNTRIES.COUNTRY_ID
  AND OEHR_COUNTRIES.REGION_ID=OEHR_REGIONS.REGION_ID
  AND OEHR_EMPLOYEES.EMPLOYEE_ID =OEHR_ORDERS.SALES_REP_ID
  AND OEHR_ORDERS.ORDER_ID=OEHR_ORDER_ITEMS.ORDER_ID
  AND OEHR_ORDER_ITEMS.PRODUCT_ID =OEHR_PRODUCT_INFORMATION.PRODUCT_ID
  AND ( instr(upper(JOB_TITLE),upper(NVL(:P2_REPORT_SEARCH,JOB_
TITLE))) > 0                OR instr(upper(DEPARTMENT_
NAME),upper(NVL(:P2_REPORT_SEARCH,DEPARTMENT_NAME))) > 0      OR
instr(upper(REGION_NAME),upper(NVL(:P2_REPORT_SEARCH,REGION_
NAME)))        > 0      OR instr(upper(PRODUCT_NAME),upper(NVL(:P2_
REPORT_SEARCH,PRODUCT_NAME)))        > 0       )
   GROUP BY grouping sets ((),(department_name,product_name),product_
name,(product_name,department_name,SALARY,region_name,job_title))
    order by product_name,department_name
```

The preceding query is more or less similar to the query of the **Tabular Report** region. The difference is in the grouping sets and some extra decode statements.

Let's start from the highlighted part at the bottom of the query.

Grouping sets defines the sets for which we want to generate subtotals. In the highlighted piece of code at the bottom of the preceding query, grouping set() generates a grand total for the entire data set. Grouping set (department_name,product_name) generates the total per department per product. product_name generates the total per product. The final grouping set, that is, (product_name, department_name,SALARY,region_name,job_title) is actually our detail level which includes all the columns in the select statement except the ones on which the aggregate function, that is, Count has been applied.

Let us now see the select clause. The HTML formatting generated by the query can be used if we change the **Display As** dropdown to **Standard Report Column**. Follow the given steps to notice this:

1. Go to the **Report Attributes** page of this region.

2. Click on the pencil link next to the **PRODUCT_NAME** column in **Column Attributes** and note that the value of the **Display As** dropdown is **Standard Report Column**. The same had been done for the **JOB_TITLE** column as well.

Let us now focus on the highlighted `decode` statement. Note that `job_title`, `department_name`, and `product_name` have the `not null` constraints on them. Our query only has equi-joins, so the only rows with null values for these columns will be the rows displaying the aggregations. The highlighted `decode` statement in the preceding query uses this fact to display a formatted custom text for various totals.

An easier way to identify the null values due to totaling is the `grouping` function. This function accepts a single column name as an argument and returns 1 if the null value is generated because of totaling. The `GROUPING_ID` function does a similar thing but it accepts one of the sets as an argument. If your `grouping sets` are such that they are generating duplicate subtotals for the same dimensions then you can use the `GROUP_ID` function to identify these duplicates.

It is important to mention that you can use other `Group by` extensions such as `Rollup` and `Cube` if you are interested in more levels of grouping.

Additional methods of formatting

This section introduces some more techniques to format the data in classic reports. I again wish to point out that most of these techniques can be used in almost any situation. The attempt is to introduce the various possible ways of formatting a classic report.

Highlighting the searched text in a report

Let's look at the steps to highlight a searched text in APEX:

1. Run page 2 of the reference application and enter `Public Relations` in the search box, and then click on the **Go** button as shown in the second screenshot under the *Implementing classic report search functionality* section.

2. You would see that the report is filtered and the **Public Relations** keyword is highlighted in the entire report region. While the filtering is done by the query, as explained under the *Implementing classic report search functionality* section, the highlighting is defined in the attributes of individual columns in the report

3. Go to the **Column Attributes** section in the **Report Attributes** page of **Tabular Report** of the reference application, and click on the pencil icon next to PRODUCT_NAME.

4. Go to the **Column Formatting** section and check out the **Highlight Words** textbox. You will see **&P2_REPORT_SEARCH.** there , as shown in the following screenshot. P2_REPORT_SEARCH is the name of the textbox item in which you entered Public Relations. This arrangement results in the highlighting of the **Public Relations** keyword as shown by the arrow mark in the second screenshot under the *Implementing classic report search functionality* section. You can certainly do a lot of formatting using CSS class, CSS style, and HTML expression textboxes shown in the following screenshot:

Show All	Column Definition	Column Attributes	List of Values	Tabular Form Attributes	Column Formatting

Column Formatting

CSS Class	
CSS Style	
Highlight Words	&P2_REPORT_SEARCH.
HTML Expression	

> If your logic of highlighting is complex, you can implement that in a page process, generate a comma-separated list of the words that you want to highlight and assign this list to a page item. You can then put this item in the **Highlight Words** textbox of the **Column Formatting** section. Note that putting a comma-separated list in the item will fiddle with our search functionality, because of the way the where clause of our region query is defined. This where clause was discussed in *Implementing classic report search functionality* section. So change the region query accordingly when you implement such a logic.

Editing a template for additional formatting

In this section, we will use a template and its attributes to implement the logic for highlighting various parts of a report. The **Tabular report using Grouping Sets with edited Template** region on page 2 of the reference application displays the formatting of reports using templates.

In this classic report region, the font type of all the totaled rows has been changed to bold. Open **Classic rollup report edited template** of the reference application and check `<b>` and `</b>` (underlined in the following screenshot) in **Column Template 1** section. `<b>` and `</b>` are responsible for making the text bold.

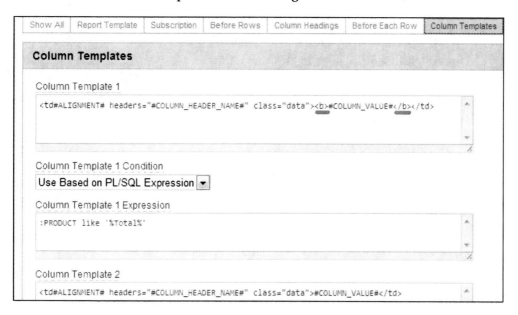

We will now understand the process of applying Column Template 1 to only the totaled rows and not to the rest of the data displayed in the report. **Column Template 1** is executed when the condition in **Column Template 1 Expression** is met, otherwise **Column Template 2** is executed. The coded condition is `:PRODUCT like '%Total%'` as shown in the preceding screenshot. It is discussed in the *Using grouping sets and HTML formatting in a query* section that our query generates the texts for the totaled rows in the `PRODUCT` column. We are doing a comparison with `%Total%`, because the texts for all totaled rows will have `Total` in them.

This template is assigned to the **Tabular report using Grouping Sets with edited Template** region on page 2 using the **Layout and Pagination** section of the **Report Attributes** page.

Run page 2 of the reference application to see this entire code in action.

> We have seen a few methods to format the output and will see a few more in the coming sections. It is important to understand that most requirements can be implemented in more than one way. The objective here is to orchestrate all the possible ways so that you can use them, wherever necessary.

Implementing a matrix report

The major learning outcomes of this section are as follows:

- Creating matrix reports
- Understanding and using the `with` clause
- Understanding and using the `pivot` operator
- Understanding string aggregation techniques
- Data highlighting using CSS, jQuery, and Dynamic Actions
- Advanced formatting using APEX templates.
- Understanding and using the Dynamic Query region in APEX

Matrix reports also known as pivoted reports are helpful when we have a measure to be sliced and diced on two or more dimensions. For example, let's say, we want to know the count of people (measure) for every combination of shirt color (Dimension 1) and pant color (Dimension 2). A matrix report for this will look like the following:

Apparel	Color		
	Green	Yellow	Blue
Pant	2	5	7
Shirt	7	0	7

We will now see the process to create one such matrix report in APEX. The tricky part in matrix report is that the number of columns change according to the data. In the preceding example, if the data had Red as the colour of a few pants or shirts then we would have had an additional column. So creation of dynamic columns and pivoting of the aggregates make a matix report different from traditional reports. Before I dig in deeper, I wish to tell you the process that we are about to follow. We will first have a look at the `with` clause to understand its importance in our report. We will then try to get a hold of the `pivot` operator, which is the heart of generating columns on the fly to create a matrix report. We will then have a look at some of the string aggregation techniques. We are using string aggregation (`listagg`) to get a comma-separated list of values which is assigned to an item (`P3_EMPLOYEE_LIST`). This item is then used for creating a dynamic `in` clause of the `pivot` operator, and for creating dynamic headings for the dynamic columns.

Understanding the with clause

If we use a sub query at multiple places in our query then we can give a name to that sub query using the `with` clause, and then reference it at multiple places in a bigger query. This helps to improve the readability and the performance of the query.

The **Matrix Report** region of page 3 of the reference application uses the `with` clause. The following query is pasted for your convenience:

```
WITH pivot_data AS ( SELECT department_id, job_id, salary
 FROM oehr_employees)
  SELECT * FROM    pivot_data
  PIVOT ( SUM(salary)         --List Clause
  FOR department_id           -- For clause
  IN  (&P3_EMPLOYEE_LIST.)  ); --Dynamic In Clause
```

The output of the query looks like the following:

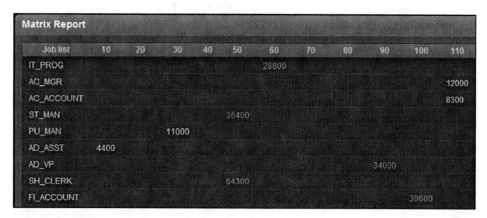

Job list	10	20	30	40	50	60	70	80	90	100	110
IT_PROG						28800					
AC_MGR											12000
AC_ACCOUNT											8300
ST_MAN					36400						
PU_MAN			11000								
AD_ASST	4400										
AD_VP									34000		
SH_CLERK					64300						
FI_ACCOUNT										39600	

Understanding the Oracle 11*g*'s pivot operator

Let me talk a little about pivot operator. This has been used in the preceding query. The basic function of a pivot query is to aggregate the data based on the function written in its `list` clause and to transpose the rows of the aggregated result as columns. The `pivot` operator has three clauses namely, the `list` clause, the `for` clause, and the `in` clause. The `list` clause describes the aggregation functions such as `sum` and `avg`. The `for` clause lists the columns which are to be grouped and pivoted. The `in` clause lists the columns which will appear in the output. The only trick in implementing a matrix report is to make a dynamic pivot `in` clause (`IN (&P3_EMPLOYEE_LIST.)`), which we will cover in the next section. Note that we have checked the **Use Generic Column Names (parse query at runtime only)** radio button under the **Region Source** in the **Source** section of the **Region Definition** page of the **Matrix Report** region. This is because the type and the number of columns generated by this query will depend on the data and we cannot have a fixed number of columns.

You would see another method of making a dynamic `in` clause in the *Implementing XML Pivot queries* section of *Chapter 9, Performance Analysis*.

Understanding string aggregation

We are talking about string aggregation because we wish to create a comma-separated list, which can not only help us in creating a dynamic in clause, but also help us in creating dynamic headings for the columns generated by the pivot operator. The following are the ways of performing string aggregations:

- Using the listagg function of Oracle 11g: We are using this method in our matrix report. listagg lets us order the data and allows us to supply a separator for the values in the list but does not allow us to use distinct. The following is the query source of the P3_EMPLOYEE_LIST item of the reference application:

```
select  listagg(department_id,',') WITHIN GROUP (ORDER BY
department_id) from (select distinct department_id from oehr_
employees)
```

  P3_EMPLOYEE_LIST is used in the region query to create a dynamic in clause. The query is pasted in the *Understanding the with clause* section. We also use P3_EMPLOYEE_LIST to create dynamic column headings. Go to the **Report Attributes** section of the **Matrix Report** region of the reference application. You would see that **PL/SQL** is selected in the **Headings Type** radio button. You would find the following code in the **Function returning colon delimited headings** section:

```
return 'Job list:'||replace(v('P3_EMPLOYEE_LIST'),',',':');
```

  This creates dynamic column headings.

- Another method to do string aggregation is wm_concat. wm_concat allows distinct, but produces only a comma-separated list and does not order the result. The syntax is as follows:

```
select wm_concat(distinct job_id) from oehr_employees
```

- String concatenation can also be done using the collect function, but the method requires the creation of a function and a type, and this involves some complexity.

- Hierarchical queries also have the potential to be used for string aggregation. We will discuss hierarchical queries in a short while.

Data highlighting using Dynamic Actions and jQuery

Now that we understand the working of matrix report, let us dedicate some time to understand a few more methods to format a classic report. We can highlight data using Dynamic Actions and jQuery. We will dedicate this section to understanding the process.

Check out the **Report dynamic action** Dynamic Action on page 3 of the reference application. Note that the value in the **Event** dropdown is set to **Page Load**. So this Dynamic Action is executed as soon as the page loads. Let's now see the JavaScript code, in the following screenshot, which is executed when the Dynamic Action is performed:

Let's understand the code in the preceding screenshot. `this.affectedElements` is a jQuery handle given by APEX to reference all the affected elements. Note that **jQuery Selector** is selected in the **Selection Type** dropdown and we have entered `.data` in the **jQuery Selector** textbox. This defines that our **Affected Elements** are the ones which have the `data` class. Why have we picked `.data`? `.data` is used because all the data in our classic report uses the `data` class. We want a handle on these elements.

How did we know that the data elements in classic reports use the `data` class? Right-click on the APEX application page and select **View Source**. This shows the HTML source of our APEX page. Search for `data` in it. You will see that the `data` class is associated with all data elements, as shown in the following screenshot:

```
<tr ><th id="COL01" class="header">Job list</th><th id="COL02" class="header">10</th><th
 class="header">30</th><th id="COL05" class="header">40</th><th id="COL06" class="header"
 class="header">70</th><th id="COL09" class="header">80</th><th id="COL10" class="header"
 class="header">110</th></tr>
<tr class="highlight-row"><td headers="COL01" class="data">AC_MGR</td><td headers="COL02"
 class="data"> </td><td headers="COL04" class="data"> </td><td headers="COL05"
 class="data"> </td><td headers="COL07" class="data"> </td><td headers="COL08"
 class="data"> </td><td headers="COL10" class="data"> </td><td headers="COL11"
 class="data">12000</td></tr>
<tr class="highlight-row"><td headers="COL01" class="data">AC_ACCOUNT</td><td headers="CO
 class="data"> </td><td headers="COL04" class="data"> </td><td headers="COL05"
 class="data"> </td><td headers="COL07" class="data"> </td><td headers="COL08"
 class="data"> </td><td headers="COL10" class="data"> </td><td headers="COL11"
 class="data">8300</td></tr>
```

In the code of the first screenshot of this section, `this.affectedElements` gives us a handle to an array of elements, and we use a `map` function to reach out to each individual element that can be controlled by the `this.affectedElements` handle. We retrieve the value of each element using `$(this).html()`, and set the color of that element to `red` if the value is greater than `20000`. The setting of the color is done by using `$(this).css({color: 'red'});`.

`$(this)` is jQuery's method to reference the current element. `html()` and `css()` are the functions referenced using the `$(this)` object. `css()` function is accepting a JSON object, that is, `{color: 'red'}` as its argument.

We can see the changed color of data elements in the screenshot under the *Understanding the with clause* section. Other jQuery handles apart from `this.affectedElements` are `this.triggeringElement`, `this.action`, `this.browserEvent`, and `this.data`.

Alright, now we have seen that our Dynamic Action affects anything that has `data` as its class. Now if we have multiple regions on our page and if we want our highlighting effect to be limited to one region, then we are in a soup. The solution is to create a copy of the template used for classic report regions, change the class name in the copied template, and then assign this template to other regions on the page. Since we would have changed the name of the class, the Dynamic Action will not apply to the regions with a new template. Let's do it in the next section.

Note that we can also limit the number of elements affected by a jQuery selector by choosing a more restrictive selector. The text has been designed to present the use case of using altered APEX templates.

Advanced formatting using APEX templates

We now have to create a template that uses some other class for formatting data and not the `data` class. This other class should have similar look and feel as the `data` class. From my experience, I know that the **Standard, Alternating Row Colors** template has a similar look and feel as a **Standard** template, so classes used in **Standard, Alternating Row Colors** template can be used for our purpose. The `dataalt` class is used in this template, and the `.report-standards-alternatingrowcolors td.dataalt` class is defined at `<directory_in_which_apex_4.1.1_en.zip_is_unzipped>/apex/images/themes/theme_3/css/theme_4_0.css`. Since the definition of the `data` and `dataalt` classes are in the `theme_4_0.css` file, we don't have to include any new CSS file in our APEX page. Now, we have to create a new template and include the `dataalt class` in it. **Matrix report template** of the reference application has the necessary changes in it. You would find `class="report-standard-alternatingrowcolors"` (highlighted in the following screenshot) in the **Before Rows** section.

```
Before Rows
<tr>
<td><table cellpadding="0" border="0" cellspacing="0" summary="" class="report-standard-
alternatingrowcolors">
```

Go to the **Column Template 1** section and note that it has `class="dataalt"`, as shown in the following screenshot:

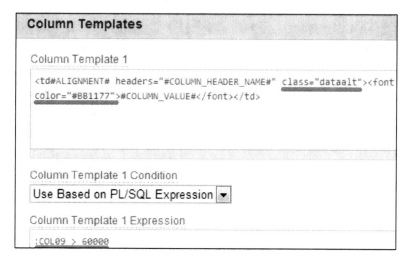

The **Matrix report changed template** region uses **Matrix report template**, and **Matrix report template** uses the `dataalt` class; so any Dynamic Action that uses the `data` class will not affect the **Matrix report changed template** region.

Note that in the preceding screenshot we have used `<font color="#BB1177">` in the **Column Template 1** section of **Matrix report template**. Again, we can conditionally apply this formatting within a report. Also note that in the preceding screenshot, we have used `:COL09 > 60000` in **Column Template 1 Expression**. This ensures that `<font color="#BB1177">` is applied to those values of `COL09`, which are greater than `60000`.

 Apart from the procedure described previously, you can have a look at the `APEX_CSS.ADD` and `APEX_CSS.ADD_FILE` procedures of the APEX API. These procedures let us add new CSS styles dynamically and us can control the whole thing from PL/SQL blocks.

We have just seen the process to use a predefined CSS class in a template. We can also write the definition of a class in a template. Check **Template for matrix report with self defined CSS in template** in the reference application. Check the **Before Rows** section. You will see CSS class definitions enclosed between the `<STYLE> </STYLE>` tags. You can see the use of these classes (`td.edited-td-template`, `th.edited-th-template`, `table.edited-table-template`) in the **Column Heading Template**, **Column Template 1**, and **Before Rows** section. **Template for matrix report with self defined CSS in template** is used in the **Matrix report with self defined CSS in template** region in the reference application.

Understanding dynamic query region in APEX

This section is an introduction to using dynamic queries in APEX reports. We will look at advanced ways of developing dynamic reports in the next chapter. This section is just to introduce the APEX's functionality of running dynamic reports and to use it for matrix reports. Go to **Region Source** of **Matrix Report with dynamic query** region of the reference application. The following screenshot is of the same region source. Note that **Region Source** contains a PL/SQL block, and this PL/SQL block returns the query that displays the report. The flexibility of writing the query as a string in a PL/SQL block gives us the freedom to make dynamic classic reports.

```
Region Source

begin
return 'WITH pivot_data AS (
            SELECT department_id, job_id, salary
            FROM   oehr_employees
            )
    SELECT *
    FROM   pivot_data
    PIVOT (
            SUM(salary)
          FOR department_id
          IN  (' || v('P3_EMPLOYEE_LIST') || ')
        )';
end;
```

Implementing hierarchical reports

The following are the major learning outcomes of this section:

- Creating hierarchical reports using drilldown links
- Dynamic messages using substitution variables
- Creating dynamic breadcrumbs for drill ups
- Understanding hierarchical queries and creating reports on them
- Creating a hierarchical report using the recursive with clause
- Creating a tree based on hierarchical data

Hierarchical reports with drilldown

Our aim is to introduce drilldowns in APEX and to use them for hierarchical data reporting.

Check the **Hierarchical reports with drilldown** region on page 4 of the reference application. The EMPLOYEE_ID column of the **Hierarchical Report** region has a link on it. Let us now see the process of creating this link. Go to the **Report Attributes** page of the region, and then click on the pencil icon next to the EMPLOYEE_ID column, which is present under the **Column Attributes** section.

Go to the **Column Link** section as shown in the following screenshot:

Note that we have #EMPLOYEE_ID# in **Link Text**. This ensures that we will have employee IDs as link texts. We have selected **Page in this Application** in the **Target** dropdown and **4** in the **Page** textbox. This ensures that page **4** (the same page on which this region exists) will be reloaded whenever the user clicks on a link. We have put P4_MANAGER_ID in the **Name** column and #EMPLOYEE_ID# in the **Value** column of the **Item 1** row. This ensures that the value (EMPLOYEE_ID) selected by the user will be stored in the P4_MANAGER_ID item which is compared with the MANAGER_ID column of the OEHR_EMPLOYEES table in the region query source. This comparison is done by the following where clause:

```
"OEHR_EMPLOYEES"."MANAGER_ID" like '%' || :P4_MANAGER_ID || '%'
```

When the page loads for the first time, P4_MANAGER_ID is empty and the like operator in the query results in displaying all the records. When any EMPLOYEE_ID is clicked, the value of P4_MANAGER_ID is set, and the records returned are only those employees whose manager is the person whose EMPLOYEE_ID has been clicked. Now these filtered records have their own links and the drilling down can continue as long as we do not reach the lowest possible node in the hierarchy chain.

Creating dynamic messages using substitution variables

We will now see the use of substitution variables for creating dynamic messages. Go to the **Report Attributes** page of the **Hierarchical reports with drilldown** region and note that we have the following in the **When No Data Found Message** text area:

The use of the `&P4_MANAGER_ID.` substitution variable ensures that a message with the selected employee ID is displayed when a user clicks on the ID of employees who do not have subordinates.

Creating dynamic breadcrumbs for drill ups

The drilldown hierarchical report (discussed in the *Hierarchical reports with drilldown* section) has no mechanism to show which employee IDs were clicked by the user to reach a particular level in the hierarchical chain. The user might have a requirement of drilling upwards, but he does not have a mechanism to do this. We can solve this problem by using dynamic breadcrumbs.

The traditional way of creating dynamic breadcrumbs is by using page items as substitution variables in the breadcrumb entry. This use of substitution variable is similar to the use of substitution variables in the **When No Data Found Message** text area in the preceding section. This type of dynamic breadcrumb works if the number of levels is fixed, and only the page number to which each breadcrumb entry refers has to be dynamic. Our problem is that the depth of the levels is different in different hierarchical chains and hence we cannot create a fixed number of breadcrumb entries. Hierarchical chain stands for the chain from a particular employee to the top most person in the organization. Clearly, the length of this chain will vary depending upon the level of the person in question.

We will have to create breadcrumb entries on the fly when the user clicks on an employee ID. We also have to destroy these entries as soon as the user moves on to a different page, because a number of hierarchical chains are possible in a hierarchical tree and the breadcrumbs used for one chain cannot be used for another.

To solve this problem, we have created the **Dynamic Breadcrumb** region in page 4 of the reference application. Note that the position of display of this region is such that it appears in the same place where a usual breadcrumb would have appeared. **Display Point** in the **User Interface** section of the **Region Definition** page is set to **Page Template Region Position 1** to get this done, as shown in the following screenshot:

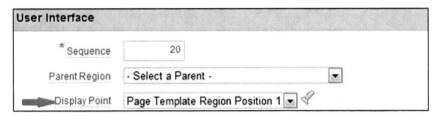

Let's now understand the method to create dynamic breadcrumbs. I checked the HTML generated for a usual breadcrumb and used it to get an idea of the kind of HTML that I should programmatically create for our dynamic breadcrumbs. The HTML of a usual breadcrumb is a good guide, because the CSS classes used for formatting the breadcrumb can be used in dynamic breadcrumb to make the look and feel consistent.

Let us look at the code to generate dynamic breadcrumbs. The anonymous PL/SQL block, in the region source of the **Dynamic Breadcrumb** region does this for us, as shown in the following code. It uses the `htp.p` procedure to transmit its HTML to the client browser. Using `sys.htp.p` instead of `htp.p` is, however, better from security point of view.

```
DECLARE
    l_vc_arr2    APEX_APPLICATION_GLOBAL.VC_ARR2;
    breadcrumbString varchar2(500);
BEGIN
htp.p('<div id="topbar"><div class="breadcrumb-region"><div
id="breadcrumbs"><ul class="breadcrumb-list">');
    If :P4_MANAGER_ID is null then
      htp.p('<li class="current">All employees</li>');

    else
      htp.p('<li class="noncurrent"><a href="f?p=&APP_ID.:4:&APP_
SESSION.::NO::P4_MANAGER_ID:">All employees</a></li>');
      end if;

SELECT *
INTO breadcrumbString
```

```
FROM
  (SELECT SYS_CONNECT_BY_PATH(last_name||'('||employee_id||')', ':')
"Path"
  FROM oehr_employees
  WHERE employee_id              = :P4_MANAGER_ID
    CONNECT BY NOCYCLE PRIOR employee_id = manager_id
  ORDER BY level DESC
  )
WHERE rownum = 1;


l_vc_arr2 := APEX_UTIL.STRING_TO_TABLE(breadcrumbString);

    FOR z IN 2..l_vc_arr2.count LOOP
       If z = l_vc_arr2.count then
        htp.p('<li class="sep">&rsaquo;</li><li class="current">'||l_
vc_arr2(z)||'</li>');
       else
        htp.p('<li class="sep">&rsaquo;</li><li class="noncurrent"><a
href="f?p=&APP_ID.:4:&APP_SESSION.::NO::P4_MANAGER_ID:'||REGEXP_
SUBSTR(l_vc_arr2(z),'[[:digit:]]+')||'">'||l_vc_arr2(z)||'</a></li>');
       end if;
    END LOOP;
htp.p('</ul></div><div class="clear"></div></div></div>');
Exception
When no_data_found then
null;
END;
If :P4_MANAGER_ID is null then
htp.p('<li class="current">All employees</li>');
```

Let's understand this. Look at the first highlighted piece of code. If P4_MANAGER_ID is null, that is, when the page is loaded, the breadcrumb starts with All employees and it does not have a link on it. So, if you move your mouse pointer to All employees in the breadcrumb region after the first load of the page, you will see that you cannot click on it.

If however, the user has drilled down, then the All Employees link should be such that it helps the user to see all the employees. This is done in the else part of the first highlighted piece of the preceding code. We pass a null value to P4_MANAGER_ID here, to achieve this.

Let's now look at the second highlighted part of the preceding code. The first query of the second highlighted piece of code returns all the rows that can be connected by the manager-employee relationship defined in the connect by clause. We are interested in only one chain, that is, the one from the employee in question to the topmost person in the organization. This chain can be used for the breadcrumb. Inner query returns the records such that the value of the level pseudo column is the highest in the topmost row which has the desired chain. Hence we have WHERE rownum = 1 in the outer query to get this topmost row. The chain is generated by using the SYS_CONNECT_BY_PATH function. We have used the level pseudo column, the SYS_CONNECT_BY_PATH function, CONNECT BY PRIOR, and NOCYCLE in this query. NOCYCLE is helpful if our hierarchical data forms a loop. The CONNECT_BY_ISCYCLE pseudo column shows the rows that have the data causing the loop.

> Other important terms related to hierarchical queries are the CONNECT BY LEVEL, START WITH, ORDER SIBLINGS BY, CONNECT_BY_ROOT operator ,and the CONNECT_BY_ISLEAF pseudo column.

Let's now look at the lower half of the second highlighted part of the code. APEX_UTIL.STRING_TO_TABLE is used to convert the employee chain string to employee chain PL/SQL table.

Finally, we use a for loop to generate the breadcrumb. The if statement, in the for loop, ensures that a link is not generated on the last node of the breadcrumb chain. Having a link on the last node of the breadcrumb does not make sense, because clicking on such a link will bring the user back to the current page. Other nodes in the chain have links and take the user to their respective levels. These links are generated in the else part of the if-else statement.

The colon-separated values generated by the hierarchical query in the top half of the second highlighted piece of code contains the last name of the manager followed by his employee_id in brackets. Now, the drilling down or drilling up works by setting the employee_id in P4_MANAGER_ID. So we have to extract the employee ID from the value returned by the query. This is done by using regular expressions in the else part of the if-else statement in the lower half of the second highlighted piece of code.

Check out the working of the **Dynamic Breadcrumb** region in the reference application.

Creating a report with hierarchical query

This section presents the use of a hierarchical query to create a hierarchical report in APEX. The **Report with hierarchical query** region is on one such hierarchical query. While **Hierarchical reports with drilldown** gives the details of the immediate subordinates of P4_MANAGER_ID, **Report with hierarchical query** gives the details of P4_MANAGER_ID. The code is similar to the hierarchical query used in the **Dynamic Breadcrumb** region. Following is a part of the query of **Report with hierarchical query** region, shared for your reference:

```
select * from (SELECT "OEHR_EMPLOYEES"."EMPLOYEE_ID" as "EMPLOYEE_ID",
    "OEHR_EMPLOYEES"."FIRST_NAME" as "FIRST_NAME",
    "OEHR_EMPLOYEES"."LAST_NAME" as "LAST_NAME", SYS_CONNECT_BY_
PATH(last_name, '/') "Path"
    FROM oehr_employees
    WHERE employee_id              = :P4_MANAGER_ID
    CONNECT BY NOCYCLE PRIOR employee_id = manager_id
order by level desc)
    where rownum = 1
```

Creating a hierarchical report using the recursive with clause

The recursive with clause is another method to fetch hierarchical data. As the name suggest, the definition of the with clause references itself to connect the rows. The following is the query of the region source of **Hierarchy with a recursive With Clause**:

```
with empl(employee_id, last_name, first_name,email,phone_number,hire_
date,salary,job_id, with_level) as (
select employee_id, last_name, first_name,email,phone_number,hire_
date,salary,job_id, 1 with_level
from oehr_employees
where employee_id  = 100
    union all
    select e.employee_id, e.last_name, e.first_name, e.email, e.phone_
number, e.hire_date, e.salary, e.job_id, empl.with_level+1 with_level
from oehr_employees e, empl
where e.manager_id=empl.employee_id)
    search depth first by last_name set ordering_sequence
    cycle employee_id set is_cycle to '1' default '0'
```

```
select replace(rpad(' ',2*(with_level-1)),' ',' ')||employee_
id||': '||last_name Names, first_name,email,phone_number,hire_
date,salary,job_id,ordering_sequence,is_cycle
  from empl
--order by is_cycle desc
--order by ordering_sequence
```

Let's do a dry run of this query. The first highlighted part of the query gives a row from which the chain begins. This query plays the same role as START WITH in a usual hierarchical query. We use `where employee_id = 100` to identify the topmost row. Note that the `with_level` column has 1 as its value. This symbolizes that the depth of the row returned by the first highlighted part of the query is 1.

The whole fun lies in the `where` clause of the second highlighted part of the query. This `where` clause compares the `employee_id` column of the row returned by the first highlighted query (`empl.employee_id`) with the `manager_id` column of the `oehr_employees` table (`e.manager_id`). Clearly, employees returned by the second highlighted query will be the immediate subordinates of the `employee_id` column returned by the first highlighted query. Now, check the formula in the `with_level` column of the second highlighted query. It has `empl.with_level+1`. The level set in the first `select` statement was 1, so the immediate subordinates get the level as 1 + 1=2. Note that this whole thing is defined inside the `empl with` clause. So, these employees with `level` set to 2 can again be referenced using the `empl.` notation and the `where` clause of the second highlighted part of the query recursively compares these `employee_id` of the `level` 2 records with the `oehr_employees` table to get the `level` 3 records. The process goes on to get the hierarchical result. The third highlighted statement identifies the cycle in a recursive `with` clause.

When we compare `nocycle` of `connect by` and `is_cycle` of the recursive `with` clause, we find that the recursive `with` clause repeats the problematic record. This is because `connect by` has an eye on the future, it checks the children which it is yet to display, while the recursive `with` clause looks back. It finds out about the cycling only after it has processed a row.

You can also see the following code in the query:

```
search depth first by last_name set ordering_sequence
```

Using `breadth first` will give the result in parent-children order, while `depth first` will show the rows of the same level together.

The syntax of `breadth first` is as follows:

```
search breadth first by last_name set ordering_sequence
```

The result is displayed to the user is governed by the final `select` statement at the bottom of the query.

We can sort the result set by using `ordering_sequence` and `is_cycle` in the order by clause of the final `select` statement.

Also note `replace(rpad(' ',2*(with_level-1)),' ',' ')` in the final `select` statement. This is done to indent the rows according to their levels. The **Display As** dropdown of the **Names** column has been changed to **Standard Report Column** for this code to be effective.

The following is the equivalent query in `connect by`:

```
select rpad(' ',2*(level-1))|| employee_id||': '|| last_name Names
   from oehr_employees
      start with employee_id = 100
      connect by nocycle prior employee_id= manager_id
      order siblings by last_name;
```

> Note that the recursive `with` clause gives us the additional power to sort the rows of the same level together.

Creating a tree based on hierarchical data

The following are the steps to create an APEX tree on hierarchical data:

1. Right-click on **Regions** and select **Create** from the menu.

2. Select **Tree** and click on **Next**.

3. Give a name to the region and select your preferred tree template.

4. Select **PACKT_SCHEMA** as the schema and **OEHR_EMPLOYEES** as the table. If the hierarchical data requires the joining of multiple tables then create a view and use it here. Click on **Next**.

5. Select **EMPLOYEE_ID** in the ID dropdown, **MANAGER_ID** in the **Parent ID** dropdown, **LAST_NAME** in the **Node Text** dropdown, **EMPLOYEE_ID** in the **Start With** dropdown, **Based on Static Value** in the **Start Tree** dropdown, and enter `100` in the **Start Value** textbox.

6. Click on **Next**.

7. The next step lets us code an optional `where` clause and an optional `order by siblings` clause. Click on **Next**.

8. The next section is to make the **Expand All** and **Collapse All** buttons, and to help us code the links on the leaves of the tree. Keep the defaults and click on **Next**.

9. Click on **Create Region**.

10. This wizard does not let us code the `NOCYCLE` parameter, so we will have to manually put it. Right-click on the newly created region and select **Edit Tree**. Enter `NOCYCLE` before **EMPLOYEE_ID** in the **Tree Query** section, and then click on **Apply Changes**.

11. The wizard generates HTML buttons. We can change them to template-based buttons by editing them.

The **Employee tree** region in the reference application is an example of this type of region.

Understanding methods to upload files in APEX

We will dedicate the next few sections to understand the uploading of files. The process of uploading as coded on page 5 of the reference application is as follows:

The user clicks on the **UPDATE** button. We have an **UPDATE** button on every row of the report in page 5. Use the following screenshot for your assistance. Clicking on this button sets the value of the `P5_EMPLOYEE_ID` page item to the selected employee ID using the **Update profiles** Dynamic Action. The code that does this is discussed in the *Using DA to set page items and side effects of PPR* section. The label of the `P5_FILEOBJECT` item uses `P5_EMPLOYEE_ID` as a substitution variable. So the label of `P5_FILEOBJECT` always has the selected employee ID in it. This code is discussed in the *Using substitution variables for labels* section. The `P5_FILEOBJECT` file browse item can now be used to select a file which we want to upload.

`setFileName`, the JavaScript function, written in the **JavaScript** section of the page, executes as soon as a value is selected in the `P5_FILEOBJECT` page item. `setFileName` automatically picks the file name and populates `P5_FILE_NAME` page item. This is discussed in the *Auto feeding one APEX item based on another* section. The user can then click on the **Apply Changes** button to upload the file.

This will upload the selected file in the `OEHR_EMPLOYEE_PROFILES` table and will also update the `FILENAME` column in the same table. The following screenshot is provided for your guidance:

 Uploading the file will generate three links, one each under the **Traditional Download**, **Download File**, and **Another Method To Download** columns. We will talk about these in the *Understanding download methods* section.

We are able to upload our file, as discussed previously, and store the selected file in `OEHR_EMPLOYEE_PROFILES` table because we had created an APEX form on the `OEHR_EMPLOYEE_PROFILES` table on page 5 in the following way:

1. We created a blank page, named it **Update profiles** and gave 5 as its page number.

2. We created a **Form** region and selected **Form on a Table or View**.

3. We then selected **OEHR_EMPLOYEE_PROFILES** in the **Table / View Name** dropdown.

4. We kept the defaults in the next step of the wizard.

5. We then checked **Select Primary Key Column(s)** in the **Primary Key Type** radio button group.

6. We selected **EMPLOYEE_ID** in the **Primary Key Column 1** dropdown and selected the **Existing sequence** radio button.

7. We selected **OEHR_EMPLOYEE_PROFILES_SEQ** in the **Sequence** dropdown, and selected **FILEOBJECT (Blob)** and **FILENAME (Varchar2)** in the **Select Column(s)** shuttle.

8. We selected **No** in **Show Create Button** and **Show Delete Button** dropdowns. We enter 5 in the **After Page Submit and Processing Branch to Page** and **When Cancel Button Pressed Branch to this Page** textboxes, and then clicked on the **Finish** button.

When the **Apply Changes** button is clicked after selecting of the file to be uploaded, Process Row of **OEHR_EMPLOYEE_PROFILES** process (created by APEX because of the form we created before) is triggered and it updates the row corresponding to the chosen employee with the uploaded file and the name of the file. The process is able to update the FILENAME and FILEOBJECT columns of OEHR_EMPLOYEE_PROFILES with the values of the P5_FILE_NAME and P5_FILEOBJECT items, because the database columns have been specified as the source of these items. The following screenshot has been shared for your convenience:

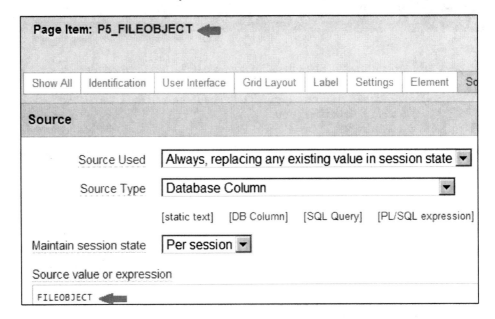

> We can also use the LOADBLOBFROMFILE and LOADCLOBFROMFILE procedures of the DBMS_LOB package to upload files. Read more about this procedure from http://docs.oracle.com/cd/ E11882_01/appdev.112/e10577/d_lob.htm.

Using DA to set page items and side effects of PPR

The objective of this section is to understand the setting of the P5_EMPLOYEE_ID item using the **Update Profiles** Dynamic Action. Let us first talk about the link (**UPDATE** buttons) that invokes this DA.

UPDATE buttons are under the **Update profiles** column in our report. Open the **Slice & Dice** region of the **Report Attributes** page, and then click on the pencil icon next to the **Update profiles** column. Go to the **Column Link** section. Note that we have set `<img src="#IMAGE_PREFIX#update.gif">` for the **Link Text**, URL set as the **Target** and `javascript:function(){}` for the URL, as shown in the following screenshot:

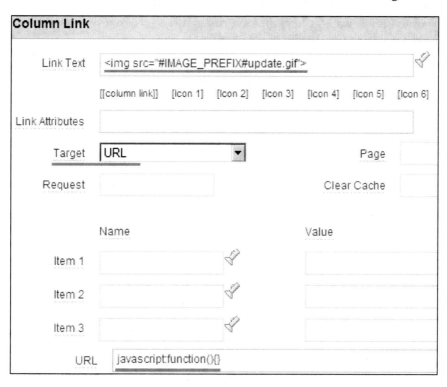

We have put an empty JavaScript function as a link in order to force APEX to create a link; a link that takes us to nowhere. The empty JavaScript function helps us to get the hand cursor when the user moves his mouse over the link. The actual action fired on the click of this link is defined by the **Update Profiles** Dynamic Action. Check out the **When** section of the **Update Profiles** Dynamic Action.

This Dynamic Action uses **JQuery selector** to identify the triggering HTML element. The **jQuery Selector** textbox says that the Dynamic Action should be fired when any of the td HTML elements with the LINK$02 header attribute is clicked. The headers of the columns created by clicking on the **Add Column Link** in the **Tasks** panel on the right hand side of the **Report Attributes** page of a report start with LINK$ and our **Update profiles** column has the LINK$02 header. Check the HTML page source of page 5 of the reference application to verify this. The following screenshot has been pasted for your convenience:

```
90F7A2AC&p_content_disposition=attachment">bells.jpg</A></td><td headers="LINK$02" class="data"><a
href="javascript:function(){}" ><img src=""/i/update.gif"></a></td><td headers="LINK$01" class="data"><a
```

Let us now see the JavaScript code that is executed by the **Update Profiles** DA, which is as follows:

```
$(this.triggeringElement).siblings().each(function(i) {if (this.
headers == 'EMPLOYEE_ID') {
apex.submit({set:{'P5_EMPLOYEE_ID':this.innerText},showWait:true});
//$s('P5_EMPLOYEE_ID',this.innerText);
}});
```

Our goal is to get the EMPLOYEE_ID column of the row on which the user clicks and set it in P5_EMPLOYEE_ID. To meet this objective, the preceding JavaScript code finds the siblings of the triggering element. The triggering element is the link of the **Update Profiles** column on which the user clicks. The siblings of the triggering element are the other columns in the same row as the triggering element. We check these siblings to find the one which has EMPLOYEE_ID as its header. We then capture the value of this sibling and set P5_EMPLOYEE_ID using apex.submit. Now for this Dynamic Action to work, we have to ensure that PPR has not been used on the page. We are using PPR to navigate to different pages of the classic report and for soft deleting a row (we will discuss soft deleting in the *Implementing soft deletion with AJAX and Apex templates* section).

A workaround to the side effects of PPR

A workaround to our problem can be that we call apex.submit when the user clicks on the **UPDATE** button instead of calling the **Update Profiles** DA. We will have to put the following in the **URL** textbox of the **Column Link** section in the **Column Attributes** page of the **Update profiles** column to make this work.

```
javascript:apex.submit({set:{'P5_EMPLOYEE_ID':#EMPLOYEE_
ID#},showWait:true});
```

This code will set P5_EMPLOYEE_ID with the value of the EMPLOYEE_ID column of the row on which the user clicks.

 Another workaround to the multiple DA problem is selecting **Dynamic** in the **Event Scope** dropdown of a DA. This will ensure that whenever a PPR happens, the DA is applied again to the "new" fields.

Using substitution variables for labels

We will now see the use of substitution variables for making dynamic labels. Have a look at the label of P5_FILEOBJECT. You will see Upload file for employee number &P5_EMPLOYEE_ID. in it. Here, &P5_EMPLOYEE_ID. is an item used as substitution variable. This ensures that the label will change with the changing value of P5_EMPLOYEE_ID.

Auto feeding one APEX item based on another

We will now see the method of extracting a value for one item based on the value entered in another. Have a look at onChange="javascript:setFileName(this.value);" in the **HTML Form Element Attributes** textbox of P5_FILEOBJECT. Any change of value in the P5_FILEOBJECT item triggers setFileName. Have a look at the definition of the setFileName function from the **JavaScript** section in the page definition of page 5 of reference application. The following code is pasted for your convenience:

```
function setFileName(p_big_file_name) {
$x('P5_FILE_NAME').value = p_big_file_name.substring(p_big_file_name.
lastIndexOf('\\')+1);}
```

The setFileName function has a single line of code which gets the value of the P5_FILE_NAME textbox and sets the part of the string after the last backslash as the value of P5_FILE_NAME. The user however has the freedom to update the **P5_FILE_NAME** textbox if required.

Note that we use \\ to find the last backslash. We need two backslashes because \ is used as an escape character in JavaScript, and hence an extra backslash is used as an escape for the other backslash. Instead of using $x().value, we can also use $s to assign a value to a page item.

The method to upload files using WWV_FLOW_FILES

I feel that this section deserves a place here since we are discussing ways to upload files in APEX. Till now, we are using an approach where we create a form and APEX creates all the necessary items and processes required for us to upload files. We can, however, create our own **File Browse...** page item with the **Storage Type** of **TABLE WWV_FLOW_FILES**. When we select a file in this item and submit the page, the file selected in the item gets uploaded and we can access the file from `apex_application_files` along with some other details such as file name, mime type, and doc size. We can then use this file according to our own desires. Trying this out is left as an exercise for the reader.

Understanding download methods

This section is dedicated to understanding various methods to download reports in APEX. The following are the major learning outcomes of this section:

- Understanding the process to download using APEX format mask.
- Understanding the process to download using developer-defined, stored procedure.
- Understanding the process to download using `APEX_UTIL.GET_BLOB_FILE_SRC`.
- Understanding the process to download using the `p` procedure

Before we jump to understanding these methods, we will look at the following region source query of the **Slice & Dice** region. This query holds the secrets of downloading files using all the ways listed previously. We will talk about the various parts of this query in a short while.

```
select     "OEHR_EMPLOYEE_PROFILES"."EMPLOYEE_ID" as "EMPLOYEE_ID",
   "OEHR_EMPLOYEES"."FIRST_NAME" as "FIRST_NAME",
   "OEHR_EMPLOYEES"."LAST_NAME" as "LAST_NAME",
dbms_lob.getlength("OEHR_EMPLOYEE_PROFILES"."FILEOBJECT") as "Download
file",
       "OEHR_EMPLOYEE_PROFILES"."FILENAME" as "Traditional
download",
       HTF.ANCHOR(curl => APEX_UTIL.GET_BLOB_FILE_SRC(p_item_name
=> 'P5_FILEOBJECT', p_v1 => "OEHR_EMPLOYEE_PROFILES"."EMPLOYEE_ID",
p_content_disposition => 'attachment'),ctext => "OEHR_EMPLOYEE_
PROFILES"."FILENAME") as "Another method to download"
from   OEHR_EMPLOYEES,OEHR_EMPLOYEE_PROFILES
where  OEHR_EMPLOYEES.JOB_ID like nvl(:P5_JOB_FILTER,'%')
```

```
and     OEHR_EMPLOYEES.SALARY like nvl(:P5_SALARY_FILTER,'%')
and OEHR_EMPLOYEES.EMPLOYEE_ID = OEHR_EMPLOYEE_PROFILES.EMPLOYEE_ID
and OEHR_EMPLOYEES.DELETE_FLAG = 'N'
```

The `like` operator in the `where` clause is used to ensure that all records are displayed when no filter is selected. We will talk about these filters in the *DML operations and report filtering using DA, JavaScript, and Page Processes* section. The preceding query uses `dbms_lob.getlength`, `HTF.ANCHOR`, `APEX_UTIL.GET_BLOB_FILE_SRC` and `"OEHR_EMPLOYEES"."DELETE_FLAG" = 'N'`. Each one of these has a specific function and we will talk about these one by one now. Let us start with `dbms_lob.getlength` first in the next section.

Download using APEX format mask

We will check out the use of the APEX format mask to help us generate a link on a `blob` column that can help us download the data in it. This format mask is as follows:

```
DOWNLOAD:Table Name:Column containing BLOB:Primary Key Column
1:Primary Key Column 2:MIME type Column:Filename Column:Last Update
Column:Character Set Column:Content Disposition:Download Text
```

The first four in the preceding format mask are necessary while the rest are optional. If we use this format mask on a `blob` column, and if that column is passed as an argument to `dbms_lob.getlength` in the region source query then APEX will generate a link on the column that will let us download the blob. The **Download file** column of the **Slice & Dice** region is one such column that has `dbms_lob.getlength("OEHR_EMPLOYEE_PROFILES"."FILEOBJECT")` in the region source, and has `DOWNLOAD:OEHR_EMPLOYEE_PROFILES:FILEOBJECT:EMPLOYEE_ID:::::attachment:Profile` as the format mask in the **Number / Date Format** textbox of **Column Attributes** of the **Download file** column.

Download using developer-defined stored function

We will now have a look at a method by which we can define our own function that can help us download the data in the `blob` columns. The link under the **Traditional Download** column of page 5 of the reference application uses the `download_file` procedure defined in the `chapter2` package. When the user clicks on a link in the **Traditional Download** column, the corresponding `employee_id` value of the link is passed to the `chapter2.download_file` procedure by the following URL:

```
packt_schema.chapter2.download_file?p_employee_number=#EMPLOYEE_ID#
```

This URL is present in the **URL** textbox of the **Column Attributes** of the **Traditional Download** column.

Before you can start to download files using this method, you will have to put the following entry in the `defaults.xml` file and restart WebLogic:

```
<entry key="security.inclusionList">apex, p, v, f, wwv_*,y*, c*,
PACKT_SCHEMA.*, packt_schema.*, apex_util.*</entry>
```

> Note that the entry in `defaults.xml` is case sensitive. So we have `PACKT_SCHEMA.*`, `packt_schema.*`, in it.

`packt_schema.*` in the preceding list helps us to call all procedures of `packt_schema` from the URL. We will also have to give the following command:

```
grant execute on chapter2 to apex_public_user
```

Let us now look at the code of the `packt_schema.chapter2.download_file` function, which is as follows:

```
PROCEDURE DOWNLOAD_FILE ( p_employee_number number) IS
  l_length     NUMBER;      l_file_name VARCHAR2 (4000);
  l_file BLOB;              l_ext VARCHAR2 (4000);
BEGIN
  SELECT fileobject, filename, DBMS_LOB.getlength (fileobject)
  INTO l_file, l_file_name, l_length
  FROM oehr_employee_profiles
  WHERE employee_id = p_employee_number;

  If INSTR (l_file_name, '.', -1, 1) > 0 then
      l_ext := SUBSTR (l_file_name, INSTR (l_file_name, '.', -1, 1) +
1);
  End if;

  IF (UPPER (l_ext) = 'PDF') THEN
    OWA_UTIL.mime_header ('application/pdf', FALSE);
  ELSIF (UPPER (l_ext) = 'DOC') THEN
    OWA_UTIL.mime_header ('application/msword', FALSE);
  ELSIF (UPPER (l_ext) = 'TXT') THEN
    OWA_UTIL.mime_header ('text/plain', FALSE);
  ELSIF (UPPER (l_ext) = 'HTML') THEN
    OWA_UTIL.mime_header ('text/html', FALSE);
```

```
    ELSE
      owa_util.mime_header('application/octet', FALSE );
    END IF;
    HTP.p ('Content-length: ' || l_length);
    -- the filename will be used by the browser if the users does a save
as
    HTP.p ( 'Content-Disposition: attachment; filename="' || l_file_name
|| '"' );
    OWA_UTIL.http_header_close;
    WPG_DOCLOAD.download_file (l_file);
END DOWNLOAD_FILE;
```

This procedure accepts an `employee_id` as an argument. This `employee_id` is used to fetch the corresponding `blob` object, filename, and file size. We then find the extension of the file by using `SUBSTR`. Based on the extension, we create the header for the file. Once the header is set, we use the `WPG_DOCLOAD.download_file` procedure to download the `blob` object.

Download using APEX_UTIL.GET_BLOB_FILE_SRC

The `APEX_UTIL` package also has methods that can help us download our blob. Let us see the process for this. The **Another method to download** column of the reference application is an example of this method. Check the highlighted code in the query shared in the *Understanding download methods* section. `HTF.ANCHOR` generates the anchor tag which is basically the HTML code for displaying the hyperlink. The URL to which the redirection should happen when a user clicks on this link is given by the `APEX_UTIL.GET_BLOB_FILE_SRC` function. The arguments of this function are a page item of **File Browse...** type, the value of the primary key, and text which says whether the download should be `inline` or an `attachment`.

> Another method of getting a file is the `APEX_UTIL.GET_FILE` function. `APEX_UTIL.DOWNLOAD_PRINT_DOCUMENT` has four signatures and is used to download reports. We have used `APEX_UTIL.DOWNLOAD_PRINT_DOCUMENT` on page 4 of the reference application of *Chapter 7, Integrating APEX with OBIEE*. `APEX_UTIL.GET_PRINT_DOCUMENT` is another procedure that can be used for similar purposes.

Download using p process

I want to talk about the p process, since I have been talking about the various ways to download files from APEX. You won't find an implementation of this in the reference application. Consider the following text as a to-do assignment. p, like f, is a procedure of APEX. To use this for download, we will have to put p?n=#ID# in the URL textbox of **Column Attributes** of a column and we will have to change the storage type of the P5_FILEOBJECT item to **Table WWV_FLOW_FILES**. Only the files uploaded after changing the storage type can be downloaded using this method. You should already be familiar with the syntax of p?n=#ID#. Here, p is the procedure and n is its argument. Now, n needs an ID. You can get this ID from the ID column of APEX_APPLICATION_FILES. The file itself can also be retrieved from the BLOB_CONTENT column of APEX_APPLICATION_FILES.

> Note that you will not be able to see your file in APEX_APPLICATION_FILES, if you are querying outside of your APEX session. This is because of the way APEX_APPLICATION_FILES is designed. Use the following query to view your data outside of your session. Replace 107 with your application ID:
>
> ```
> select id, name,filename from wwv_flow_file_
> objects$ where flow_id = 107
> ```

This brings us to the end of the section in which we discussed various ways of downloading a report. Let us now move on to understand soft Deletion with AJAX.

Implementing soft deletion with AJAX and APEX templates

Soft deletion is done if we want to retain the record and the user wants to delete it. In soft deletion, when a delete operation is triggered on a table by the user, a flag is updated instead of deleting the record altogether. All queries on this table use the flag column to display only the records for which the flag has not been set. The query in the **Slice & Dice** region uses this flag ("OEHR_EMPLOYEES"."DELETE_FLAG" = 'N') to display only the records which have not been deleted by the user.

Let us now understand the process of creating a link on a column to soft delete a record. The **AJAX emp delete** column of the **Slice & Dice** region has <img src="#IMAGE_PREFIX#del.gif" alt="APP_PROC_DELETE"> in **Link Text**, URL in **Target**, and javascript:delEmployee(#EMPLOYEE_ID#); in URL of the **Column Link** page, as shown in the following screenshot:

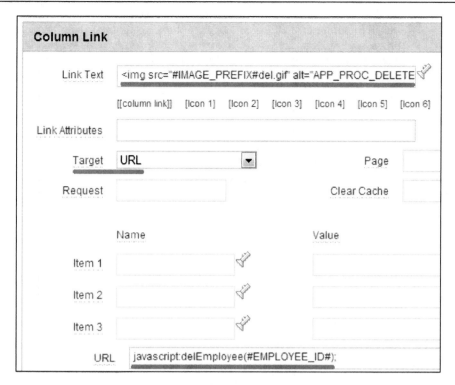

#EMPLOYEE_ID# of javascript:delEmployee(#EMPLOYEE_ID#); passes the
EMPLOYEE_ID value of the row on which the user has clicked to the delEmployee
JavaScript function. Check out the delEmployee function definition in the **JavaScript**
section of the page definition of page 5. The same is shared in the following code for
your convenience:

```
function delEmployee(p_emp_id) {
var ajaxObject = new htmldb_Get( null, html_GetElement('pFlowId').
value, 'APPLICATION_PROCESS=Delete employee', $v('pFlowStepId'));
    ajaxObject.addParam('x02',p_emp_id);
var ajaxReturn = eval(ajaxObject.get()); ajaxObject = null;
/*$('#SLICE_AND_DICE').trigger('apexrefresh'); We can use this if we
set a static id for the region*/
$a_report_Split($x('report_SLICE_AND_DICE').region_id.substr(1),
'1_15_15',null);}
```

The delEmployee function gives an AJAX call to the **Delete employee** page process,
which soft deletes the row, that is, sets "OEHR_EMPLOYEES"."DELETE_FLAG" to 'Y'.

I wish to point out that we can use the following syntax to call the page process. process_id here is the name of the process. This syntax can also be used in JavaScript by passing it as an argument to the window. open function as follows:

```
f?p=application_id:page_id:session:APPLICATION_
PROCESS=process_id
```

The delEmployee JavaScript function passes the employee_id value to the **Delete employee** page through the ajaxObject.addParam ('x02',p_emp_id); function call. Note that we are setting x02 in this place. We will have to fetch the corresponding variable in the **Delete employee** page process.

The following is the code of the **Delete employee** page process:

```
DECLARE l_emp_id NUMBER := wwv_flow.g_x02;
Begin
  update oehr_employees set delete_flag = 'Y' where employee_id = l_
emp_id;
--htp.p ('javascript:apex.submit({request:this.id,showWait:true});');
End;
```

Note that we are capturing the value passed by ajaxObject.addParam ('x02',p_emp_id) using wwv_flow.g_x02. We are using g_x02 because we passed the value using x02. You can see a commented htp.p statement in this page process. This statement can be used to submit the page and hence refresh the region from the page process itself. We don't need it because we have the partial page refresh mechanism in place in the delEmployee JavaScript function. Let's see this now. The final important piece of code in the delEmployee JavaScript function is as follows:

```
$a_report_Split($x('report_SLICE_AND_DICE').region_id.substr(1),
'1_15_15',null);
```

Before I talk about $a_report_Split, I want you to open the page 5 of the reference application and right-click on the **Next** link at the bottom of the report, and then select **Copy Shortcut**. Now paste this in a text editor. Until APEX 4.1 $a_report_Split was used for report pagination. The function still exists for backward compatibility. In APEX 4.2, apex.widget.report.paginate is used. So we can use apex.widget. report.paginate as well instead of $a_report_Split. $a_report_Split needs the region_id value of the region which has to be refreshed. To capture the region_id value, we have put a static ID and we are using this static ID to get the region_id value. You can see SLICE_AND_DICE in the **Static ID** textbox in the **Region Definition** tab of the **Slice & Dice** region.

The **Slice & Dice** region uses the **Standard** report template and we have tinkered it a little to capture the `region_id` value of this region. Open the **Standard** report template of the reference application and go to the **Before Rows** section. You will see the following code in it:

```
id="report_#REGION_STATIC_ID#" region_id="#REGION_ID#"
```

Putting this in the template, generates an HTML which is similar to `id="report_SLICE_AND_DICE" region_id="R9573132397694942"`. Since `report_SLICE_AND_DICE` is static for the region, so this can be used as a handle to get `R9573132397694942`. We have precisely done this by putting `$x('report_SLICE_AND_DICE').region_id.substr(1)` in the `delEmployee` JavaScript function. `Substr` is required because `$a_report_Split` expects the `region_id` value without `R` prefixed to it. The second argument of `$a_report_Split`, that is, `'1_15_15'` will show you the first 15 rows of the report. So every delete will bring you to the first 15 records.

We can also implement partial page refresh by using `$('#SLICE_AND_DICE').trigger('apexrefresh');`.

In the preceding example, we are capturing the region ID using templates. We can also get the region ID by using the following query:

```
SELECT region_id, page_id, application_id
FROM    apex_application_page_regions
WHERE   static_id     = 'SLICE_AND_DICE' /*Here SLICE_AND_DICE is your
static region id.*/
```

This brings us to the end of the soft delete section. Click on any link in the **AJAX emp delete** column of the reference application to see soft deletion with partial page refresh in action.

DML operations and report filtering using DA, JavaScript, and page processes

This section is dedicated to understand the following two methods of report filtering and DML operations:

- Filtering report and logging user selection using Dynamic Actions.

- Filtering report and logging user selection using JavaScript and Page Process. We will see Advanced AJAX and two way communication between page process and JavaScript in this section.

We have two select lists, namely, P5_JOB_FILTER and P5_SALARY_FILTER on page 5 of the reference application. The first select list is a list of jobs and the second select list is a list of salaries. We will now use P5_JOB_FILTER to see the filtering of a report and logging of values using Dynamic Actions.

Filtering reports and logging values using Dynamic Actions

This section is dedicated to using Dynamic Actions for submitting the page and logging the values. Let's check it out. The **Filter selected job id** DA and the **Ajax using Dynamic Actions** DA are fired when a value changes in P5_JOB_FILTER. The **Filter selected job id** Dynamic Action submits the page. This results in the setting of P5_JOB_FILTER with the selected value. Since the region source of the **Slice & Dice** region uses P5_JOB_FILTER in the where clause, the report is filtered with the value of P5_JOB_FILTER. We can see this filter in the query under the *Understanding download methods* section. Have a look at the following screenshot of the **Filter selected job id** Dynamic Action:

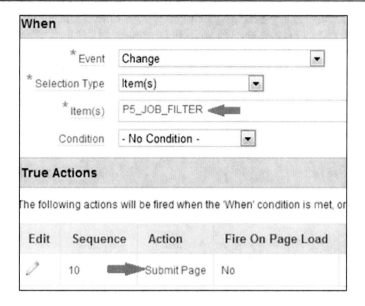

The **Ajax using Dynamic Actions** Dynamic Action runs a PL/SQL code that logs the value of P5_JOB_FILTER in CHAP2_P5_SLICE_AND_DICE_LOG.

We have filtered records and logged values using Dynamic Actions. There are many more triggers of Dynamic Action and many more ways in which Dynamic Actions can work. Exploring these is left to you as homework.

Let's now see the method to filter a report and log the selected value using traditional methods.

AJAX – a two-way communication between page process and JavaScript

In this section, we will see a method to use page processes and JavaScript to refresh the page and to log values. The important thing to note here is that we having a two way communication between the page process and the JavaScript function. Edit P5_SALARY_FILTER and note that we have onChange="apex.submit({request:this.id,showWait:true});insertInLogTable();" in **HTML Form Element Attributes**.

In this code, we are invoking two JavaScript functions namely, `apex.submit` and `insertInLogTable`, when the value in `P5_SALARY_FILTER` changes. `apex.submit` is used here to just submit the page, but it can also be used to set any item. `showWait:true` in `apex.submit` is used to show a cool progress bar when APEX is submitting the page. The `insertInLogTable` is a JavaScript function and can be found in the **JavaScript** section of **Page Attributes**. Here is the code for your convenience:

```
function insertInLogTable() {
var ajaxObject = new htmldb_Get( null, html_GetElement('pFlowId').
value, 'APPLICATION_PROCESS=INSERT_SALARY_IN_LOG_TABLE',
$v('pFlowStepId'));
   ajaxObject.addParam('x01',$v('P5_SALARY_FILTER'));
   var ajaxReturn = eval(ajaxObject.get());
 if (ajaxReturn)
  {
    for ( var i=0; i<ajaxReturn.length; i++ )
       {alert(ajaxReturn[i].data + ' ' + ajaxReturn[i].id);}
  }
   ajaxObject = null;
}
```

The `insertInLogTable` JavaScript function calls the `INSERT_SALARY_IN_LOG_TABLE` page process using AJAX. The important thing to note here is that the page process is returning data to the JavaScript function. This two way interaction can be used to do a variety of things. The `INSERT_SALARY_IN_LOG_TABLE` page process (the following code) returns all the employees whose salaries match with the salary selected in `P5_SALARY_FILTER`. The final part of the `insertInLogTable` JavaScript function discussed previously is used to display the array of returned values using the `alert` JavaScript function. The following is the code for this `INSERT_SALARY_IN_LOG_TABLE` page process:

```
DECLARE
   l_salary NUMBER := wwv_flow.g_x01;
   CURSOR my_cur (p_salary VARCHAR2)  IS
     SELECT employee_id,     last_name,       rownum r
     FROM oehr_employees
     WHERE salary = p_salary;
BEGIN
  INSERT
  INTO CHAP2_P5_SLICE_AND_DICE_LOG VALUES
     (       :P5_SALARY_FILTER ||' has been selected in the salary
filter'    );
     HTP.prn (    '['  )  ;
   FOR c IN my_cur (    l_salary  ) LOOP
```

```
    HTP.prn    (    CASE    WHEN c.r > 1 THEN    ','    ELSE
NULL      END
 || '{ id: "' || c.employee_id || '", data: "' || c.last_name || '"}'
)    ;
  END LOOP;
  HTP.prn  (    ']'  )  ;
END;
```

In the `INSERT_SALARY_IN_LOG_TABLE` page process, `wwv_flow.g_x01` is used to capture the value passed from the `insertInLogTable` JavaScript. This code in `INSERT_SALARY_IN_LOG_TABLE`, inserts into `CHAP2_P5_SLICE_AND_DICE_LOG` and the rest of the code is to form the JSON name-value pair object that can be returned to the calling JavaScript function. The `HTP.prn` facilitates this interaction between JavaScript code and page process.

We have now reached the end of the section. Let's now move on to see tabular forms in APEX.

Implementing a tabular form

The name tabular form says it all. We are talking about a table and a form. So the entire table appears before us in editable format. We can use **Column Attributes** to change the type of HTML element from textbox to any other input type according to our convenience. I believe that this form arms us with all the tools necessary to cater the requirements of editable tables. APEX has a good wizard which lets us create a tabular form. I have quickly listed the steps I followed to create a tabular form.

Creating a tabular form

The following are the steps for creating a tabular form:

1. Create a new page.
2. Select **Form** as the page type, and then select **Tabular Form**.
3. Select the desired table (`OEHR_EMPLOYEES`).
4. Select all columns except `DELETE_FLAG`.
5. Select **Update**, **Insert**, and **Delete** as the **Allowed Operations**.
6. Select **Yes** in **User Interface Defaults**.
7. Select **Primary Key Column(s)** in **Primary Key Type**.

8. Select **1. EMPLOYEE_ID (Number)** in **Primary Key Column**.

9. Enter OEHR_EMPLOYEES_SEQ in **Existing Sequence**.

10. Select all columns as updatable.

11. Give the page number as 6 and choose your page name and region name.

12. Create all four buttons namely, **Cancel**, **Submit**, **Delete**, and **Add Row**.

13. Create the form.

This creates a long list of validations on each of the columns, multi row update and multi row delete processes, branches, and a report. Page 6 of the reference application has this form. After the page is created, we can do any number of changes with the column types, the layouts, and other formatting.

Let me quickly introduce the next section to you. Our mission in the next section is to create a tabular form which looks like a usual classic report, but when a user clicks on any value of the report, the read-only value is replaced by a textbox with the value in it. The user is then allowed to edit as many values as he likes. The user is then allowed to commit the changed values on the click of the button.

Changing item type on user event

Our objective is to create a tabular form with HTML elements whose type changes on the fly. Let me share the screenshot of the final result of this exercise with you, which looks as follows:

 The code has been tested using Internet Explorer 8.

Note that the values **Donald, Feeney,** and **DOCONNEL** are editable. We will first create a tabular report and then use a Dynamic Action to change the types of HTML elements. Page 7 of the reference application has a usual tabular form of OEHR_EMPLOYEES and we have selected EMPLOYEE_ID, FIRST_NAME, LAST_NAME, EMAIL, and PHONE_NUMBER in the form. EMPLOYEE_ID is our primary key, so the wizard allowed us to mention only the other four columns as updatable. We then went to the **Column Attributes** section of each of the four editable columns and changed **Display As** from **Text Field** to **Display as Text(Saves State)**. We then created the **DA to change cell types** DA to change cell types. Let me now explain the code of the **DA to change cell types** DA.

In our **Standard** report template, the formatting of any data in the classic report is done using a class called data. The **DA to change cell types** DA is fired when a user clicks on any HTML element which has the data class as one of its attributes. The code performing this is present in the **When** section of the DA. We have selected **jQuery Selector** in the **Selection Type** dropdown and have put .data in the **jQuery Selector** textbox to achieve this. Let me paste sample HTML which qualifies to be the object of this Dynamic Action. Have a good look at the following code, because I will use this to explain the JavaScript code that follows:

```
<td headers="LAST_NAME" class="data"><input type="hidden" name="f04"
value="King" /><label for="f04_0001" class="hideMeButHearMe">Last
Name</label><span id="f04_0001">King</span></td>
```

Let's now get into the JavaScript code executed by the **DA to change cell types** DA. The following code is pasted for your convenience:

```
var oldHTML = $(this.triggeringElement).html();
if (oldHTML.indexOf('type=text') == -1)
{
var lab = oldHTML.substr(oldHTML.indexOf('<LABEL'),oldHTML.indexOf('</
LABEL>')-oldHTML.indexOf('<LABEL')+8);
var name = $(this.triggeringElement).children().attr('name');
var id;
$(this.triggeringElement).children().each(function(i){if(this.id){id =
this.id;}});
var val = $(this.triggeringElement).children().attr('value');
$(this.triggeringElement).html(lab + '<INPUT id="'+id+'"
value="'+val+'" maxLength=2000 size=16 type=text name="' + name + '"
autocomplete="off">');
}
```

As can be seen in the HTML code above this JavaScript code, the `td` element has the `data` class. Since we had defined our **jQuery Selector** as anything that has the `data class`, so `$(this.triggeringElement)` holds the handle to `td`, and `$(this.triggeringElement).html()` returns the HTML encapsulated by the `td` tag.

The HTML that would have been returned by `$(this.triggeringElement).html()` for the preceding sample code is as follows:

```
<input type="hidden" name="f04" value="King" /><label for="f04_0001"
class="hideMeButHearMe">Last Name</label><span id="f04_0001">King</
span>
```

This value is stored in the `oldHTML` variable. Our strategy is to change the `input` type of this HTML to `text`. The second line of JavaScript code is `if (oldHTML.indexOf('type=text') == -1)`. It ensures that the JavaScript is not executed if the `type` of any data element has already been changed to `text`. The code following this is an attempt to get the values of attributes such as `name`, `value`, and so on. These values are used in the final line of the code to frame the new HTML.

If you wish to know the exact values that are captured in each of the variables then use the `alert` JavaScript function to get the value of the variables as prompts.

I presented this example to demonstrate the amazing uses of Dynamic Action. This method can also be used for conditional formatting.

 It's important to mention about jqGrid in this place. jqGrid is a JQuery based solution which can be used to implement similar functions such as searching in tables and virtual scrolling. More information on jqGrid can be found at `http://www.trirand.com/blog/jqgrid/jqgrid.html`.

Implementing a master detail report and displaying complex types

The name says it all. Let me explain how master detail report works in APEX. This report is a combination of a classic report on the master table and a drilldown child report, which shows one selected master record along with its child records. All values in the child report are editable. However, if required we can obviously tweak this master detail report in our own way. Before we do that, let's first create and understand one master detail report.

APEX assumes that a master detail report will be created on a set of tables which are having parent-child relationship between them, and it creates the processes for all kinds of DML operations, corresponding buttons, and a link between the master and detail level.

Let's switch on to actually creating a master detail report. I have picked the oehr_customers table as my master and the oehr_orders table as my child. We can create a master detail report by selecting a new **Master Detail Form** from the **Create Form** page of the wizard. The wizard lets us select the columns for both the master and the detail reports. The wizard is also intelligent enough to use the foreign key relations established at the database level to show only the relevant child tables to us after we have selected a master table. If physical foreign key does not exist between the tables of interest then APEX will expect us to code the relationship using the wizard.

The wizard lets us set the primary keys for both master and detail tables if we select **Select Primary Key Column(s)** in the **Define Primary Key** step. Setting of the primary key for the master table dictates the column value, which APEX will use to link the master report with the detail report. APEX also uses this ID for any update on the selected master record. The ID of the detail report is used for updating the records of the detail table.

The **Include master report?** radio button in the **Master Options** step of the wizard lets us specify whether we want a master report or not. If we select **No** in **Include master report** radio button then the wizard will then only generate the detail report.

The wizard also lets us bifurcate the details page into two pages. The first page would contain the items of the selected master record and the second page would contain the detailed records for the selected master record. I find this bifurcation clumsy, so I have opted for **Edit detail as tabular form on same page**.

Have a look at the master detail report created as an example on page 13 and page 14 of the reference application.

Displaying complex types and varray in a report

The **Cust Address** and **Phone Numbers** columns of the `oehr_customers` table are of complex data types, so we have to put some extra effort to display these. Check the definition of the `OEHR_CUSTOMERS` table to verify this. To deal with this situation, we will have to tweak our query a little. **Cust Address** is actually a structure of native data types, which together will form a user-defined data type. We can access each of the native data type columns of this collection by individually. For example `postal_code` can be accessed by the `c.CUST_ADDRESS.postal_code` syntax. The query in the **Customers Master Report** region of page 13 of the reference application has this in place. The following query is pasted for your convenience. Check the second highlighted piece of the following code:

```
SELECT c.cust_first_name,  c.cust_last_name,  c.customer_id,
   c.CREDIT_LIMIT,  c.CUST_EMAIL,
   (SELECT first_name || ' ' || last_name FROM oehr_employees
   WHERE employee_id = c.ACCOUNT_MGR_ID ) Manager,
   listagg(p.column_value,',') WITHIN GROUP (ORDER BY cust_first_name)
"PHONE_NUMBERS",

   c.CUST_ADDRESS.street_address ||',' || c.CUST_ADDRESS.postal_code
||',' ||c.CUST_ADDRESS.city
   ||',' ||c.CUST_ADDRESS.state_province ||','
   ||c.CUST_ADDRESS.country_id Address

FROM "OEHR_CUSTOMERS" c, TABLE (c.PHONE_NUMBERS) p
GROUP BY c.cust_first_name, c.cust_last_name, c.customer_id,
   c.CREDIT_LIMIT, c.CUST_EMAIL, c.ACCOUNT_MGR_ID, c.CUST_ADDRESS.
street_address, c.CUST_ADDRESS.postal_code,
   c.CUST_ADDRESS.city, c.CUST_ADDRESS.state_province,
   c.CUST_ADDRESS.country_id
order by c.customer_id
```

`phone_numbers column` is a little different. It is actually a column containing a varray. To display the values for this column we will have to use the `table` function. We will discuss the `table` function again when we discuss advanced dynamic queries in the next chapter. The `table` function accepts a collection of rows (either collection types or ref cursors) and treats them as physical database tables. We are using the `listagg` string aggregation function to aggregate the values returned by the `table` function. Note the cross join between the `c` and `p` aliases. `c.PHONE_NUMBERS` is passed as an argument to `p` so the join is actually been done by passing the argument in the third highlighted piece of code.

This brings us to the end of master detail report. Let's now see reports related to time series.

Implementing time series reports

In this section, we will learn about some of the time series functions which help in the development of analytical reports in APEX.

I have created `OEHR_TIME_DIM` for displaying some of the time series reports. Most OLAP reports use a time dimension for analysis. The reports introduced in this section are special because of their queries. This section is designed to primarily display the quantum of analytical processing possible using SQL.

Creating aggregation on a partitioned time dimension region

We have seen grouping sets in the *Using grouping sets and HTML formatting in a query* section. Here we are going a step further by using the `cube` extension of the `group by` clause. We will also see the use of some aggregation on partitioned time dimension.

`cube` produces aggregation results of each combination of the columns. Go to page 9 of the reference application and see the region source query of the **Aggregation on partitioned time dimension** region. The following query is pasted for your convenience:

```
select DECODE(GROUPING(t.quarter_year)+GROUPING(o.order_mode)
              , 0, t.quarter_year
              , 1, DECODE(GROUPING(t.quarter_year),0,'Total for '||t.
quarter_year,'Total for '||o.order_mode)
              ,2 , 'Grand total'
              ) "Quarter",        decode(GROUPING(t.quarter_
year)+GROUPING(o.order_mode),0, o.order_mode,null) "Order mode",
sum(order_total) "Sum of order amount",
TO_CHAR(100 * RATIO_TO_REPORT(SUM(order_total)) OVER (PARTITION BY
(GROUPING(o.order_mode) ||
 t.quarter_year)),'990D0') "% of contribution in a quarter"
from oehr_orders o, oehr_time_dim t where o.time_dim_id = t.time_dim_
id
group by cube(quarter_year,order_mode)
order by to_number(substr(t.quarter_year,4)),to_number(substr(t.
quarter_year,2,1)) o.order_mode
```

The decode statements in this query are to display correct texts when the aggregated rows are displayed. Note the use of the RATIO_TO_REPORT analytical function to show the percentage contributions of each order_mode in a particular quarter. Also note the use of oehr_time_dim. Note that the partitioning is done using a combination of the quarter_year column and the order_mode column. Direct and online are the only two order modes in the oehr_orders table. So the sum of percentages of direct and online for every quarter will be 100. Therefore, by partitioning over a combination of the quarter_year column and the order_mode column, we are able to show the contributions by both the modes of receiving orders in any quarter. Some analytical functions allow us to specify a rolling window using the windowing clause. The ROWS and RANGE keywords can be used along with a specification of the set of rows on which we want to apply the windowing clause. ROWS gives us the freedom to apply our function on physical set of rows, while RANGE can be used for a logical set of rows. Run page 9 of the reference application to see the preceding query in action.

Time series analysis with analytical functions and time dimension

We will dedicate this section for doing time series analysis using analytical functions. Have a look at the query of the region source of the **Comparison of aggregations with previous & next time periods** region. The query is more or less similar to the query of the **Aggregation on partitioned time dimension** region, but has the lead and lag functions. These functions have been used to compare the values of one quarter relative to other quarters. We have one dropdown each for selecting the number of months to lead and the number of months to lag. Comparing the performance over time is an important analytical business requirement and this region helps us achieve this.

Functions such as sum and avg, which are traditionally used with the group by clause can also be used in the analytical form. In the analytical form, we can specify different partition by clauses and hence have different windows of different functions.

In the query of the **Comparison of aggregations with previous & next time periods** region, we see that we are multiplying: P9_LAG_MONTHS by three for creating a column with a lagging period, and similarly we are multiplying: P9_LEAD_MONTHS by three to create a column for a leading period. So if a user selects 1 in the **P9_LAG_MONTHS** dropdown, we create a lag of three rows because we assume that there will be one row each for direct and online modes and another for quarter total in every quarter.

So we have a total of three rows per quarter. So if we want to compare the values of the previous quarter with the current quarter, we have to lag by three rows. Now, when we say this, we assume that every quarter will have values for both `direct` and `online` modes but this might not always be the case and our logic will fail then. One way out of this trouble is to make sure that our table has data for every quarter and for every mode. The other way is to densify data on the fly. We have done this data densification in this query by using the query `partition by` clause.

Using the query partition clause for data densification

This part is dedicated to understanding the process to dense the data on the fly. This solves the problem discussed in the previous section. Have a look at the region source of the **Aggregation on partitioned time dim with data densification** region. The following query is shared for your convenience:

```
select DECODE(GROUPING(t.quarter_year)+GROUPING(o.order_mode)
            , 0, t.quarter_year
            , 1, DECODE(GROUPING(t.quarter_year),0,'Total for '||t.
quarter_year,'Total for '||o.order_mode)
            ,2 , 'Grand total'
            ) "Quarter",              decode(GROUPING(t.quarter_
year)+GROUPING(o.order_mode),0, o.order_mode,null) "Order mode",
            nvl(sum(order_total),0) "Sum of order amount",
            TO_CHAR(100 * nvl(RATIO_TO_REPORT(SUM(order_total))
OVER (PARTITION BY (GROUPING(o.order_mode) ||
 t.quarter_year)),0),'990D0') "% of contribution in a Quarter"
from     oehr_time_dim t      LEFT OUTER JOIN
         oehr_orders o PARTITION BY (o.order_mode)
         ON (o.time_dim_id = t.time_dim_id)
         where t.dat < to_date('02-Aug-2000','dd-Mon-yyyy')
         group by cube(quarter_year,order_mode)
         order by to_number(substr(t.quarter_year,4)),to_
number(substr(t.quarter_year,2,1))
    ,       o.order_mode
```

Focus on the highlighted part. The query `partition by` clause extends the functionality of traditional outer joins. It performs the outer join with each partition returned by the query partition clause rather than joining the whole table. We are partitioning on `o.order_mode`, so we will have two partitions of the table, one for `direct` and the other for `online`. The left outer join ensures that all the data is selected for all the quarters, and the query partition clause ensures that the join of each quarter happens with both the partitions; hence we get data for all quarters and all modes.

Some of the other functions which can be used in the analytical form and might interest you are `LAST_VALUE`, `FIRST_VALUE`, `RANK`, `DENSE_RANK`, `ROW_NUMBER`, `FIRST`, and `LAST`. `LAST_VALUE` and `FIRST_VALUE` can be used for handling null values. `KEEP FIRST` can be used in conjugation with `DENSE_RANK` to apply aggregations on a set of rows which have the first rank.

Creating aggregations using the model clause

The model clause is a whole school in itself. It lets us define rules, perform aggregations, and much more. My example in the query of the **Aggregations using Model clause** region on page 9 of the reference application is a very basic one, and the attempt is to introduce the `model` clause to you. This clause can however be used to perform much more complex calculations and is a powerful tool in the hands of business intelligence developers. Let me share the following query for your convenience:

```
select month_year, product_name,cnt_of_orders from (select
count(ord.order_id) as cnt_of_orders,
product_name,month_year
 from   oehr_product_information prod_info,
        oehr_order_items ord_itm,
        oehr_orders ord,oehr_time_dim tim_dim
 where     ord_itm.product_id = prod_info.product_id
 and ord.order_id = ord_itm.order_id
 and ord.time_dim_id = tim_dim.time_dim_id
 and prod_info.product_name in ('KB 101/EN','LaserPro 600/6/
BW','Screws <B.28.S>')
group by product_name, month_year)
model
dimension by (product_name, month_year)
measures (cnt_of_orders)
RULES
(upsert all cnt_of_orders[ANY,'Total'] =sum(cnt_of_orders)[cv(PRODUCT_
NAME),MONTH_YEAR],
upsert all cnt_of_orders[' Total','Grand'] =sum(cnt_of_orders)
[PRODUCT_NAME,MONTH_YEAR])
order by product_name desc,month_year
```

In the region source of the **Aggregations using Model clause** region, we have an inner query that generates three columns as its output. One of these three columns is a measure, and the other two are the dimensions on which this measure can be sliced and diced. Dimensions are specified by DIMENSION BY, and measures by MEASURES in the highlighted part of the query. I have also written a few rules to demonstrate the use of rules in the model clause. Upsert updates the value in the output if any row matches the value specified in the corresponding rule. This makes it very powerful, because we are able to display a value based on a rule which is different from the original value without physically updating the table. The Any keyword matches any value of the corresponding dimension (PRODUCT_NAME in this case). The Cv() function is used to fetch the value from the left side of the expression. So the Any keyword matches all the values of the product_name, and cv function picks the product name. So this rule effectively says that the sum function should work for all the values of product_name and should sum the output for every month_year. The second rule helps us upsert the grand total value.

This more or less brings us to the end of the section where we saw the use of classic reports to fulfill almost any business requirement. The next section will be focused on data-level security.

Implementing data-level security

Data-level security essentially means that a user should not be able to see the records which do not fall under the rights of his business role.

Using VPD

We will dedicate this section to understand the use of VPD for implementing data-level security.

 VPD is only available in the enterprise edition.

Open the **VPD Report** region on page 10 of the reference application and check out the commented code in the region source. Execute this after logging in as SYS. Note that we are creating CHAP2_VPD_OEHR_EMPLOYEES, so that other reports built on OEHR_EMPLOYEES are not affected by the VPD policy.

The commented code in the region source is as follows:

```
create table PACKT_SCHEMA.CHAP2_VPD_OEHR_EMPLOYEES as select * from
PACKT_SCHEMA.OEHR_EMPLOYEES

CREATE OR REPLACE FUNCTION chap2_data_lev_scrty_usng_vpd (
p_schema IN VARCHAR2 DEFAULT NULL,
p_object IN VARCHAR2 DEFAULT NULL)
RETURN VARCHAR2 AS
BEGIN
RETURN 'upper(email) = v(''APP_USER'')';
END;
--Dont grant execute on the above function to anyone

BEGIN DBMS_RLS.add_policy
(object_schema => 'PACKT_SCHEMA',
object_name => 'CHAP2_VPD_OEHR_EMPLOYEES',
policy_name => 'EMPLOYEE_VPD', function_schema => 'SYS',
policy_function => 'CHAP2_DATA_LEV_SCRTY_USNG_VPD',
statement_types => 'SELECT'); END;
```

Let us understand the `chap2_data_lev_scrty_usng_vpd` function now. `chap2_data_lev_scrty_usng_vpd` returns `'upper(email) = v(''APP_USER'')'`. This string is appended to all queries which fall under the `EMPLOYEE_VPD` policy, and hence all affected queries will filter out the records which belong to the currently logged in user. Also note the use of `v()` in this place.

The uncommented code in the **VPD Report** region on page 10 is selecting from `CHAP2_VPD_OEHR_EMPLOYEES` and only the record of the logged in user is displayed when we view this page.

This example was just to demonstrate the process of creating a VPD. This mechanism can obviously handle more complex scenarios.

Using query filters

We will now look at the approach of using query filters for implementing data level security. The **Data Level Security using Query Filters** region of page 10 of the reference application is probably the simplest of all regions we have seen so far. It uses `v('APP_USER')` in its `where` clause and hence shows the records of only the currently logged in user. So the net effect of this query and the VPD is the same.

Summary

We saw a number of reports in this chapter and a majority of the reports orchestrated here have been the classic reports. This attests the multiple utilities of classic reports. We also saw some ways to highlight specific parts of the report. We will take this highlighting exercise to a higher level in the next chapter and will also try to understand some of the important features of interactive reports. Since we will mostly be looking at the functionalities of APEX, it should be a lot lighter than this one. Time for a break and see you soon in *Chapter 3, In the APEX Mansion – Interactive Reports.*

3
In the APEX Mansion – Interactive Reports

Welcome back. I hope that the last two chapters were informative and exciting. Let me quickly summarize our learning till now. *Chapter 1, Know Your Horse Before You Ride It*, was about the architecture and installation, while *Chapter 2, Conventional Reporting in APEX*, spoke about classic reports and various experiments on them to make them more useful. When it comes to usefulness, nothing can be as good as **Interactive Reports** (**IR**). This is because of the ease with which an interactive report can help us generate the reports for the most complex requirements and because of its beautiful look.

An interactive report is a huge leap towards making APEX a good reporting tool. The advantage of an IR not only lies in the fact that it lets us perform calculations and conditional formatting without much effort, but it also lies in the fact that once an IR is developed, a user can personalize an IR and save his modifications as a new report for himself. So, a user can easily create a pie chart out of the columns in an IR, and can also create some new columns which are based on the calculations of existing columns. Again, these reports can be used to run **flashback queries**, which can help us get a report on data which existed a few minutes back. We will see all of this in a short while. I will dedicate a major portion of this chapter to show the inbuilt features of IR, and will then move on to explain some advanced features of APEX.

The following are the major learning outcomes of this chapter:

- Learning important features of an IR
- Linking IRs
- Learning about the configurations of the **Icon View**, **Detail View**, **Advanced**, and **Column Group** sections
- A number of ways to create an IR using CSS
- A generic process to customize any IR
- Using APEX views to created links for various saved IRs
- Method to put multiple IRs on the same page
- Conditional report columns based on authorization and method to create an Interactive Report Dashboard.
- Dynamic IR using the following:
  ◦ Collection approach
  ◦ The native table function approach: We will learn about both pipelined and parallel enabled table functions
  ◦ Dynamic reporting using interface approach

Alright, let's start digging.

About the reference application

Before we start to understand the intricacies of IR, I suggest that you first install the reference application for *Chapter 3, In the APEX Mansion – Interactive Report*, (4-98-9_03_APEX_Chapter03.sql). The script to install the reference application also has the code to install the supporting objects. The code has been tested using IE 8 so I suggest that you use the same.

External table authentication that uses OEHR_EMPLOYEES is used in this chapter. The authentication is dependent on the Chapter2 package. So, make sure that the Chapter2 package (4-98-9_02_chapter2.sql) is compiled before running this application. Check *Chapter 2, Conventional reporting in APEX*, to see how external table authentication is set. I have saved a number of IR reports using the SKING user so you will have to log in using SKING/SKING (all CAPITALS) to see these.

Important features of the interactive report

Let's first have a look at the out of the box features of APEX, and we will then continue our quest to make things better.

The following is a screenshot of a typical IR. We will now talk about the **Actions** menu and the **Search** functionality of IRs.

The Search functionality

The components that implement this feature include a drop-down menu to select a column if we want to search only a single column, a text box to enter the string to be searched, and a **Go** button to let us search for the entered text. These items are highlighted in the previous screenshot.

There was a **Search** functionality in classic reports as well. In classic reports, APEX had put an enveloping query to facilitate the search. In IRs, AJAX calls are made to implement the functionality.

Let us now talk about the **Actions** menu. This menu is visible under the **Actions** button in the previous screenshot.

Using the Select Columns feature of the Actions menu

Select Columns is the first item in the **Actions** menu. It lets us select the columns which we want to see in our report. We can select our desired columns, and save the new report for ourselves or as a default report for everyone if we have the necessary rights. Saving is done by clicking on the **Save Report** link in the **Actions** menu. If we want to remove a column from the report, then we can either use **Select Columns** for this, or we can click on the column's heading and we will get a button to do this. The button to do this is underlined in the following screenshot.

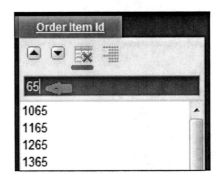

Using the filtering feature of the Actions menu

Filter is the second item in the **Actions** menu as can be seen in the screenshot under the *Important features of the interactive report* section. We can save a report with our set of filters so that we see only the information in which we are interested, whenever we log in. We can write a filter on a column by selecting the **Column** radio button after selecting **Filter** from the **Actions** menu or can write a filter on the entire table by selecting the **Row** radio button. These options can be seen in the following screenshot:

When we select the **Row** radio button, APEX gives us a list of columns and operators which can be used for framing a complex query. An example of the complex filter on the IR on the first page of the reference application can be A = 2354 and C = 'direct'. We can also filter the records on a particular column by clicking on the column heading. This option is highlighted in the screenshot under the *Using the Select Columns feature of the Actions menu* section with an arrow.

Linking the interactive reports

We can pass the filter to other IRs using the URL. To do this, we will have to put IR<Operator>_<COLUMN_ALIAS> in the item_names part of the URL and pass the filter value in the item_values part of the URL.

For example:

- http://localhost:7001/apex/f?p=131:1:376742729106701:::::IR_ ORDER_ID_4_AD_PRES:2458
- http://localhost:7001/apex/f?p=131:1:376742729106701:::::IRLT_ ORDER_ID_4_AD_PRES:2400

The following is a list of valid operators:

- EQ: Equals (this is the default)
- NEQ: Not Equal to
- LT: Less than
- LTE: Less than or equal to
- GT: Greater Than
- GTE: Greater than or equal to
- LIKE: SQL Like operator
- N: Null
- NN: Not Null
- C: Contains
- NC: Not Contains

The default is EQ. The first example URL does not have the operator, precisely for this reason.

We can also add an IR filter using APEX_UTIL.IR_FILTER.

Now if we wish to select rows which have specific texts in them, then we can use IR_ROWFILTER as shown in the following example:

```
http://localhost:7001/apex/f?p=131:3:1545633467110601::NO::IR_
ROWFILTER:6000
```

If you ever have a requirement where you have to pass the filters saved by the user in an IR to some other page, then you can make use of the APEX_APPLICATION_PAGE_IR_COND view. There are many more IR views which might help you in similar requirements. Run the following query using the SYS schema to get their names:

```
Select view_name from all_views where view_name like '%IR%' and owner
= 'APEX_040200'
```

Using the Rows per Page feature of the Actions menu

Rows per Page is the third item in the screenshot under the *Important features of the interactive report* section. It lets us select the number of rows we want in our report. This control is there with the developer in classic reports. The developer can set this in the **Pagination** section but the control has been passed to the user in IRs and has been taken out of the **Pagination** section of the **Report Attributes** page.

Customizing the number of rows in an IR

The only trouble with the **Rows per Page** feature is that a user gets a limited number of options for the number of rows per page. For example, what if the requirement was to set 45 rows per page? The answer is to go back to the HTML source for this section.

You should be able to see the following code in the HTML of any IR page:

```
<li><a href="javascript:gReport.search('SEARCH',1000)"
class="dhtmlSubMenuN" onmouseover="dhtml_CloseAllSubMenusL(this)"
title="1000"> 1000</a></li>
```

This piece of code is responsible for showing the option to set 1000 rows per page in the **Actions** menu. I pulled this out to show you that javascript:gReport.search('SEARCH',1000) is called to set the number of rows to 1000. If your requirement is to set the number of rows to 45, then you use javascript:gReport.search('SEARCH',45), and call this on loading of a page or a button or any other similar place. I have put this function in *Execute when Page Loads* section of page definition of seventh page of the reference application to reduce the number of rows per page to seven.

Using the formatting options of the Actions menu

Format is the fourth item in the screenshot under the *Important features of the interactive report* section and is the best part of interactive reporting. Reporting is all about organization of data such that the most important information stands out. This section deals with ways and means to perform this organization. A screenshot of this section is shown as follows:

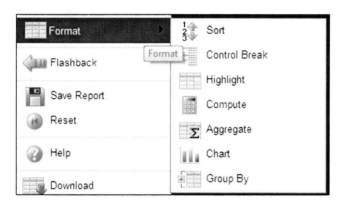

Let us now talk about the available options in this section.

Using Control Break

Control Break is the second option in the **Format** menu. The screenshot of the format menu is shown in the previous section. We had used APEX's internal grouping feature in the *Using the break formatting in classic reports* section of *Chapter 2, Conventional Reporting in APEX*. IR lets the user to do this. **Control Break** lets the user break the report into a number of groups with each group corresponding to one distinct value of the column on which he is breaking. For example, if we use **Control Break** on the order_mode column of the IR on the first page, then we will get two groups because order_mode has only two distinct values. We can apply **Control Break** on a column by clicking on the column heading as well. The screenshot of this is shown as follows for your convenience:

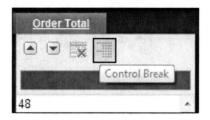

Using the Compute option

Compute is the fourth option in the **Format** menu, and is a graphical way of putting functions such as ABS, COS, and DECODE on our selected columns. This can also be used to put format masks on the columns. So basically, if we want to add some columns, do some string rearrangement of the columns, or any other manipulation, then **Compute** will do it for us. When we create a computation, a new column is created for us and our computation is applied to it. An example of a computation on the IR of the first page can be TRUNC (D). Here D is the order_date column. The new columns can be used just as we use the older ones.

Using Chart in an IR

Chart is the sixth option in the **Format** menu, and is by far the most exciting feature of IR. It easily screens the complex architecture of the charts in APEX from the end user. The user gets the freedom to build a visual treat from him. Available charting options are horizontal and vertical charts, pie charts and line charts.

Using the Flashback feature of the Actions menu

Flashback the fifth option in the **Actions** menu and is a very powerful feature. We can see this option in the screenshot under the *Important features of the interactive report* section. Let's say that an IR is developed on real-time data. A user notices a surprising change in the data and he wants to reconfirm his observation by checking out the previous data as well. The user can use this feature to check the data that existed in the past. APEX uses **Automatic Undo Management (AUM)** system to execute the flashback queries. The old data in any DML operation is stored by the AUM system. Hence, before using this system, you must configure your database for flashback technology. Refer the following documentation for more details:

```
http://docs.oracle.com/cd/E11882_01/appdev.112/e25518/adfns_
flashback.htm
```

Data from the flashback can be retrieved using the SELECT AS OF clause. We can also use the **flashback version query** if we want to retrieve older data in some time interval. **Flashback transaction query** is another method to get flashback data. However, APEX uses the SELECT AS OF clause. We can get the query in the **Flashback AJAX** call fired by APEX by running the following query by the SYS user:

```
select * from v$sql where instr(upper(SQL_FULLTEXT),'AS OF')>0
```

You should get a query similar to the following if you carry out this test for the IR on the first page of the reference application. Note that you will first have to use the flashback feature in an IR for the query to appear in `v$sql` view:

```
select
        apxws_row_pk,
        "ORDER_ID_4_AD_PRES",
        "ORDER_MODE",
        "ORDER_DATE",
        "ORDER_TOTAL",
        count(*) over () as apxws_row_cnt
  from (
select  * from (select b.ROWID apxws_row_pk, b.* from (select *  from
(
select order_id order_id_4_ad_pres,order_id order_id_4_others ,order_
mode,order_date,order_total  from oehr_orders
) ) b) as of timestamp (systimestamp - to_number(:APXWS_MINS_
AGO)/1440)   r
) r where rownum <= to_number(:APXWS_MAX_ROW_CNT)
  order by apxws_row_pk
```

Using the Save Report feature of the Actions menu

Save Report is the sixth item in the screenshot under the *Important features of the interactive report* section and let's us save a private, public, or alternate report depending on our access rights. We can access our saved reports by going to the **Reports Attributes** page of our IR and then clicking on the **View Saved Report Activity** link in the **Tasks** panel on the right-hand side of the page. We can also access saved reports by clicking on the **Saved Reports** tab next to the **Report Attributes** tab. **Save Public Report Authorization** in the **Search Bar** section in the **Report Attributes** page of an IR can be used to limit the set of users who can save public reports.

Note that the default and alternate reports can be accessed by using the following syntax:

```
f?p=&APP_ID.:&APP_PAGE_ID.:&APP_SESSION.:IR_REPORT_<REPORT_ALIAS>
```

Let's say we have certain page items which should only be displayed for some of the public reports. We can do this conditional displaying by using IR_REPORT_<REPORT_ALIAS>. We can use `Request = Expression 1` in our condition section of the item which we want to make conditional and put IR_REPORT_<REPORT_ALIAS> in the `Expression 1` textbox.

APEX puts a numeric report ID when an alternate or a default report is created. We can replace this by some more meaningful IDs. This can be done in the **Saved Reports** page of an IR report region.

The **Saved Reports** page of an IR report region can also be used to delete a saved report. Deleting of saved reports can also be done using APEX_UTIL.IR_ DELETE_REPORT.

Using the Reset and Download features of the Actions menu

Reset is the seventh item in the screenshot under the *Important features of the interactive report* section and is used to reset the currently active report settings. Resetting can also be done using the APEX_UTIL.IR_RESET procedure. **Download** is the eighth item in the screenshot under the *Important features of the interactive report* section and it gives us four download format options. Let's look at each one of them now.

Configuring the Email functionality

We are talking about e-mail configuration, because e-mailing exists as one of the options to download an IR. This e-mailing option will not work unless the configuration described in this section is executed. Configuration of e-mail and subscription functionality can be used in the following way:

1. Login in to the **INTERNAL** workspace using your admin credentials.
2. Go to the **EMAIL** section of **Manage Instance** from **Instance Settings** for configuring this.
3. Put your SMTP mail server address, the port number, and your credentials which will be used to send the mails.

Once this is done, you will be able to use the **Email** functionality and the **Subscription** functionality. The **Email** functionality can be used to get the report immediately while **Subscription** can be used to get mails on a fixed time of the day and on recurring basis.

We will have to check the desired file format checkbox in the **Download** section of the **Report Attributes** page of an IR for the download link of the corresponding format to be visible in the **Actions** menu. The **Download** section also lets us dictate the filename of the downloaded file and lets us specify the separators of the CSV file which is to be downloaded.

Downloading in CSV and HTML formats

Apart from using APEX's feature to download an IR in the CSV and HTML format, we can create our own download link for CSV and HTML formats by putting `CSV` and `HTMLD` in the `REQUEST` section of the URL. So, a link for downloading the IR on the first page of the reference application will look like the following:

```
http://localhost:7001/apex/f?p=131:1:376742729106701:CSV
```

If you want to create a button for CSV download, then put the following in its target:

```
f?p=&APP_ID.:&APP_PAGE_ID.:&SESSION.:CSV
```

Similarly a Target for HTML download will be `f?p=&APP_ID.:&APP_PAGE_ID.:&SESSION.:HTMLD`.

Downloading in PDF format

PDF requires us to configure a PDF engine again. APEX does not have a PDF engine of its own, but APEX Listener can be configured for report printing.. This PDF configuration is also done in **Instance Settings** of the **Manage Instance** page after logging in the **INTERNAL** workspace. We have to go to the **Report Printing** section for this. Available options are **Oracle APEX Listener**, **Oracle BI Publisher**, and **External (Apache FOP)**. Once this section is configured, we can also use the **Print Attributes** page of both IR and classic reports to get the reports in different formats.

Using the Subscription feature of the Actions menu

Subscription is the last item in the screenshot under the *Important features of the interactive report* section and this lets us schedule the delivery of reports by e-mail. We can check the mail by logging in the **INTERNAL** workspace under **Monitor Activity**. The mail log can also be queried from `apex_040200.wwv_flow_mail_log`. We can access our subscriptions by going to the **Reports Attributes** page of our IR and then clicking on the **Manage Subscriptions** link in the **Tasks** panel on the right-hand side of the page.

Subscriptions can be deleted from the IR page or can be deleted using `APEX_UTIL.IR_DELETE_SUBSCRIPTION`.

Other configurable attributes of an IR

Alright, now let's go to the **Report Attributes** page of the IR on the first page of the reference application, and check out some of the other configurable attributes there. If you go to the **Search Bar** section, you will see that you have a few textboxes such as **Button Template, Finder Image,** and **Actions Menu Image**. These textboxes are accompanied with a number of checkboxes which help in beautifying and customizing the IR. A screenshot of these checkboxes is displayed as follows for your convenience:

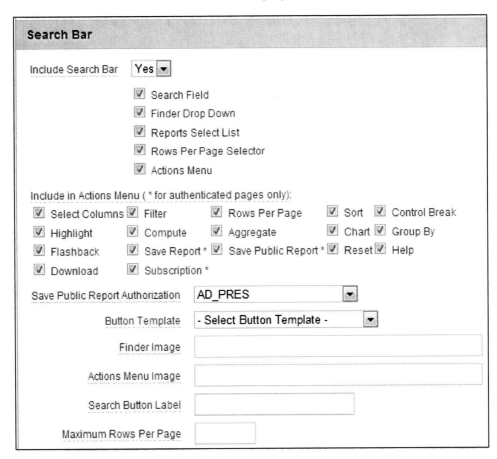

This section dictates which IR features will be available to the users. The names of most of these checkboxes clearly explain their purpose.

Using the Link Column section of the Report Attributes page

Go to the **Link Column** section of the **Report Attributes** page of the IR on the first page of the reference application. Screenshot is shown as follows for your convenience:

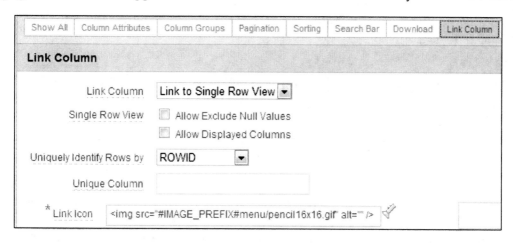

This is IR's way of giving a drilldown. We can obviously use the **Column Link** section of the **Column Attributes** page to create drilldowns, but APEX always gives more than what we dream. If we select **Link to Single Row View** in the **Link Column** dropdown, APEX will create a column with a pencil icon and will provide a drilldown to a view which will exclusively shows the row on which we drill down. We can obviously choose any other icon of our choice by editing the **Link Icon** textbox. Run the first page and click on the pencil icon on any row of the IR to see the single-row view. If we select **Link to Custom Target** in the **Link Column** dropdown, APEX will allow us set our own drilldown. Note that we can use RIR and CIR in the **ClearCache** textbox of the **Link Column** section of the **Report Attributes** page of an IR and also of the **Column Link** section on the **Column Attributes** page of every column in an IR. RIR is used to reset to the default IR (clear all filters and formats) on the target page and CIR is used to clear all report settings.

RIR and CIR can also be used in the clearCache section of the URL. For example, if we wish to clear all report settings on the third page using URL, we should use the following URL:

```
http://localhost:7001/apex/f?p=131:3:551282089043201::NO:3,CIR:P3_
REPORT_ID:5833116732248613#
```

Using the Icon View section of the Report Attributes page

If we select **Yes** in the **Icon View Enabled** dropdown of the **Icon View** section of the **Report Attributes** page, APEX adds a link in the search bar to view the report as icons. To view a report in this mode, we will have to have a query which has a column for image source, a column for the label of the icon, and a column for the target of the icon.

Using the Detail View section of the Report Attributes page

The name does not quite say what it does. This view is APEX's method to let a developer arrange the data furnished by a query in his own sweet way. You can create wonders with this view, but you will need a good understanding of HTML for that. The data returned by the query can be accessed by using the #COLUMN_ ALIAS# substitutions. For example, we can use `<tr><td align="right">#ORDER_ ID_4_AD_PRES#</td></tr>` in the **For Each Row (Use #COLUMN_ALIAS# substitutions)** text area, the **Before Rows** section can have `<TABLE>`, and **After Rows** can have `</TABLE>`. IR on the first page of the reference application has the following code in this section:

```
<style type="text/css">
p {font-family:"Times New Roman";
background-color:#dddddd;
color:red;} </style> <p>#ORDER_MODE#</p>
```

Run the first page and click on the **View Detail** button next to the search bar to view this code in action. The result is shown as follows and the **View Detail** button is highlighted for your convenience:

Using the Advanced section of the Report Attributes page

Go to the **Advanced** section of the **Report Attributes** page of the IR on the first page of the reference application. The following is a screenshot of this section:

Region Alias is to help us reference an IR region in our code. We can give a unique alias to an IR using this textbox, and then use APEX_APPLICATION_PAGE_IR to fetch the various attributes of the IR in our code. The alias must be unique within the application.

Report ID Item is a very important feature of IR. It lets us set different default views for different users. We can initially save a number of reports and then code a page item to pick the report ID of one of those saved reports depending on the user who has logged in. This page item which holds the ID of the report can then be mentioned in this textbox to let the user view the selected report as his default report. Report IDs can be retrieved from the apex_application_page_ir_rpt view. This functionality can also be used to create a report on the saved reports of an IR. We can use this functionality to give links to open different saved reports of an IR. Run the third page of the reference application to see the classic report which has links of different saved reports of the IR on the same page.

Using the Column Group section of the Report Attributes page

Go to the **Column Group** section of the **Report Attributes** page of the IR on the first page of the reference application. You will see the **Numeric data** column group. Find the screenshot as follows:

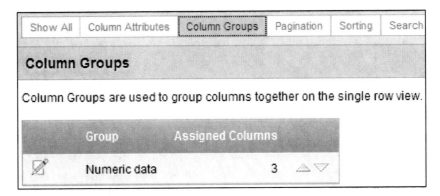

We have grouped ORDER_ID_4_AD_PRES, ORDER_ID_4_OTHERS and ORDER_TOTAL together in the **Numeric data** column group. The **Column Group** section is used to group the columns in the single-row view. We can check out the single-row view by running the first page and then clicking on the pencil icon in any row of the IR on the first page. We will always be able to see only two of these three columns because of the authorizations put on ORDER_ID_4_AD_PRES and ORDER_ID_4_OTHERS. Find the following screenshot. Note that **Order Id 4 Ad Pres** and **Order Total** are grouped together:

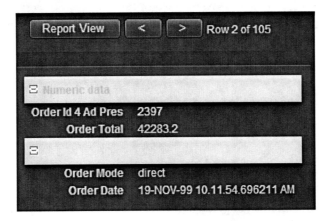

Using Dynamic Actions (DA) to add custom functions in the Actions menu

Now that we have a good idea about the functions and features of IRs in APEX, it's time to get back to our mischief. We have extensively used DAs to customize classic reports and now we will use DAs to customize magical IRs. We will use it to add a new item in the Actions menu of an IR.

The process of doing this, however, remains the same. The first step is to view the HTML source of the page. The first page of the reference application has **Actions** menu. We just have to see the HTML code generated by APEX to render the **Actions** menu and then code similar HTML using DAs. If you view the HTML source of the first page, you should be able to find the following code:

```
<li>
<a href="javascript:gReport.dialog2('SHOW_COLUMN','COLUMN');"
class="dhtmlSubMenuN" onmouseover="dhtml_CloseAllSubMenusL(this)"
title="Select Columns"><img alt="" src="/i/ws/edit_col_32.gif" />
Select Columns</a></li>
```

This code is responsible for showing the **Select Columns** link in the **Actions** menu. When we click on this link, a call to `gReport.dialog2` is made.

We will create a similar HTML code to add a new link to the **Actions** menu. We will keep the same classes so that the look and feel remains the same. Our link will be a single element and will not have lists under it, so we do not need `onmouseover="dhtml_CloseAllSubMenusL(this)"`. Title is not required, so we will remove it. The `src` attribute dictates the image which will be shown for our new item of the **Actions** menu. I am putting `#IMAGE_PREFIX#menu/pencil16x16.gif` as the `src` attribute. This is the same image that is displayed for the `Link` column. We can also upload images in the **Images** section present in **Supporting Components** and then use them. The text between `/>` and `</a>` will appear next to the `#IMAGE_PREFIX#menu/pencil16x16.gif` image in the menu.

Alright, now we have to get a handle on the **Actions** menu. The `li` code tag as shown previously is prefixed with the following code in the HTML source:

```
<ul id="apexir_ACTIONSMENU" htmldb:listlevel="2" class="dhtmlSubMenu"
style="display:none;">
```

This tells us that `apexir_ACTIONSMENU` is the ID of the **Action** menu and we can use this ID to get a handle on the menu. Now, we can write any JavaScript function of our choice to be called from the **Actions** menu, but since my purpose is to only show the process, I will use our old buddy, the `alert` function. Open the **Adding submenu to Actions menu** DA in the first page of the reference application. The code in this DA is as follows:

```
$('#apexir_ACTIONSMENU').prepend('<li><a href="javascript:alert(&
quot;Hello World&quot;);" class="dhtmlSubMenuN"><img src="#IMAGE_
PREFIX#menu/pencil16x16.gif">     Alert</a></
li>');
```

`prepend` is a standard jQuery function to prepend HTML text to some HTML handle. ` ` is to add blank spaces between the image and the alert text so that the formatting is proper. `&quot;` is for double quotes. We cannot put " character because it messes with the other " characters in the code.

The **Adding submenu to Actions menu** DA fires on **Page Load**. See the **When** section of the DA for verifying this. The **Adding submenu to Actions menu** DA affects only the master report region. The final result of this exercise is the following:

Using CSS in IR

Before I discuss the different ways of using CSS in an IR, I want to introduce you to the technique of writing code in a CSS file and using the file in APEX pages. It is also important to understand that the **Actions** menu can be used to handle many of the business requirements handled here. The following section only serves the purpose of informing you about the various possibilities to code in APEX.

Formatting a column using another column

The objective of this section is to format a column, based on another column of the query of a region source. Let me first talk about the CSS files in APEX, because one such CSS file is used in the query of region source.

CSS code files can be uploaded under the **Cascading Style Sheets** section of **Shared Components**, and then referencing these files in the APEX application can be done by putting the following in page header or region header:

```
<link rel="stylesheet" href="#WORKSPACE_IMAGES#4-98-9_03_chapter3.css"
type="text/css" />
```

I have put the previous `link` tag code in the header section of the page 101 because it will be the first page to execute since page 101 is my login page. CSS and JavaScript files are cached by the browser as soon as they are referenced. So make sure that you do not have references to a lot of these files in the login page because that will spoil user experience as the user will have to wait for a longer time for the login page to appear. If your application does not use an APEX login page, then you can put it in page 0, because doing this will load your CSS file as soon as your application is opened and hence you will be able to use the classes defined in it, everywhere in the application. You can also put these references on individual pages in APEX. When you put the previous code in your page or region header, your browser usually stores your **CSS** file and can use any class defined in it whenever a reference is made to any class in it. So, if you want to change certain attributes of a **CSS** class in the standard APEX templates, and you want these changes to only apply to certain places and not affect the application as a whole, then you should put the code in the header of the target region or page. It is also important to note that putting CSS in the page headers can increase the size of APEX pages, and hence increase the load time of the page, which can hamper user experience. Again, code in the headers might affect other regions which use the same class. If you are defining your own class in the **CSS** file, then there is no risk since you would be coding the references of these classes in only the necessary places, and the rest of the application will work perfectly well.

A side effect of the browser storing the **CSS** file is that any change made to the **CSS** file might not be reflected until we clear the temporary Internet files, since the browser might be using the older version of the file. Browsers store the file so that they don't have to load it on every page view. This storing improves the performance. I have written few classes, which are responsible for formatting the classic report on the third page of the reference application, in `4-98-9_03_chapter3.css` and I have uploaded it in **Shared Components**.

You can check the code in the `4-98-9_03_chapter3.css` file by going to the **Cascading Style Sheets** section of the **Shared Components** page. A section of the `4-98-9_03_chapter3.css` file is shown as follows for your convenience:

```
.new_pink_class {color: pink;}
.new_darkgoldenrod_class {color: #B8860B;}
.new_default_class {color: greenyellow;}
```

I have used the CSS classes, defined previously, in the REPORT_NAME column of the classic report on the third page. I have added a column called css_class in the query of the region source which returns the names of these CSS classes using a decode function. This query of the region source is shown as follows for your convenience:

```
select report_id,
       coalesce(report_name, 'Primary Report') report_name,
       decode(report_name,'Group by report', 'new_pink_class', 'Report
with computation', 'new_blue_class', 'Flashback report', 'new_purple_
class', 'Report using Column Break', 'new_red_class', 'Report using
Column Break and Aggregation', 'new_orange_class', 'Column Filter',
'new_brown_class', 'Vertical bar chart', 'new_white_class', 'Row
filter', 'new_crimson_class', 'Pie chart', 'new_darkgoldenrod_class',
'Horizontal bar chart','new_darkred_class','Salary groups','new_gold_
class','new_default_class') css_class
  from apex_application_page_ir_rpt
 where application_id = :APP_ID and page_id = :APP_PAGE_ID
   and (status = 'PUBLIC' or
        (status = 'PRIVATE' and application_user = :APP_USER))
   and report_type != 'SESSION'
```

I have then used the css_class column in the **Link Attributes** section of the **Column Attributes** page of the REPORT_NAME column. The same can be done in an IR as well. We can also use the **HTML Expression** text area of the **Column Attributes** page of both classic and interactive reports to use the column retuning CSS class names.

 The classes defined in the CSS file can also be defined in the region header.

APEX_CSS.ADD and APEX_CSS.ADD_FILE can also be used to add CSS content in an APEX application.

If you are not able to see the rows of the classic report appearing in different colors, then it means that your browser is not storing the **CSS** file. In this case, you should put the definition of the CSS classes defined in 4-98-9_03_chapter3.css in the header of the third page so that the **CSS** are available when the page is opened.

Putting the **CSS** code in the templates is also fine because the code in the region remains neater this way.

Using CSS in the page header to format APEX data

It is important to understand that `font-weight` is just an example and the process can be used for making any change to the display of pages in APEX. If you look at the HTML source of the third page of the reference application, you will find that `apexir_WORKSHEET_DATA` is the class of the HTML table of our IR. So, we can use this class to get a handle on the entire region. We can use it to search for the required element and add our formatting. For example, if we want to highlight the `Salary` column, then we could put the following code in the **Region Header** text area in the **Headers and Footer** section of the **Region Definition** page of the IR. You can see the following code in action in the third page of the reference application:

```
<style>.apexir_WORKSHEET_DATA td[headers="SALARY"] {font-weight:
bold;}</style>
```

It is difficult to spot the highlighted text of the `Salary` column because all the data of all the columns is highlighted due to the `new_class` class. We will talk about `new_class` in the *Using a user-defined CSS class in APEX* section. Change the previous code to the following. This will change the font color of the data in the `Salary` column to `red`. The changed color can easily be spotted.

```
<style>.apexir_WORKSHEET_DATA td[headers="SALARY"] {color: red;}</
style>
```

Note that we aren't defining any new CSS class here. We are getting the handle on a part of the APEX page and then using the handle to change the appearance of various parts on the page.

The `.` character in the preceding code helps us get the handle of the element which have `apexir_WORKSHEET_DATA` as their class. We then search for the `td` elements which have `SALARY` as the value of their `header` attribute and change their property.

Changing the font color of alternate rows in APEX

I took the whole CSS thing a little too far and changed the font color of the `td` elements, having `even` as the value of their `class` attribute, to `green`. You can see this code in the **Header and Footer** section of the **Features of IR** region on the third page of the reference application. The code is shown as follows for your convenience:

```
<style>.even td{color: green;}</style>
```

The important thing to note here is that we can change the attributes of a CSS class. Here, all elements that use the `even` class are getting formatted and the `even` class is a part of the APEX theme which we have chosen for our reports.

Using a user-defined CSS class in APEX

Another method of achieving formatting in APEX is by defining our own CSS class and using it. We have the following code in the region header of the **Features of IR** region of reference application. We have `class = "new_class"` in the **Region HTML table cell attributes** textbox of the **Attributes** section of the **Region Definition** page. The following definition of the class can be seen in the **Header and Footer** section of the **Features of IR** region on the third page of the reference application:

```
<style>.new_class {font-weight: bold;}</style>
```

This code changes the font of all data elements in the IR to bold. Run the third page to verify this.

Conditionally highlighting a column in IR using CSS and jQuery

Now if we wish to highlight all orders with `order_total` greater than `50000`, then we put the following code in the IR footer region. This code can be found in the IR of the first page and has also been shown as follows:

```
<script type="text/javascript">
$('td[headers="ORDER_TOTAL"]').each(function() {
  if ($(this).text() > 50000) {
    $(this).css('color','red');
}});</script>
```

Formatting an IR using a region query

Another method in this series is to define a CSS class in the **Header** section of the **Region Definition** page and to concatenate the column names in the query with the CSS class name to produce conditional formatting. I have done this to change the font color of the `Finance` values of the **Department Name** column. Go to the region source of the **Features of IR** region and note that we are using `decode(department_name,'Finance','<span class="finance_class"> ' || department_name || '</span>', '<span> ' || department_name || '</span>')`. This decode statement assigns `finance_class` to the rows which belong to the `Finance` department. The definition of `finance_class` is in the **Header and Footer** section of **Features of IR** region on the third page of the reference application. The code is `<style>.finance_class {color: blue;}</style>`.

Note that the value in the **Display Text As** dropdown has been changed to **Standard Report Column** for the formatting to be effective. I, however, suggest that you refrain from using this method because the users will have tremendous difficulty in framing the right filters in the IR. If they set a filter on just the value, they will not get the records because the value actually contains the class name as well. You will find this problem when you create filters using the **Actions** menu on the report on the third page of the reference application.

Understanding the process of any customizations in IR

I intend to lay down a process to customize an IR by presenting an example:

1. Log in to the reference application using SKING/SKING and click on the **Features of IR** tab.

2. Click on **Row filter** in the **Reports on IR** region. Note the icon next to **Saved Report = "Column Filter"** on the page.

   This icon will change by the end of this section. Screenshot is shown as follows and the icon is highlighted for your convenience:

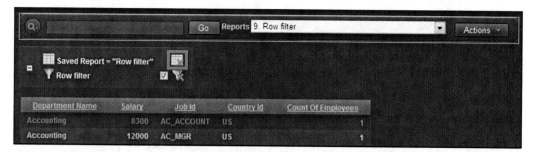

3. Move your mouse over this icon. You will see **Delete Report** as the tip. This is our clue. We will search for **Delete Report** in the HTML source and will then manipulate the HTML element containing **Delete Report** as the value of one of its attributes.

4. Search the HTML source for **Delete Report**. I found this:

```
<img src="/i/ws/report_remove_20x18.gif" height="18" width="20"
title="Delete Report" alt="Delete Report" />
```

`report_remove_20x18.gif` is the highlighted icon in the previous screenshot. Our task is to change this icon. We see that `Delete Report` is a value of the `alt` attribute. We will use this to get a handle on the `img` tag and change its `src` attribute to a new value.

5. Our target is to replace `report_remove_20x18.gif` with a different image. I have picked `trash_32.gif` for this purpose. Place the following code in either the region footer of the IR region or the page footer:

```
<script type="text/javascript">
$("img").each(function() {if($(this).attr("alt") == "Delete
Report"){$(this).attr("src","/i/ws/trash_32.gif");}});
</script>
```

In the preceding code, we first get all the handles of the `img` tag. We then filter the `img` tag which has `Delete Report` in its `alt` attribute. Finally, we replace the value of the `src` attribute by our desired value. I have placed it in the region footer of the **Features of IR** region. We chose to put the JavaScript code in the footer and not in the header because we are grabbing handles of the HTML tags in this JavaScript. These handles will not be available until the page is loaded. So, this JavaScript has to be in the footer. I have commented the code; you can uncomment it to see the effect. Refresh the third page and note the changed icon next to **Saved Report = "Column Filter"**. Screenshot is shown as follows and the changed icon is highlighted for your convenience:

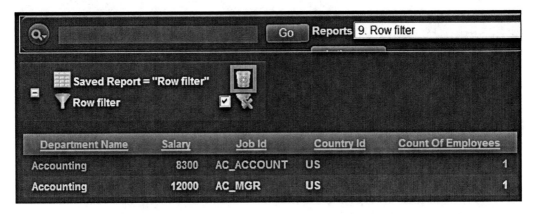

The key to any customization in an IR is to know the value of any one of the attribute such as `id`, `class`, or `alt` of the target HTML element. APEX makes this work easier by prepending `apexir` to the ids of a majority of the HTML elements in an IR. View the page source of an IR and search for `apexir`. I suggest that you have a look at each of these elements whose ID is prefixed with `apexir`. Doing this will give you a good understanding of the organelles which together form an IR.

Coding against the internal structures of APEX is a two-headed sword. It can help to meet any requirement but can also create problems post upgrading an APEX instance because the internal structures of APEX might change in the newer versions.

Using APEX views to create a classic report on saved IRs

In this section, we create a classic report that gives us links to access the saved reports of an IR. We can query the information about saved reports from the `apex_application_page_ir_rpt` view. This view holds the metadata of IR reports. One row of this report corresponds to one of the saved IRs. Log in as SKING/SKING and run the third page of the reference application. Screenshot has been shown as follows and the heading of the classic report is highlighted for your convenience:

The **Reports on IR** classic report lets us select one of our saved reports. Its function is similar to the **Reports** dropdown. We are using the `report_id` column of `apex_application_page_ir_rpt` to help us uniquely identify each saved report. We are assigning this `report_id` value to a page item and this page item is put in the **Report ID Item** textbox of the **Advanced** section of the **Report Attributes** page of the IR. The entire query can be found in the *Formatting an IR using region query* section.

Capturing report ID using JavaScript

We can also capture the report IDs using the following JavaScript code:

```
<script type="text/javascript">
$("#apexir_SAVED_REPORTS").children().children().each(function() {
alert($(this).val());}); </script>
```

Here, I am using `apexir_SAVED_REPORTS` to get a handle on the report drop-down list and I am then extracting the report IDs from the dropdown.

Creating multiple IR on the same page

In APEX 4.2, we can have only a single IR on one page. Let us outfox this problem. The truth is, we can have only one IR on one APEX page and APEX won't let us create more. So, we will have to create one IR each on two separate pages and then put them together in one. This has been done in the reference application using first and second pages. We have used the `object` HTML tag to get the report of the second page on the first page. Report on the first page is a report on `order_items` while that on the second page is on `order_line_items`. I wanted to create a master-detail relation between the two reports, so I had to pass the `order_id` value from the first page to the second page. We cannot use the usual column links to set some page item because the report which we get on the first page, using the `object` HTML tag, can only be affected by the `data` attribute of the `object` tag. So I am using application items to set a link between the two pages. When the user clicks on a link in the **Order Id 4 Ad Pres** or **Order Id 4 Others** column of the report on the first page, we set the `G_ORDER_ITEM` application item and submit the first page. Since we have set an application item, the newly set value is visible from the second page as well. Hence, we can filter the records on the second page using `G_ORDER_ITEM` without having the hassle of passing any value from the first page to the second page. The final result looks like the following:

Let us now see the process of creating this report using the following steps:

1. Create one IR on the first page and the other on the second page. Do not create a tab or breadcrumb for the second page. Make sure that **No** is selected in the **Link to Single Row View** dropdown in both the reports. I see that **One Level Tabs - Right Sidebar (optional / table-based)** is the template of my page. Make sure that you also have the same template, because we will have to edit it in step 5.

   Copy the queries of the region sources of the two IR's from the reference application. The `order_id` column has been selected twice in the query of the region source on the first page and I will reveal the reason for this shortly. Query in the IR of the second page is again a simple query on `oehr_order_items`. This query has a `where` clause that uses the `G_ORDER_ITEM` application item.

2. Create the `G_ORDER_ITEM` application item.

3. We are now creating a meaningful report alias for our primary report. Right-click on the report on the second page and select **Edit Saved Reports**. Put **IR_OEHR_ORDER_ITEMS** in the **Report Alias** column and click on **Apply Changes**. If you do not see anything when you select **Edit Saved Reports**, then you will have to run the page and then select **Save Report** from the **Actions** menu. You will have to select **As Default Report Settings** from the **Save** dropdown. You will also have to select the **Primary** radio button and then hit the **Apply** button. This will now show the default report when you select **Edit Saved Reports**.

   This report is the primary default report for the IR on the second page. Using the same IR region, every user can customize the report in his way and save his version of the report. So, many customized versions of an IR can exist. Some of these can be public.

4. Create a new HTML region on the first page. Call it **Detail report** and put the following as region source in it. Note the `IR_REPORT_` prefix in `IR_REPORT_IR_OEHR_ORDER_ITEMS` in the following code. Prefixing `IR_REPORT_` to a report alias lets us access the public report we created on the second page as shown in the following snippet:

```
<object type="text/html" data="f?p=&APP_ID.:2:&APP_
SESSION.:IR_REPORT_IR_OEHR_ORDER_ITEMS:::::" style="width:100%;
height:750px"></object>
```

This code will put the contents of the second page on the first page. We can use **substitution variables** in the `data` attribute of the `object` tag. So, we can perform some computation and put a report alias based on our computation in a page item. We can then use this item as the substitution variables in the `data` attribute to make our child report vary according to certain conditions. The `APEX_APPLICATION_PAGE_IR_RPT` view can be used to dynamically get report alias.

5. Go to **Shared Components | Security Attributes** and then go to the **Browser Security** section in it. Select **Allow from same Origin** in the **Embed in Frames** dropdown and click on **Apply Changes**.

   We will now create a copy of our template. The aim is to create a copy of the page template, edit the copied template, and apply it only on the second page. This way, we get to customize one page without disturbing the look and feel of the others. We are editing the template in order to remove tabs and other links from the second page. We want to remove these things because the second page is embedded in the first and we have these on the first page.

6. Go to **Shared Components** and create a copy of the **One Level Tabs - Right Sidebar (optional / table-based)** template.

   Edit the newly created template. Go to the **Body** section of it. Delete the following from it:

```
<div id="header">
  <div id="logo"><a href="#HOME_LINK#">#LOGO##REGION_
POSITION_06#</a></div>
  #REGION_POSITION_07#
  <div id="navbar">
    <div class="app-user">#WELCOME_USER#</div>
    #NAVIGATION_BAR#
    #REGION_POSITION_08#
  </div> </div>
<div id="tabs">
  <div class="frame">
    <div class="bg">
      <div class="tab-holder">
        #TAB_CELLS#
      </div>    </div>  </div>    </div>
<div id="topbar">#REGION_POSITION_01##REGION_POSITION_04#</div>
```

This code is responsible for showing the logged in username, the logout link, and the bar that holds the tabs on the top of the page. We are embedding the second page in the first page and we don't want these things to appear in the embedded section on the first page.

We should also remove the version number which appears at the bottom of the page. For this, go the footer section and delete the following:

```
<div class="app-version">#APP_VERSION#</div>
  #REGION_POSITION_05#
</div>
```

7. Now apply this newly created template to the second page.

 We can also use Dynamic Actions to remove these from our page. We will examine the Dynamic Actions method when we discuss **Interactive Report Dashboard**.

8. Go to the **Report Attributes** page of the report on the first page and click on the **ORDER_ID_4_AD_PRES** column. Go to the **Link** section. Enter `#ORDER_ID_4_AD_PRES#` in the **Link Text** textbox, select **Page in this Application** in the **Target** dropdown, enter 1 in the **Page** textbox, **G_ORDER_ITEM** in the **Item 1** textbox, and **#ORDER_ID_4_AD_PRES#** in the corresponding **Value** textbox. Follow a similar process for the **ORDER_ID_4_OTHERS** column as well.

This step puts a link on the **ORDER_ID_4_AD_PRES** and **ORDER_ID_4_OTHERS** columns and it sets the `order_id` value in **G_ORDER_ITEM** when the user clicks on the link on any row.

All this work has been done in the reference application. Run the first page of the reference application to see the result.

Authorizing user groups to view report columns

The business problem which we will solve here is related to the rights of an individual user. Let's say that we have a requirement where we want the users with `AD_PRES` `job_id` to do fancy IR stuff such as highlighting, sorting and filtering on the `order_id` column, and we do not want these features for other users. We can solve this business problem by setting different authorizations on two columns which display the same data. **ORDER_ID_4_AD_PRES** and **ORDER_ID_4_OTHERS** are the two such columns in the reference application.

Let's now have a look at the CHAPTER3.AD_PRES_AUTHORIZATION function. This function takes the user ID of the currently logged in user and returns true if the job_id value is AD_PRES, otherwise it returns false. We have built an APEX authorization called AD_PRES around this function. AD_PRES authorization is responsible for passing the user ID of the currently logged in user to the CHAPTER3.AD_PRES_AUTHORIZATION function. Note that we can use v('APP_USER') in CHAPTER3.AD_PRES_AUTHORIZATION to get the value of the user ID. The use of v('APP_USER') is costly because it leads to a lot of switches between the SQL and the PL/SQL engine. This switching is primarily because v() is a PL/SQL function and this function will be executed in an SQL statement to check the JOB_ID value of the currently logged in user. So, passing the value is a lot better.

The AD_PRES authorization is used in the **Security** section of the **Column Attributes** page of the **ORDER_ID_4_AD_PRES** column (the **ORDER_ID_4_AD_PRES** column is in the **Master report** region of the first page of the reference application). The AD_PRES authorization ensures that the **ORDER_ID_4_AD_PRES** column is only visible to the person with the AD_PRES job_id. When we created the AD_PRES authorization scheme, APEX created a {Not AD_PRES} scheme for us. You will not be able to see this scheme listed in the **Authorization Schemes** section in the **Shared Components** page, but you will be able to use it. This scheme has been used in the **ORDER_ID_4_OTHERS** column. We have introduced a functional difference between the two columns by unchecking all the checkboxes in the **Allow Users To** checkbox group present in the **Column Definition** section of the **Column Attributes** page of the **ORDER_ID_4_OTHERS** column. The screenshot has been shown as follows for your convenience:

This prevents the Non AD_PRES users from doing any IR activity such as highlighting on the **ORDER_ID_4_OTHERS** column.

Creating Interactive Report Dashboard

Building on the concepts introduced to you till now, I have created an **Interactive Report Dashboard**. Check the fourth page of the reference application to have a feel of it. I have handpicked six of the eleven saved reports of the third page and arranged them in different regions on the fourth page so that they look like gadgets. Check the screenshot at the bottom of this section to get a feel of the Interactive Report Dashboard. Let us now look at the code of one of the gadgets in the Interactive Report Dashboard to understand the implementation. Open the region definition of the **Row filter** region and go to the **Source** section. The code has been shown as follows for your convenience:

```
declare
l_row_fltr_rpt_id number;
begin
select report_id into l_row_fltr_rpt_id from apex_application_page_ir_
rpt where application_id = :APP_ID and page_id = 3 and report_name =
'Row filter' and report_type = 'PRIVATE';
htp.p('<object type="text/html" data="f?p=&APP_
ID.:3:&SESSION.::NO:3,CIR:P3_REPORT_ID:'||l_row_fltr_rpt_id||   '"
style="width:100%; height:290px"></object>');
end;
```

Let us now understand this code. The `Htp.p` function has been used to put an HTML object on the browser. I am using `apex_application_page_ir_rpt` to get the region IDs. Region ID, fetched from `apex_application_page_ir_rpt`, is assigned to **P3_REPORT_ID**. The assignment is done using the URL which appears in the `data` attribute of the HTML `Object` element.

Notice that each region on the fourth page only shows a report while the URL in the region source is the URL of the third page. So ideally, each region on the fourth page should show the entire third page. We are able to cut only the relevant section of the third page because we have the **replaceByRegionHTML** DA on the third page which replaces the HTML code of the page with the HTML of a region if the URL of the window does not have `:3:` in it. This basically means that the DA will replace the HTML of the third page with the HTML code of the required region when the request comes from the fourth page. The code of this DA is shown as follows:

```
if ($u_SubString(window.location.href,":3:"))
return;
else
$('#wwvFlowForm').html($(this.triggeringElement).html());
```

We can also remove the **Action** menu and the search bar using the techniques learned in this chapter.

Note that the gadgets in the dashboards are arranged in three columns and three rows. The width of the columns have been changed by editing the **Region Table Attributes** text area of the **One Level Tabs - Right Sidebar (optional / table-based)** template. The height of every column is adjusted by putting the following code in the page header:

```
<style>.rc-body {height: 300px;}</style>
```

Height and width of HTML `object` element which is inside the region source of the PL/SQL region is adjusted using the `style` attribute in the `htp.p` function in the region source. A screenshot of the Interactive Report Dashboard is shown as follows:

Understanding Dynamic Interactive Reports

We had seen that we can make a dynamic classic report by picking **Function Returning SQL Query** as the region source in the *Dynamic query region in APEX* section of *Chapter 2, Conventional Reporting in APEX*. We do not have this liberty in IRs, but we can use the `table` function using both native and interface approach and APEX collections to create dynamic reports in IR.

Let us first talk about the `table` function. It accepts a collection or a ref cursor and is used in the `from` clause of a query. The `table` function can be used as any other physical table. Two important features associated with a `table` function are **pipelining** and **partitioning**. We will see information about both of these in the coming sections. Note the subtle point here. table() accepts a ref cursor or a collection as an argument. We can define a stored function that returns either one of these and pass the function as an arguement to `table()`. Until now, we have been referencing table() as table function but the stored functions that return a collection or ref cursor are also often called table functions.

Using native PL/SQL table function approach and conditional columns

In the native PL/SQL `table` function approach, we declare a `table` function to return a collection (nested table or `varray`) by pipelining every row in the result. I have used this in the fifth page of the reference application. The query in the region source is:

```
select * from table(chapter3.ir_dynmc_rpt_ntv_aprch(:P5_TABLE_
NAME,decode(:P5_TABLE_NAME,'OEHR_ORDERS',:P5_CUSTOMER_ID,:P5_ORDER_
ID)));
```

Pipelining an output means that data is not cached and is delivered as soon as it is generated. This also helps to save the memory as the entire result set does not have to be cached anywhere.

Run the fifth page of the reference application. The dynamic query returns three columns when the `OEHR_ORDERS` table is selected and returns two columns when the `OEHR_ORDER_ITEMS` table is selected. The table function, however, is declared to return a table of the `chap3_ntv_aproch_tbl_type` type. `chap3_ntv_aproch_tbl_type` is an object of the `chap3_ntv_aproch_type` type and `chap3_ntv_aproch_type` has three attributes.

So where do we hide the third attribute, that is, `ORDER_MODE` when `OEHR_ORDER_ITEMS` is selected? We have made the **Order Mode** column conditional. The **Order Mode** column is displayed only when `OEHR_ORDERS` is selected in the `P5_TABLE_NAME` item. We can check this in the **Conditions** section of the **Column Attributes** page of the **Order Mode** column. We can certainly have a different logic to hide our column.

 Collection approach uses a completely different logic to hide the column. We will see collection approach in a short while. In the collection approach, we feed `null` in the third attribute of `chap3_ntv_aproch_type` when `OEHR_ORDER_ITMES` is selected. We use it to frame a condition that the **Order Mode** column should be displayed only when at least one value in the column is not `null`.

The important point to understand here is that the chap3_ntv_aproch_type type should have the maximum expected columns in the output. If under certain conditions, some of the columns should not be displayed, then we can feed null in those attributes and make the columns conditional in APEX.

The chapter3 package has the ir_dynmc_rpt_ntv_aprch function. As discussed earlier, this function is used in the fifth page of the reference application. Let us talk about it now. ir_dynmc_rpt_ntv_aprch returns the chap3_rprt_table_type type by pipelining rows of the chap3_rprt_type type. The following is the code of this function:

```
FUNCTION ir_dynmc_rpt_ntv_aprch
  (  p_tab_name VARCHAR2,   p_filter   NUMBER)
  RETURN chap3_ntv_aproch_tbl_type PIPELINED
IS
  single_rec chap3_ntv_aproch_type := chap3_ntv_aproch_
type(NULL,NULL,NULL);
TYPE rc IS   REF   CURSOR;
    l_rc rc;
    l_oehr_orders constant VARCHAR2 (11 CHAR):= 'OEHR_ORDERS';
    l_query       VARCHAR2 (100 CHAR);
    l_id          NUMBER;
    l_price       NUMBER;
    l_order_mode  VARCHAR2(20 CHAR);
  BEGIN
    IF upper(p_tab_name) = l_oehr_orders THEN
      l_query          := 'SELECT ORDER_ID, ORDER_TOTAL   , ORDER_MODE
FROM oehr_orders
WHERE   customer_id = :p_customer_id';
    ELSE
      l_query := 'SELECT ORDER_ITEM_ID, unit_price
FROM oehr_order_items  WHERE   ORDER_ID = :p_order_id';
    END IF;
    OPEN l_rc FOR l_query USING p_filter;
    LOOP
    IF upper(p_tab_name) = l_oehr_orders THEN
      FETCH l_rc INTO l_id, l_price, l_order_mode;
      single_rec := chap3_ntv_aproch_type (l_id, l_price, l_order_
mode);
    ELSE
      FETCH l_rc INTO l_id, l_price;
      single_rec := chap3_ntv_aproch_type (l_id, l_price, null);
    END IF;
    EXIT
  WHEN l_rc%NOTFOUND;
    PIPE ROW (single_rec);
```

```
    END LOOP;
    CLOSE l_rc;
    RETURN;
  END ir_dynmc_rpt_ntv_aprch;
```

Let us understand this code. We first create a cursor based on the input arguments. We then run a loop and store every row returned by the cursor in `single_rec` which is a variable of the `chap3_ntv_aproch_type` type. Every row in `single_rec` is then pipelined to return the entire result set. Since `ir_dynmc_rpt_ntv_aprch` returns a number of rows of the `chap3_ntv_aproch_type` type, `ir_dynmc_rpt_ntv_aprch` is declared to return `chap3_ntv_aproch_tbl_type` which is a table of the `chap3_ntv_aproch_type` type. `ir_dynmc_rpt_ntv_aprch` accepts the table name and a filter value as its arguments. These arguments are passed to `ir_dynmc_rpt_ntv_aprch` from the `from` clause of the query in the region source of the IR on the fifth page. `P5_TABLE_NAME` is always passed and only one of `P5_CUSTOMER_ID` or `P5_ORDER_ID` is passed to `ir_dynmc_rpt_ntv_aprch`. So, in any call to the `table` function, only two of the three values are passed.

Using parallel-enabled table functions

Parallel execution means that the execution is distributed among a number of slave processes which operate in parallel, and hence speed up the execution. The partitioning approach used by a `table` function is declared in its specification. In a partitioned `table` function, slave processes first do the partitioning and the partitions are then executed by slave processes to retrieve data in the second step.

The following two conditions must be met for parallel execution to happen:

- The `table` function should have the `PARALLEL_ENABLE` clause in its declaration
- The function should accept at least one ref cursor as its argument and one of these ref cursors should be specified with a `partition by` clause

`chapter3.prllel_enbld_tbl_funct` is one such function. This function is not used in our APEX application, and there are better ways of fetching records from the `oehr_employees` table, but this function is written to demonstrate parallel-enabled `table` functions:

```
FUNCTION prllel_enbld_tbl_funct
  ( p_cursor chapter3.emp_ref_cursor)
  RETURN chap3_prllel_enbl_tabl_typ PIPELINED
  PARALLEL_ENABLE (PARTITION p_cursor BY range (department_id)) is
  TYPE emp_tab_type IS TABLE OF oehr_employees%ROWTYPE;
  l_emp_tab emp_tab_type;
```

```
BEGIN
    FETCH p_cursor BULK COLLECT INTO l_emp_tab;
        FOR i IN l_emp_tab.FIRST .. l_emp_tab.LAST loop
            PIPE ROW (chap3_prllel_enbl_typ(l_emp_tab(i).EMPLOYEE_ID,
            l_emp_tab(i).FIRST_NAME,l_emp_tab(i).LAST_NAME,
            l_emp_tab(i).EMAIL,l_emp_tab(i).PHONE_NUMBER,
            l_emp_tab(i).HIRE_DATE, l_emp_tab(i).JOB_ID,
            l_emp_tab(i).SALARY,l_emp_tab(i).COMMISSION_PCT,
            l_emp_tab(i).MANAGER_ID,l_emp_tab(i).DEPARTMENT_ID
            ));
            end loop;
    CLOSE p_cursor;
    RETURN;
END prllel_enbld_tbl_funct;
```

Let me briefly talk about the bits of code involved in making this function work. We have an `object` type called `chap3_prllel_enbl_typ` and a table of this type called `chap3_prllel_enbl_tabl_typ`. `p_cursor` is of the `chapter3.emp_ref_cursor` type. `emp_tab_type` is declared inside `prllel_enbld_tbl_funct` and is a table of `oehr_employees%rowtype`. We created this table type so that we could collect the entire dataset of the input cursor in a single shot using `bulk collect`. `prllel_enbld_tbl_funct` then runs a `for` loop to fetch single row from `l_emp_tab` and `pipe` the `row` object to the calling function.

 `bulk collect` improves performance of DML statements.

We will be passing `cursor (select * from oehr_employees)` as an argument to `prllel_enbld_tbl_funct` and will be collecting the rows of this cursor in `l_emp_tab` which is of `emp_tab_type`, so `emp_tab_type` has to be a table of `oehr_employees%rowtype`. `prllel_enbld_tbl_funct` returns `chap3_prllel_enbl_tabl_typ`. `prllel_enbld_tbl_funct` range partitions the data based on `department_id`.

We can also **hash partition** the data. Range and hash can only be specified if we are putting a list of columns in the `partition by` clause. We can also write ANY keyword instead of a list of columns. If ANY is used, then the data is randomly partitioned among slave processes.

We can check the output of this function using the following query:

```
SELECT * FROM TABLE(chapter3.prllel_enbld_tbl_funct(CURSOR
  (SELECT * FROM oehr_employees  )))
```

Unterstanding interface table function approach

In the native approach, we created a type with attributes that match with the columns of the select clause of our query. We then pipelined a set of rows of this type. Now, if we do not know the columns in the select clause at the time of development, then we cannot create a type and hence the query of native approach cannot handle dynamic queries with different columns in the select clause. The workaround is to conditionally display the columns. This has been presented to you in the *Native PL/SQL table function approach* section. We will now see a method to use the table function to handle dynamic queries that return different columns in the select clause. This approach is called the **interface approach**.

In the interface approach, we create types at runtime. We call it the interface approach because we implement the ODCITable interface. Interfaces are a set of function declarations. Implementing the interface means that we create the function definitions for the functions in the interface. The signature of the functions should match with the declarations in the interface. The ODCITable interface has the six functions listed in the following section in the order of their execution. These functions will be used in the data retrieval process. Interface methods can be written in PL/SQL, Java, or C++.

ODCITableDescribe and ODCITablePrepare are optional to implement, but we will have to implement them because we do not know the types and the number of columns in our dynamic select statement. Let me first share the specification and the body of the CHAP3_INTRFC_APROCH_TYP type:

```
create or replace TYPE CHAP3_INTRFC_APROCH_TYP AS OBJECT
  ( dymc_rcrd_typ ANYTYPE ,
    STATIC FUNCTION ODCITableDescribe
    ( p_dynmc_objct_tbl_typ OUT ANYTYPE,
      p_dynmic_imput_stmt IN VARCHAR2 ) RETURN NUMBER ,
    STATIC FUNCTION ODCITablePrepare
    ( p_dymc_tbl_obj_scn_cntxt OUT CHAP3_INTRFC_APROCH_TYP,
      p_tf_info            IN sys.ODCITabFuncInfo,
      p_dynmic_imput_stmt IN VARCHAR2 ) RETURN NUMBER ,
    STATIC FUNCTION ODCITableStart
    ( p_dymc_tbl_obj_scn_cntxt IN OUT CHAP3_INTRFC_APROCH_TYP,
      p_dynmic_imput_stmt       IN VARCHAR2 ) RETURN NUMBER ,
    MEMBER FUNCTION ODCITableFetch
    ( self                  IN OUT CHAP3_INTRFC_APROCH_TYP,
      p_orcl_exptd_no_of_rows IN NUMBER,
      p_nxt_btch_of_rows OUT ANYDATASET ) RETURN NUMBER ,
```

```
      MEMBER FUNCTION ODCITableClose
      ( SELF IN CHAP3_INTRFC_APROCH_TYP ) RETURN NUMBER );
create or replace TYPE BODY CHAP3_INTRFC_APROCH_TYP
AS
   STATIC FUNCTION ODCITableDescribe
   ( p_dynmc_objct_tbl_typ OUT ANYTYPE,
     p_dynmic_imput_stmt IN VARCHAR2 ) RETURN NUMBER IS
   l_dynmc_objct_typ ANYTYPE;
BEGIN
   chapter3.g_cursor := DBMS_SQL.OPEN_CURSOR;
   DBMS_SQL.PARSE( chapter3.g_cursor, p_dynmic_imput_stmt, DBMS_SQL.
NATIVE );
   DBMS_SQL.DESCRIBE_COLUMNS2( chapter3.g_cursor, chapter3.g_col_cnt,
chapter3.g_descrip );
   DBMS_SQL.CLOSE_CURSOR( chapter3.g_cursor );
   ANYTYPE.BeginCreate( DBMS_TYPES.TYPECODE_OBJECT, l_dynmc_objct_typ
);
   FOR i IN 1 .. chapter3.g_col_cnt
   LOOP
     l_dynmc_objct_typ.AddAttr( chapter3.g_descrip(i).col_name,
     CASE
     WHEN chapter3.g_descrip(i).col_type IN (1,96,11,208) THEN
       DBMS_TYPES.TYPECODE_VARCHAR2
     WHEN chapter3.g_descrip(i).col_type = 2 THEN
       DBMS_TYPES.TYPECODE_NUMBER
     WHEN chapter3.g_descrip(i).col_type = 12 THEN
       DBMS_TYPES.TYPECODE_DATE
     END, chapter3.g_descrip(i).col_precision, chapter3.g_descrip(i).
col_scale, chapter3.g_descrip(i).col_max_len, chapter3.g_descrip(i).
col_charsetid, chapter3.g_descrip(i).col_charsetform );
   END LOOP;
   l_dynmc_objct_typ.EndCreate;
   ANYTYPE.BeginCreate( DBMS_TYPES.TYPECODE_TABLE, p_dynmc_objct_tbl_
typ );
   p_dynmc_objct_tbl_typ.SetInfo( NULL, NULL, NULL, NULL, NULL, l_
dynmc_objct_typ, DBMS_TYPES.TYPECODE_OBJECT, 0 );
   p_dynmc_objct_tbl_typ.EndCreate();
   RETURN ODCIConst.Success;
END;
STATIC FUNCTION ODCITablePrepare
   ( p_dymc_tbl_obj_scn_cntxt OUT CHAP3_INTRFC_APROCH_TYP,
     p_tf_info           IN sys.ODCITabFuncInfo,
```

```
    p_dynmic_imput_stmt IN VARCHAR2 ) RETURN NUMBER IS
  l_dummy_num NUMBER;
  l_type ANYTYPE;
  l_name      VARCHAR2(30);
  l_typecode NUMBER;
BEGIN
  l_typecode                := p_tf_info.rettype.GetAttrElemInfo( 1, l_
dummy_num, l_dummy_num, l_dummy_num, l_dummy_num, l_dummy_num, l_type,
l_name );
  p_dymc_tbl_obj_scn_cntxt := CHAP3_INTRFC_APROCH_TYP(l_type);
  RETURN ODCIConst.Success;
END;
STATIC FUNCTION ODCITableStart
  ( p_dymc_tbl_obj_scn_cntxt IN OUT CHAP3_INTRFC_APROCH_TYP,
    p_dynmic_imput_stmt      IN VARCHAR2 ) RETURN NUMBER IS
  l_num_dummy NUMBER; l_type ANYTYPE; l_name VARCHAR2(30);
  l_typecode NUMBER;
BEGIN
  chapter3.g_cursor := DBMS_SQL.OPEN_CURSOR;
  DBMS_SQL.PARSE( chapter3.g_cursor, p_dynmic_imput_stmt, DBMS_SQL.
NATIVE );
  DBMS_SQL.DESCRIBE_COLUMNS2( chapter3.g_cursor, chapter3.g_col_cnt,
chapter3.g_descrip );
  FOR i IN 1 .. chapter3.g_col_cnt LOOP
    l_typecode := p_dymc_tbl_obj_scn_cntxt.dymc_rcrd_typ.
GetAttrElemInfo( i, l_num_dummy, l_num_dummy, l_num_dummy, l_num_
dummy, l_num_dummy, l_type, l_name );
    CASE l_typecode
    WHEN DBMS_TYPES.TYPECODE_VARCHAR2 THEN
      DBMS_SQL.DEFINE_COLUMN( chapter3.g_cursor, i, '', 32767 );
    WHEN DBMS_TYPES.TYPECODE_NUMBER THEN
      DBMS_SQL.DEFINE_COLUMN( chapter3.g_cursor, i, CAST(NULL AS
NUMBER) );
    WHEN DBMS_TYPES.TYPECODE_DATE THEN
      DBMS_SQL.DEFINE_COLUMN( chapter3.g_cursor, i, CAST(NULL AS DATE)
);
    END CASE;
  END LOOP;
  chapter3.g_execute := DBMS_SQL.EXECUTE( chapter3.g_cursor );
  RETURN ODCIConst.Success;
END;
MEMBER FUNCTION ODCITableFetch
  ( self                    IN OUT CHAP3_INTRFC_APROCH_TYP,
```

```
      p_orcl_exptd_no_of_rows IN NUMBER,
      p_nxt_btch_of_rows OUT ANYDATASET )  RETURN NUMBER IS
   l_get_val_4_varchar_col VARCHAR2(20);
   l_get_val_4_nmbr_col    NUMBER; l_get_val_4_date_col DATE;
   l_name       VARCHAR2(30); l_typecode  NUMBER;
   l_attr_type ANYTYPE;  l_num_dummy NUMBER;
BEGIN
  IF DBMS_SQL.FETCH_ROWS( chapter3.g_cursor ) > 0 THEN
     ANYDATASET.BeginCreate( DBMS_TYPES.TYPECODE_OBJECT, self.dymc_
rcrd_typ, p_nxt_btch_of_rows );
     p_nxt_btch_of_rows.AddInstance();
     p_nxt_btch_of_rows.PieceWise();
     FOR i IN 1 .. chapter3.g_col_cnt LOOP
       l_typecode := self.dymc_rcrd_typ.GetAttrElemInfo( i, l_num_
dummy, l_num_dummy, l_num_dummy, l_num_dummy, l_num_dummy, l_attr_
type, l_name );
       CASE l_typecode
       WHEN DBMS_TYPES.TYPECODE_VARCHAR2 THEN
         DBMS_SQL.COLUMN_VALUE( chapter3.g_cursor, i, l_get_val_4_
varchar_col );
          p_nxt_btch_of_rows.SetVarchar2( l_get_val_4_varchar_col );
       WHEN DBMS_TYPES.TYPECODE_NUMBER THEN
         DBMS_SQL.COLUMN_VALUE( chapter3.g_cursor, i, l_get_val_4_nmbr_
col );
          p_nxt_btch_of_rows.SetNumber( l_get_val_4_nmbr_col );
       WHEN DBMS_TYPES.TYPECODE_DATE THEN
         DBMS_SQL.COLUMN_VALUE( chapter3.g_cursor, i, l_get_val_4_date_
col );
          p_nxt_btch_of_rows.SetDate( l_get_val_4_date_col );
       END CASE;
     END LOOP;
     p_nxt_btch_of_rows.EndCreate();
  END IF;
  RETURN ODCIConst.Success;
END;
MEMBER FUNCTION ODCITableClose
  ( SELF IN CHAP3_INTRFC_APROCH_TYP )  RETURN NUMBER IS
BEGIN
  DBMS_SQL.CLOSE_CURSOR( chapter3.g_cursor );
  RETURN ODCIConst.Success;
END;
END;
```

Understanding the ODCITableDescribe function

The ODCITableDescribe function is executed at query-complication time. This function is called when a dynamic query is fired for the first time. We created two ANYTYPE objects namely, l_dynmc_objct_typ and p_dynmc_objct_tbl_typ in the ODCITableDescribe function. Creation is done by the ANYTYPE.BeginCreate procedure. We parse the dynamic query using DBMS_SQL to get information such as precision and scale of the data types of the columns in the select clause. We then execute DBMS_SQL.DESCRIBE_COLUMNS2 and we loop through each column info returned by DBMS_SQL.DESCRIBE_COLUMNS2 and then add attributes to l_dynmc_objct_typ. So we get an object (l_dynmc_objct_typ) that has attributes which represent the columns of the input dynamic query. We then create p_dynmc_objct_tbl_typ as a table of l_dynmc_objct_typ.

Understanding the ODCITablePrepare function

The ODCITablePrepare function is also executed only once per query. Just like ODCITableDescribe(),ODCITablePrepare() is executed when the dynamic query is fired for the first time. ODCITablePrepare has an OUT parameter of the CHAP3_INTRFC_APROCH_TYP type. This type has been defined in the using clause of chpater3.tbl_funct_intrfc_aproch. The p_tf_info.rettype.GetAttrElemInfo function has a number of arguments. Apart from the first one, the rest are the OUT arguments and out of all these arguments, we are only interested in l_type. Since the rest are unnecessary, I fetch all the number type arguments in one variable called l_dummy_num. This simplifies and shortens the code. l_type returned here is having the attributes of l_dynmc_objct_typ and l_type is actually a variable of ANYTYPE. This might be confusing but the interface is designed in such a way that p_tf_info is a handle to get the attributes of the table type created in ODCITableDescribe, that is, p_dynmc_objct_tbl_typ. Since p_dynmc_objct_tbl_typ is a table of l_dynmc_objct_typ, so we are able to fetch it. The type of l_type is ANYTYPE because this will let l_type capture any structure. We use l_type to create an object of CHAP3_INTRFC_APROCH_TYP. We are able to do a casting from ANYTYPE to CHAP3_INTRFC_APROCH_TYP because CHAP3_INTRFC_APROCH_TYP also has an ANYTYPE attribute called dymc_rcrd_typ. Check the specification of CHAP3_INTRFC_APROCH_TYP to verify this. This newly created object, p_dymc_tbl_obj_scn_cntxt, is called the **scan context**. Scan context is created only when the dynamic query is fired for the first time because ODCITablePrepare() is fired only when a dynamic query is fired for the first time. On subsequent firing of the same query, the scan context created in the first query execution is reused. This scan context is passed to ODCITableStart() when ODCITableStart() is called at the beginning of the query execution.

Understanding the ODCITableStart function

The `ODCITableStart` function initiates the scan of the `table` function. We are only interested in getting the `l_typecode` value. Look what is happening here. We are parsing the dynamic query again. The parsing done in `ODCITableDescribe` cannot be reused because `ODCITableDescribe` runs only when the dynamic query is executed for the first time, and hence the parsed query will not be available in subsequent calls. We are doing this parsing because we want to define the columns that will appear in our `select` clause. This defining is done by `DBMS_SQL.DEFINE_COLUMN`. Defining of columns lets Oracle know about the type of the columns it should expect in the dynamic query. Our `scan` context was also created by parsing the `p_dynmic_imput_stmt` variable and the same variable is again used in the parsing here, so the output of the two parsing will be the same and hence we can use the scan context to get `typecode`. Values of `typecode` correspond to the data type of the columns of the dynamic SQL statement. So we have different cases for each possible data types in dynamic SQL. Note that the code here can only handle the `number`, `varchar2`, and `date` columns. If you anticipate your dynamic query to have a column that returns `timestamp` value, then you will have to add an extra case for `timestamp` in this place.

After defining the columns, we then execute the dynamic query using `DBMS_SQL.EXECUTE`.

Another thing to note in this function is the use of variables defined in the `chapter3` package, namely, `chapter3.g_cursor`, `chapter3.g_col_cnt` and `chapter3.g_descrip`. We have to assign the returned values to variables in the package and not some local variables in the function because we will need these variables in `ODCITableFetch()` and local function variables in `ODCITableStart` will not be visible in `ODCITableFetch()`.

Understanding the ODCITableFetch function

This is the place where we fetch the data and put it in an `ANYDATASET` object. Note that `chapter3.tbl_funct_intrfc_aproch` is also declared to return an `ANYDATASET` object so it makes sense that `ODCITableFetch()` puts the data in the `ANYDATASET` object. Retrieving of value is done by the `DBMS_SQL.COLUMN_VALUE` procedure. Again, if you expect that your columns will not be of `varchar2`, `date`, or `number` type, then you will have to put an extra `case` statements here.

Understanding the ODCITableClose function

This is to close `chapter3.g_cursor` which was opened in `ODCITableStart`.

I have created an APEX page with an interactive report that uses `chapter3.tbl_funct_intrfc_aproch`. I have hardcoded a select string but you could either store your `select` query in a page item and use it in the interactive report region source as a substitution variable, or could write a function returning a VARCHAR2 query string and pass that function name as an argument to `chapter3.tbl_funct_intrfc_aproch`.

A report on interface approach can be seen on the seventh page of the reference application. The query in the region source is:

```
SELECT * FROM    TABLE( chapter3.tbl_funct_intrfc_aproch(  'SELECT *
FROM oehr_employees'  ) )
```

Understanding the collection approach

The collection approach is easier to implement the dynamic queries when compared to the previous approaches. APEX has an entire API, and we will use it for our advantage. APEX collections have a `blob` column, a `clob` column, a XMLTYPE column, five `date` columns, six `number` columns including a sequence ID, 52 varchar2 columns which include a column for MD5 check, and another for collection name. Data in these columns can be manipulated using the APEX_COLLECTION API. Some of the important functions in this API are APEX_COLLECTION.COLLECTION_EXISTS, APEX_COLLECTION.CREATE_COLLECTION_FROM_QUERY, and APEX_COLLECTION.DELETE_COLLECTION.

To make the report dynamic, we have to make the report columns conditional so that they are displayed only if the columns have data. This sixth page of the reference application uses the collection approach. You can go to the **Column Attributes** and note that the following query has been placed in the **Conditions** section of the C001 column:

```
select c001 from apex_collections where collection_name = 'DYNAMIC_IR_
P6' and c001 is not null
```

Other columns also have the same condition with their own column names in the query. I have hidden COLLECTION_NAME, SEQ_ID, CLOB001, BLOB001, XMLTYPE001, and MD5_ORIGINAL columns. Headings are made more meaningful by using page items as substitution variables. These page items are fed by the Feed Headers page process. Page process can be used to synchronize column headings with the column data. Note that I have created only two page items, namely P6_C001 and P6_C002, for the headers. The number of items that should be created for headers should be equal to the maximum number of expected columns in the result. The purpose of P6_TABLE_NAME, P6_CUSTOMER_ID, and P6_ORDER_ID is the same as that of the corresponding items on the fifth page.

It is interesting to note that if collections are used with the classic reports, and if any column in a classic report did not have the header and data, then that column would not have been displayed even if the **Show** checkbox for the column had been checked. We can find the **Show** checkbox of a column in the **Report Attributes** page of a report. I have checked this using theme 3 and the same might not happen in other themes. If this does not work, then you can obviously make the whole thing work by making the column conditional, just the way we are doing it in IR. I have created one classic report on the sixth page which uses collection and shows only the two columns which have header and data. Note that the column C003 is not displayed even when the **Show** checkbox in the **Report Attributes** page for this column is checked. Let us have a look at the **Report Attributes** page first. Note that the heading is blank and **Show** checkbox is checked:

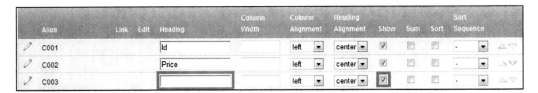

The output of the classic report is:

If we check the **Show** checkbox of all columns and if we prudently synchronize the heading and column data, then we can create dynamic classic reports based on collections without having to do the laborious work of putting conditions on every column. It is important to note that we can set the headings using PL/SQL code in classic reports so it is easy to synchronise it with the data and hence we do not have to create page items for every column in a classic report in order to make the column heading dynamic.

The collection used in interactive and classic report on the sixth page is fed from the **Feed Collection** process which runs **On Load – Before Regions**. So basically, whenever any `select` list is changed, the page is loaded and **Feed Collection** is executed **On Load – Before Regions** with the values of the select lists. The **Feed Collection** process in turn calls `chapter3.ir_dynmc_rpt_colction_aprch` which deletes `DYNAMIC_IR_P6` if it already exists, and then creates a new one. The following is the code for the **Feed Collection** page process and the `chapter3.ir_dynmc_rpt_colction_aprch` procedure:

```
begin
If nvl(:P6_TABLE_NAME,'OEHR_ORDERS') = 'OEHR_ORDERS' then
chapter3.ir_dynmc_rpt_colction_aprch(nvl(:P6_TABLE_NAME,'OEHR_
ORDERS'),nvl(:P6_CUSTOMER_ID,101));
else
chapter3.ir_dynmc_rpt_colction_aprch(nvl(:P6_TABLE_NAME,'OEHR_ORDER_
ITEMS'),nvl(:P6_ORDER_ID,2366));
end if;
end;

PROCEDURE ir_dynmc_rpt_colction_aprch
   ( p_tab_name VARCHAR2, p_filter   NUMBER) IS
     l_oehr_orders constant VARCHAR2 (11 CHAR):= 'OEHR_ORDERS';
     l_query        VARCHAR2 (100 CHAR);
   BEGIN
     IF upper(p_tab_name) = l_oehr_orders THEN
       l_query          := 'SELECT ORDER_ID, ORDER_TOTAL
FROM oehr_orders  WHERE  customer_id = ' || p_filter;
     ELSE
     If p_filter - p_filter = 0 then
       l_query := 'SELECT ORDER_ITEM_ID, unit_price
FROM oehr_order_items  WHERE  ORDER_ID = ' || p_filter;
     End if;
     END IF;
IF APEX_COLLECTION.COLLECTION_EXISTS (
     p_collection_name => 'DYNAMIC_IR_P6') then
APEX_COLLECTION.DELETE_COLLECTION (
     p_collection_name => 'DYNAMIC_IR_P6');
end if;
APEX_COLLECTION.CREATE_COLLECTION_FROM_QUERY (
     p_collection_name => 'DYNAMIC_IR_P6',
     p_query => l_query);
END ir_dynmc_rpt_colction_aprch;
```

It is important to note that every APEX session will have its own `DYNAMIC_IR_P6` collection and when `chapter3.ir_dynmc_rpt_colction_aprch` deletes the `DYNAMIC_IR_P6` collection, it deletes the one of the current APEX session. Again, when we fetch the collection using the `APEX_COLLECTIONS` view, the collection of the current APEX session is displayed. This whole arrangement ensures concurrency.

Since the loading of the `DYNAMIC_IR_P6` collection happens **On Load – Before Regions**, the collection is always ready for report regions to use.

Summary

We are standing at the end of *Chapter 3, In the APEX Mansion – Interactive Reports*, and we have seen different ways and means to use interactive reports in this chapter. We started this chapter with talking about some of the most important features of IR. We then switched to a series of ways of formatting IRs. We used DAs to build a dashboard with a number of gadgets in it. This was followed by coding a mechanism to put multiple IR's on a page. The chapter ended with going through various ways to generate dynamic IRs. The dynamic query techniques can also be used in our classic reports. In fact, these techniques can be used is any place where we are writing a SQL query. The next chapter will be about all the other reporting options in APEX. The next chapter will be dedicated to discuss the features provided by APEX so expect to get more results without spending a lot of time in doing manipulations. It's time for a break, I will see you in *Chapter 4, The Fairy Tale Begins – Advanced Reporting*.

4
The Fairy Tale Begins – Advanced Reporting

Let's rewind. We saw the architecture in the first chapter, classic reports in the second, and interactive reports in the third. The first chapter was about laying the foundation, the second one gave more visible output by using classic reports for various purposes, and the third one took the whole thing a step further by letting the user control a lot of things which were in the hands of the developer in classis reports. This chapter talks about making pretty graphs and charts. The following are the major learning outcomes of this chapter:

- **LDAP (Lightweight Directory Access Protocol)** Authentication and the use of JXplorer for it.
- Creating sparkline charts.
- Creating a report with slider.
- Creating HTML charts using the APEX HTML chart functionality. We will also see a method to generate HTML on our own. This chapter will show a method of generating reports using the XMLDB query syntax
- Using Google visualization charts in APEX.
- Creating flash charts. This includes the creation of doughnut chart, bar chart, line chart, gauge chart, gantt chart, scatter chart, candlestick chart, and 3D stack chart.
- Creating HTML image maps and Flash image maps.

- Creating calendars in APEX.

- Ways to create a report which displays images in a column.

- Creating dialog boxes in APEX using jQuery.

- Creating context menus in APEX using jQuery.

- Creating wizards and setting validations on page processes.

About the reference application for this chapter

Install the reference application for this chapter (4-98-9_04_APEX_Chapter04. sql). Install the supporting objects as well when you are prompted to do so, while installing the application. I have created a new table called oehr_galaxy_corp and have modified OEHR_TIME_DIM and oehr_employees. The changes have been made so that the charts presented in this chapter make more sense. I have extensively used DBMS_RANDOM to populate values. This package works like a charm if you have to create a lot of records with different values. You can check out the **Modification and addition of a few objects** script in **Supporting Objects** of this application to see the use of the DBMS_RANDOM package.

To log in to the reference application of this chapter, you would have to change the hostname, port, and DN in the LDAP authentication scheme. We will discuss the place and the process to so in the *Using LDAP authentication* section.

Using LDAP authentication

Since this is advanced reporting, let's start this chapter by talking about some advanced ways of authenticating the user. Until now, we have only seen the external table authentication scheme. We do not have to do any configuration for APEX authentication scheme so we haven't dedicated a section to it. This section will introduce LDAP authentication to you.

We are using WebLogic to host our APEX listener and WebLogic has an LDAP server of its own. This LDAP server works on the admin server port. We can use the same LDAP server to create some users for our application and also create an authentication scheme based on this LDAP server. Let's see how it's done:

1. Login to the WebLogic console (Typical URL: `http://localhost:7001/ console`) using your WebLogic admin credentials. Here `7001` is the port on which the admin server is running.

2. Click on **Security Realms** present in the **Domain Structure** panel on the left side of the page.

3. Click on **myrealm** and then click on the **User and Groups** tab.

4. Create a user here by clicking on the **New** button. Select the provider as **Default Authenticator**. Enter the username and the password for this new user.

5. Click on your domain name under **Domain Structure**, click on the **Security** tab and then on **Embedded LDAP**. The first two textboxes are for the credentials of the administrator of the embedded LDAP server. Set a password for the admin user and click on the **Save** button. Restart WebLogic now.

> Please note that **Anonymous Bind Allowed** should not be checked because that will be a major security concern.

6. Now let's move on to the APEX part where we create a scheme for use this new user. Go to the the **LDAP Authentication** scheme of the reference application.

7. In the **Settings** section, **Host** is the hostname of our Weblogic admin server or external LDAP server. **Port** is the port number of our admin server or the external LDAP server. We can check whether an LDAP server is running on a port and can check out its connectivity to the server by doing any one of the following two tests:

    - Using the `ldapbind` command on command prompt:

        ```
        C:\> ldapbind -h localhost -p 7001 -D "cn=Admin" -w Admin
        ```

        You should get a `bind successful` message.

    - Enter `ldap://localhost:7001/` on your browser. A dialog box should open that lets you find users.

    Replace `localhost` and `7001` with your ldap server host and port numbers. If your LDAP server (embedded in WebLogic or external) uses SSL, then select **Yes** in the **Use SSL** dropdown and configure a wallet for the APEX instance.

8. Select **Yes** in the **Use Exact Distinguished Name (DN)** dropdown and put your DN in the **Distinguished Name (DN) String** textbox. My DN looks similar to the following:

```
uid=%LDAP_USER%,ou=people,ou=myrealm,dc=apex_weblogic_domain
```

Here, `%LDAP_USER%` is the place holder of the user ID, which is used to log in. `myrealm` is the security realm in which I have created my user, `apex_weblogic_domain` is my WebLogic domain. The DN mentioned here is used in a call to `DBMS_LDAP.SIMPLE_BIND_S`, which synchronously authenticates to the directory server using the DN and the password. We can use JXplorer (an open LDAP browser) to get the DN, which you can then be used in your authentication scheme.

Process to get the necessary DN from JXplorer

Perform the following steps to get the DN from JXplorer:

1. Download JXplorer. I had to download a patch as well which had a BAT file which finally made JXplorer work. So I downloaded `jxplorer-3.3.01-windows-installer.exe` and `JXv3.2.2rc1deploy.zip`. Install the `.exe` file and unzip the zipped file. Open `jxplorer.bat` present in `<directory in which JXv3.2.2rc1deploy.zip is unzipped>\JXv3.2.2rc1deploy\jxplorer`.

2. Enter the hostname (`localhost`) and the port(`7001`).

3. Select **LDAP v3** as the protocol.

4. Enter `dc=apex_weblogic_domain` as the **Base DN** value. Here, `apex_weblogic_domain` is the domain in which APEX listener is installed.

5. Enter `User + Password` as the level.

6. Enter `cn=Admin` as the user DN value and the password which you had set in step 5 of the above section. Click on **Ok**.

7. You should be able to see the following screen with your domain and security realm:

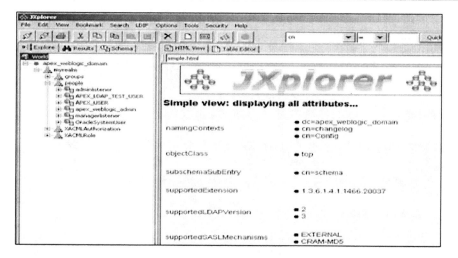

8. Now, right-click on the LDAP user you created and select **Copy DN** as shown in the following screenshot. This DN can now be used in authentication scheme in APEX.

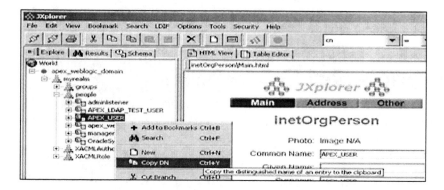

9. Note that we have **f?p=&APP_ID.:101** in the **Session Not Valid** section of the authentication scheme. 101 is the login page of the application.

We can also use the following code for our LDAP authentication from a PL/SQL block. I am using the admin user credentials of the LDAP server, but we can use any other user as well with appropriate DN as follows:

```
declare
    l_retval        pls_integer;
    l_session       dbms_ldap.session;
begin
    l_session   := dbms_ldap.init('localhost','7001');
```

```
    l_retval   := dbms_ldap.simple_bind_s(l_session, 'cn=Admin',
'abcd1111'); -- uid=APEX_USER,ou=people,ou=myrealm,dc=apex_weblogic_
domain
    dbms_output.put_line( 'Return value: ' || l_retval );
    dbms_output.put_line(DBMS_LDAP.SUCCESS);
    l_retval   := dbms_ldap.unbind_s( l_session );
    exception when others
  then
    dbms_output.put_line ('Error:'||rawtohex(substr(l_session,1,8)));
    dbms_output.put_line( 'error: ' || sqlerrm||' '||sqlcode );
    l_retval   := dbms_ldap.unbind_s( l_session );
  end;
  /
```

We can also have a look at some of the other functions in the `DBMS_LDAP` and `DBMS_LDAP_UTIL` packages. Some of the important functions are `dbms_ldap.search_s`, `dbms_ldap.next_entry`, `dbms_ldap.next_entry`, and `dmbs_ldap_util.get_user_dn`.

APEX also has a package called `APEX_LDAP`, which is dedicated to LDAP. `APEX_CUSTOM_AUTH.GET_LDAP_PROPS` obtains the LDAP attributes of the current authentication scheme for the current application.

Creating sparkline reports

Let us now talk about Sparkline reports. Have a look at the screenshot at the bottom of the section to get a feel of how a sparkline report looks. Page 1 of the reference application has sparkline reports on it. This report has been tested on IE 8.

Sparkline reports are unique because they show the detail level info at the parent level. For example, we can use sparklines if we wish to make a report on the shares being traded in an exchange and we also wish to see the performance of each individual share in the last month. In such a report, we can have a column of sparkline which shows the performance of a share in the over one month and have other columns that show other attributes of the share. So every row in the report can correspond to a share and can have a sparkline column to list the performance of the share over a period of a month.

The sparklines are created by the `sparklines` class which is defined in the `jquery.sparkline.min.js` file. This file can be downloaded from `http://archive.plugins.jquery.com/project/sparklines`, `http://omnipotent.net/jquery.sparkline/#s-download`.

You should be able to find the `jquery.sparkline.min.js` file when you click on **Static Files** in **Shared Components** of the reference application.

Go to the **Header text** text area of the **Header and Footer** section of the page definition of page 1 of the reference application. You should see a reference to the `jquery.sparkline.min.js` file here. We have put the reference in the header of the page so that the definition of the `sparklines` class is available before the loading of the region. Note the use of the `#WORKSPACE_IMAGES#` substitution string references a file uploaded in the application's workspace.

Go to the query in the region source of the **Sparkline Report** region on page 1 of the reference application. The following is the code:

```
select oehr_ORDERs.order_id, listagg(unit_price,',') WITHIN GROUP
(order by order_item_id) "Price of Order items 1" from oehr_orders,
oehr_order_items where oehr_orders.order_id = oehr_order_items.order_
id group by oehr_orders.order_id
```

Note the use of the `listagg` function in the region source. Note the use of `order by` in this function. The ordering is done on the `order_id` column which might not be beneficial, but had this report been on the shares traded in an exchange then we could have ordered the prices of each share by date, which would have helped a user to understand the pattern of trading of each individual share while comparing different shares.

Go to the **Report Attributes** tab of the **Sparkline Report** region on page 1 of the reference application. Click on the **Price Of Order Items 1** column and then go to the **Column Formatting** section. You will find the following code in the **HTML Expression** textbox under **Column Formatting**:

```
<span class="sparklines" sparkType="bar" sparkBarColor="blue">#Price
of Order items 1#</span>
```

The preceding code along with the list of values in the region source query creates a sparkline bar chart for us. Run page 1 of the reference application to see the code in action.

Every type of sparkline graph has its own set of attributes, which can be controlled to get a more customized graph. One of these attributes is `sparkBarColor`. We have used this attribute to give different colors to line, bar, and discrete sparkline graphs. We can also control the attributes of a sparkline from JavaScript by using jQuery. The values of the attributes are passed as a JSON object. The syntax is as follows:

```
$('#<html_id_of_sparkline_column>').sparkline(myvalues, {
<attribute>:<value>});
```

Note that the names of the attributes in the HTML syntax are different from the names of the attributes in the jQuery and the JSON syntax. So if you have a working piece of code in HTML and you try to use the same attribute name in jQuery then it might not work.

Go to the **Report Attributes** tab of the **Sparkline Report** region and note that **Price of order items 2** and **Price of Order items 3** are the column links. Both these column links use `#Price of Order items 1#`. These three columns differ in the `sparkType` attribute.

This more or less brings us to the end of the sparkline report. The sparkline report looks as follows:

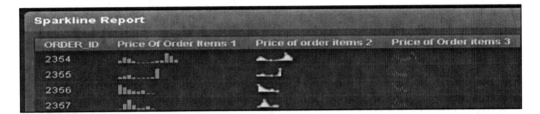

We will now talk about creating a report which has a column with a slider in it for every row. The slider can be used to change the value and we can submit the report to commit the changed value in the database.

Creating a report with slider

We will now talk about creating a report which has a column with a slider in it for every row. The slider can be used to change the value and we can submit the report to commit the changed value in the database.

Note that this report has been tested using IE 8. Like the previous section, this section is also hugely dependent on jQuery. jQuery is embedded in APEX and hence a lot of classes required for using the jQuery features are already there in APEX. Go to the folder in which you had the `_4.1.1_en.zip` unzipped APEX at the time of installation, and navigate to the following directory:

```
<directory in which apex_4.1.1_en.zip is unzipped>\apex\images\
libraries\jquery-ui\1.8\ui
```

You should be able to find `jquery.ui.slider.js` in it. We had given the path of the `<directory in which apex_4.1.1_en.zip is unzipped>\apex\images` folder while creating `i.war`, and `i.war` was deployed on WebLogic at the time of installation. So the `jquery.ui.slider.js` file can be used by APEX. Have a look at some of the other `.js` files in the same folder as these might be of use to you.

Some of these such as `jquery.effects.explode.js`, `jquery.effects.pulsate.js`, `jquery.effects.shake.js`, and `jquery.effects.slide.js` are really exciting.

Look at the **Header Text** text area of the **Header and Footer** section of the page definition of page 3 to find out the method to reference the files present in `i.war` in your application. The syntax is also shared below for your convenience:

```
<script type="text/javascript" src="/i/libraries/jquery-ui/1.8/ui/
minified/jquery.ui.slider.min.js"></script>
```

Information about the slider can be found at `http://jqueryui.com/demos/slider/`.

The slider has been implemented in page 3 of the reference application. We have created a tabular form which lets us edit the values of the OEHR_EMPLOYEES table. The `salary` column has a slider. I made the following choices in the wizard that creates a tabular form:

1. I did not select EMPLOYEE_ID, DELETE_FLAG, DATE_OF_LEAVING and COMMISSION_AMOUNT in the **Identify Table or View and Columns** section.
2. I selected **Update, Insert,** and **Delete** in the **Allowed Operations** dropdown.
3. I chose EMOPLYEE_ID as the primary key and OEHR_EMPLOYEES_SEQ in the **Defaults for Primary and Foreign Keys** section, and selected all columns to be updatable apart from FIRST_NAME and LAST_NAME in the **Updateable Columns** section.

The magic is done by a little piece of code in the **Region footer** section of the **Slider** region, which is as follows:

```
<script type="text/javascript">
$('[headers="SALARY"]').each(function() {
$(this).html($(this).html().replace("text","hidden"));
if ($(this).find($("input")).val() != "")
{ $(this).attr("style","width:200px;");
var default_value = $(this).find($("input")).val();
$(this).slider({ range: "min",min: 4000,max: 24000,value: default_value,
change: function (event,ui) {alert('new salary:' + ui.value); $(this).
find($("input")).val(ui.value);}
});}});
</script>
```

Starting from the top, `[headers="SALARY"]` gives us a handle to all the rows of the SALARY column of the HTML table. The `each` function lets us perform operations on each of these rows. We then hide the textbox of the `salary` column inside the `each` function. Note that we cannot select Hidden in the **Display As** dropdown of the **Column Attributes** page to hide the textboxes of the `salary` column, because doing this will hide the entire column and we will not be able to capture the current value of the salary.

We need the current value of the salary to set the default position of the slider. We then set the `width` attribute of the `salary` column to `200px`. Now each `td` tag has an `input` tag and a `label` tag. The `salary` value is inside the `input` tag. So we use the `find` function to reach the `input` tag and then capture the current salary using the `val` function. Finally we call the `slider` function to put a slider with a minimum value of `4000`, a maximum value of `24000` and a default value as the current salary.

When a user changes the value using the slider, the change should happen in the HTML form element because the values of the HTML form are passed using the `wwv_flow.accept` function to the APEX engine, which then takes the necessary action (modifying the `OEHR_EMPLOYEES` table in this case). We have seen a small paragraph about `wwv_flow.accept` in the *Decoding APEX page submissions* section of *Chapter 1, Know Your Horse Before You Ride It*. Alright, so to make sure that the change is passed to the `form` element, we use the `input` tag and then use the `val` function to set its value. We have also put an `alert` box, so that the user knows the exact salary which he has set for an employee. You can see the code in action in page 3 of the reference application, as shown in the following screenshot:

Creating HTML charts

Before we move on to the more fancy Flash charts, let's first check out the other charting options in APEX.

HTML charts are faster than Flash charts because of the simplicity of the architecture. HTML charts are a combination of images, HTML, CSS, and JavaScript which produce a chart. Let's see how it's done.

Creating a bar chart using APEX's HTML chart functionality

While this subcategory falls under the broad category of charts which use HTML, JavaScript, CSS, and images; this subcategory of HTML charts is relatively simple because APEX does most of the work for us.

Creating an APEX HTML chart

Create a new region, select **Chart** as the type of region and then select **HTML5 Chart in the Chart Rendering** dropdown. Enter the query for the chart. The query should have three columns. The first one is for the link (we can have null here in the Bar chart region on page 5 of the reference application, if we do not wish to have a drilldown on the chart), the second column is for the label, and the third one is for the value.

Most of the attributes under the query text area are self-explanatory. **Axis** dropdown present in **Chart Attributes** page is a good option. It gives us the freedom to draw a graph relative to a certain value in the series. Let's say that the last value in the series is 40, and the **Axis** has been set to **Last Value in Series** then all the values which are less than 40 will have their bars facing downwards and the length of the bars will be proportional to the deviation of their value from 40. Similarly, values greater than 40 will have their bars facing upwards and the length will be proportional to the deviation form 40. The group of **Summary** check boxes in the **Chart Attributes** page of an HTML5 Chart lets us list a few characteristics of the chart at the end of the chart. The **Bar chart** region of page 5 of the reference application has an example of this type of chart, which is as follows:

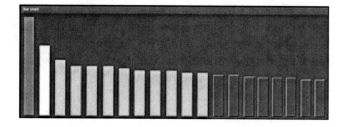

Displaying the top N and the bottom N rows in an HTML chart

Go to the **Chart Attributes** page of the **Bar chart** region of page 5 of the reference application. The **Display** textbox in the **Chart Attributes** page holds the value of the maximum number of values that should appear on one page of the chart. We can use this feature to our advantage if we wish to show the top N or the bottom N rows, where N is any positive integer. We can have an order by clause in our query and set the **Display** textbox to N. We can then set **Pagination** to **No Pagination**. The wizard to create the region does not give the option to set **Pagination**, but we can set **Pagination** by going to the **Chart Attributes** page. If the query is ordered in ascending order then we get the bottom N, and if it is sorted in descending order we get the top N records.

Note that we will miss the summary section of the chart if we do this. We can however add our own summary by writing the HTML in the **Region Footer** section. Any calculation required in the **Region Footer** section can be done using standard techniques of computation in APEX and the value of the computation can be fed to a page item. The page item can then be used as a substitution variable in the **Region Footer** section.

The **Bar chart** region on page 5 of the reference application uses this technique to display the total number of values. Run page 5 of the reference application and look at the bottom of the **Bar chart** region to see this. Note that we also get an option to choose the color of the bars on the **Chart Attributes** page. We can draw both horizontal and vertical bar charts using an HTML chart.

Understanding the APEX HTML bar chart behind the scenes

Behind the scenes, this subcategory of HTML charts makes very little use of JQuery or JavaScript. The APEX engine has bars of different colors stored in it as GIF files. You can check out these files in `<directory in which apex_4.1.1_en.zip is unzipped>\apex\images`. You can check out `green.gif` in this directory. `green.gif` is used to create a green bar in the chart. When you open this file, you will probably not be able to see the bar. This is primarily because it is more a dot than a bar. You will have to zoom in to see it. Similarly, there are `.gif` files for other bar colors as well. Depending on the value of the bar, the height is set at runtime using the `height` and `width` attribute of the `img` tag.

Understanding self-generated HTML charts

Taking a leaf out of APEX's book, we can create our own HTML charts; we can upload images and associate them with our APEX application or with the workspace. We can then create a PL/SQL region and use the `htp.p` procedure to send these images to the browser. The heights of these images can be dynamically adjusted using HTML, just the way APEX does it. Now, I must mention that we can achieve similar results using a SQL query region as well. We have seen how we can use the HTML generated by a query in formatting the results of the query, in *Chapter 2, Conventional Reporting in APEX*.

The **Self generated HTML** region on page 5 of the reference application uses this technique. Let's look at the region source now, which is given in the following code:

```
declare
increment integer;
begin
htp.p('  <table class="css_n_html_chart">
      <tr>
```

```
        <th>Department name</th>
        <th>Count of employees per department</th>
    </tr>');
for i in (select count(employee_id) cnt_of_emp_per_
dept,max(count(employee_id)) over () max_emp,min(count(employee_id))
over () min_emp, department_name from oehr_employees,oehr_departments
where oehr_employees.department_id = oehr_departments.department_id
and delete_flag = 'N' group by department_name) loop
increment := 200/(i.max_emp - i.min_emp);
    htp.p('<tr> <td>' || to_char(i.department_name) ||'</td><td><img
src="#WORKSPACE_IMAGES#value_bar.png" width="'||to_char(i.cnt_of_emp_
per_dept*increment)||'" height="15" />'|| to_char(i.cnt_of_emp_per_
dept) || ' </td> </tr> ');
end loop;
htp.p(' </table>');
end;
```

The region source starts with setting `css_n_html_chart` as the class of an HTML
table. This class is defined in `4-98-9_04_chapter4.css` in the **Cascading Style Sheet**
section of the **Shared Components** tab. The only big use of this class is to set the `color`
attribute of the `th` (table header) to `pink`. Run page 5 of the reference application and
note that the color of the headers in the **Self generated HTML** region is pink, as shown
in the following screenshot:

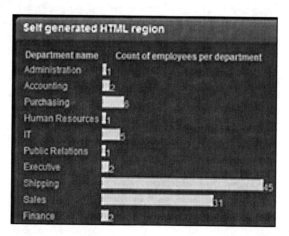

You can have much more CSS in this place. My motive is just to show a possible
method of adding CSS to this type of region. Honestly, you can define classes in any
legal place such as templates, region and page headers, and so on, and then use the
class here. After declaring the table with a class, we add a few headers to the HTML.
This is followed by running a loop which generates the bars of different widths.
Note the syntax used to reference `value_bar.png` which has been uploaded in the
Images section of the **Shared Components** tab and has been associated with this
application's workspace.

We can also achieve the same result using CSS instead of using images. We can use CSS to create blocks of different colors. This will also help to improve the performance.

Creating a report from XMLTYPE

The **Report from XMLTYPE** region on page 5 is not exactly a chart, but I wish to bring it here because we are discussing the use of PL/SQL to generate HTML and this region also does the same.

The syntax of this region might look a little unfamiliar, but that is only because we have never used it till now in this book. We had a little dealing with XMLDB when we were talking about the architecture of APEX, and we had a little natter about the XML DB HTTP server which breathes in XML DB.

The basic theme behind this region is that XML DB can be used to generate XML tags and an HTML page is also a set of tags, just that the tags in HTML hold special meanings. Deducing the meaning of these tags is the job of the parser, so the generator of these tags can be agnostic to the fact that the tags hold special meanings as long as the right structure is generated. XML DB is a little religious about XML. It does not forgive any mistake in the XML formation. The region source of XML DB is as follows:

```
Declare
XML_RETURN CLOB;
l_temp varchar2(32767);
Begin
select xmlquery('
<table class="report-standard">
<tr><th id="EMPLOYEE_ID" class="header">EMPLOYEE_ID</th><th
id="JOB_ID" class="header">JOB_ID</th><th id="FIRST_NAME"
class="header">FIRST_NAME</th><th id="LAST_NAME" class="header">LAST_
NAME</th><th id="EMAIL" class="header">EMAIL</th><th id="PHONE_
NUMBER" class="header">PHONE_NUMBER</th><th id="SALARY"
class="header">SALARY</th><th id="HIRE_DATE" class="header">HIRE_
DATE</th></tr>
{
for $i in ora:view("PACKT_SCHEMA","OEHR_EMPLOYEES")/ROW
order by $i/EMPLOYEE_ID descending
return
<tr class="highlight-row">
<td headers="EMPLOYEE_ID" class="data">{$i/EMPLOYEE_ID/text()}</td>
<td headers="JOB_ID" class="data">{$i/JOB_ID/text()}</td>
```

```
<td headers="FIRST_NAME" class="data">{$i/FIRST_NAME/text()}</td>
<td headers="LAST_NAME" class="data">{$i/LAST_NAME/text()}</td>
<td headers="EMAIL" class="data">{$i/EMAIL/text()}</td>
<td headers="PHONE_NUMBER" class="data">{$i/PHONE_NUMBER/text()}</td>
<td headers="SALARY" class="data">{$i/SALARY/text()}</td>
<td headers="HIRE_DATE" class="data">{$i/HIRE_DATE/text()}</td>
</tr>
}
</table>
' returning content).getClobVal() into XML_RETURN from dual;
loop
if length(XML_RETURN) > 32767 then
l_temp:= substr(XML_RETURN,1,32767);
htp.p(l_temp);
XML_RETURN:= substr(XML_RETURN,length(l_temp)+1);
else
l_temp := XML_RETURN;
htp.p(l_temp);
exit;
end if;
end loop;
end;
```

In the preceding region source, we are using the CSS classes used in our APEX theme to maintain the look and feel.

Let me first share the approach here. We are using the XMLQUERY function which returns an XMLTYPE value. We are using the syntax for XML queries inside this function. The getClobVal function is used to convert the XMLTYPE value to a CLOB. This CLOB value is broken into pieces and fed to the htp.p function, which finally puts it on the browser.

The else section of the If statement is to mark the exit of the loop. If the execution reaches the else section then it means that we are in the final lap of displaying the CLOB value. The final part of the CLOB value is sent to the browser using htp.p and we then exit the loop.

Inside the XMLQUERY function, we start by the HTML table tag followed by a few th tags. Each of these tags is for displaying a header of a column in the report. This is followed by a loop which generates a single tr (table row) tag. order by $i/EMPLOYEE_ID descending orders the result set in the descending order of employee_id. $i/EMPLOYEE_ID/text() is used to have a tag for EMPLOYEE_ID in the output HTML (XML).

The following is a screenshot of a report:

Report from XMLTYPE							
EMPLOYEE_ID	JOB_ID	FIRST_NAME	LAST_NAME	EMAIL	PHONE_NUMBER	SALARY	HIRE_DATE
206	AC_ACCOUNT	William	Gietz	WGIETZ	515.123.8181	8300	1994-06-07
205	AC_MGR	Shelley	Higgins	SHIGGINS	515.123.8080	12000	1994-06-07
204	PR_REP	Hermann	Baer	HBAER	515.123.8888	10000	1994-06-07
203	HR_REP	Susan	Mavris	SMAVRIS	515.123.7777	6500	1994-06-07

This brings us to the end of HTML charts. I haven't added any frills to this section but if you have to add any effects or animation then you know that CSS and JQuery is the way to go.

Creating Google visualization charts

Before we discuss the Flash chart of AnyChart, it is worthwhile to have a look at the charting option given by Google. I intend to present a small example of a line chart using Google visualizations and I am sure that you can extrapolate the technique to create other types of charts using this method. One big advantage of Google visualizations is that it has some new type of charts, for example, area charts. So if you are ever stuck in a place where Flash charts do not provide the necessary charting option, and creating your own HTML chart is too tedious, then Google visualization is the way to go.

Page 14 of the reference application creates the Google visualization line chart. You would need an Internet connection for this because the libraries used for these are stored on Google's server.

You can visit the following link for more information on Google visualization charts:

```
https://developers.google.com/chart/interactive/docs/index
```

The following is a screenshot of the chart from the reference application:

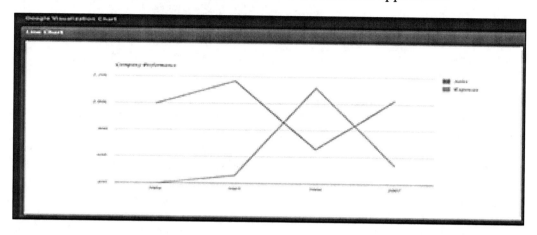

Creating Flash charts

AnyChart is a flexible Flash/JavaScript (HTML5) based charting solution which has been tightly integrated with APEX.

Customizing an XML chart

The **Chart Attributes** page of a region based on AnyChart lets us set the properties of the chart. Most of the attributes of the **Chart Attributes** page are self-explanatory, so we don't need to discuss them here. We can use the **Chart XML** section to change and customize certain properties of the chart. We have to set the value in the **Use Custom XML** dropdown to **Yes** to edit the XML. Flipping the dropdown will show us the default XML. Check the following link to know about the use of each tag of the XML:

http://anychart.com/products/anychart/docs/xmlReference/index.html

The user guide can be found in the following link:

http://www.anychart.com/products/anychart/docs/users-guide/index.html

There are tons of configurable tags and I suggest that you have a good look at these, so that you can twist and turn your charts and make them dance to your own tunes. For example, you can enable the download of the Flash chart to an image file by setting the path of a AnyChartPNGSaver.jsp file in the settings section of the XML. You would have to package this JSP as a WAR file (web archive) and deploy it on the WebLogic server.

Once it is deployed, it can be used for printing the report as an image. Similarly, we can also configure to print the region in a PDF file .You can download `AnyChartPNGSaver.jsp` from the following link:

`http://www.anychart.com/products/anychart/docs/users-guide/SaveAsImage.html`

Let us now look at an example of customizing the XML of a AnyChart region to improve its usability. Logarithmic chart on page 15 of the reference application showcases the massive difference in the usability by configuring certain parameters, but configuring attributes is not just about usability, it's also about appearance and animation. `<scale type="Logarithmic" />` has been put in the `<y_axis >` tag in the **Custom XML** text area of the **Logrithmic chart changed scale** region of page 15. This changes the scale to a logarithmic scale and helps in better projection of the data. Data values on x axis have also been customized. Run page 15 of the reference application and note that the comma separating the thousands value is not appearing in the **Logrithmic chart changed scale** region. We can also flash the 'scale is logarithmic' message on the **Logrithmic chart changed scale** region of page 15, but I leave that task to you.

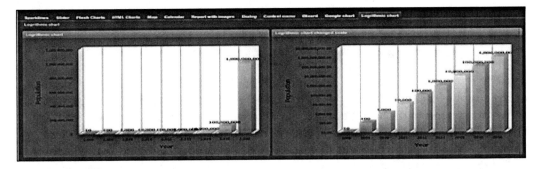

I want to bring it to your notice that the order of the column in the query in the **Chart Series** section of the **Chart Attributes** page of a chart based on AnyChart is important. For example, the series in a 2D doughnut chart should have the column holding the value of the link, followed by the column holding the value of the label, and finally the value column. So check out the query in the series of every chart in page 2 of the reference application to find the correct order.

Understanding Anychart options using a doughnut chart

We will now look at Doughnut chart of the reference application and use it as an example to understand some more options of charts created using AnyChart. Doughnut charts are used to show the percentage contribution of each of the values. Go to the **Chart Series** page of the **Doughnut chart** region on page 2 of the reference application. The important thing to note in Flash charts is the **Maximum Rows** textbox, which is present at the bottom of the query for the series that generates the chart. If the series has 20 records and we have put 17 in the **Maximum Rows** textbox, then the last few values will be grouped together and labeled as **Other** so that the number of values displayed remains 17. If we have a drilldown from the chart then we will not be able to drill down from the **Other** value, because **Other** is actually a collection of values. **Color Scheme** in the **Chart Settings** section on the **Chart Attributes** page has a set of seven schemes, which can be used to change the appearance of the chart. We can define our own scheme by selecting **Custom** in the **Color Scheme** dropdown.

The series of a doughnut chart should have three columns, the first one should be the link text, the second one should be the label, and the third one should be the value. APEX also gives us the freedom to write a function that returns a query, if we want to generate the query dynamically. The dynamic query should, however, have the same three columns in the same order.

In the **Chart Series** page, you will see an **Action Link** section. The **Action Link** dropdown in the **Action Link** section has only two values and one of them has to be selected. When **Use Value of LINK Column** is selected, then the **Link** column value of the chart series is used as a link in drilling down from the chart. When **Link to Custom Target** is selected then APEX lets you write any custom link which you might want.

The reference application for this chapter shipped with the book, has examples for bar charts, line charts, combination charts (bar and line charts combined), gauge charts, gantt chart, candle stick chart, scatter chart, 3D stacked chart, and logarithmic charts. Since the process to create these charts is similar, a detailed discussion is not required. I would however talk about the business requirements of some of the less known chart types.

Discussion on scatter and 3D stacked charts

Let me briefly say that scatter charts are a plot of points with respect to two metrics. One metric is on the x axis while the other is on the y axis. Points are plotted on the XY-quadrants depending on the value of the points on both these metrics.

A 3D stacked chart is a bar chart with segments in every bar. For example, we can have a 3D stacked chart to show the total income of an employee and we can show the bifurcation of the income as salary and commission by having two segments in the bar. The first segment can stand for the salary and the second one can stand for commission.

Discussion on a gauge chart

If you are dealing with the percentage of contributions to a bigger entity and one of the special entities holds special meaning to you, then a doughnut graph might not be able to do justice to you, since doughnut shows all the entities that make a bigger entity and the bigger the contribution by an entity the more prominently it appears in a doughnut chart. A gauge chart can be drawn exclusively for one single entity. Gauge chart is the fourth chart on page 2, as shown in the following screenshot:

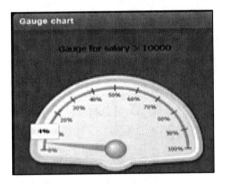

Discussion on a gantt chart

I must confess that I saw this chart for the first time when I was dealing with informatica. Informatica has a number of workflows which are sequenced to execute one after the other. So a gantt chart is displayed by the tool which creates a workflow, which starts from the start time and ends at the end time. When this is done for every workflow, we get a chart which shows the exact time of the starting and stopping of all workflows. This helps us find the workflow which took the longest duration and helps us discover the order of execution of the workflows. Chart number five on page 2 of the reference application is a gantt chart.

The reference for customizing the XML for this chart can be found in the following link:

`http://anychart.com/products/anygantt/docs/xmlReference/index.html`

The following is the screenshot of a gantt chart:

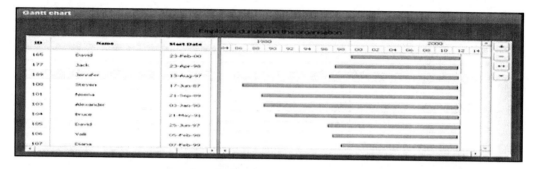

Discussion on a candlestick chart

Candlesticks are a more fancy way of showing data related to share trading. While a typical line graph can show us the price of the share at any point of the day, be it the beginning of the day or the end of the day over a period of time, candlestick graphs show us four different properties of the share trading. Candlesticks show us the opening price, the closing price, the highest value, and the lowest value of the share every day over a period of time. This helps in better analysis in judging the volatility and fluctuations of a particular share. Chart number seven on page 2 of the reference application is a candlestick chart. The following is the screenshot of a candlestick chart:

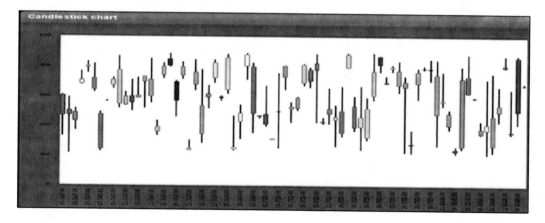

Creating Flash image maps

Anychart has a flash object that lets us create a Flash image map. We have an image map of Europe in page 6 of the reference application. Our OEHR_EMPLOYEES table did not have a lot of European countries, so I have used the decode statement to translate other country names to European country names. You should be able see some data for France and Ireland on the image map of the reference application as follows:

HTML image maps are similar to AnyChart image maps in their functionality, but the limitation is the limited number of shapes, and the effort required to define the boundary of the typical nation using HTML. HTML image maps are more helpful where regular shapes are involved.HTML image maps are discussed in the beginning of the next chapter.

Creating a calendar

Calendars in APEX are of two types, namely, Easy calendar and SQL calendar. Enabling the **Drag and Drop** dropdown in the Easy calendar lets the user drag-and-drop the data of one date to some other date. SQL calendar lets you write an SQL statement which returns the display value, the primary key, and the date on which the display value has to be attached on the calendar. An SQL calendar has been created for your reference on page 7, which is as follows:

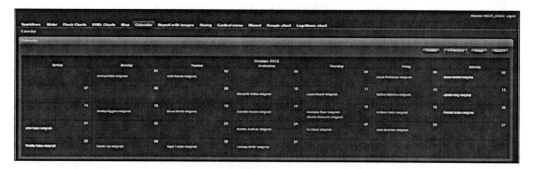

Creating a report with images

Use the reference application of *Chapter 2, Conventional Reports in APEX* to upload images instead of profiles in the OEHR_EMPLOYEE_PROFILES table. This table is used for reporting in this section and only the rows which have some value in the FILEOJBECT column are displayed in this report. If using the application of *Chapter 2, Conventional Reporting in APEX* is a lot of work then you can also use the exported OEHR_EMPLOYEE_PROFILES file which has been shipped with this book. I use this opportunity to introduce the DBMS_DATAPUMP package to you. The Expdp and impdp utilities are close kin of this package. Apart from the exported file(OEHR_EMPLOYEE_ PROFILES.DMP), the code pack also has a bunch of four scripts. Two of these scripts are used for exporting the data and two are used for importing. You obviously have to use only the import scripts because I have attached shipped the exported file with this chapter. Let me talk a little about these four scripts. 4-98-9_04_grants_for_ dbms_datapump_import.sql is executed after connecting to the sys schema. It gives the necessary privileges to export the table. 4-98-9_04_export_emp_profiles_ table.sql does the export. It first creates a directory object and then uses the dbms_datapump package to export data. 4-98-9_04_grants_for_dbms_datapump_ import.sql should be executed after connecting to the sys schema and it grants the necessary privileges to the schema which has to import the table. 4-98-9_04_ import_emp_profiles_table.sql finally imports the table. This script has some remapping in it. The metadata of the exported file has packt_schema as the schema and APEX_1342511262016249 as the tablespace. Your tablespace and schema will be different, so a remapping has to be done to make sure that the data is imported in the right schema. The script prompts for the schema where the data has to be imported. It also prompts for the default tablespace of this schema. You can get the default tablespace using the following query:

```
select DEFAULT_TABLESPACE from dba_users where username = 'PACKT_
SCHEMA';
```

You can know more about the `dbms_datapump` package from the following resource:

`http://docs.oracle.com/cd/E18283_01/appdev.112/e16760/d_datpmp.htm`

Page 9 of the reference application shows the various ways of displaying images in APEX. We will talk about two techniques here. Let's first talk about the **Another method to download** column of the **Report with images** region of page 9 of the reference application. Go to the region source of the **Report with images** region, which is as follows:

```
Select              dbms_lob.getlength("OEHR_EMPLOYEE_
PROFILES"."FILEOBJECT") as "Download file",
HTF.IMG(curl => APEX_UTIL.GET_BLOB_FILE_SRC(p_item_name => 'P9_IMAGE_
ITEM', p_v1 => "OEHR_EMPLOYEE_PROFILES"."EMPLOYEE_ID", p_content_
disposition => 'inline'),cattributes=>'style="float:left;width:32px;he
ight:24px;"') as "Another method to download"
from        "OEHR_EMPLOYEES" "OEHR_EMPLOYEES","OEHR_EMPLOYEE_PROFILES"
"OEHR_EMPLOYEE_PROFILES"
where       "OEHR_EMPLOYEES"."EMPLOYEE_ID" = "OEHR_EMPLOYEE_
PROFILES"."EMPLOYEE_ID"
and "OEHR_EMPLOYEES"."DELETE_FLAG" = 'N'
and "OEHR_EMPLOYEE_PROFILES"."FILEOBJECT" is not null
```

Note that the `APEX_UTIL.GET_BLOB_FILE_SRC` procedure of APEX API is used to display the **Another method to download** column. This method requires a file browse item and `P9_IMAGE_ITEM` is for this purpose. `HTF.IMG` helps us in creating an HTML `img` tag and we have set **Standard Report Column** in the **Display As** dropdown of the **Column Attributes** page of the **Another method to download** column, so that the `img` tag does not appear as text but as an image on the APEX page. The `style` attribute is used in the above query to set the width and height of the image. The **Download file** column on the other hand uses a totally different technique. In this technique, the query source should not query the `blob` column but should pass the column as an argument to the `dbms_lob.getlength` procedure. The rest of the magic is done by the format mask. Now check out the **Number / Date Format** column of the **Column Attributes** page of the **Download file** column. It says `IMAGE:OEHR_EMPLOYEE_PROFILES:FILEOBJECT:EMPLOYEE_ID::::::attachment:Profile`.

The general syntax of the format mask is: `IMAGE:Table Name:Column containing BLOB:Primary Key Column 1:Primary Key Column 2:MIME type Column:Filename Column:Last Update Column:Character Set Column:Content Disposition:Alt Text` `IMAGE` in the beginning of the format is to tell APEX that we wish to see the image and not a link to it. This is followed by the table name, and then by the column which holds the blob image. We then have the primary key of the table which holds the `blob` object. The next slots are respectively the second column of the primary key of the table, the mime type, column containing the filename, last updated date, character column set, content disposition, and the alt text.

Let us talk about this format mask now. Images do not need the filename. Filename, in the format mask, might be important if we wish to download the file using a link, but not if we wish to see the file as an image. However, column containing the filename still occupies a section in our download format so that the same format can be used to download a file as well as to see it as an image. The same logic holds true for character column set and content disposition. The last part, that is, alt text is used to fill the `alt` attribute of the `img` tag of HTML that will be generated to display the image. If the last updated date section has a column in it, then the HTTP header gets this value which enables browsers to cache the `blob` object. This can result in significant performance improvement depending on the size of the `blob` objects.

Creating a dialog box

When we click on some help text in APEX wizards, we get a dialog box which has some meaningful info about the role of the corresponding item. Guess what, we can create the same dialog box for our reports as well. Check page 10 of the reference application and click on any one of the order IDs.

You will see that a dialog box opens which shows the order lines of all the order on which you clicked. So, how did we do it?

Page 10 of the reference application actually has two regions. The **Detail report** region has been given a static ID, called `Detail`, in the **Attributes** section of the region definition page so that we can get a handle to this region, whenever required.

Go to the **JavaScript** section of page definition of page 10 of the reference application. The code in the JavaScript section is as follows:

```
function openDialog (p_order_id)
{ var ajaxObject = new htmldb_Get( null, html_GetElement('pFlowId').
value, 'APPLICATION_PROCESS=Set P10_ORDER_ID', $v('pFlowStepId'));
    ajaxObject.addParam('x01',p_order_id);   var ajaxReturn =
eval(ajaxObject.get());
    ajaxObject = null;$a_report_Split($x('Detail').region_id.substr(1),
'1_15_15',null);
$("#Detail").dialog("open");
}
  $.fx.speeds._default = 1000;
  $(function() {
    $( "#Detail" ).dialog({
    autoOpen: false,   width: 600,  modal: true,
                   open: function(event, ui){},beforeClose:
function(event, ui) {},
                         closeOnEscape : true
    }); });
```

It defines a JavaScript function called openDialog. This function accepts the order_id value. It passes the same by an AJAX call to a page process which sets the P10_ORDER_ID page item. We then get a handle to the **Detail report** region using $x('Detail').region_id.substr(1). Note that we are able to get the handle because we had defined Detail as the static id of the region. This handle is used to refresh the report using the a_report_Split function. Since the **Detail report** region uses P10_ORDER_ID, and since we have already set P10_ORDER_ID so the PPR refreshes the report with the new value. We then use the jQuery's dialog function to open the dialog. The openDialog JavaScript function defined by us ends here. The rest of the code in the **JavaScript** section of page definition is outside the openDialog JavaScript function and is hence executed on page load. Check out the autoOpen attribute of the $("#Detail").dialog. This attribute prevents the dialog box from opening when the page load although the $("#Detail") dialog itself is executed on page load. The Open and beforeClose attributes are also important as they let you define any custom operation of your choice based on the events on the dialog box. modal: true part of the code dims the background. The result of the dialog box region is shared in the following screenshot:

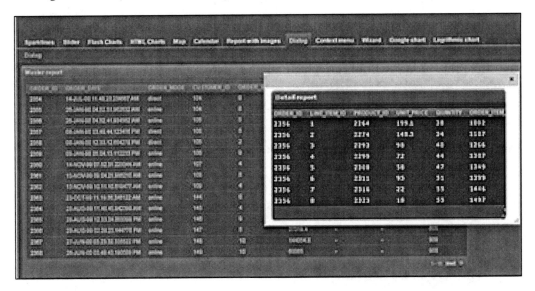

Note that the $("#Detail").dialog code which executes on page load is also responsible for the magical disappearance of the **Detail report** region in the parent page.

 The preceding code has been tested in IE 8.

Creating a context menu

This is another one of those features which has been borrowed from APEX environment. When you right-click on any of the region in APEX, you will see a menu which gives you options to perform different operations on the region. Similar menus can be created in our application by using the context menus. I have used two resources to create a context menu on page 11 of the reference application, which are as follows:

```
http://archive.plugins.jquery.com/project/jqueryContextMenu
```

```
http://www.trendskitchens.co.nz/jquery/contextmenu/
```

The following screenshot of the context menu region is pasted for your convenience:

Let us now talk about the code of context menus. The **Header text** text area of the **Headers and Footers** section of the page definition of page 11 has the following text:

```
<script type="text/javascript" src="#WORKSPACE_IMAGES#jquery.
contextmenu.r2.js"></script>
```

jquery.contextmenu.r2.js has been imported in the **Static Files** section under **Shared Components** and has been associated with the application's workspace. Hence we are able to reference jquery.contextmenu.r2.js using the #WORKSPACE_IMAGES# substitution string. We have also created an HTML region which has a few ul and li tags, which is as follows:

```
<span id="menuCreateItems"><b>Right click to create items</b></span>
    <div class="contextMenu" id="createItems">
    <ul>
      <li id="SelectList">Create select list</li>
      <li id="TextBox">Create text box</li>
      <li id="DateItem">Create date item</li>
    </ul>
    </div>
```

The classes used in this region source are defined in `jquery.contextmenu.r2.js` and are an essential part of the architecture for creating context menus. Now come to the **Region Footer** text area of the **Context menu** region, the code in this region is as follows:

```
<script type="text/javascript">
    $('#menuCreateItems').contextMenu('createItems', {
      bindings: {
        'SelectList': function(t) {
          alert('\nAction was to Create a select list');
        },
        'TextBox': function(t) {
          alert('\nAction was Create a text box');
        },
        'DateItem': function(t) {
          alert('\nAction was to Create a date item ');
        }
      }
    });
</script>
```

The `bindings` attribute has a case for each `li` tag it sets, and the function to be used when the user selects a particular item from the context menu. Each `li` tag becomes an item in the context menu. The `bindings` attribute gets a handle on each `li` tag using its `id`. Needless to say, we can have a PL/SQL region to generate this context menu dynamically.

Creating a wizard and using hierarchical queries and regular expressions

Let us now understand the process of creating wizards in APEX. When we create a wizard, APEX creates pages for us and connects those pages with the **Next** and **Previous** buttons. A wizard has been created for you in the reference application as a sample and it spans over pages 12 and 13. The wizard in the reference application lets you create a table. Page 12 can be used to enter the name of the table and then you can use page 13 to define the columns of the table and their types. We could have done the whole thing in a single page as well. The wizard for creating wizards lets you create an some information region and it also lets you specify a region template, which can be used for all the regions created by the wizard across all the pages. I have, however, deleted the region created by the wizard on page 13 and created one of my own. The region source uses `APEX_ITEM.SELECT_LIST` and `apex_item.text` to dynamically create items based on the value entered by the user in the `P13_ITEM1` item. Note the use of hierarchical query to dynamically create the number of rows depending on the value of `P13_ITEM1`.

Note that you will have to press Enter (Return key) to submit the page after entering a value in P13_ITEM1 text box. Submission of the page will generate a number of text boxes according to the value entered in P13_ITEM1. The values in the dynamically created items are fed to the Create table process on submit, which uses APEX_APPLICATION.G_F01.COUNT to count and process the items for the creation of the table. The Create table process page process is introducing the APEX_DEBUG_MESSAGE package to you. This package lets you write your own log messages. Usually custom tables are created for logging messages, but APEX_DEBUG_MESSAGE is a lot cleaner and standardized way of doing the same thing. To use APEX_DEBUG_MESSAGE we first have to mention the log level at which we will like to capture the messages using the APEX_DEBUG_MESSAGE.ENABLE_DEBUG_MESSAGES procedure. The logging is then finally done using the APEX_DEBUG_MESSAGE.LOG_LONG_MESSAGE procedure.

We also have regular expressions and REGEXP_LIKE in the Create table process to make sure that the user enters valid oracle identifiers for column names. A similar regular expression validation also exists on page 12 to make sure that a valid table name is entered by the user.

Setting different validations for different parts of a page process

Note the use of the raise_application_error function in the **Process** text area and #SQLERRM_TEXT# in the **Process Error Message** text area of the Create table process. Let's say that you want to have different validation messages for different parts of your page process then you could use the raise_application_error function to raise an error with your custom text in it, and then use #SQLERRM_TEXT# in the **Process Error Message** text area to print this custom error message on the page.

Summary

This chapter was dedicated to graphical reporting. We started this chapter with LDAP authentication and then moved on to create sparkline charts. We saw how we could merge the DML processing in APEX with sliders. We also had a look at the various ways of creating HTML charts in APEX. This chapter also included a report that used XMLDB query syntax for reporting. We then moved on to use the freely available, exceptionally pretty, and easily usable Google Visualizations API for creating charts in APEX. We also explored a different dimension of flash charts using AnyChart. This was followed by different ways to show images as a report column. We then started exploring jQuery for reporting and saw the use of jQuery context menus and dialog boxes in APEX. We brought this chapter to an end by creating a wizard and looking at a method to code validations on page processes in APEX. The next chapter will be an extension to this and my attempt will be to demonstrate a few things to beautify your application. See you in *Chapter 5, Flight to Space Station – Advanced APEX*.

5
Flight to Space Station: Advanced APEX

Let me begin this chapter from where I had left the previous one. This chapter will introduce some of the things which were missed out of the previous chapter. The following are the major learning outcomes from this chapter:

- Creating client side and server side HTML image maps
- PL/SQL server pages (PSP)
- Loadjava utility
- Understanding Oracle OLAP cubes
- Understanding APEX plugins
- Understanding Oracle advanced queuing
- Overview of APEX views, APEX advisor, data loading wizard, and database object dependencies report
- Understanding the process for downloading APEX applications using APEX utilities
- Understanding APEX websheets
- Understanding APEX shortcuts
- Understanding Resource Templates
- Using FusionCharts to create a funnel chart
- Understanding background jobs in APEX
- Creating tag clouds in APEX
- Brief discussion on some of the important PL/SQL packages
- The process to configure mail in APEX

So there is a lot in our kitty. Before we begin, install the reference application (4-98-9_05_chapter05.sql) for this chapter. The reference application uses APEX authentication scheme.

Creating HTML image maps

In the previous chapter we saw a pretty Flash image. We will now have a look at **HTML image maps**. HTML image maps can be used in places where basic shapes are involved, as carving out complex shapes using HTML might be a bit tedious. HTML image maps can be of the following two types:

- Server side image maps
- Client side image maps

We will have a look at these now.

Server-side image maps

In the **server side image map,** we put an image in the src attribute of the img tag and set the ismap attribute of the img tag. The following is the code in the **Server side image map** region on the first page of the reference application:

```
<a href="f?p=&APP_ID.:1:&APP_SESSION.:::::::">
<img src="#WORKSPACE_IMAGES#Image map.png" alt="" ismap></a>
```

When the user clicks on the image, the coordinates of the point on which the user clicks are appended to the target URL of the image as highlighted in the screenshot below. If you click on the image in **Server side image map** region, you would get an alert as shown in the next screenshot. This alert has been generated by `<script type="text/javascript"> javascript:alert( window.location); </script>` code present in the region **Header and Footer** section. If the user is not using a mouse then the coordinates will be (0, 0).

The coordinates have intentionally been appended to the end of the URL so that they don't fiddle with the APEX URL. This is done by adding a number of colons in the value of the `href` attribute in the previous code. We can collect the coordinates from server side image maps and use them to create client side image maps.

Client-side image maps

In the **client side image maps**, the HTML source itself contains the code to make a link out of certain portions of the image. We can mark a rectangular, circular or polygonal region of an image as a link.

Check the code in the client side image map on the first page of the reference application. A link on the rectangular part of an image has been created by the following code:

```
<area shape="rect" coords="110,28,167,83" href=http://www.yahoo.com>
```

The arguments of the `coords` attribute are the coordinates of the top left corner (`110,28`) and the bottom right corner (`167,83`) of the rectangle.

A link on the circular part of the image has been created by the following code:

```
<area shape="circle" coords="45,45,32" href="http://www.google.com">
```

The arguments of the `coords` attribute are the coordinates of the center of the circle followed by its radius. Click on the circular and rectangular parts of the image in **Client side image map** region and you will be redirected to `google.com` and `yahoo.com` respectively. The following screenshot is provided for your convenience:

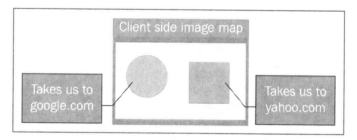

A polygonal link on an image can be created using `shape="poly"` and passing the pair of coordinates of all the end points of the polygon. A comma should be used as the separator for a pair of coordinates and also as a separator of the X-coordinate value from the Y-coordinate value of the same point.

Creating PL/SQL Server Pages (PSP)

This section introduces **PL/SQL Server Pages (PSPs)** to you. PSPs are a mechanism of writing PL/SQL and HTML code together to produce a webpage. APEX developers can use this technology to their advantage. Coding in PSPs is more comfortable than coding a stored procedure that does web interaction using the `htp` and `htf` packages. If you have worked with Java then you will realize the similarity between PSP and **Java Server Pages (JSP)**. Just like Java and HTML can be coded in a JSP, both PL/SQL and HTML can be coded in a PSP. Check out the following documentation for more details:

```
http://docs.oracle.com/cd/E11882_01/appdev.112/e25518/adfns_psp.htm
```

The code pack contains `show_emps.psp`. This file serves the purpose of a readymade example to check out the PSPs in action. You can put this file in the database using the following command on the command line:

```
loadpsp  -replace -user packt_schema/packt_schema "<Directory of show_
emps.psp>\show_emps.psp"
```

Note that the extension of the file has to be `.psp`.

On successful execution of the command you should get a message similar to the following in the command prompt:

```
"D:\Work\Final code stack\Chapter 05\show_emps.psp": procedure "show_
employees" created.
```

The following is the code of the PSP:

```
<%@ page language="PL/SQL" %>
<%@ page contentType="text/html" %>
<%@ plsql procedure="show_employees" %>
<%-- This example displays the last name and first name of every
employee in the employees table. --%>
<%!
  CURSOR emp_cursor IS
  SELECT last_name, first_name
  FROM oehr_employees
  ORDER BY last_name;
%>
<html> <head> <meta http-equiv="Content-Type" content="text/html">
  <title>List of Employees</title> </head> <body TEXT="#000000"
    BGCOLOR="#FFFFFF">
  <h1>List of Employees</h1>
```

```
<table width="40%" border="1">
  <tr> <th align="left">Last Name</th>
    <th align="left">First Name</th> </tr>
<% FOR emp_record IN emp_cursor LOOP %>
  <tr> <td> <%= emp_record.last_name %> </td>
    <td> <%= emp_record.first_name %> </td> </tr>
<% END LOOP; %>
</table></body></html>
```

After the successful execution of the command, you should be able to see `show_employees` procedure in `packt_schema`. We have mentioned the name of the procedure using `plsql procedure` directive in the PSP file. If we do not use `plsql procedure` directive then Oracle assumes the name of the PSP file to be the name of the PL/SQL procedure. The newly created `show_employees` procedure is a translation of the code in `show_emps.psp` file. All PSP related syntax is replaced by calls to PL/SQL web toolkit functions in the newly created procedure. We can now call this procedure using **DADs (Database Access Descriptors)** or APEX Listener. Check the *Database and Web interaction in both DAD and Listener configurations* section of the *Appendix* to learn more about this topic.

Once the Listener/DAD has been configured, we can see the list of employees using `http://localhost:7001/apex/PACKT_SCHEMA.show_employees`.

My `defaults.xml` has `<entry key="security.inclusionList">apex, p, v, f, wwv_*, y*, c*, PACKT_SCHEMA.*, packt_schema.*, apex_util.*</entry>` and my output looks like the following screenshot:

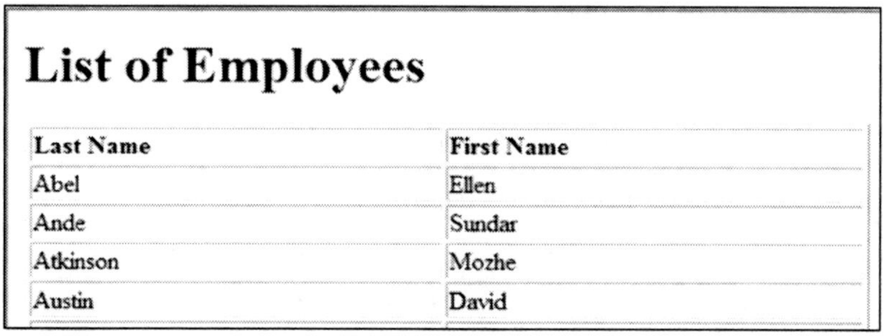

List of Employees

Last Name	First Name
Abel	Ellen
Ande	Sundar
Atkinson	Mozhe
Austin	David

Understanding and using loadjava utility

`loadjava` is another command line utility like `loadpsp`. This utility is not widely used and hence is not widely known. The utility can be used in situations where we have to use a java class in APEX to meet the objective. Let us look at a simple example of using a java class in a PL/SQL program.

The `hello_world.java` file is a part of the code pack and contains a java class called `hello_world`. Note that the name of the java class and the java file should match. The `hello_world` class contains a static function called `hello_world` which returns the `Hello world` string.

Open command prompt and get into the folder which holds `hello_world.java` (supplied in the code pack) and run the following command:

```
javac hello_world.java
```

This will create `hello_world.class` file. A `.class` file is the byte code for the **Java virtual machine (JVM)**. We will upload this `.class` file, and our uploaded `.class` file will be used by the inbuilt JVM of Oracle server. Run the following command to upload the `.class` file as a database object on the Oracle server:

```
loadjava -user packt_schema/packt_schema "<Directory of hello_world.
class>\hello_world.class"
```

> You can also compile the java class directly against the JVM of the database server. I like this approach because this avoids version problems. If the version of the JVM on your machine is higher than the version of the JVM on the database server then there is a possibility that a java class might compile in your machine but give errors when it is executed on the database server. The following is the syntax to compile the java class against the JVM of the database server:
>
> ```
> loadjava -user packt_schema/packt_schema "<Directory
> of hello_world.class>\hello_world.java"
> ```

Oracle Java development is a whole big area and this small paragraph is just an introduction to it. Check out the following documentation if you wish to sink deeper:

http://docs.oracle.com/cd/E18283_01/java.112/e10588/toc.htm

After creation of the class, a PL/SQL wrapper has to be created around the class so that the code can be used in a PL/SQL program. The following code creates the wrapper:

```
FUNCTION helloworld RETURN VARCHAR2 AS
  LANGUAGE JAVA NAME 'hello_world.hello_world () return java.lang.
String';
```

You can find this code in `chapter05` package. `chapter05` package is compiled in the database at the time of the installation of your reference application.

To test this wrapper, open `sqlplus` and connect using `packt_schema` and run the following code:

```
Set serveroutput on
Exec dbms_output.put_line(chapter05.helloworld);
```

You should be able to see the `Hello world` string which is returned by the `hello_world.hello_world` java function.

You might also want to check the `DBMS_JAVA` package which provides a library of java related database functions. See the following URL:

```
http://docs.oracle.com/cd/E11882_01/java.112/e10588/appendixa.htm
```

Creating funnel charts using FusionCharts

Just like AnyChart, **FusionCharts** also has a few products which can be used as charting options and just like AnyChart, FusionChart is a flash charting option as well. The best part is that just like Google Visualization API, FusionChart is free. You can find more about FusionChart in the following place. The third page of the reference application has a funnel chart created using FusionCharts:

```
http://www.fusioncharts.com/goodies/fusioncharts-free/
```

Let us now see the process of creating funnel charts using FusionCharts.

We will first have to download and unzip `FusionChartsFree.zip`. The `Charts` folder in the unzipped contents has a bunch of `.swf` files. Different types of flash charts have different `.swf` files. I uploaded `FCF_Funnel.swf` for funnel chart in the **Static Files** section of the **Shared Components** of reference application. We also have to upload the `FusionCharts.js` file from the `JSClass` folder to **Static Files** section of the **Shared Components**.

Let us now talk a little about the code in **Funnel chart** region in third page of the reference application. The following code is shared for your reference:

```
DECLARE
  l_xml_data            VARCHAR2 (32767);
  l_width  VARCHAR2 (10):='700'; l_height VARCHAR2(10):='565';
BEGIN
  l_xml_data := '<chart numberPrefix=''$''>';
  FOR i IN
```

```
        (SELECT first_name,salary FROM oehr_employees WHERE rownum < 15) LOOP
            l_xml_data := l_xml_data || '<set name=''' || i.first_name || '''
    value=''' || i.salary || ''' />';
    END LOOP;
        l_xml_data := l_xml_data || '</chart>';
        HTP.p ('<div id="funnelChart" align="center"/><script
    language="JavaScript" src="#WORKSPACE_IMAGES#FusionCharts.js"></script>
        <script type="text/javascript">
        var funnelChart = new FusionCharts("#WORKSPACE_IMAGES#FCF_Funnel.
    swf", "funnelChartId", "' || l_width || '", "' || l_height || '", "1");
        funnelChart.setDataXML("' || l_xml_data || '");
        funnelChart.render("funnelChart");
        </script>');
    END;
```

In this code, `l_xml_data` holds the XML data in the format in which FusionChart's swf object expects. We then use `HTP.p` function to put some JavaScript code to the browser. The JavaScript code starts by declaring `FusionCharts.js` as the source of the JavaScript functions. The code then creates a JavaScript FusionCharts object which accepts the `.swf` file along with some more attributes such as `height` and `width` as arguments. This is followed by a call to `setDataXML` which binds the XML data with the newly created object. Finally, the `render` function renders the chart. `FusionCharts.js` and `FCF_Funnel.swf` have been associated with the workspace and hence the use of the `#WORKSPACE_IMAGES#` substitution string in the code. The following is a screenshot of our funnel chart:

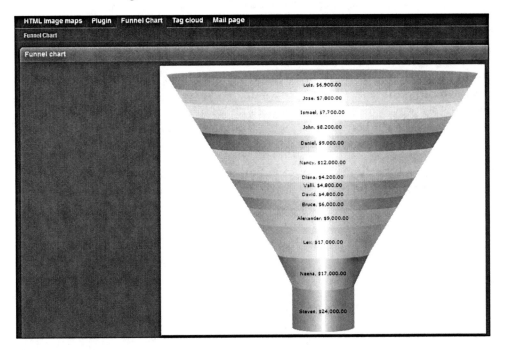

Creating tag cloud

Tag cloud is a fancy name given to something that is one of the basic features of Oracle APEX. In the *Implementing classic report search functionality* section of *Chapter 2, Conventional Reporting in APEX*, we had seen that APEX puts an enveloping query if we wish to enable the **search** functionality on a **classic report** region. In this **search** functionality, the user has to put a text which is searched in the database. There might be some scenarios where a user might want to get a list of options, one of which can be selected to search. A tag cloud fills this gap by providing a list of options to search. It is called a cloud because the list is often presented as a collection of links forming a cloud-like shape instead of a list. The following is a screenshot of the tag cloud from the reference application:

To create a tag cloud, we first need a report in which the selected string will be searched. This report is more like a drilldown report. The cloud is created using a PL/SQL region. You can find the sample code in the fourth page of the reference application. The same has been shared for your convenience:

```
begin
  htp.p('<style type="text/css">A:hover {color: red;} </style>');
  for i in (SELECT LISTAGG(htf.anchor(ctext => first_name,curl =>
'f?p='||:APP_ID||':4:'||:APP_SESSION||':::::'||'P4_SEARCH:'||first_
name), ',') WITHIN GROUP (order by first_name) AS employees
    FROM  (select first_name,mod(rownum,25) mod_rownum from oehr_
employees)
    GROUP  BY
      mod_rownum) loop
    htp.p(i.employees);
  end loop;
end;
```

In this code, LISTAGG is used for string aggregation and htf.anchor is used for the generation of the links. mod (rownum,25) is used to group the results such that the tag cloud occupies a relatively smaller width on the screen. P4_SEARCH holds the value which is selected by the user. For the sake of demonstration, let us assume that the first names of the employees are tags.

In a real world, you can store tags in a table and use those tag names instead of employee first names. Note that my region query is comparing all columns of employee table with the page item containing the selected first name value because a tag is not generally associated with a column. It is a generic text and is searched in the whole set of data. So even though, we realize that the first names will not result in any match in the other columns, we are comparing them with the other columns to show the process. This type of query will benefit from Oracle text indexes. Learn more about Oracle text indexes from `http://docs.oracle.com/cd/E11882_01/` `text.112/e24436/whatsnew.htm`.

We can also use JQuery to generate our tag clouds. Following is the link to explore this option:

`http://archive.plugins.jquery.com/node/3109`

Creating plugins

We have used a lot of **JQuery** code and have tinkered with the APEX standard features to attain our motives. What if you had many applications and all of these required the same tinkering? The solution is called **plugin**. Plugins let you write a definition of an item, region, process, dynamic action, authentication, or an authorization type. This definition can then be plugged in any application and can be used as the standard item or page or region or dynamic action, or authentication or authorization type. Plugins are APEX's way of involving the developers in the tool enhancement process. A repository of all plugins created by developers around the globe can be found at `http://apex.oracle.com/plugins`.

To implement a plugin, you have to define a set of functions with predefined signatures. These functions are called `interface` functions. The name of the functions can be of your own choice but the argument list and the type of the arguments must match with the predefined structure. This standardization helps the APEX engine in processing a plugin.

Creating item and page process plugin

We will first see the process of creating item plugins. We will see two item plugins. The first one (`packt_render_text_box_item`) just formats the appearance of the item when it is displayed on an APEX page while the second one (`packt_render_text_box_item_improvd`) is an improved plugin and it is capable of sending the values entered in the item to the APEX engine.

If you wish to define an item plugin, then the function that renders the item must look like the following code:

```
function <name of function> (
   p_item in apex_plugin.t_page_item, p_plugin in apex_plugin.t_plugin,
   p_value in varchar2, p_is_readonly in boolean, p_is_printer_friendly
   in boolean )
   return apex_plugin.t_page_item_render_result
```

Similarly, if the item plugin uses **Asynchronous JavaScript and XML (AJAX)** to load additional data, then the function that is executed on an AJAX call should look like the following code:

```
function <name of function> ( p_item   in apex_plugin.t_page_item, p_
plugin in apex_plugin.t_plugin ) return apex_plugin.t_page_item_ajax_
result
```

A function that performs a validation on the items of the item plugin type should look like the following code:

```
function <name of function> ( p_item   in apex_plugin.t_page_item,
p_plugin in apex_plugin.t_plugin, p_value  in varchar2 ) return apex_
plugin.t_page_item_validation_result
```

We can either define these functions in the **PL/SQL** region in the **Source** section of the plugin itself or can have stored database functions and then mention those function names in the plugin definition.

`packt_render_text_box_item` plugin in the reference application is an APEX item plugin and the rendering function for this plugin has been put in `chapter05` package. The rendering function has `htp.p('<input type="text" style="background-color: #F00" />');` which displays a text box with a red background.

It is important to note that a plugin is your own baby. So, APEX will not do anything to make your life easier if your plugin becomes a problem. For example, in our plugin, we create an HTML text box with red background and APEX did just that for us but how do we use this text box now? From the *Decoding APEX page submissions* discussion in *Chapter 1, Know Your Horse Before You Ride It*, we know that APEX puts a system generated value in the `name` attribute of the HTML tag generated for page items. This value, in the `name` attribute, is used by `wwv_flow.accept` process. The name of the APEX item becomes the `id` of the corresponding tag in HTML. `wwv_flow.accept` is responsible for getting the values in the client side HTML page to the server side APEX engine. So the big question is, in the case of our plugin item, who will do this job?

The answer is that we have to do this. The good news is that we have APEX_PLUGIN and APEX_PLUGIN_UTIL to help us do this. We can solve the problem of sending the value of the HTML element to the APEX engine by using APEX_PLUGIN.GET_INPUT_ NAME_FOR_PAGE_ITEM. The packt_render_text_box_item_improvd plugin uses this function. The rendering function of this plugin is chapter05.render_text_ box_item_improvd and we have the following code in it:

```
htp.p ('<tr><td><label for="'||p_item.name||'">'||p_item.name||'</
label></td>'||'<td><input type="text" style="background-color: #F00"
'||
   'name="'||APEX_PLUGIN.GET_INPUT_NAME_FOR_PAGE_ITEM (p_is_multi_value
=> false)||'"/></td></tr>);
```

Here p_item is a variable of type apex_plugin.t_page_item which is a part of the signature of the interface function. Check APEX_PLUGIN and APEX_PLUGIN_UTIL for some other important functions in the packages.

The second page of the reference section has the **Log plugin value** procedure which logs the value of two page items namely, P2_PLUGIN_ITEM and P2_IMPROVED_ PLUGIN_ITEM. P2_PLUGIN_ITEM is created using packt_render_text_box_item plugin and P2_IMPROVED_PLUGIN_ITEM is created using packt_render_text_box_ item_improvd plugin. Open the second page of the reference application, enter some values in the **Plugin Item** and **P2_IMPROVED_PLUGIN_ITEM** text boxes and click on the **Submit** button. Run the following query to see that the value of P2_PLUGIN_ ITEM is not captured while the value of P2_IMPROVED_PLUGIN_ITEM is captured:

```
select * from apex_debug_messages where application_id = 102 and page_
id = 2 and message_level = 5
```

Change the application_id if you have installed the reference application with a different ID.

Let us now check out some of the other properties of item plugins. Open the **packt_ render_text_box_item** plugin from **Shared Components | Plug-ins** to make more sense of the talk. If **Is Visible Widget** check box of **Standard Attributes** (highlighted in the next screenshot) is checked, then we see an extra step in the **Create Item** wizard that lets us enter certain attributes such as **height** and **width** of the item based on the plugin.

Standard Attributes

Attributes:

☐ Is Visible Widget ◀━━━   ☐ Session State Changeable   ☐ Has Read Only Attribute   ☐ Has Escape Special Characters Attribute
☐ Has Quick Pick Attributes   ☑ Has Source Attributes   ☐ Format Mask Date Only   ☐ Format Mask Number Only
☑ Has Element Attributes   ☑ Has Width Attributes   ☐ Has Height Attribute   ☐ Has Element Option Attribute
☐ Has Placeholder Attribute   ☑ Has Encrypt Session State Attribute   ☐ Has List of Values   ☐ List of Values Required
☐ Has LOV Display Null Attributes ☐ Has Cascading LOV Attributes

Custom Attributes

Substitute Attribute Values   Yes ▾

No attributes defined

[Add Attribute] ◀━━━   --

The visible attributes will depend on the checking of the checkboxes in the
Standard Attributes section and defining of attributes in the **Custom Attributes**
section of the plugin.

A plugin developer can create his own attributes in the **Custom Attributes**
section of a plugin. When we click on the **Add Attribute** button (highlighted in
the preceding screenshot), we are taken to a page that lets us define an attribute
for the plugin. Most of the fields in this page are self-explanatory. The **Scope**
drop-down list is important. If you select the scope as **Component** then you get to
set the attribute you are defining for every item that uses the plugin. If you select
the scope as **Application** then the attribute in question can only be defined once
per application. The values fed into the **Custom Attributes**, at the time of using
the plugin to create items, regions, and other such objects, can be accessed in the
plugin code. The `interface` functions of an item plugin have a variable of `apex_
plugin.t_page_item` type. A variable of `apex_plugin.t_page_item` type can be
used to get the value of custom attribute of an item created using an item plugin.
Let us say that the name of a variable of `apex_plugin.t_page_item` type is `p_item`.
The first custom attribute associated with the plugin can then be accessed using
`p_item.attribute_01`. Similarly, if we were creating a process type plugin then
we could access the first custom attributes using `p_process.attribute_01` where
`p_process` is a variable of `apex_plugin.t_process`, and `apex_plugin.t_process`
is one of the arguments present in the interface for process plugins. The success
message defined at the time of creating a plugin can be accessed using `p_process.
success_message`. `packt_da_plugin` in the reference application has a custom
attribute and uses it in the `interface` functions. Let us talk about `packt_da_
plugin` now.

Creating DA plugin

Dynamic action (DA) plugins are a little different than the other plugins because the end task of a DA is to execute a JavaScript/JQuery code. So the operational logic in case of a DA plugin is generally in a .js file while in case of other plugins, the operational logic is in PL/SQL blocks.

We will do the following in this section. We will create a custom attribute and capture its value in the rendering function (da_alert). We will then pass this captured value to a JavaScript function (apex_alert) present in a .js file (da_plugin.js). The code in this .js file will use this value and display it as a text in an alert box. This process will help us understand most of the components of a DA plugin.

Open **packt_da_plugin** DA and check out the following custom attributes shown in the following screenshot:

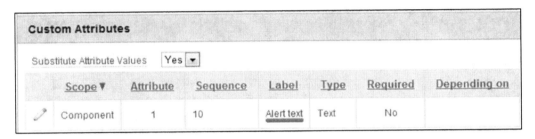

Let us now understand the interface function (da_alert) code in the **Source** section of **packt_da_plugin** DA.

```
function da_alert (
  p_dynamic_action  in apex_plugin.t_dynamic_action,
  p_plugin          in apex_plugin.t_plugin )
  return apex_plugin.t_dynamic_action_render_result
is
  l_attr1     varchar2(100) := p_dynamic_action.attribute_01;
  l_result apex_plugin.t_dynamic_action_render_result;
begin
  apex_javascript.add_library ( p_name        => 'da_plugin',
  p_directory =>p_plugin.file_prefix, p_version   => null );
  l_result.javascript_function := 'packt_da_plugin.apex_alert';
  l_result.attribute_01         := l_attr1;
  return l_result;
end da_alert;
```

The arguments of da_alert are according to the interface for the rendering function of a DA. We capture the first attribute using p_dynamic_action.attribute_01. The first attribute in our case is the attribute with **Alert text** label which is shown in the previous screenshot. We assign its value to l_attr1 in the first highlighted piece of the previous code. This is followed by the declaration of l_result. We then use apex_javascript.add_library function to add da_plugin.js file. Every plugin has its own files and the files can be accessed using the #PLUGIN_PREFIX# substitution string. This string is defined in the **File Prefix** text box of the **File** section of a plugin. Typical files which are uploaded are the CSS files, images, and JavaScript files used in the plugin.

In a dynamic action type plugin the JavaScript function is put in a string and that string is assigned to l_result.javascript_function in our rendering function. Any properly escaped JavaScript code or a call to a JavaScript function can be assigned to l_result.javascript_function. We are calling packt_da_plugin. apex_alert JavaScript function here. This can be seen in the second highlighted piece of the previous code. The definition of packt_da_plugin.apex_alert is in da_plugin.js file. The da_plugin.js file has the following code:

```
packt_da_plugin={
  apex_alert:function()
    {alert(this.action.attribute01)}};
```

We are able to capture the value of the custom attribute in the JavaScript code of da_plugin.js using this.action.attribute01. The value is passed to this. action.attribute01 by assigning l_attr1 to l_result.attribute_01. Refer to the previous code to verify this.

Handles such as this.affectedElements and this.browserEvent which are used in a normal DA can also be used in DAs which are based on a plugin. The use of handles such as this.affectedElements will obviously depend on whether you have checked their corresponding check boxes in the **Standard Attributes** section of the plugin page. If these checkboxes are not selected then a developer using the plugin will not be able to use them.

Alert on load DA on the first page of the reference application uses packt_da_ plugin and displays an alert textbox when first page is executed. Edit **Alert on load** DA and then click on the pencil icon under **True Actions** section. You would see your custom attribute under **Settings** section. The text in this section is displayed in the alert box when you run the first page of the reference application.

Creating websheet application

This is the newest feature in APEX 4.*x* and warrants a deeper look. **Websheets** empower the end user to create applications of their own. The metadata of the websheets is stored in APEX generated tables which change according to the design of the websheet. The end user on the other hand can be blissfully ignorant about the complexities that lie underneath. A websheet application can be created in a couple of clicks on the **Create Application** wizard unlike the traditional database application wizard which expects you to mention the theme, the homepage, tabs, and breadcrumbs. Once a websheet application is created, a developer can click on the **Edit Properties** button to configure a few properties for the websheet.

Import the websheet reference application (`4-98-9_05_chapter05_websheet.sql`). Select **File Type** as **Websheet Application Export** while importing the application. The websheet reference application has an ACL for authorization. After importing the reference websheet application, click on the **Edit** button of the application and go to the **Authorization** section. Click on the **Edit Access Control List** button and add the user ID of the admin user of your workspace.

Check out the **Authentication** section of the reference websheet application. A few things missing in the **Create Application** wizard of a websheet are present here. If you believe that your end user is PL/SQL educated, then you can select **Yes** in the **Allow SQL and PL/SQL** drop-down of the **SQL and PL/SQL** section. After doing this, you can select a list of objects which can be used by the end user to create his objects in the application. This list of objects can be used to create reports in a websheet.

Before opening the websheet application, add `ws*` to `security.inclusionList` of `defaults.xml` file as discussed in the *Database interaction and Web interaction in both DAD and Listener configuration* section of the *Appendix*. Restart WebLogic after this.

Open the reference application of the websheet and check out the panel on the right hand side of it. We will discuss the most important of these links now.

Let us now have a deeper look at the set of controls shown in the previous screenshot. Note that the **New Report** link is only available because we had edited the properties of the websheet application and selected **Yes** in the **Allow SQL and PL/SQL** drop-down. This selection also gets a new type of section which lets you write PL/SQL code as source. We can see this **PL/SQL** section highlighted in the next screenshot. This **PL/SQL** region can be used to fire owa web toolkit functions such as htp.p which will display the section on the page.

The first two links (**New Section** and **Edit Sections**) in the preceding screenshot can be used to create and edit sections in a websheet. The following are the possible types of sections. The definition of the all the sections created by us can be found in the APEX$_WS_WEBPG_SECTIONS table.

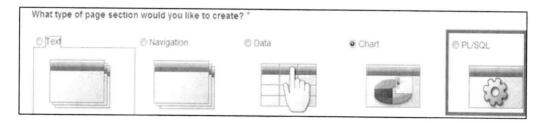

If you are creating a **Text** section then you can click on the small black arrow to reveal a whole set of tools to beautify your text. Refer the following screenshot:

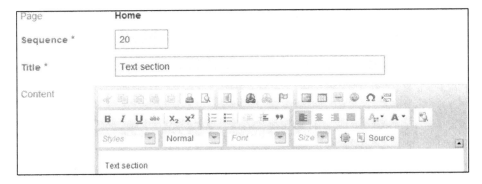

Let us now look at the prominent features of websheets.

Understanding datagrid

A **datagrid** is an incredibly useful tool that has many interesting implementations. You can either create a datagrid from scratch or can copy the data from a spreadsheet. Spreadsheet data can be copied in a text area while creating a datagrid and APEX will generate a report based on this data for you. Moreover, the report has most of the features of interactive reports in it. The data in the websheet can be found in APEX$_ WS_ROWS table in packt_schema.

Understanding reports

The final link in the **Control Panel** group in the screenshot under *Creating websheet application* section helps us to create a report. Report can either be a report on an SQL query or can be reports on the objects which you might have selected in the **SQL and PL/SQL** section while editing the properties of the websheet. This report is also an interactive report.

Understanding the features of administration and view drop-downs

Certain administrative tasks such as checking out the activity in the websheet application, finding the properties set for the application can be done using the **Administration** link on the top. The following screenshot of the menu under the **Administration** link is given for you convenience:

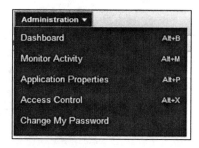

Similarly, the **View** menu (Refer the next screenshot) has a few functions to help you track the activities done on the application such as viewing the different objects created on the application, viewing the uploaded files, tags, notes, and page history. **Presentation Mode** is to show the whole application without the widgets that create objects. The feel of **Presentation Mode** is the same as that of any database application.

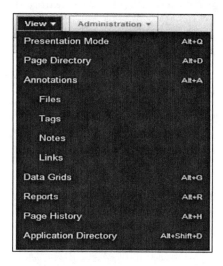

Understanding Websheet Help menu

A user can get help by clicking on the **Help** link (Refer the next screenshot) present on the top of a websheet application.

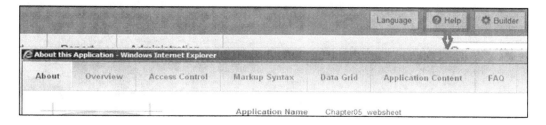

A good understanding of the things mentioned in the **Help** link is vital for the development of websheet applications. The **Application Content** tab (Refer the next screenshot) of the **Help** includes the markup syntax to add images to the websheet application and the syntax to get the link of the reports, datagrids, and other objects created in the application.

If we had to show an image on our websheet application, then we will first have to upload the image in the **Files** section and the syntax for displaying the uploaded image on the websheet can be found in the **Markup Syntax** tab of the **Help** link. Check the **Text** section of the reference websheet application for an example of an uploaded image.

Queries of datagrids have their own syntax. You can check queries for each of your datagrids in this special syntax by going in the **Data Grids** tab of the **Help** link. You can copy this and paste it in a **Text** section of your websheet to generate the same datagrid. A sample of this technique can be seen in the **Text** section of the reference websheet application.

The **Access Control** tab of the **Help** link gives considerable information on the various levels of privileges in a websheet. Let us talk about privileges in websheets and sharing them.

Sharing websheets using ACL

Websheets can be shared with multiple users. Let's see a process to do the same:

1. In the **Application Builder**, go to the websheet application and click on the **Edit** Properties and then go to the **Authorization** section.

2. Click on the **Edit Access Control List** button and then click on the **Create Entry** button.

3. Put PACKT_ADMIN as the user name and **Administrator** as the privilege and then click on the **Create** button.

4. Go back to the properties of the application and then select **Custom** in **Access Control List Type** radio button and click on the **Apply Changes** button.

5. Run your websheet application and then click on the **Administration** link on your Websheet application and select **Access Control**.

6. Click on **Create Entry**.

7. Enter the proposed user ID of the user with whom you wish to share the websheet.

8. Select the **Reader** role in the radio button list.

A user with **Reader** privileges has only read-only access. A user with **Contributor** privileges can read and edit while a user with **Administrator** privileges can create ACLs and can delete the application.

Until this point, we have set the authorization of the new user but we also have to set the authentication so that the user is able to log in. If we go to the Properties of the reference application and then go to the **Authentication** tab of it, we will see that **Application Express Account** authentication has been set for it. To enable a websheet user to be authenticated, we have to create a workspace user. We can obviously have other authentication mechanisms. We have already seen most of them in the previous chapters.

Configuring the mail

At present, Oracle 11.2.0.2 Version is only available for Linux 64-bit OS and I am doing all my installations on my personal Windows 7 laptop. So I am working on Oracle 11.2.0.1.0. I am sure that when you will be reading this book, Oracle 11.2.0.2 will be available for windows as well.

To demonstrate the mail configuration, I wish to use a Gmail account. The Gmail SMTP server accepts only SSL requests. UTL_SMTP of Oracle 11.2.0.1 cannot send such requests but one of the 11.2.0.2 can. Following is a link to the documentation which confirms this:

```
http://docs.oracle.com/cd/E11882_01/server.112/e22487/chapter1_2.htm
```

So, configuring Gmail on 11.2.0.2 will be a lot easier than it was at the time this book was written, and you will probably be saved from all the extra hard work.

In 11.2.0.2, the signature of `open_connection` function is different from the one in 11.2.0.1.0. In 11.2.0.2, the function accepts a wallet path and it's password as arguments. So we would basically have to create a wallet using **Oracle's Wallet Manager** with **Equifax Secure Certificate Authority** trusted certificate in it. We can get this certificate from `http://www.geotrust.com/resources/root-certificates/`. We would then have to do a handshake by using `utl_smtp.ehlo` function. We can then use `utl_smtp.starttls` which secures SMTP connection using SSL/TLS. Finally, `utl_smtp.auth` can be used to authenticate against the SMTP server.

I will use stunnel to create a SSL wrapper between the client (Oracle database server) and the server (Gmail SMTP server). I must mention that the following website was a great support in helping me configure the mail functionality:

`http://monkeyonoracle.blogspot.in/2009/11/plsql-and-gmail-or-utlsmtp-with-ssl.html`

Check out the following link to know more about stunnel and to download it:

- `https://www.stunnel.org/index.html`
- `https://www.stunnel.org/downloads/stunnel-4.54-installer.exe`

Create the ACL to enable the network service to create a connection. Use the following code for it:

```
begin
  dbms_network_acl_admin.create_acl (
    acl => 'gmail.xml', description => 'Normal Access',
    principal => 'CONNECT', is_grant => TRUE,
    privilege => 'connect', start_date => null,
    end_date      => null );
end;
/
begin
  dbms_network_acl_admin.add_privilege (
    acl        => 'gmail.xml', principal     => 'PACKT_SCHEMA',
    is_grant    => TRUE, privilege    => 'connect',
    start_date    => null, end_date    => null)
end;
/
begin
  dbms_network_acl_admin.assign_acl (
```

```
    acl => 'gmail.xml', host => 'localhost',
    lower_port => 1925, upper_port => 1925);
end;
/
commit;
```

Put the following code in `stunnel.conf` file. You can find `stunnel.conf` in the folder in which you have installed stunnel:

```
; Use it for client mode
client = yes
[ssmtp]
accept  = 1925
connect = smtp.gmail.com:465
```

By doing this, you have created an SMTP server on your local machine that operates on port 1925. You can confirm this by the following command. The code in the `stunnel.conf` file redirects this request to Gmail's SMTP server after wrapping it in the SSL layer. Open stunnel before running the following command in the command prompt:

telnet localhost 1925

We can now send the mails using the following code:

```
declare
  g_smtp_host      varchar2 (256)      := 'localhost';
  g_smtp_port      pls_integer         := 1925;
  l_conn utl_smtp.connection; nls_charset    varchar2(255);
  p_sender varchar2 (255):= 'packt.apex@gmail.com';
  p_recipient varchar2 (255):= 'packt.apex@gmail.com';
  p_subject varchar2(255):='Hii';
  p_message varchar2 (255):= 'Hii';
  -- Write a MIME header
  procedure write_mime_header (
    p_conn in out nocopy utl_smtp.connection,
    p_name in varchar2, p_value in varchar2)
  is
  begin
    utl_smtp.write_data ( p_conn,
      p_name || ': ' || p_value || utl_tcp.crlf);
  end;
begin
  -- get characterset
  select value into   nls_charset from   nls_database_parameters
```

```
        where parameter = 'NLS_CHARACTERSET';
        -- establish connection and authenticate
        l_conn    := utl_smtp.open_connection (g_smtp_host, g_smtp_port);
        utl_smtp.ehlo(l_conn, 'any value');
        utl_smtp.command(l_conn, 'auth login');
        utl_smtp.command (l_conn,utl_encode.text_encode('packt.apex@gmail.
com', nls_charset, 1));
        utl_smtp.command(l_conn, utl_encode.text_encode('abcd1111', nls_
charset, 1));
        -- set from/recipient
        utl_smtp.command(l_conn, 'MAIL FROM: <'||p_sender||'>');
        utl_smtp.command(l_conn, 'RCPT TO: <'||p_recipient||'>');
        -- write mime headers
        utl_smtp.open_data (l_conn);
        write_mime_header (l_conn, 'Subject', p_subject);
        write_mime_header (l_conn, 'Content-Type', 'text/plain');
        utl_smtp.write_data (l_conn, utl_tcp.crlf);
        -- write message body
        utl_smtp.write_data (l_conn, p_message);
        utl_smtp.close_data (l_conn);
        -- end connection
        utl_smtp.quit (l_conn);
        exception
        when others then
    begin         utl_smtp.quit(l_conn);
        exception when others then          null;      end;
        raise_application_error(-20000,'Failed to send mail due to the
following error: ' || sqlerrm);
    end;
```

This should successfully send the mails. We have dug the tunnel and any vehicle can pass through it. We just saw an example of utl_smtp using the tunnel and now we will see how apex_mail package can be used to deliver the mails using the tunnel. We have to start by putting APEX_040200 in the ACL. Execute the following from a sysdba account:

```
begin
  dbms_network_acl_admin.add_privilege (
  acl        => 'gmail.xml', principal    => 'APEX_040200',
  is_grant   => TRUE, privilege     => 'connect',
  start_date   => null, end_date    => null);
end;
commit;
```

Note that Gmail requires that the all mail IDs be enclosed in angle brackets (second highlighted piece of the previous code). The mail ID used for authentication is an exception to this rule (first highlighted piece of the previous code).

APEX has an inbuilt mail feature and an APEX_MAIL package. We can use these only if we configure the SMTP server in the **Email** section of the **Instance** Settings page after logging in the **INTERNAL** workspace. The final configuration of email looks like the following screenshot:

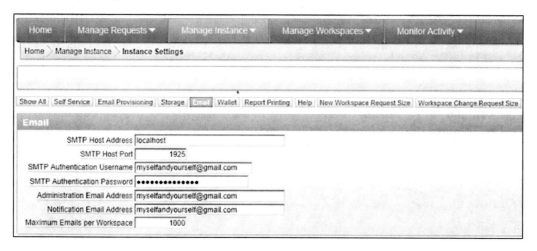

The **Mail** process on the fifth page of the reference application is a PL/SQL process and uses APEX_MAIL.SEND package to send message. The following code is shared for your convenience:

```
DECLARE
  l_id NUMBER; l_blob BLOB; l_filename varchar2(50);
  l_row_exists_flag integer: = 0;
BEGIN
  select count(1) into l_row_exists_flag from oehr_employee_profiles
where fileobject is not null and rownum = 1;
  IF l_row_exists_flag > 0 THEN
    select fileobject, filename into l_blob, l_filename from oehr_
employee_profiles where fileobject is not null and rownum = 1;
    l_id:= APEX_MAIL.SEND(
      p_to        => '<myselfandyourself@gmail.com>',
      p_from      => '<myselfandyourself@gmail.com>',
      p_subj      => 'APEX_MAIL with attachment',
      p_body      => 'Attachment in mail.',
      p_replyto   => '<myselfandyourself@gmail.com>');
APEX_MAIL.ADD_ATTACHMENT(p_mail_id    => l_id,
```

```
            p_attachment => l_blob,
            p_filename   => l_filename,
            p_mime_type  => 'application/octet');
    commit;
     ELSE
       l_id:= APEX_MAIL.SEND(
         p_to        => '<myselfandyourself@gmail.com>',
         p_from      => '<myselfandyourself@gmail.com>',
         p_subj      => 'APEX_MAIL without attachment',
         p_body      => 'No attachments.',
         p_replyto   => '<myselfandyourself@gmail.com>');
    commit;
     END IF;
    end;
```

Check the syntax of passing the arguments in the page process. **Mail process** on the fifth page of the reference application uses a different technique. It uses the Mail page process of APEX to send mail. Check the arguments of the process in the reference application. A screenshot of the delivered mails can be seen as follows:

APEX_MAIL_QUEUE view shows the queued tasks that use the APEX internal mail configuration and APEX_MAIL_LOG view shows the logs of these tasks. We can delete the tasks from the mail queue by going to **Manage Instance** and then clicking on the **Mail Queue** in APEX Administration. We can also trigger the mails in the mail queue from the **Manage Instance** page.

Downloading APEX application without web server

We generally download APEX applications from the web server but honestly, we put an extra layer in the process because the applications themselves are stored in the database. Again there are situations where the web server of the DEV environment goes down and you have to work on a critical CR. You can either use a SQL developer to get your application or could use APEXExport command line utility for this purpose.

Downloading an application from a SQL developer is straight forward. You have to login to the schema which is the owner of the application and you will see an **Application Express** link under the connection. You can expand the link to see the application and then you can right-click on the desired application to export it.

The other way is to use the APEXExport command line utility which is as follows:

```
D:\My softwares\apex\utilities>java -classpath "C:\OracleProducts\
Oracle11GDatabase\product\11.2.0\dbhome_1\owb\wf\lib\ojdbc14.jar;D:\My
softwares\apex\utilities" oracle.apex.APEXExport
```

Executing the preceding command will give an output which will list the various options which can be used with APEXExport. Note that the classpath argument should have the ojdbc14.jar file and the apex\utilities folder. You have to get into the apex\utilities folder to execute the previous command. You can find the utilities folder in <Directory in which apex_4.1.1_en.zip is unzipped>/apex/utilities.

We can use oracle.apex.APEXExportSplitter on an exported APEX file if we wish to create subfolders for each component type.

Understanding Oracle OLAP cubes

We can use **OLAP (online analytical processing)** cubes for reporting instead of our traditional relational tables. Let's see the process to create a cube and use it in APEX. Oracle's OLAP engine is fused into the 11G Version of the database so the creation of an OLAP cube only requires an **Analytic Workspace Manager** which gives the UI to create an OLAP cube. A cube gives you a method to collect the measures of the same dimensionality. The edges of a cube are **dimensions**. Multiple cubes in the same analytical workspace may share a dimension. The order of the listing of dimensions in a cube affects the performance.

The first dimension in a cube has to be the one with fewest number of dimension members. OLAP cubes can handle sparse data and we can compress them so that I/O is minimized and hence performance is improved. Cubes in OLAP 11G come with a new feature called **cost-based aggregation**. If the cube is compressed, then we can specify a percentage amount and Oracle OLAP will pre-compute the most costly aggregations based on our input. We can have stored (or base) measures and calculated measures in a cube.

Execute the following statement as `sysdba` to give the necessary privileges to `packt_schema` to create an analytic workspace:

```
GRANT create procedure, create session, create dimension, Create
materialized view, advisor, olap_user, olap_xs_admin, unlimited
tablespace to packt_schema;
```

Open **Analytic Workspace Manager** and create a workspace as shown in the following screenshot:

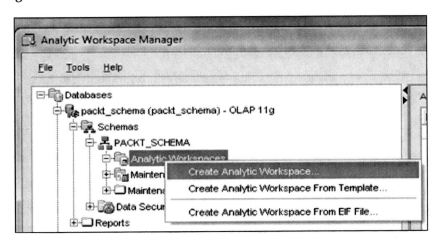

Once we have defined an analytic workspace, we can start creating our dimensions. We can create a **REGION** dimension and then create a hierarchy on top of this dimension. In a **REGION** dimension, the highest level can be **ALL REGIONS** followed by the **COUNTRY** level, and **CITY** can be the lowest level of the **REGION_HIERARCHY**. We can also define a few attributes for the dimension. Once the dimension is ready, we can map our physical tables to the analytical workspace by getting into the **Mappings** section. With all these things in place, our analytic workspace should look like the following screenshot:

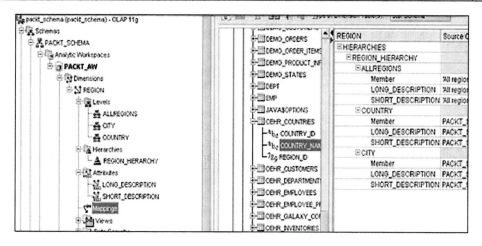

The stage is now set to create OLAP cubes using the available dimensions. When we are creating a cube, we can check the **Use Compression** check box under the **Storage** tab to compress the storage of the cube. Doing this significantly improves the performance. If any dimension of the cube is sparse, then we can check the **Sparse** check box of the dimension and OLAP will create a special index for the dimension which will automatically manage sparsity. We can classify a dimension as sparse if a large number of measure cells become null when we add this dimension to the model. For example, the ratio of the amount of products bought by any one customer to the total number of products in a supermarket will be small. So the product dimension can be classified as sparse because adding the product dimension to the model will result in a lot of measure columns as null. **Precompute** tab under the **Aggregation** tab can be used to specify cost based aggregation percentage if we have chosen to compress our cube. We can use this to direct OLAP to pre-compute the costliest aggregations based on our input here. Finally we can create measures in the cube and map our columns to the relational sources. OLAP cubes can also be represented as cube organized materialized views that offer significant performance improvement over traditional **Materialized Views (MVs)**. The query rewrite feature automatically converts the queries on the relational tables to cube MVs leading to significant performance gains. These are particularly helpful in summary management of BI applications.

OLAP creates views for every cube. These views are visible in the AWM and can be used to query cube data. **PACKT_CUBE_VIEW**, in the next screenshot, is one such view:

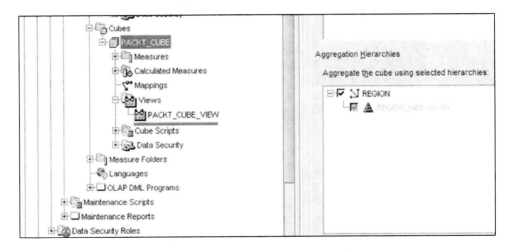

Analytical workspace or cubes can be exported to **Oracle Business Intelligence Enterprise Edition (OIBEE)** but to do that you will have to configure the OBIEE plugin for AWM. More details on it, you can refer to the following link:

`http://st-curriculum.oracle.com/obe/db/11g/r1/olap/biee/`
`createbieemetadata.htm`

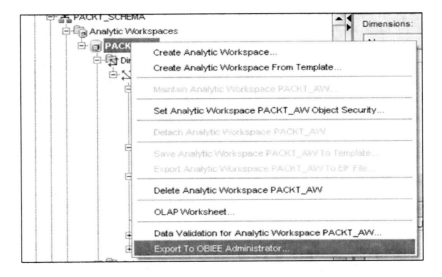

The views of a cube present the measures and dimension attributes and typically no aggregation is required on top of the data presented by these views since the data is already summarized in the OLAP engine. A single query with different values in the `where` clause can be used to get the data at different levels. Every OLAP hierarchy and dimension view contains a **LEVEL_NAME** column. The value in this column is the name of the OLAP hierarchy level object. By specifying a value for this column in the `where` clause we can aggregate the data at the specified level of the hierarchy. Since the queries on cubes can be executed using views we can easily use OLAP cubes in APEX in both interactive and classic reports.

Please visit the following documents for more information:

- `http://www.oracle.com/technetwork/database/options/olap/index.html`
- `http://st-curriculum.oracle.com/obe/db/11g/r1/olap/cube/buildicubes.htm`
- `http://st-curriculum.oracle.com/obe/db/11g/r1/olap/cube/querycubes.htm`
- `http://st-curriculum.oracle.com/obe/db/11g/r1/olap/apex/usingapex4olap.htm`

`DBMS_CUBE`, `DBMS_CUBE_LOG`, and `DBMS_CUBE_ADVISE` package have been built to assist you in dealing with OLAP cubes. You might want to check the functions and procedures in them. `DBMS_AW_STATS` can be used to manage optimizer statistics for cubes and dimensions.

Understanding Oracle's advanced queuing

Oracle provides an advanced queuing functionality to enable the developers to do asynchronous messaging. We will now try to understand **advanced queues** (AQs) and will look at some of the packages which can help us use them in APEX. AQs enable reliable communication among different systems with different workloads in the enterprise and gives improved performance. Since AQs are built in the database, they leverage all operational benefits of the database such as reliability and scalability. The following are the two major terms associated with an AQ:

- **Message**: This is the message that one part of the enterprise wants to send to another.

- **Message queues**: Messages are stored in queues which are empowered with all queuing functions like enqueue, dequeue and so on. These queues can be of any type including ANYDATA data type. If you remember, we used this ANYDATA to run dynamic queries from table function. ANYDATA almost does the same function here by enabling the user to queue messages of different data type in a single queue.

Message routing is possible using message attributes which can be transformed using complex logic. Messages can either be persistent if the need is to store them for a longer duration for audit purposes or can be transient. Security is ensured by the granting of appropriate privileges to the users. Users can either have queue level privileges or can be an administrator. A user becomes an AQ administrator if he/she is granted aq_administrator_role role. AQ users have aq_user_role role and have execute privileges on the queue. Execute privilege on the queue can be granted using DBMS_AQADM.GRANT_QUEUE_PRIVILEGE. Privileges can be granted by the DBA. Subscribers can be added using DBMS_AQADM.ADD_SUBSCRIBER and the transformations of the messages can be done using DBMS_TRANSFORM.CREATE_TRANSFORMATION. Queuing operations such as enqueuing and dequeuing can be done using functions such as DBMS_AQ.ENQUEUE and DBMS_AQ.DEQUEUE. Message queue propagation enables the user to put the message from one queue to another. This propagation can either be a back ground job or can be executed on a need-by-need basis.

To implement a queue, we must follow the given steps:

1. Create a type. This type will be the type of all our messages.
2. Create a queue table using DBMS_AQADM.CREATE_QUEUE_TABLE and a queue using DBMS_AQADM.CREATE_QUEUE.
3. Start a queue using DBMS_AQADM.START_QUEUE.

Some of the packages, other than DBMS_AQADM, that may interest you are DBMS_AQ, DBMS_AQELM, DBMS_AQIN, and DBMS_AQJMS. While DBMS_AQELM can be used for email notification, DBMS_AQIN and DBMS_AQJMS can be used to provide secure access to Oracle JMS interfaces. Read the following document for more details on AQ:

```
http://docs.oracle.com/cd/E11882_01/server.112/e11013/toc.htm
```

Understanding other APEX features

This book is focused on reporting and I haven't done justice to some of the interesting features of APEX. I wish to dedicate this small section to such features; you can read about these in more detail in the documentation, should you find them interesting.

Understanding locking and unlocking of pages and team development

If a team of developers are working on an application, then each developer can lock the page on which he is working by the lock icon on the top right corner of the page. If the lock on the page is up for grabs then the lock symbol will be open as shown in the following screenshot:

If the lock has been acquired then the lock symbol will be locked as shown in the following screenshot:

We can click on the **Application Utilities** button on an APEX page, and then click on the **Cross Page** Utilities to get a link for **Page Locks** administration. The last link in the following screenshot is for the **Page Locks** administration:

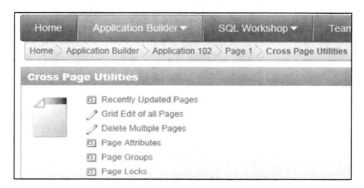

Another related concept is team development. We can click on the **Team Development** menu on the top of our workspace to find a number of options for managing your projects and bugs. These options are shown in the following screenshot:

Understanding database object dependencies report

Database object dependencies report is also an interesting feature as it lets us create a checklist of all the objects used in an application. It lists all the dependent objects of the current application but it does not list the objects used in your stored packages, functions, and procedures.

Understanding advisor

The advisor utility suggests ways to improve your written code. For example, it names the reports which should have a default order and items which should have a help text.

Understanding shortcuts

APEX shortcuts are a way of reducing code redundancy. Plugins also do the same thing, but plugins can easily be put from one application to the other, while shortcuts are local to an application and are a means of putting the same piece of code in multiple places in the same application. A shortcut can be created for a PL/SQL code or an image or an HTML code, or JavaScript. Obviously, CSS can also be bundled with the HTML code. The link to create shortcuts can be seen in **Shared Components**.

Understanding data loading wizard

You can create a page of type **Data Loading** which will help you create a wizard for loading data into the database. The page creation wizard that helps you create a **Data Loading** page also gives you options of configuring lookup tables and transformations. The **Create page** wizard results in the creation of four pages instead of a single page. This set of four pages helps you load data with each page corresponding to each step in the data loading process. You have a **Data Loading** link in the **Shared Components** of an application. This link can be used to change the Data Load Definition which includes transformation and lookups.

Understanding application express views

APEX views are a great help. These views give more information about APEX objects created by you. For example, `APEX_APPLICATION_PAGE_FLASH5` lists the information such as chart type, chart name, region ID, component signature, or any other information that you might want about your charts. I suggest that you have a look at these. These views are available in your APEX schema.

Understanding background jobs in APEX

Background jobs might be required to perform certain operations that are required for the proper functioning of the application. These jobs can include tasks such as triggering an ETL operation. The story of background jobs in APEX starts at `APEX_PLSQL_JOB` package and ends with it. This package in turn calls `DBMS_JOB` which actually does the job. Functions available in this package are `SUBMIT_PROCESS`, `UPDATE_JOB_STATUS`, `TIME_ELAPSED`, `JOBS_ARE_ENABLED` and, `PURGE_PROCESS`.

`DBMS_JOB` has been superseded by `DBMS_SCHEDULER` which is the recommended package to use these days. `DBMS_SCHEDULER` was introduced in 10G and has a number of features such as job history and event based jobs. One important distinction between `DBMS_JOB` and `DBMS_SCHEDULER` is that `DBMS_SCHEDULER` performs an implicit commit while `DBMS_JOB` does not. This non committing feature increases the usability of `DBMS_JOB`. `DBMS_SCHEDULER` in 11gR2 and has email job notification as well. `CREATE_FILE_WATCHER` of `DBMS_SCHEDULER` procedure helps you in consuming feeds which you might receive from other systems. It triggers a job when a file arrives. `DBMS_SCHEDULER.GET_FILE` helps you fetch a file from a folder on your machine and returns its contents in `file_contents OUT` parameter. `DBMS_SCHEDULER.PUT_FILE` can be used to put a file on any system that does not have Oracle database installed on it. **Oracle remote scheduler agent** should however be there on such a system. `UTL_FILE` can be used for similar purposes but it will need an Oracle installation. `DBMS_SCHEDULER.CREATE_CHAIN` can be used to create a chain of programs. This is helpful if the output of one task is fed as an input to the other.

Before using other functions of `APEX_PLSQL_JOB`, execute `APEX_PLSQL_JOB.JOBS_ARE_ENABLED` to find out whether job scheduling is enabled on the database or not. `APEX_PLSQL_JOB.SUBMIT_PROCESS` returns a job ID when you create a job using it. This job ID is useful to do all job related operations such as purging for the job. Since you can call web services from PL/SQL procedures, you can use APEX's job scheduling to trigger jobs in some other parts of the enterprise.

Knowing about important functions from the API

We will now talk about some of the important packages which can help you in the development process. We haven't seen examples of the implementation of some of these packages but I hope that this little discussion will give you a good idea about the use of these packages. Let's begin.

Knowing about the APEX API

APEX_APPLICATION_INSTALL is built to give you a substitute to the usual UI install. It lets you set the values like the application number which you usually set when you are using the UI to install an application. I once used this package to install one application multiple times in a workspace using a single export. All export files in APEX 4.*x* contain reference to values set by this package. Values that can be set include the owner schema, application id, workspace id, alias, and image prefix.

APEX_CSS can be used to include CSS files in the HTML generated by APEX. It can also be used to put CSS code in the HTML page. The fact that this is a PL/SQL package gives you the freedom to call it form almost anywhere in your application. Its close brother is APEX_JAVASCRIPT package which lets you put JavaScript code in your application using PL/SQL.

APEX_CUSTOM_AUTH deals with APEX session management. Procedures like DEFINE_USER_SESSION can be used for creating a session ID for a user. GET_COOKIE_PROPS helps you find out the properties of the cookies associated with APEX session management. GET_LDAP_PROPS helps you get the properties of the current LDAP session (if LDAP security is used). This package also has a number of procedures to get various properties of a session such as the session ID and the user name. Login procedure does the authentication and registers an APEX session for you. Logout does the opposite.

APEX_ERROR can be used to give more teeth to your error handling mechanisms. ADD_ERROR can be used to add your own error to an existing error stack. The package has its own result type that lets you bundle all error related information in a single structure.

If you are one of those who believe, that logging into the INTERNAL workspace for admin related tasks like creating workspace, setting the email, and printing server configurations is a lot of work then APEX_INSTANCE_ADMIN package is for you. ADD_SCHEMA procedure can be used to add a schema to an existing workspace, workspaces can be created using ADD_WORKSPACE, email and printing server configurations can be set by using SET_PARAMETER function. Check the following link to find the list of parameters that can be set:

http://docs.oracle.com/cd/E37097_01/doc/doc.42/e35127/apex_instance.htm

The package also has procedures to remove schemas, applications, and saved interactive reports.

The APEX_ITEM package can be used to dynamically create most of the items you see in the **Create Item page** wizard.

APEX_MAIL is built on top of UTL_SMTP and is used for sending mails. It provides easier procedures and functions to do tasks which can also be done using UTL_SMTP. Procedures and functions include ADD_ATTACHMENT, and SEND. PUSH_QUEUE is another method which can be used to send all the unsent messages which exist in APEX_MAIL_LOG table. These mails also include the mails send by APEX mail page processes and the mails generated on account of the subscriptions in APEX such as those of interactive reports. Similarly, APEX_LDAP has been built to simplify the process of extracting information stored in an LDAP server. You can get the same information using DBMS_LDAP and DBMS_LDAP_UTIL as well.

APEX_LANG is to facilitate the translation of text from one language to the other.

If you are thinking about creating a plugin then you should first have a deep and good look at APEX_PLUGIN and APEX_PLUGIN_UTIL packages. Every function in these packages is unique in its own way and has a very specific purpose in the plugin creation process.

APEX_UI_DEFAULT_UPDATE lets you set some default values in the APEX development environment and might help you save some development time.

APEX_UTIL is by far the most useful package for an APEX developer. DOWNLOAD_PRINT_DOCUMENT and GET_PRINT_DOCUMENT are two very important functions for report printing. These functions need template (rtf or xsl-fo) and your data to generate a report. You will however have to pass the URI of a printing engine which will do the processing.

You can store the report query and layout in your **Shared Components** as well, if you do not have them as BLOBs or CLOBs. dbms_xmlgen.getxml comes in handy while using these two functions because it lets you convert the data returned by your query to an XML. APEX_UTIL has many procedures and these procedures do not fall in any single category. My humble suggestion is to go through this package, because the functions in this package will ease of your development workload and you will spend lesser time in reinventing the wheel. The same suggestion applies for the JavaScript API of APEX.

Knowing about the database API

Change data capture systems load data in the data warehouses and Oracle helps you do that using DBMS_CDC_PUBLISH, DBMS_CAPTURE_ADM, and DBMS_CDC_SUBSCRIBE packages.

DBMS_CQ_NOTIFICATION is a trigger in many ways. It can send notifications and does certain job on the execution of DDL and DML on the objects associated with the queries that are registered with DBMS_CQ_NOTIFICATION.

DBMS_CRYPTO and DBMS_OBFUSCATION_TOOLKIT are for encryption and decryption purposes. DBMS_CRYPTO is the newer one of the two.

DBMS_DATA_MINING and DBMS_DATA_MINING_TRANSFORM are for your data mining requirements. DBMS_DATA_MINING implements a number of mining models which help you predict the future based on your historical data while DBMS_DATA_MINING_TRANSFORM holds a number of transformation functions. DBMS_PREDICTIVE_ANALYTICS takes data mining a step further by helping you to mine the data so that it is meaningful to a wider audience.

DBMS_COMPARISON is to compare data in different databases and update the objects in one database based on those in the other.

DBMS_DEBUG helps in the debugging of the target session using another session.

You can create dimensions using the Create Dimension statement. Creating dimensions is not necessary but if you are working in a data warehouse with star schema and hierarchies then creating dimensions can enable more complex types of query rewrite which can significantly improve your performance. DBMS_DIMENSION package and the **Enterprise Manager Dimension** wizard can be used for the management of these.

DBMS_ERRLOG is useful in cases where your data isn't clean enough and the insertion of records often fails because, one row out of some thousand odd rows was not good enough to be inserted. DBMS_ERRLOG can help you create a log table which can hold the bad record while the good ones are inserted. We can log errors in DML statements by adding an extra clause like the following:

```
LOG ERRORS INTO ERROR_LOG_TABLE REJECT LIMIT 1
```

In the preceding clause ERROR_LOG_TABLE stands for the table created with DBMS_ERRLOG package. A table created by DBMS_ERRLOG is a normal table with a few columns used for error logging purpose.

DBMS_FILE_TRANSFER is for file related operations like coping and transferring of files. There are other ways to do this, but this one is the easiest.

DBMS_FLASHBACK_ARCHIVE and DBMS_FLASHBACK are for retrieving and managing flashback data.

DBMS_REFRESH and DBMS_MVIEW are for materialized views.

UTL_RECOMP is for recompiling invalid objects.

DBMS_XMLPARSER is used for the parsing of XML documents.

Summary

This chapter was meant to introduce some of the advanced features of APEX and Oracle database. We started this chapter with HTML image maps and then moved on to learn about PSPs and the loadjava utility. This chapter introduced FusionCharts to you which is a freeware and can be used for the generation of FlashCharts and can be a good substitute for AnyChart. Tag clouds can be seen in almost all places on the internet so it was prudent to see a method to create tag clouds in APEX. We saw websheets and plugins which are the two most important improvements in APEX 4.*x*. We also saw the method to configure mails in APEX and to download APEX applications without webserver. We learned about Oracle OLAP cubes and Oracle Advanced Queues. We also explored some of the interesting features of APEX and some of the lesser known PL/SQL packages of APEX and Oracle.

The next chapter will focus on other technologies which can be coupled with APEX to give an enriched user experience. The next chapter talks about some of the PL/SQL packages which can generate reports. We will also explore **Jasper** and **Eclipse BIRT** in it. We will then move on to a chapter about **OBIEE 11G,** which will include a detail discussion on **BI Publisher** as well. The next chapters will focus on integrations of tools and migration of reports from other technologies to APEX. The final chapter will be on tuning. Till now, our boat was in the river of APEX and we are about to enter the sea of reporting. I hope you like the adventure.

6

Using PL/SQL Reporting Packages, Jasper, and Eclipse BIRT

The focus of this chapter is to explore ways and means to generate reports using reporting solutions such as **PL/PDF, PL_FPDF, Apache FOP, Apache Cocoon, Jasper,** and **Eclipse BIRT**. The following are the major learning outcomes of this chapter.

- Generating reports using PL/PDF
- Generating reports using PL_FPDF
- Creating XLS, RTF, CSV, and HTML documents using PL/SQL
- Generating reports using Apache FOP
- Generating reports using Apache Cocoon
- Creating reports in Jasper and integrating it with APEX
- Creating reports in Eclipse BIRT and integrating it with APEX

Before we begin, let us install the Chapter 6 reference application (`4-98-9_06_chapter6.sql`) and the Chapter 06-B reference application (`4-98-9_06_chapter6-B.sql`).

APEX reporting using PL/PDF and PL_FPDF

Both PL/PDF and PL_FPDF can be used for the generation of PDF documents. We will start our discussion with PL/PDF and then move on to creating PDF documents using PL_FPDF.

Creating PDF using PL/PDF

The process of creating documents using PL/PDF begins by downloading the installation pack (Version 2.7.0) from `http://www.plpdf.com/`. The installation pack installs the trial version, which can help us generate a maximum of five-page long PDF documents.

It is good to logically separate this code from the rest of the application code so `plpdf.com` suggests creating a separate schema. Unzip `plpdf-v270.zip` (installation pack) and execute `1_create_user.sql` from the `sys` user to create the `plpdf` schema and to grant necessary privileges to it. These grants include `select` on `sys.V_$DATABASE` and `execute` on `sys.DBMS_CRYPTO` to `plpdf`. The password of this schema is also `plpdf`. Log in as `plpdf` and execute `2_install_objects.sql` to install the necessary objects for pdf printing. Execute `3_compile_schema.sql` as `plpdf` to compile any invalid objects. The `3_compile_schema.sql` script uses `dbms_utility.compile_schema` to compile all objects of the schema, which is passed to it as an argument.

We can have the PLPDF code in any page process APEX, and call the page process on the click of a button. You can check out an example to create a PDF document in the **PL PDF** region on the third page of the reference application. The button to download it is in the first page of the application. Note that if any object of the `plpdf` schema is used, then the corresponding grants will have to be given to `packt_schema`. So execute the following to enable the use of PLPDF in our APEX application.

```
Grant execute on plpdf.plpdf to packt_schema;
Create public synonym plpdf for plpdf.plpdf;
```

Let us now look at the code.

```
declare
l_blob blob;
begin
Plpdf.init; Plpdf.NewPage;
Plpdf.SetPrintFont('Arial',NULL,12);
```

```
Plpdf.PrintCell(50,10,'Hello World');
Plpdf.SendDoc(l_blob);
owa_util.mime_header('application/pdf',FALSE);
htp.p('Content-Length: ' || dbms_lob.getlength(l_blob));
owa_util.http_header_close;
WPG_DOCLOAD.download_file (l_blob);
END;
```

The code starts with `Plpdf.init`. Every new page should start with `Plpdf.NewPage`. `Plpdf.SetPrintFont` is to set the font and `Plpdf.SendDoc` has an out argument which returns the PDF document as a `blob`. This `blob` can then be downloaded by first setting the header, and then invoking the `WPG_DOCLOAD.download_file` procedure. The header is set using the highlighted code.

Run first page of the reference application and hit the **PL PDF** button to get a PDF document generated using PL/PDF. Note that the trial version of PL/PDF puts a water mark on the documents.

The important point is that PL/PDF gives a viable alternative to the report printing needs in Oracle APEX. Traditionally, BI Publisher is used for PDF printing, but if your report printing needs are limited, then you could save your BI Publisher license money by using the trial version of PL/PDF.

 Plpdf has also come up with plxls, which as you might have guessed, lets you generate an XLS document using PL/SQL. It is also important to note that APEX Listener 2.x can also help us with our report printing requirements.

Creating PDF using PL_FPDF

`PL_FPDF` is another package that can help us in PDF printing. The first F in `PL_FPDF` stands for *free*. `PL_FPDF` is a PL/SQL wrapper around FPDF which is a PHP class and does the business of generating PDF files. More info on the FPDF library can be found at `http://www.fpdf.org/`. Check out the following link to know more about `PL_FPDF`:

`http://www.erasme.org/PL-FPDF,1337?lang=en`

You can download the package from the following link:

`https://github.com/Pilooz/pl_fpdf`

The lack of good documentation is the biggest problem with PL_FPDF. So if you wish to know about the functions and procedures in the pl_fpdf package then you will have to have a good scan of the entire code package. Compile the package, create a synonym, pl_fpdf, in packt_schema for the package, and grant execute on pl_fpdf to package packt_schema.

Let us now look at the code in the reference application that uses PL_FPDF. Have a look at the **PL FPDF** region of the third page of the reference application. The code is responsible to print a PDF document with Hello World in it. It starts with setting the page layout. This is followed by the opening of the document, addition of a page, setting of the font, putting the text in a cell, and finally outputting the document.

```
begin
    pl_fpdf.FPDF('P','cm','A4');
    pl_fpdf.openpdf; pl_fpdf.AddPage();
    pl_fpdf.SetFont('Arial','B',16);
    pl_fpdf.Cell(0,1.2,'Hello World',0,1,'C');
    pl_fpdf.Output();
end;
```

This brings us to the end of the section dealing with PDF generation. We will now look at a few methods to generate reports in other formats.

Process to create RTF, XLS, CSV, and HTML documents

If we wish to generate simple RTF, XLS, CSV, and HTML files, then we can code them ourselves. This involves a little effort, but it's worth it, as it saves us the license cost.

RTF, CSV, and HTML printing

RTF documents have their own syntax just like HTML documents. Write the text, which you wish to show, in WordPad and save it as an RTF file. Open this file in Notepad and you will see the code responsible for generating the document. We can use this to frame the text, which can then be downloaded using wpg_docload. download_file. I used this process to build the following code sample. This has been implemented in the **RTF document generator** process on the third page of the reference application. The button to run this process is on the first page of the reference application.

```
declare
l_blob blob;
begin
dbms_lob.createTemporary(l_blob, true);
dbms_lob.open(l_blob, dbms_lob.lob_readwrite);
dbms_lob.append(l_blob,utl_raw.cast_to_raw('{\rtf1\ansi\ansicpg1252\
deff0\deflang1033{\fonttbl{\f0\fnil\fcharset0 Calibri;}}
{\*\generator Msftedit 5.41.21.2510;}\viewkind4\uc1\pard\sa200\sl276\
slmult1\lang9\f0\fs22 Hello, I am \b bold\b0\par
}'));
   dbms_lob.close(l_blob);
owa_util.mime_header('application/msword',FALSE);
htp.p('Content-Disposition: attachment; filename=abc.rtf');
htp.p('Content-Length: ' || dbms_lob.getlength(l_blob));
owa_util.http_header_close;
WPG_DOCLOAD.download_file (l_blob);
END;
```

I suggest that you use WordPad instead of Microsoft Word for this purpose, because Microsoft Word generates a lot of formatting code, which might not be necessary for our purpose. If you plan to use this approach to generate RTF files, then the following three links will be useful:

```
http://www.pindari.com/rtf1.html
```

```
http://www.pindari.com/rtf2.html
```

```
http://www.pindari.com/rtf3.html
```

To generate HTML documents, you just have to replace the RTF code with HTML code. You will have to set the header for HTML and then download the blob using `wpg_docload.download_file`.

The same process works for CSV files as well. CSV files have comma separated values, so you will have to make sure that the columns of your output are comma separated. String aggregation functions such as `listagg` will prove helpful here. APEX also gives you the option to download reports in CSV files. So you honestly do not have to put an extra effort for CSV download.

XLS document generation

XLS documents can be created using XML. Special tags with namespaces can be used for the creation of an XLS document. This XML contains all kinds of formatting required for an XLS file. We can save this XML file as `.xls` and open it using Microsoft Excel. The use of XML, for generating XLS documents, is similar to HTML, which has its own special tags but is inherently an XML document. We can put "Hello, I'm bold" in an XLS file using the following code:

```
<?xml version="1.0"?>
<Workbook xmlns="urn:schemas-microsoft-com:office:spreadsheet"
 xmlns:spreadsheet="urn:schemas-microsoft-com:office:spreadsheet">
 <Worksheet spreadsheet:Name="Example">
 <spreadsheet:Table>
    <spreadsheet:Row>
<spreadsheet:Cell>
    <spreadsheet:Data spreadsheet:Type="String"
    xmlns="http://www.w3.org/TR/REC-html40">
        Hello, I am <B>Bold</B>.</spreadsheet:Data>
</spreadsheet:Cell>
    </spreadsheet:Row>
</spreadsheet:Table>
 </Worksheet>
</Workbook>
```

Open a text editor and save the file as `example.xls` and then open it in Microsoft Excel. We can put the above code in a `blob` column and download the file using `wpg_docload.download_file` in APEX. We can get more information about the tags used for the generation of XLS documents from `http://msdn.microsoft.com/en-us/library/office/aa140066(v=office.10).aspx`.

> Tom Kyte has developed the `owa_sylk` package, which can also be used for XLS document generation. The following links will be informative:
>
> `http://en.wikipedia.org/wiki/SYmbolic_LinK_(SYLK)`
>
> `http://asktom.oracle.com/pls/asktom/`
> `f?p=100:11:0:::::P11_QUESTION_ID:728625409049`

APEX reporting using fop and Cocoon

Report printing using the **fop** package and **Cocoon** are one of the standard ways of report printing in APEX. So let's see how it's done.

We first have to create an ACL to enable external network access in the Oracle database. Use the following code snippet for this:

```
SQL> exec DBMS_NETWORK_ACL_ADMIN.CREATE_ACL('apex_users.xml','APEX
Users','APEX_040200', TRUE, 'connect');
SQL> exec DBMS_NETWORK_ACL_ADMIN.ASSIGN_ACL('apex_users.xml','*');
SQL> commit;
```

Do not forget to add `commit` at the end.

Once ACL has been set, we have to deploy `fop.war` on Weblogic. `fop.war` can be found in `<Directory in which apex_4.1.1_en.zip is unzipped>\apex\utilities\fop`.

> APEX Listener 2.x has fop tightly integrated in it. So, you don't have to do the configuration described in the next section if you are using APEX Listener 2.x. You can just select Oracle APEX Listener in the Print Server dropdown by navigating to **Manage Instance | Instance Settings | Report Printing** section to enable report printing using APEX Listener.

APEX reporting using fop.war and WebLogic

> The code pack consists of fop directory. You can deploy this open directory on WebLogic to install fop. You can also follow the process below to install `fop`.

The steps involved to install `fop.war` on WebLogic are:

1. Unzip `fop.war`.

   This step is required because report printing requires classes such as `DOMParser` and `XMLProcessor`. Before deploying, our fop application should have a JAR that has these classes. The `xmlparserv2.jar` file in `<Oracle_database_home>/lib` has these classes. So we unzip `fop.war`, and then put `xmlparserv2.jar` in `WEB-INF/lib` of the unzipped `fop.war` file directory. Now this unzipped directory can be installed as an application in WebLogic, just as we install a war file.

2. Login to the WebLogic console using the admin credentials.

3. Click on the **Deployments** link under the **Domain Structure** panel on the left-hand side of the page.

4. Click on the **Install** button.

5. Browse for the directory that contains the contents of the `fop.war` file along with the `xmlparserv2.jar` file in the **Path** browse item and click on **Next**.

6. Select the **Install this deployment as an application** radio button and click on **Next**.

7. Select **DD Only: Use only roles and policies that are defined in the deployment descriptors** in the **Security** section, and **Use the defaults defined by the deployment's targets** in the **Source accessibility** section. Then click on **Next**.

8. Select **Yes, take me to the deployment's configuration screen** and click on the **Finish** button. Click on the **Save** button after the deployment is done.

9. Go to the list of deployments again and make sure that the newly deployed fop application is in the **Active** state.

Now, we have to configure APEX to use `fop.war`. Login to the **INTERNAL** workspace, by going to **Manage Instance | Instance Settings | Report Printing** section and change the settings as shown in the following screenshot:

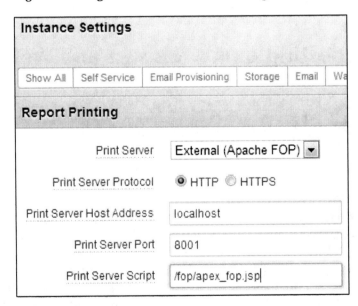

Note that you will have to change Print Server Host Address and Print Server Port according to your environment. Now we can create a report and then go to the **Print Attributes** page of it. This page gives us a number of options for configuring our report. The link in the **Print URL** textbox can be used as a target of any button if we wish to generate our own report printing link. The **Output Format** text box lets us select the desired output format of our report. Selecting **Yes** in the **Enable Report Printing** dropdown gives us a link at the bottom of the report region on our application page. You can find one such report with a download link on the second page of the reference application.

APEX reporting using Apache Cocoon and WebLogic

Apache Cocoon is a XML and XSLT-based Java application that helps in publishing reports in most of the known formats. Although Cocoon can use a number of different data sources, we will use it for the publishing of APEX reports. Cocoon can be configured as a report printing agent for APEX. The following are the steps to do the same:

 The code pack consists of the cocoon directory. You can deploy this open directory on WebLogic to install cocoon. You can also follow the process below to install cocoon.

1. Download cocoon-2.1.11-src.zip from `http://www.apache.org/dist/cocoon/` and unzip it.

2. Set the JAVA_HOME environment variable and test it using the following command:

    ```
    C:> echo %JAVA_HOME%
    ```

    The above command should return a value similar to the following:

    ```
    C:\Program Files (x86)\Java\jdk1.6.0_26
    ```

3. Open a command prompt and go to the `<Directory in which cocoon-2.1.11-src.zip is unzipped>\cocoon-2.1.11` folder and run the `build.bat` file.

4. Get `fop_post.zip` from `http://apex.oracle.com/i/carl/apex_cocoon/fop_post.zip` and unzip it.

5. Put the unzipped `fop_post` folder in `<Directory in which cocoon-2.1.11-src.zip is unzipped>\cocoon-2.1.11\build\webapp`.

6. Open a command prompt and change the directory to `<The directory in which cocoon-2.1.11-src.zip is unzipped>\cocoon-2.1.11>` and then run the following:

```
C:> build war
```

This `build` command executes the `build.bat` file which uses the ANT utility shipped in `cocoon-2.1.11-src.zip` to build a web application for us. If everything works well then you should get a message similar to the following:

```
BUILD SUCCESSFUL
Total time: 2 minutes 48 seconds
```

7. You will find `cocoon.war` in `<Directory in which cocoon-2.1.11-src.zip is unzipped>\cocoon-2.1.11\build\cocoon`.

This WAR file can be deployed on OC4J without any troubles, but you would need the `weblogic.xml` file to deploy on WebLogic. To add `weblogic.xml`, we will have to unzip `cocoon.war` and then put `weblogic.xml` (supplied in the code bundle), with the necessary code, in the `WEB-INF` directory, of the directory containing the unzipped files. The code pack has the `weblogic.xml` file with the necessary configuration. This `weblogic.xml` file is needed so that the `org.apache.log.*` package is loaded from the web class loader and not from the WLS system class loader. We can deploy the open directory of the code pack in WebLogic just as we deployed the fop application. Log in to the WebLogic console and make sure that the deployed application is active.

This ends the Cocoon installation. We now have to configure APEX to use Cocoon. Change the value of the **Print Server Script** textbox in the **Report Printing** section of the **Instance Settings** page to `/cocoon/fop_post/`. My final settings for Cocoon look like the following:

Restart WebLogic once you have changed the settings. Note that you will have
to change **Print Server Host Address** and **Print Server Port** according to your
environment. You can then use the report on the second page of the reference
application for testing Cocoon report printing as well. The same link was used
to test the FOP implementation in the previous section. The report link remains
unaltered, but the backend system to generate the reports has changed.

Creating Jasper reports

Jasper is a reporting tool that can be used to implement a variety of reporting
requirements. While it is possible to install Jasper reports server on WebLogic, we
will see the use of Jasper using a typical install, which includes the **bundled tomcat**
server and the **PostgreSQL** database. If you wish to get the WAR application that
you intend to deploy on a WebLogic server, then you will have to contact the
customer support at `http://support.jaspersoft.com`.

 If you are good at Java then you could deploy the Jasper
library on your web server and then bypass the use of the
Jasper Report Server. This method is more economical
than using the Jasper Report Server.

Let's look at the process of creating a simple report in Jasper and then using it in APEX.

1. Go to the following place and download the installer for your OS:

   `http://www.jaspersoft.com/thanks-download-30-day`

   The same page contains the link to download **iReports**. Get that as well.
   If you don't want the hustle of installing, then you can use the 3 day trial
   period on Jasper's cloud server. Check out the following link for this.
   You will however have to install iReports.

   `https://www.jaspersoft.com/jaspersoft-live-trial`

   Install Jasper server and iReports.

   We will use our `packt_schema` objects for building our reports, so you don't
   have to worry if PostgreSQL does not sound familiar. I will assume that you
   have a Jasper Report Server on Tomcat with PostgreSQL.

2. Now, to use our `oehr_employees` table in our report, we need an Oracle
   connection from the report and for that we need a driver. Copy `ojdbc14.jar`
   from `<ORACLE_HOME>\owb\wf\lib` to `<iReports installation folder>\`
   `platform9\lib`. For example, `C:\Program Files (x86)\Jaspersoft\`
   `iReport-4.7.1\platform9\lib`.

Also put it in `<JasperReports Server install root>/apache-tomcat/lib` for the server.

3. Open iReports and you will see a link to create a database connection on the welcome window itself. A screenshot of this link is shared for your convenience.

Step 1: Create a database connection or setup a data source. Click on the icon to run the connection setup wizard.

Select **Database JDBC connection** in the popup that opens after clicking on that link.

4. Fill in the details to create a connection for the `packt_schema` shown in the following screenshot and hit the **Save** button.

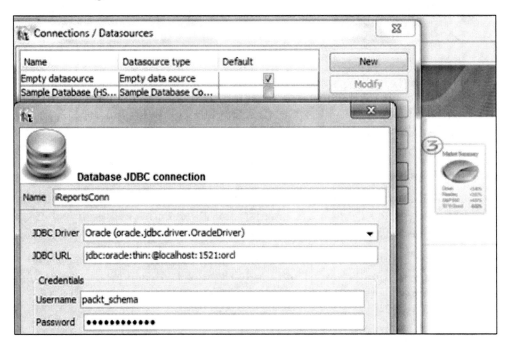

5. Now click on the **step 2** link on the welcome window of iReports. You will get a bunch of options, but you keep the default options. Keeping the defaults will create a blank A4 report for you.

6. Name the report as shown in the following screenshot:

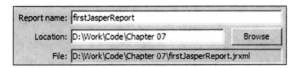

7. Put select * from oehr_employees in the **Query** step of the wizard and select the necessary columns in the **Fields** step of the wizard. The selected columns will appear in the **Fields** section of the **Report Inspector**. Click on **Next** twice and then click on **Finish**.

    You should be able to see the ready arena for you to make a new report. Refer to the following screenshot for your convenience. The lines in the following screenshot are for marking the regions in the report. These regions include the **Title** and **Page header**. You can move these lines by hovering your mouse over them and then dragging them. If you do not want a **Page Header** then reduce its width to zero by dragging. The layout to create the report looks like the following.

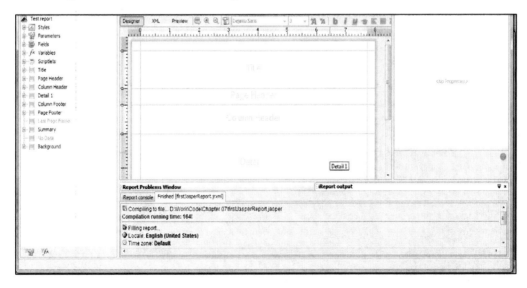

8. Drag a few columns from the **Fields** section present in the **Report Inspector**, which is there on the leftmost side of the window. Drag these columns on the **Detail 1** section. A tool tip can be seen in the **Detail1** section of the previous screenshot. This should help you identify the **Detail1** section.

Right-click on any of these fields/columns and you will find **Edit Expression** on the top of the menu. There are a number of other options to format the field, and I am sure you will have a look at them whenever the need arises. The following screenshot shows the **Palette**, the **Expression editor**, and also the highlighted column.

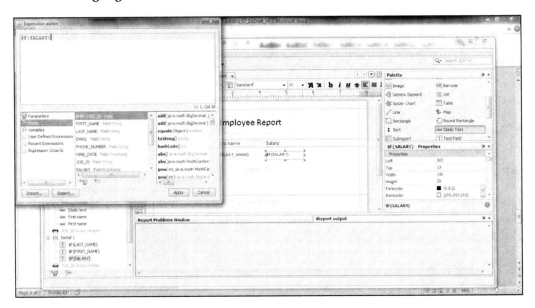

9. You can then drag the **Static Text** item from the **Palette** window on the rightmost side. **Static Text** can be used to create the headings of the columns.

   If **Palette** is not visible then you can select it from the **Window** menu on the top. Check the **Window** menu so that you are aware of the tools you have at your disposal for generating the reports. There are wizards spread all over the window, so I suggest that you explore a little. For example, the highlighted button below helps us to play with the query.

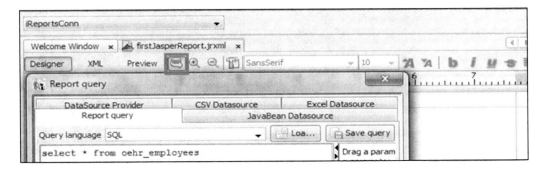

10. Creation of the report is done. Now let's deploy it to the Jasper server. Create a Jasper Server connection by going to the **Repository Navigator** which is present next to **Report Inspector** as shown in the following screenshot. We can get the **Repository Navigator** panel by selecting **JasperReports Server Repository** from the **Window** menu (highlighted in the following screenshot). The first button in the **Repository Navigator** is to add a new server. The following screenshot shows the button:

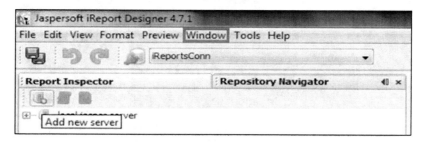

This server connection uses web services to do its job. So we have to give the URL of the repository service to create a connection. The default installation creates jasperadmin/jasperadmin as the admin user, so the same has been used to create the connection. The following screenshot shows the values which help us configure the connection.

11. If you expand the server connection, you will be able to see all the objects on the Jasper server now. Right-click on the folder in which you intend to deploy your report and select **Add | JasperServer Report** as shown in the following screenshot:.

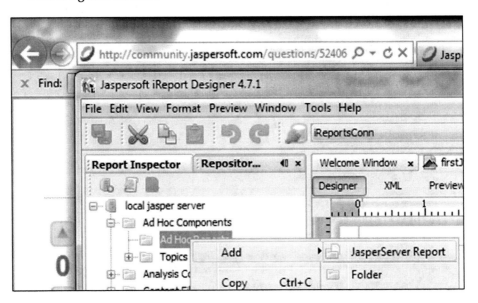

12. The wizard expects you to name the report and then makes you pick the report to be deployed. You can click on the **Get source from current opened report** button. Clicking on the button picks a .jrxml file of the currently open report. This file is converted to a .jasper file, which is used by the Jasper Server.

13. The wizard then expects you to give a data source for the report to run on the server. Select **Locally Defined** and then click on the **Edit local datasource** button and perform the steps as described by the following screenshot:

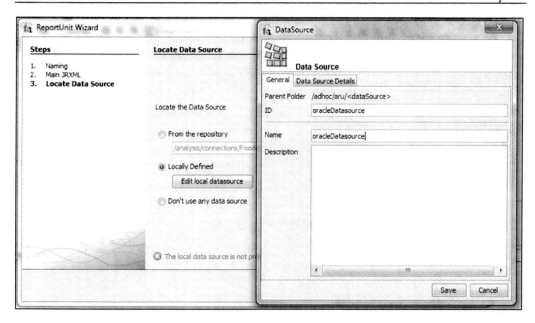

14. Click on the **Data Source Details** tab and then click on the **Import from iReport** button. Select the `packt_schema` connection which you had created earlier. Click on the **Save** and **Finish** buttons.

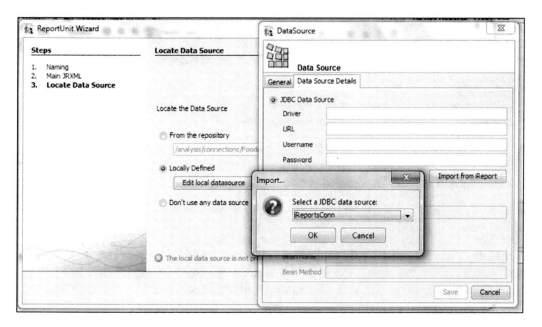

Reports can explicitly be compiled using the compile button on the development window. Compilation is the process of converting the .jrxml file to the .jasper file, which is finally used by the jasper server. The jrxml file is an XML file that contains all the information we had coded using the UI of iReports.

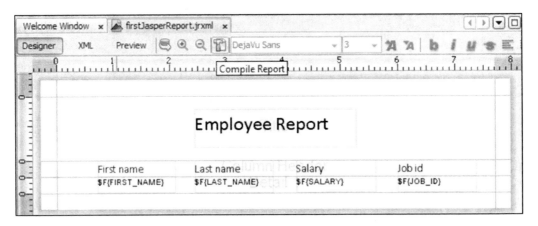

Using Jasper in APEX

There are a number of ways to use Jasper reports in APEX.

Jasper 4.7 gives us both, the **SOAP** and **REST** web services, for using Jasper reports in any third party tool. We will use the RESTful web service to get our reports here. You can check out the detailed web service documentation of Jasper at the following URL:

```
http://community.jaspersoft.com/sites/default/files/docs/
jasperreports-server-web-services-guide.pdf
```

Before we check out the use of RESTful web service, I wish to tell you that Opal-consulting has also come up with a solution which uses freely available methods of integrating APEX with Jasper, and you can find more about it at the following URL:

```
http://www.opal-consulting.de/apex/f?p=20090928:4
```

Go to the second page of the Chapter 6-B reference application. I have hardcoded the values since the purpose is only to display the use of RESTful web service. I guess we have enough experience now to use APEX items in the PL/SQL region, in a bid to make the whole process dynamic. The code is shared as follows for your convenience.

Note that for the code to work you will have to change the hostname, port, report paths, and credentials in the **Rest Jasper** page process on the second page of the reference application.

```
DECLARE
    l_http_req UTL_HTTP.req;  l_http_resp UTL_HTTP.resp;
    l_web_serv_end_pt_url VARCHAR2 (2000) :=
    'http://localhost:8444/jasperserver-
    pro/rest_v2/reports/reports/samples/AllAccounts.pdf';
    l_blob BLOB;  l_raw  RAW(32767);
BEGIN
    l_http_req := UTL_HTTP.begin_request (l_web_serv_end_pt_url,
    'GET', 'HTTP/1.1');
DBMS_LOB.createtemporary(l_blob, FALSE);
        utl_http.set_authentication(r => l_http_req, username =>
        'jasperadmin', password => 'jasperadmin', scheme => 'Basic',
        for_proxy => FALSE);
l_http_resp := UTL_HTTP.get_response (l_http_req);
    BEGIN
      LOOP
        UTL_HTTP.read_raw(l_http_resp, l_raw, 32767);
        DBMS_LOB.writeappend (l_blob, UTL_RAW.length(l_raw), l_raw);
      END LOOP;
    EXCEPTION
      WHEN UTL_HTTP.end_of_body THEN
        UTL_HTTP.end_response(l_http_resp);
    END;
owa_util.mime_header('application/pdf',false); htp.p('Content-
length: ' || dbms_lob.getlength(l_blob));
owa_util.http_header_close; wpg_docload.download_file(l_blob);
end;
```

Let us now understand this code. Right after beginning the request using UTL_ HTTP.begin_request, we authenticate the session using admin jasperadmin/ jasperadmin credentials. The response is collected using UTL_HTTP.get_response, and we then convert the response object to a blob and then put the blob as an argument to wpg_docload.download_file, after setting the header.

A shorter method of doing the same thing is using the HTTPURITYPE.createuri function. The code using this function has also been put as a comment in the **Rest Jasper** page process. The authentication credentials are passed in the URL in this commented code.

The above code uses the `UTL_HTTP` package to send an HTTP request to the RESTful web service. The general syntax of invoking the `Get HTTP` method of the Jasper RESTful web service is given as follows:

```
http://<jasper server hostname>:<jasper server port number>/
jasperserver-pro/rest_v2/reports/<path/to/report>/<Reoprt
name>.<desired report format>
```

Here `rest_v2/reports` is the web service. There are a few more v2 web services. Check the PDF on Jasper web services for more info on this.

An example of the URL Get request to a RESTful webs service is:

```
http://localhost:8444/jasperserver-pro/rest_v2/reports/reports/
samples/AllAccounts.html
```

We can also use the traditional APEX method of creating a RESTful web service reference and then creating a page process that runs the web service. Then, we can use the collection which holds the response to get the document.

This brings us to the end of the discussion on Jasper Reports. We will continue our quest of exploring reporting technologies and the process of gluing them with APEX. The next section is dedicated to Eclipse BIRT, which is one such technology.

Creating reports using Eclipse BIRT and integrating with APEX

Business Intelligence and Reporting Tool (BIRT) is an open source JEE solution that can be used to create high fidelity report outputs in most of the know file formats. BIRT has three major APIs. The first one, called the **Design engine API**, is to help you create your BIRT reports. The second one, called the **Report engine API**, is for consuming your report files on a web server, and the third one, called the **chart engine**, is for displaying the charts on a web server. Let's start the process of creating a report in BIRT.

1. Get your Eclipse BIRT package from the following place:

   ```
   http://download.eclipse.org/birt/downloads/
   ```

2. Unzip the package and then run the **Eclipse Juno** application.

If you get the `Failed to load the JNI shared library "C:\Program Files (x86)\Java\jdk1.6.0_20\bin..\jre\bin\client\jvm.dll"` error while opening `eclipse.exe`, then make sure that your JDK and OS are either both 32 bit or both 64 bit. Then open command prompt and run the following command after getting in the directory which holds `eclipse.exe`:

`D:\Work\Code\Chapter 07\eclipse>eclipse -vm "C:\Program Files\Java\jdk1.6.0_26\bin"`

3. Set your workspace directory.

4. Open the workbench and press *Ctrl + N*.

5. Go to **Business Intelligence and Reporting Tools**.

6. Select **Report Project** and click on **Next**.

7. Enter the name of the project and click on **Finish**.

8. Again press *Ctrl + N* and select **Report** instead of **Report Project**, and click on **Next**.

9. Select your created project and give a name to the report. I named it as `eclipseReport`. The extension of the report design file is `rptdesign`. Click on **Next**.

10. Select **My First Report** as the template and click on **Finish**.

11. You will see the **Data Sources** link in the **Data Explorer** tab present on the left-hand side of the workbench. Right-click on it and select **New Data Source**.

12. Select **JDBC datasource** and click on **Next**.

13. Click on the **Manage Drivers** button.

14. Add `ojdbc14.jar`. The `ojdbc14.jar` file should be present in `<Oracle database home>\owb\wf\lib`. Click on the **OK** button after adding it.

15. After the addition process is completed, you should be able to see **oracle.jdbc.OracleDriver (v10.2)** in the **Driver Class** drop-down. Select the same.

16. Put your database username/password and put `jdbc:oracle:thin:@localhost:1521:orcl` as the **Database URL** and then test the connection. Click on **Finish**.

17. Click on the **Save All** button which is present next to the **Save** button.

18. The next step is to build the data set for the report. Click on **Data Sets** in the **Data Explorer** tab and select **New Data Set**.

19. Select the newly created data source. Let **Data Set Type** be **SQL Select Query**. Put the **Data Set Name** as `Employee Data Set`. Click on **Next**.

20. Put `select * from oehr_employees` in the **Query Text** field and click on **Finish**.

21. You should now get a window listing all the columns of the `oehr_employees` table. You will find **Preview Results** in this window. Select it to verify that the query is able to set the records. Click on **OK**.

    Since you had selected **My First Report** as the template, a table element is inserted by default in your workspace. A table element iterates through all the data rows of a data set.

22. Change the heading of the column and the report as shown in the following screenshot:

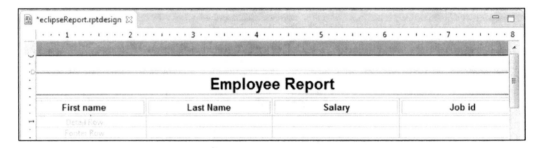

23. Now drag the columns from the **Data Set** section created by you in the **Detail Row** section, which is right beneath the label.

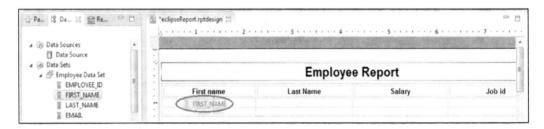

24. Select the **FIRST_NAME** data column and then click on the **Property Editor – Data** tab (highlighted in the following screenshot), present in the lower half of the window.

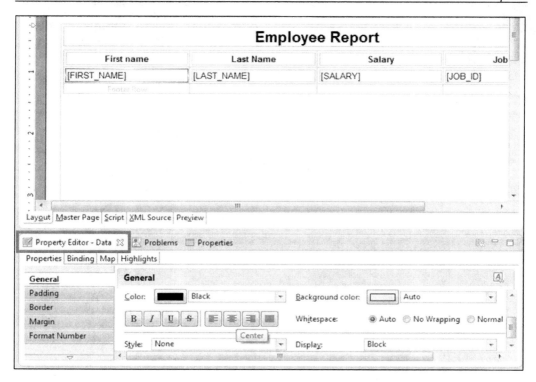

You can use this tab for formatting the data column. Use it to center-align the data column's text. Do the same for other columns as well and save your report.

If you move your mouse pointer to the lower left corner of the table then you will see a **Table** button (highlighted in the following screenshot). If you click on this button then you get to set the properties of the entire table.

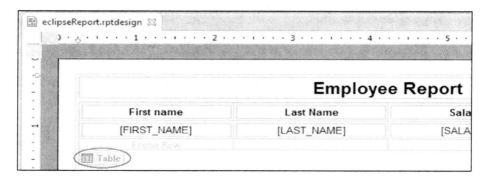

Eclipse BIRT helps you create charts, filter reports, sort and aggregate data, cross tab reports, create interactive views, and so on. Since the code is ours, we can tinker and customize it wherever we want to do so.

You have a **Palette** tab (highlighted in the following screenshot) next to the **Data Explorer** tab. It performs, more or less, the same function as **Palette** in iReports. Right under it are some quick tools for **Aggregation** and for the **Relative Time Period** analysis (highlighted in the following screenshot):

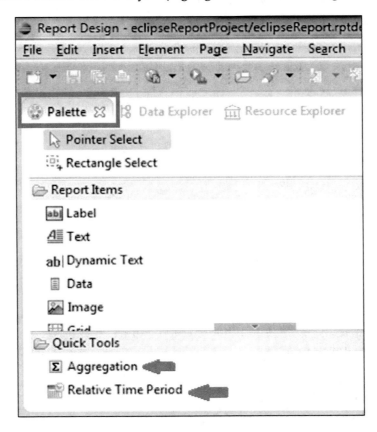

25. You can get a preview in a number of formats by clicking on the preview icon as shown in the following screenshot:

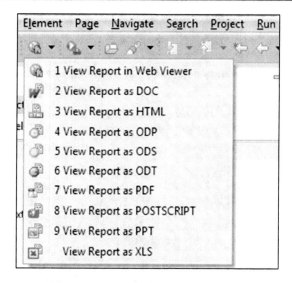

Running the BIRT report on WebLogic

Perform the following for running the BIRT report on WebLogic:

 The code pack consists of the `birt` directory. You can deploy this open directory on WebLogic to install BIRT runtime. You can also follow the process below to install BIRT runtime.

1. Click on the **Runtime** button which is present at the bottom of the button stack in the following link, to download the runtime viewer:

    `http://download.eclipse.org/birt/downloads/`

    Note that deploying BIRT on WebLogic has the following bug:

    `https://bugs.eclipse.org/bugs/show_bug.cgi?id=383926`

    The workaround this bug is to unzip the birt.war file (present in the runtime viewer downloaded from the preceding link) and remove the `org.apache.xerces_2.9.0.v201101211617.jar` file from it.

2. The `<Eclipse workspace directory>/<BIRT project name directory>` folder will have the `.rptdesign` file, that you created in step 9 of the previous list of steps. Put this file in the folder that contains the unzipped `birt.war` file. The same unzipped directory has a `test.rptdesign` file.

3. Log in to the WebLogic console and click on **Deployments**.

4. Click on the **Install** button and browse for the `birt` directory (which was generated after unzipping the `birt.war` file) in the **Path** browse item and click on **Next**.

5. Select the **Install this deployment as an application** radio button and click on **Next**.

6. Select **DD Only: Use only roles and policies that are defined in the deployment descriptors** in the **Security** section, and **Use the defaults defined by the deployment's targets** in the **Source accessibility** section. Then click on **Next**.

7. Select **Yes, take me to the deployment's configuration screen** and click on the **Finish** button. Click on the **Save** button after the deployment is done.

8. Go to the list of deployments again and make sure that the newly deployed BIRT application is in the **Active** state.

9. Open `http://localhost:7001/birt/index.jsp` and click on the **View Example** link. You should be able to see the following report:

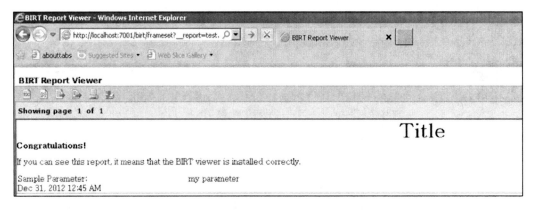

The BIRT installation contains the `eclipseReport.rptdesign` file which was created using Eclipse. We had put this file in step 2. We can execute the report using the following URL:

`http://localhost:7001/birt/frameset?__report=eclipseReport.rptdesign`

Note that previous link has the web server and port of my WebLogic installation. You will have to replace the same with your WebLogic information. The same alert applies to other links in this section. We get links to download out report in a number of formats, but in this case, we are using the `frameset` operation. Our aim is to run the report outside the frame so that we can have a URL to download the report from APEX. To do this, run the report using the following link:

```
http://localhost:7001/birt/run?__report=eclipseReport.rptdesign
```

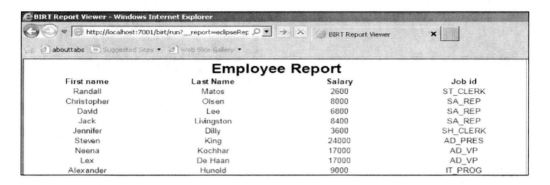

This gives the report in its default format. We can specify the desired format of the report by adding the `_format` option. So if we wish to get the report in PDF format then we can use the following URL:

```
http://localhost:7001/birt/run?__report=eclipseReport.
rptdesign&__format=pdf
```

If you have defined any parameter in the report design, then the parameters can also be passed in the URL, and is separated by ampersand. Check out the following link to find more options:

```
http://www.eclipse.org/birt/phoenix/deploy/viewerUsage.php
```

These URLs can now be invoked from APEX.

10. Linking this in APEX is equally simple. Add a button in APEX and set the **Action** drop-down to **Redirect to URL** in the **Action When Button Clicked** section. The URL can be framed as discussed in step 9.

Clicking on the button will give you your report in the desired format. You can obviously let the user select his desired format at the APEX end and dynamically construct the URL. All this is done for you in the third page of Chapter 06-B reference application. You will have to set the environment as chalked out in the preceding steps to use the reference application.

Ideally, your BIRT report viewer Weblogic web server will be protected by your company's firewall, so security should not be a concern. Questions have however been raised on the security of the URL parameter method of Web Viewer. You can find more information at the following link:

```
https://bugs.eclipse.org/bugs/show_bug.
cgi?id=336767
```

Summary

This chapter brought the understanding of some tools which can be linked with APEX without much impact on the pocket. We started with some packages which have PL/SQL wrappers around them. These include PL/PDF and PL_FPDF. We also had a look at Apache FOP and Apache Cocoon, which can be used as report generation engines in APEX. This was followed by a discussion on Jasper, which is licensed, but is often used with APEX for report generation. The final section was on Eclipse BIRT, which can work wonders with the report without a big footprint on the pocket. We will take this approach of introducing newer tools which can be integrated with APEX, by talking about OBIEE 11*g* in the next chapter. OBIEE has been the the face of Oracle's reporting solution for a number of years now and certainly warrants some discussion on it. OBIEE 11*g* is a part of the Fusion Middleware architecture of Oracle and comes with a lot of exciting new features which can be leveraged. I will try my best to inform you sufficiently so that you can make a decision about using this tool whenever required. See you in *Chapter 7, Integrating APEX with OBIEE*.

Integrating APEX with OBIEE

7

With this chapter we will launch in a different and a very special space. We are now planning to link APEX with a specialized enterprise reporting technology. When we talk about **Business Intelligence (BI)**, few tools are as elaborate as OBIEE is. This chapter will not only focus on the exotic BI features of OBIEE, but will also talk about BI Publisher 11*g*, which looks very different from its 10*g* avatar. OBIEE is enormous and certainly needs a separate book on it. I will however, assume that you are new to it and will try to make you as comfortable as possible with this technology. The motive here is to give you a brief idea of OBIEE, so that you are familiar with its powers and hence in a position to use it in APEX, whenever required. I must mention that BI Publisher is often used as a printing engine and can be configured for a spectrum of reporting solutions with APEX. So, we will talk about BI Publisher in detail. We will see all this in a while. Let us start by building a little understanding of OFM.

Install the reference application (4-98-9_07_chapter07.sql) for this chapter before going through the chapter. Note that credentials in all web service references and processes will have to be changed for the code to work. You will also have to create an ACL. OBIEE presentation server host and IP address will also have to be changed in all web service references and processes. You will also have to ensure that BI Publisher reports and OBIEE answers exist in the path mentioned in the web service references and page processes.

Understanding Oracle fusion management architecture

Before we start talking about OBIEE, I believe we should talk a little about the fusion architecture and get a hang of the tasks which we will be doing in the rest of the chapter. Let us first have a look at the architecture.

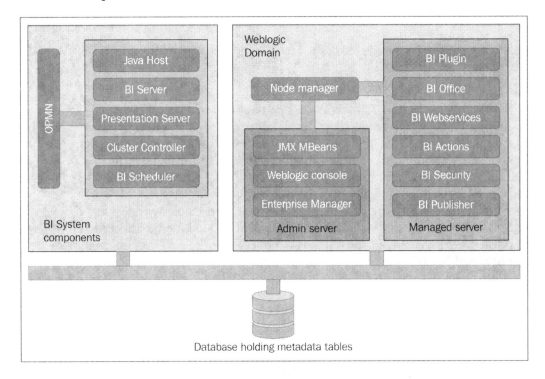

Note that **Managed server** can be absent in the desktop class installations. In such installations, all the Managed server components are deployed on **Admin server** itself. On a broader basis, we can say that JEE components can be easily managed in Weblogic and **OPMN (Oracle Process Manager and Notification)** takes care of non-JEE components. These non-JEE components are called **System Components** and a combination of a number of such components along with controlling OPMN is called a **fusion middleware instance**. In order to allow the control of System Components from a UI, a fusion middleware instance is registered with a weblogic domain. Because of this registration, Enterprise Manager can be used to control the components of a fusion middleware instance. Enterprise Manager is in fact a nerve center for starting and stopping all JEE and System Components in a **farm**.

We can also control the components of OPMN from the command line. It is possible to register a number of fusion middleware instances in a weblogic domain. The config file (opmn.xml) of the OPMN, that has our OBIEE components registered in it, can be found in <BI_Middleware_Home>\instances\instance1\config\ OPMN\opmn. The non-JEE System Components of OBIEE includes Oracle BI **Cluster Controller** component, Oracle BI **Java Host** component, Oracle BI **Presentation Server** component, Oracle **BI Scheduler** component, and Oracle **BI Server** component. We can see these components using the opmnctl command in the following screenshot:

```
C:\OracleProducts\BI_Middleware\instances\instance1\bin>opmnctl status

Processes in Instance: instance1
--------------------------------+--------------------+-------+---------
ias-component                   | process-type       |   pid | status
--------------------------------+--------------------+-------+---------
coreapplication_obiccs1         | OracleBIClusterCo~ |  8572 | Alive
coreapplication_obisch1         | OracleBIScheduler~ |  5684 | Alive
coreapplication_obijh1          | OracleBIJavaHostC~ |  4668 | Alive
coreapplication_obips1          | OracleBIPresentat~ |  5092 | Alive
coreapplication_obis1           | OracleBIServerCom~ |  8424 | Alive
```

Understanding OBIEE

We have seen that OBIEE System Components consist of a Cluster Controller component, a Java Host component a Presentation Server component, a BI Scheduler component, and a BI Server component.

Let us now talk about the BI Server component.

The assumption here is that OBIEE is installed. SampleAppLite_ BI0001.rpd, and the corresponding default web catalog is online. This repository and its default web catalog are online by default when we do a desktop class installation of OBIEE.

Understanding the BI Server component

BI Server hosts a repository often called **rpd**. This repository is a store of all the metadata which is used by OBIEE for the creation of the reports. Let us have a brief overview of the repository. This rpd has three layers namely, **Physical, Business Model and Mapping (BMM)**, and **Presentation**. A repository opened using the Admin tool of OBIEE is shared for your convenience in the following screenshot:

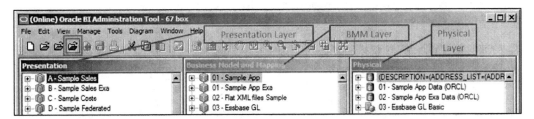

Connections to the data source are made in the **Physical** layer (highlighted in the preceding screenshot) using connection pools. OBIEE can use a variety of data sources which include relational data sources, XML files, Essbase data sources, Hyperion Financial Management data sources, OLAP data sources, and ADF data sources. The relationships among the different tables as they exist in the data source are brought to the notice of the BI Server component in the **Physical** layer. The model created by connecting the tables in the **Physical** layer is called the physical model. The next layer is the **Business Model and Mapping (BMM)** layer (highlighted in the preceding screenshot) where we define the business model. Let's say that we have a fact table, we have aggregated some of the measures and stored the aggregated value in a new table. We will then have the same information at different levels in different tables. In such a case, two sources of information should map in the same logical table because business-wise the information is the same. Logical tables are tables that exist in the **Business Model and Mapping** layer. Multiple tables of the **Physical** layer can be sources of a logical table.

The final layer is the **Presentation** layer (highlighted in the preceding screenshot). This layer is finally exposed to the user in the portal. Apart from these three layers, repositories also have wizards for job, session, and cache managements. It is also a storehouse for the OBIEE variables: repository and session. Hierarchies are also created in the repository. Hierarchies enable us to link one level in a dimension to another level. If a user generates a report with a dimension column and if a hierarchy has been defined on the dimension, then a drilldown link automatically appears on the column and the user can then drilldown to see a more detailed level of information.

A new concept called Lookups has been introduced in OBIEE 11*g*. Both physical and logical tables can be marked as Lookup tables by checking the **Lookup table** checkbox. Setting the table as a lookup lets OBIEE bypass certain checks which it performs on facts and dimensions. If configured correctly, Lookups can offer substantial performance benefits.

Another important concept which is new to OBIEE 11*g* is double columns. It lets us set one column as an ID and another column as a description. So, OBIEE uses the description column in the report and uses the ID column to join the table containing the description column with other tables which are required a business query.

OBIEE 11*g* has introduced a new column called Hierarchical column. If a column in the presentation layer is defined as a hierarchical column then this column in OBIEE is presented as a collapsible column, which can be expanded to see the different levels of hierarchy.

The BI Server component holds the repository and it exposes the tables in the **Presentation** layer to the outside world as an ODBC data source.

Both the analytics application (the OBIEE portal) and the admin tool connect to the repository hosted on the BI Server component using ODBC. The admin tool is the BI server's interface, which helps us modify the repository. The preceding screenshot is of the **Oracle BI Administration Tool** that helps us see the repository.

This finishes a quick overview of the BI Server component. Let us now look at BI Presentation Server.

Understanding the BI Presentation Server

We will use this section to understand the various features provided by the BI Presentation Server component.

Understanding Dashboards, analysis (answers), and filters

Let us go through the following steps to understand and get a feel of the various features of OBIEE Dashboards and analysis.

1. Open the OBIEE portal (typical URL:`http://<obiee_presentation_server_ip>:<obiee_presentation_server_port>/analytics/saw.dll?bieehome`) and navigate to the **New | Analysis** link (highlighted in the following screenshot).

2. This will open up a menu which will show you the subject areas that are present in the **Presentation** layer of the repository. Select the **SampleApp Lite** subject area.

3. Expand the **Time | More Time Objects** dimension folder.

4. Double-click on **Calendar Date**. Similarly expand **Base Facts**, and then double-click on **Revenue**.

These two columns have been selected in the following screenshot:

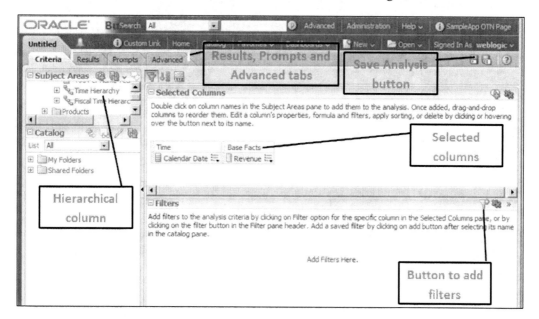

We can see a button to add filters in the preceding screenshot. These filters let us limit the number of records in our analysis. If we create a new filter and select the **is prompted** in the **Operator** checkbox then our analysis will be affected by prompts. Prompts let the user select the filtering criteria in a dashboard or on a dashboard page. Prompts can be created using the **Prompts** tab (displayed next to the **Results** tab).

Let me now introduce the selection steps of OBIEE. The fundamental difference between filters and selection steps (highlighted in the following screenshot) is that filters filter the data and then the aggregations on the columns are performed. Selection steps are applied after the aggregations are performed so they only control the display of data. Selection steps are a collection of steps and the order of steps affect the final result. Each step processes the result of the previous step to generate the final result.

5. Click on the **Save Analysis** button (highlighted in the preceding screenshot). Create a New Folder called `Packt` in the **Shared Folders** and save the analysis as `First Analysis`.

6. Now click on the **Results** tab (highlighted in the following screenshot).

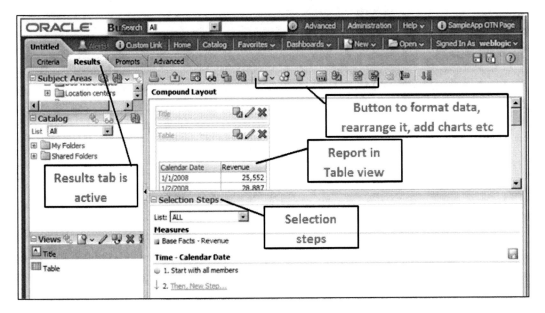

You will see a lot of buttons on the top. These buttons (highlighted in the preceding screenshot) are used to format the result in a desired format. These can help us create all sorts of charts using the selected data. The **Advanced** tab shows us the logical SQL that is sent to the BI Server component. We also get link to get a web query (.iqy) file which can be used to directly get the data from the analysis in an excel sheet in the Advanced tab. The tab also gives us the freedom to directly edit the XML of the analysis. This XML is the definition of the report. The **Bypass Oracle BI Presentation Services Cache** checkbox in the **Advanced** tab lets us bypass the presentation server cache. The final sections of the **Advanced** tab are used to do some advanced SQL operations and to take a few steps to improve the performance of the analysis.

A collection of analysis and other presentation objects are put together in a Dashboard that enables a Dashboard to give a 360 degree view of the business to the user. A typical Dashboard is shared for your convenience in the following screenshot:

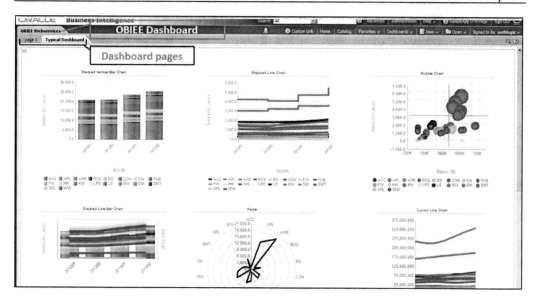

Understanding KPIs and KPI watchlist

KPI stands for Key Performance Indicator. This is one of the most frequently used terms in Business Intelligence circles. Although APEX does not have a region similar to the KPI functionality in OBIEE, but with our knowledge of APEX, creating KPIs in APEX should not be tough. For the time being, however, let's see the KPIs of OBIEE. KPIs are an advanced version of our old measures. In KPIs we have an actual measure and a target measure. Actual measure is compared against the target measure and is then the values of the actual measure are grouped. We pin certain dimensions which can be used to slice and dice and we define ranges, which tell us whether the performance has been good, average, or bad. The screenshot of a typical KPI is shared as follows:

Revenue KPI

Revenue KPI

Per Name Month	Product	Actual	Target	Status	Variance	% Variance
2008 / 01	V5x Flip Phone	3,151.45	3,160.14	⚠	(8.69)	-0
	CompCell RX3	3,718.21	2,189.30	✓	1,528.91	70
	Touch-Screen T5	2,167.05	1,062.05	✓	1,105.00	104

A collection of KPIs can be put together in a **KPI Watchlist**. We can slice and dice a watchlist on runtime. A screenshot of one such KPI Watchlist is shown as follows:

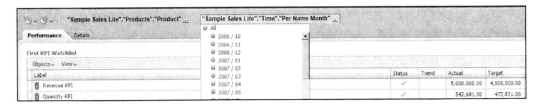

Understanding Actions

The concept of Actions is new to OBIEE 11*g*. It provides limbs to OBIEE, which can be used for handshaking with other systems. Actions can be used to navigate to an analysis, the Dashboard, or a web page or can be used to invoke a browser script, a web service, a Java method in an EJB, or send an HTTP requests. Actions can be initiated from an analysis, the Dashboard, agents, balanced scorecards, and KPIs. A list of Actions is called an Action Link Menu.

Using Actions is a simple process. An action was used to invoke the `logon` method of the `SAWSessionService` web service of OBIEE. A screenshot of the result is shared as follows:

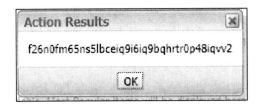

Using browser script Actions can however, become a little tricky. Let us talk about browser script Actions.

If we use Actions to invoke a browser script then the script should be in the `UserScripts.js` file. The path of this file in my system is `<BI_Domain>\ servers\<BI_Server>\tmp\_WL_user\analytics_11.1.1\silp1v\war\res\b_ mozilla\actions`.

Every Action has two different parts with a fixed syntax. A typical signature of a first part is `USERSCRIPT.funct_name = function(array_of_parameters) { <Code> };`.

Here `funct_name` is the name of the function and the actual code gets in this part. The second part to be coded has the following syntax:

```
USERSCRIPT.funct_name.publish = { parameters:[new JAVASCRIPT.parameter
("<variable name without angle brackets>","<description without angle
brackets>","<default value without angle brackets>")]};.
```

This second part describes the parameter list for the function. The preceding code is the prototype for just one parameter but you can have a list of parameters. The list maps to the `array_of_parameters` function of the first part. Let's say that the name of one of the parameters in the second part is `abc`, then you can use this parameter in the code in the first part using `array_of_parameters.abc`. The values to the parameters declared in the parameter list of the second part can be fed from OBIEE when we use a browser script Actions.

Understanding OBIEE Mapviewer

OBIEE Mapviewer is new in OBIEE 11*g*. It lets us seamlessly integrate third-party maps such as Google and Navteq with OBIEE. The advantage of this integration is that we can lay our BI data on top of these maps and can create a number of layers on top of the base maps to make more sense of the data. Layers can be used for setting advanced zoom levels in maps. These zoom levels can be considered as a drilldown method while using maps. We can also create our own maps in Oracle Spatials. We can learn more about Oracle Spatials from `http://www.oracle.com/technetwork/database-options/spatialandgraph/overview/index.html`.

Information on the configuration of Spatial Analytics in OBIEE can be found at `http://download.oracle.com/otndocs/products/spatial/pdf/osuc2012_presentations/osuc12_advbi_lappsharma.pdf`.

An example of location intelligence and Spatial Analytics is shared as follows:

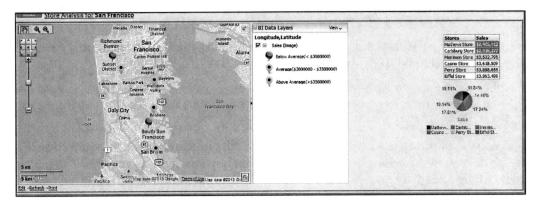

Understanding strategy management

OBIEE's strategy management has been designed to reflect the business strategy of the customers. It lets us define objectives, connect them, and put weightage on the results so that we can focus on the important KPIs of the system. A **Strategy Tree** (shown in the following screenshot) displays the rolling up of each of our objectives to higher objectives. It also shows whether each of the objectives is meeting expectations or not using red, yellow and green color coding. A **Strategy Wheel** (shown in the following screenshot) is another representation of the objective hierarchy and it shows the objectives in a circular diagram. The **Cause and Effect Map** (shown in the following screenshot) are used to display dependencies among various objectives and show KPIs in a fish bone diagram. The **Strategy Map** (shown in the following screenshot) is another method of displaying these dependencies.

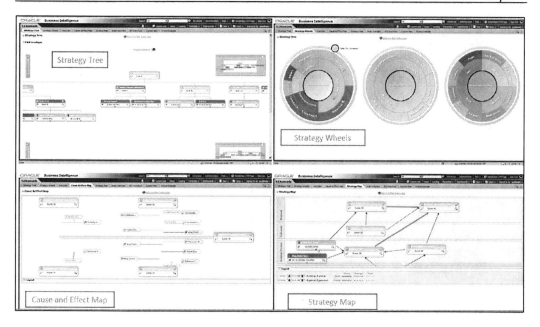

Configuring the Gmail SMTP server in OBIEE

We will use this section to check out the configuration of the Gmail smtp server for
e-mail delivery using agents. We will talk about OBIEE agents after we are done with
the SMTP server configuration. We had used stunnel to configure mail functionality
in APEX because our database Version (11.2.0.1.0) is not capable of sending SSL
requests to the mail server and Gmail accepts only SSL requests. We can use Stunnel
for OBIEE as well. It is important to point out that OBIEE is capable of sending SSL
requests to the SMTP server.

Note that the configurations mentioned here are according to the `stunnel.conf`
file described in the *Configuring the mail* section of *Chapter 5, Flight to Space Station
– Advanced APEX*. Let us now configure OBIEE for e-mail delivery.

1. Log in to **Fusion Middleware Control**.
2. Expand **Business Intelligence** in **Farm_bifoundation_domain**
   in the left panel.
3. Click on **coreapplication** and then on the **Deployment** tab.
   Select the **Mail** tab under the **Deployment** tab.

4. Click on the **Lock and Edit Configuration** button and enter the following details:
    - ° **SMTP server**: `localhost`
    - ° **Port**: `1925`
    - ° **Display name of sender**: Your choice
    - ° **Email address of sender**: Gmail ID
    - ° **Username**: Gmail ID
    - ° **Password**: Your Gmail password

5. Apply and activate changes. You will be taken to a screen that helps you restart the BI components. Restart them.

Once the web server is configured, we can now create an agent on top of an OBIEE analysis.

Understanding agents

OBIEE agents are used to schedule OBIEE tasks. Agents run the report on a specific schedule and deliver the output to a configured device. The jobs executed by the agents can be seen in the Job Manager. Link to open the Job Manager is present in the Oracle Business Intelligence program group. We can use our weblogic admin credentials to log in to the Job Manager.

A screenshot of the Job Manager is shared as follows:

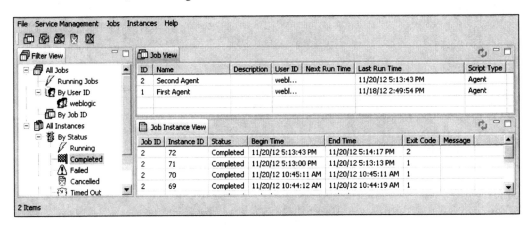

Let us now create an agent, using the following steps:

1. Log in to the analytics portal via `http://<obiee_presentation_server_ip>:<obiee_presentation_server_port>/analytics/saw.dll?bieehome&startPage=1`.

2. Move your mouse pointer on top of the **New** link and select **Agent** (highlighted in the following screenshot) from it.

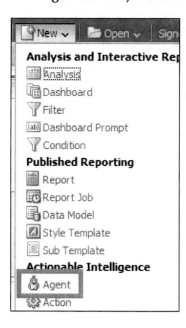

This will take us to a screen that will help you configure agents. I created an agent with the following configuration:

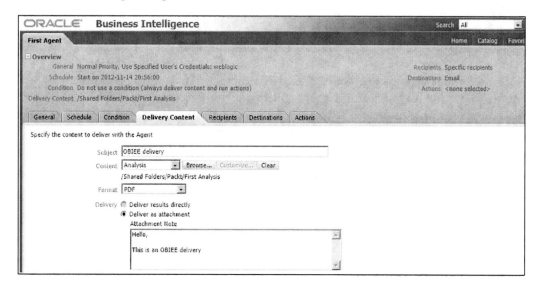

The tabs in the previous screenshot are self-explanatory. The **General** tab is for impersonation and priority setting. Impersonation uses the data level security configuration of the user to which the session is impersonated and the agent is executed accordingly. **Priority** is to set the priority of the delivery. The **Schedule** tab lets us set the schedule of the agent. The **Condition** tab can help us make the running of the agent subject to certain conditions. These conditions can be based on both KPIs and analysis. **Delivery Content** is the analysis, Dashboard, or the briefing book, which we want to deliver to the user. **Recipients** are the users who will receive the delivery of this agent. The **Destination** tab lets us select a number of devices to which the content can be delivered. For example, you can configure the delivery of an agent to both the dashboard of the user and to his e-mail.

I got an e-mail in my Gmail inbox after executing the agent shown in the preceding screenshot.

OBIEE server reaching out to Stunnel to deliver the e-mail can be seen in the Stunnel's log. If you see that Stunnel is getting used, then you can be sure that your OBIEE configuration is correct. If you do not get the e-mail, then the Stunnel log file should tell you the problem. A successful connection will give you a log similar to the following one:

```
2012.11.20 17:12:15 LOG5[1680:7764]: Reading configuration from file
stunnel.conf
2012.11.20 17:12:15 LOG5[1680:7764]: FIPS mode is enabled
2012.11.20 17:12:16 LOG5[1680:7764]: Configuration successful
2012.11.20 17:13:43 LOG5[1680:4456]: Service [ssmtp] accepted
connection from 127.0.0.1:58947
2012.11.20 17:13:44 LOG5[1680:4456]: Service [ssmtp] connected remote
server from 223.178.246.29:58948
```

```
2012.11.20 17:14:17 LOG5[1680:4456]: Connection closed: 129655 byte(s)
sent to SSL, 435 byte(s) sent to socket
```

Integrating OBIEE with APEX

Integration of OBIEE with APEX can be done using web services, OBIEE's Go URL, or using ODBC connections. There are a number of limitations of the ODBC technique, so a section is not dedicated to it. It is important to understand that if we use ODBC, then, we are leveraging OBIEE's BI Server component, but we are not leveraging OBIEE's Presentation Server component. ODBC method connects to the BI Server component and accesses the presentation tables of OBIEE to query data. The data will be fetched using the relationships established in the BI repository.

The other two methods are web services and Go URL. We will have a look at them now.

Integration using web services

Before we dig into understanding a few web services of OBIEE, I wish to point out that we can only use manually created web services reference for OBIEE's integration with APEX because OBIEE's WSDL contains multiple SOAP bindings.

The SOAP envelopes can easily be generated using SoapUI. The WSDL page of OBIEE web services is `http://<obiee_presentation_server_ip>:<obiee_presentation_server_port>/analytics/saw.dll/wsdl/v7` or `http://<obiee_presentation_server_ip>:<obiee_presentation_server_port>/analytics/saw.dll/wsdl/v6`. SoapUI will use this WSDL to generate the right structure of the SOAP envelope required to fire the call.

Alright, let us now check out a few web services.

Delivery of OBIEE reports can happen either by first fetching the reports to APEX and then delivering it from APEX, or the delivery can happen by using OBIEE agents and agents can be called from APEX. The `executeIBotNow` method of the `iBotService` service can be used to execute an agent. We have already seen a number of ways to execute a web services method from APEX and the `executeIBotNow` method is no different. A typical SOAP envelope to execute an agent looks like the following code:

```
<soapenv:Envelope
  xmlns:soapenv="http://schemas.xmlsoap.org/soap/envelope/"
    xmlns:v7="urn://oracle.bi.webservices/v7">
<soapenv:Header/>
```

```
<soapenv:Body>
  <v7:executeIBotNow>
    <v7:path>/shared/Packt/Agents/First Agent</v7:path>
<v7:sessionID>dr913u5fd53tpj0nq64ck5m15fj5m3hdnes557q</v7:session
ID>
  </v7:executeIBotNow>
</soapenv:Body>
</soapenv:Envelope>
```

The session ID highlighted in the preceding piece of code is in the response to the
`logon` method of the `SAWSessionService` service. The `logon` method accepts a
user ID and a password to generate a valid OBIEE session. The result of a successful
execution of the agent looks like the following code:

```
<soap:Envelope
  xmlns:soap="http://schemas.xmlsoap.org/soap/envelope/"
    xmlns:xsi="http://www.w3.org/2001/XMLSchema-instance"
      xmlns:xsd="http://www.w3.org/2001/XMLSchema"
        xmlns:soapenc="http://schemas.xmlsoap.org/soap/encoding/"
          xmlns:sawsoap="urn://oracle.bi.webservices/v7">
  <soap:Body>
    <sawsoap:executeIBotNowResult/>
  </soap:Body>
</soap:Envelope>
```

I wish to talk about HTMLViewService here. This service is used to get an online
OBIEE report for any client that uses this service. An example of a soap envelope that
invokes an OBIEE report using HTMLViewService is shown in the following code:

```
<soapenv:Envelope
  xmlns:soapenv="http://schemas.xmlsoap.org/soap/envelope/"
    xmlns:v6="urn://oracle.bi.webservices/v6">
<soapenv:Header/>
<soapenv:Body>
  <v6:getHtmlForPageWithOneReport>
    <v6:reportID>simpleReport</v6:reportID>
    <v6:report>
      <v6:reportPath>/shared/Packt/simpleReport</v6:reportPath>
      <v6:reportXml></v6:reportXml>
    </v6:report>
    <v6:reportViewName></v6:reportViewName>
    <v6:reportParams>
      <v6:filterExpressions></v6:filterExpressions>
      <v6:variables>
        <v6:name></v6:name>
```

```
        <v6:value></v6:value>
      </v6:variables>
      <v6:nameValues>
        <v6:name></v6:name>
        <v6:value></v6:value>
      </v6:nameValues>
      <v6:templateInfos>
        <v6:templateForEach></v6:templateForEach>
        <v6:templateIterator></v6:templateIterator>
        <v6:instance>
          <v6:instanceName></v6:instanceName>
          <v6:nameValues>
            <v6:name></v6:name>
            <v6:value></v6:value>
          </v6:nameValues>
        </v6:instance>
      </v6:templateInfos>
      <v6:viewName></v6:viewName>
    </v6:reportParams>
    <v6:reportOptions>
      <v6:enableDelayLoading>false</v6:enableDelayLoading>
      <v6:linkMode></v6:linkMode>
    </v6:reportOptions>
    <v6:pageParams>
      <v6:idsPrefix></v6:idsPrefix>
      <v6:dontUseHttpCookies>true</v6:dontUseHttpCookies>
    </v6:pageParams>
    <v6:sessionID>dr9l3u5fd53tpj0nq64ck5m15fj5m3hdnes557q</v6:
      sessionID>
  </v6:getHtmlForPageWithOneReport>
</soapenv:Body>
</soapenv:Envelope>
```

The end point for the above SOAP envelope has the following form `http://<obiee_
presentation_server_ip>:<obiee_presentation_server_port>/analytics/
saw.dll?SoapImpl=htmlViewService`

`report_id` (highlighted in the preceding code) can be any value. `report_path`
(highlighted in the preceding code) is the path of the analysis in OBIEE web catalog.
The output of the preceding invocation looks like the following code:

```
<noscript>To use Oracle BIEE, please enable javascript in your
browser.
</noscript>
```

```
<script type="text/javascript" src="http:// <obiee_presentation_
server>:<obiee_presentation_server_port>/analytics/res/b_mozilla/
browserdom.js"></script>
<script type="text/javascript">try{saw.doFrameBust(0);function
sawC2U(s)
{return
   "http:// <obiee_presentation_server>:<obiee_presentation_server_
port>/analytics/saw.dll?__xyz__".replace("__xyz__",s);}function
sawP2U(s)
  {return
     "http:// <obiee_presentation_server>:<obiee_presentation_
server_port>/analytics/saw.dll/__xyz__".replace("__xyz__",s);}var
sawEmptyHtm="http:// <obiee_presentation_server>:<obiee_presentation_
server_port>/analytics/res/empty.htm";var obips_fmapId="APwjeg";var
obips_scid="KlrYtT9JNWfOXC2JfSl5";var obips_maxStylesheets=100;var
g_LocaleInfo={sDateSeparator:"/",sTimeSeparator:":",sDecimalPoint:"."
,sThousandsSeparator:",",sAM:"AM",sPM:"PM",b24:false,sDateOrder:"mdy"
,nFDOW:6,nYearPadding:4,nMonthPadding:2,nDayPadding:2,nHourPadding:2,
sListSeparator:",",sNegativeNumberTemplate:"-#"};var obips_seeded_res
= [{p:"styleproperties.res",v:{exprs:{"dialogHelpPosition":"header",
"shuttleButtonSpace":"true","shuttleButtonLabel":"false","shuttleTab
leCellSpace":"6","shuttleDropdownWidth":"7px","shuttleDropdownHeight"
:"4px","menubarSeparator":"false","pageShadowBackground":"true","hea
derRightBorder":"true","pageBorderBottomRequired":"true","tabBarStar
tCellWidth":"5px","tabBarStartImgRequired":"true","bihRoundCorner":"
false","adminBannerBackground":"false","breadCrumbHeight":"15"}}}];}
catch(e){if (window.console && console.error) console.error('Header
script error:' + e.message);}</script><script type="text/javascript"
src="http://<obiee_presentation_server>:<obiee_presentation_
server_port>/analytics/res/b_mozilla/common/obips.ImportMeFirst.
js"></script><script type="text/javascript" src="http:// <obiee_
presentation_server>:<obiee_presentation_server_port>/analytics/
res/b_mozilla/common.js"></script><script type="text/javascript"
src="http:// <obiee_presentation_server>:<obiee_presentation_
server_port>/analytics/res/b_mozilla/viewhelper.js"></script><script
type="text/javascript" src="http:// <obiee_presentation_
server>:<obiee_presentation_server_port>/analytics/res/b_mozilla/
common/obips.JavaScriptExtensions.js"></script><script type="text/
javascript" src="http:// <obiee_presentation_server>:<obiee_
presentation_server_port>/analytics/res/b_mozilla/common/ajax.
js"></script><script type="text/javascript" src="http:// <obiee_
presentation_server>:<obiee_presentation_server_port>/analytics/
res/b_mozilla/common/ondemandload.js"></script><div id="simpleReport2"
Effective_simpleReport2_ReportObj_ID="simpleReport2_ReportObj"  >
<img class="SrchImg" border=0 src="http:// <obiee_presentation_
server>:<obiee_presentation_server_port>/analytics/res/s_FusionFX/
views/searching.gif" alt=""></div>
```

```
<SCRIPT type="text/javascript">
  try{simpleReport2_ReportObj = new saw.ondemandload.
EmbededReport('simpleReport2');
  var reportObject = simpleReport2_ReportObj;
  reportObject.setSessionId
    ('q9dbef0d519166nss2m3751pr9dkg63pa3al1ji');
  reportObject.setSearchId('tdi2f2upm13eu0e62mo36e2m8a');
  reportObject.setAjaxGoUrl('http:// <obiee_presentation_
server>:<obiee_presentation_server_port>/analytics/saw.dll?ajaxGo');
  reportObject.show();
}catch(e){if (window.console && console.error) console.error('Load
embedded report error:' + e.message);}
</SCRIPT>
```

This response fires an AJAX request to the BI Presentation Server component. The AJAX request is highlighted in the preceding code. This AJAX request is responsible for helping us get our desired report. The result looks like the following screenshot:

Year	Severity	No. of Critical SRs	No. of Open SRs	Average Days SR is Open	Total No. of SRs	No. of Closed SRs	Average Days Open	No. of SRs Closed in First Call
2007	4-Low	10	7	58.0	10	0	57.1	0
2007	2-Medium	23	16	56.0	23	1	55.9	0
2009	1-Critical	35	54	55.0	82	33	55.0	0
2009	2-High	49	73	51.0	122	92	50.7	0
2008	3-Medium	49	89	51.0	143	39	50.7	0
2008	2-High	53	112	51.0	186	54	50.1	0
2009	4-Low	17	25	48.0	42	16	47.5	0
2009	3-Medium	32	44	48.0	74	43	47.3	0
2008	1-Critical	34	59	47.0	102	28	46.4	0
2008	4-Low	18	39	46.0	67	21	45.4	0
2007	1-Critical	16	9	46.0	16	0	45.0	0
2007	2-High	32	19	45.0	32	1	44.1	0

Refresh - Print - Export

Note that if the OBIEE Presentation Server and APEX Listener server are hosted on different web servers, then we will have to set a bridge. This bridge will broker the requests between APEX Listener and OBIEE Presentation. More information on setting the bridge can be found at `http://docs.oracle.com/cd/E21764_01/bi.1111/e16364/methods.htm#i1011107`.

A bridge can be coded in any language but should deployed on the same domain as the BI Presentation server. HTMLViewService has a setBridge method which should be used before making a call to get any report from OBIEE. Once we have invoked the `setBridge` method, our web service response will change a little. Following code is a part of the web service response after the invocation of `setBridge`. Compare it with the response shared earlier.

```
<SCRIPT type="text/javascript">
try{tab_rpt_ReportObj = new saw.ondemandload.EmbededReport('tab_rpt');
var reportObject = tab_rpt_ReportObj;
```

```
repor-tObject.setSessionId('b3ea95e7dngnr89k4bf016ng7ejslru074onuli');

reportObject.setSearchId('e1diij9vrjr9oc29757smpk2sm');
reportObject.setAjaxGoUrl('http://localhost:7001/bridgeJSP.jsp?Redirec
tURL=http%3a%2f%2flocalhost%3a7001%2fanalytics%2fsaw.dll%3fajaxGo');
reportObject.show();
}catch(e){if (window.console && console.error) console.error('Load
embedded report error:' + e.message);}
```

To get the above response, `http://localhost:7001/bridgeJSP.jsp` was passed as an argument to setBridge method. Note that the bridge code, `bridgeJSP.jsp` in this case, has to be implemented and is not a part of OBIEE tool. Note the highlighted part of the code. Instead of calling the OBIEE resources directly, the web service response now calls http://localhost:7001/bridgeJSP.jsp and passes the required resources to it (the bridge) as an argument. It is now the responsibility of the bridge to call OBIEE resources and send the response back to APEX. So the bridge should be able to capture the headers and cookies from APEX and the BI Presentation server and use them to make both HTTP GET and HTTP POST calls to the BI server. The headers and cookies will also have to be set while sending the response back to APEX.

Integration with APEX using Go URL

OBIEE lets external systems use its services using Go URL. The URL lets us pass filters to the OBIEE analysis and Dashboards. The only problem in this approach is the security. If we are firing a Go URL from an external system, then we will be prompted for a password. We can escape this by passing the credentials in the URL.

The following URL is an example of a Go URL:

```
http://<obiee_presentation_server_ip>:<obiee_presentation_
server_port>/analytics/saw.dll?Go&Path=%2Fshared%2FSample%20
Lite%2FKPIs%2FAvg%20Order%20Size&NQUser=weblogic&NQPassword=weblog
ic123.
```

Here, the path of the **Avg Order Size** KPI in the catalog is `/shared/Sample Lite/` `KPIs` and `weblogic/weblogic123` are the credentials of the weblogic user. If we wish to show only a particular view of the analysis then we can use `&ViewName=<view_name>` in the Go URL, where `<view_name>` is the name of the view, which we want to show.

We can get the view name of all the views in the analysis by going to the **Analysis XML** section in the **Advanced** tab of an analysis. There are some more options, associated with goURL, which we can check. A detail list can be found in OBIEE's Integrator's guide from the following location: `http://docs.oracle.com/cd/E23943_01/bi.1111/e16364/apiwebintegrate.htm#CACCHBHC`.

OBIEE Dashboards can be accessed using the syntax similar to the following URL: `http://<obiee_presentation_server_ip>:<obiee_presentation_server_port>/analytics/saw.dll?Dashboard&PortalPath=%2Fshared%2FSample%20Lite%2F_portal%2FQuickStart&NQUser=weblogic&NQPassword=weblogic123`.

Pages inside the Dashboard can be accessed using `http://<obiee_presentation_server_ip>:<obiee_presentation_server_port>/analytics/saw.dll?Dashboard&PortalPath=%2Fshared%2FSample%20Lite%2F_portal%2FQuickStart&Page=Scorecard&NQUser=weblogic&NQPassword=weblogic123`.

Note the use of `&Page=Scorecard` here.

If you hate OBIEE buttons on your page then you can use Portal Pages as shown in the following example: `http://<obiee_presentation_server_ip>:<obiee_presentation_server_port>/analytics/saw.dll?PortalPages&PortalPath=%2Fshared%2FSample%20Lite%2F_portal%2FQuickStart&Page=Scorecard&NQUser=weblogic&NQPassword=weblogic123`.

We can also fire queries on the presentation tables using Go URL. The following is an example: `http://<obiee_presentation_server_ip>:<obiee_presentation_server_port>/analytics/saw.dll?Go&SQL=select+Products.Product,Products.Brand+from+"Sample+Sales+Lite"`.

We can use goURL as targets of any link in APEX. goURL can be set as the targets in classic and interactive reports, buttons, branches and any other place to use URLs in APEX.

Integration using iFrames in APEX

We can also use iFrames in APEX to display OBIEE content. Integration using iFrames is an extension of integration using GoURL. We will have to do the following configurational changes and restart OBIEE before using OBIEE reports in APEX iFrames:

1. Put the following in `instanceconfig.xml`.

    ```
    <Security>
    <InIFrameRenderingMode>allow</InIFrameRenderingMode>
    </Security>
    ```

2. Put the following in web.xml present in <Middleware_Home>\oracleBI1\
    bifoundation\web\app\WEB-INF.

```
<context-param>
<param-name>oracle.adf.view.rich.security.FRAME_BUSTING</param-name>
<param-value>never</param-value>
</context-param>
```

3. Once these configurations are done, we can use the following code in
    APEX HTML region to get OBIEE reports.:

```
<html>
<title> OBIEE iFrame demo</title>
<body>
<iframe src="http://<OBIEE_Presentation_server_ip>:<OBIEE_
Presentation_server_port>/analytics/saw.dll?Go&Path=<report_path_
in_obiee_web_catalog>&NQUser=<OBIEE_user_id>&NQPassword=<OBIEE_
password>" width="700" height="400"></iframe>
</body>
</html>
```

The following is an example of the argument of the `src` attribute of the `iframe` tag.

```
http://localhost:7001/analytics/saw.dll?Go&Path=/shared/Test/Test%20
Report&NQUser=weblogic&NQPassword=Admin123.
```

Understanding BI Publisher

A few years back, BI Publisher was called XML publisher. Oracle bought it, baptized
it in its own way, and started calling it BI Publisher. The basic architecture of the
tool still remains the same. It is a widely used reporting solution because of the ease
with which it can be integrated with almost any interface and its ability to work on
almost any kind of data source. The data sources can even be files and web services.
However, the most important feature of BI Publisher is the ability to design the
output format (template) using MS Word (rtf format). One can use the BI Publisher
plugin of MS Word to make this template. The template with the data source is
then used to produce the report. However, rtf is not the only possible format for
designing the template. We can also make templates in the `pdf`, `eTEXT`, `flash`, and
`excel` formats.

BI Publisher is essentially a JEE **web archive (WAR)** application and until 10*g* it worked almost independent of OBIEE answers and Dashboards. OBIEE answers and Dashboards is the erstwhile Siebel Analytics. It is possible to use answers (now analysis) as data sources in BI Publisher. In 11*g*, we can have a shared repository of objects and the two tools are more tightly integrated.

> We will talk about creating the BI Publisher reports in greater detail because BI Publisher is often used as a report printing engine in APEX. Functions such as APEX_UTIL.DOWNLOAD_PRINT_DOCUMENT and APEX_UTIL.GET_PRINT_DOCUMENT can use the rtf template along with report data and send these to BI Publisher to create a report.

Creating and mailing reports in BI Publisher

We will use rtf templates for creating our sample reports because it is generic (can be used to generate almost any format of the output) and is easy to use. The other template formats are xls, pdf, flash, and eTEXT.

Let's now begin the process of creating a simple BI Publisher report. Log in to BI Publisher (typical URL http://<obiee_presentation_server_ip>:<obiee_presentation_server_port>/xmlpserver/login.jsp).

We have to first create a data model, then a template, and will finally put both of these together.

Creating data model in BI Publisher

The first step in the creation of a BI Publisher report is the creation of a data model. This defines the method of fetching data. We will be using a SQL Query as the data source and will create a report on our very own oehr_employees table. BI Publisher can use **SQL Query, MDX Query, Oracle BI Analysis, ADF View Object, Web Service, LDAP Query, XML file, Microsoft Excel file** and **HTTP (XML Feed)** as data sources.

1. Let us first create a data source. Click on the **Administration** link (highlighted in the following screenshot) on the top-right corner of the page after logging into BI Publisher.

2. Click on **JDBC Connection** under the **Data Sources** group.

3. Click on the **Add Data Source** button.

4. Enter Oracle Query Data Source as **Data Source Name**. **Data Source Name** can be any name. Let **Driver Type** be **Oracle 11G** and **Database Driver Class** be **oracle.jdbc.OracleDriver**.

5. Enter jdbc:oracle:thin:@<db_host>:<db_post>:<sid> as **Connection String**. Replace <db_host>:<db_post>:<sid> with your database information. Enter packt_schema credentials in the **Username** and **Password** textboxes. Put the **Data Source Name** as **Oracle Query Data Source**.

6. Click on the **Test Connection** button after doing this. You should get the **Connection established successfully** message at the top of the browser window.

7. Click on the **Apply** button.

8. Click on the **Home** link (highlighted in the preceding screenshot).

9. Click on the **Data Model** link (highlighted in the following screenshot).

10. Select **Oracle Query Data Source** (highlighted in the following screenshot) as **Default Data Source**. Note that we had created this Data Source in step 5.

11. Click on the **Data Sets** link (highlighted in the preceding screenshot) in the left panel and then click on the **New Data Set** button under the **Diagram** tab and select **SQL Query** as shown in the following screenshot:

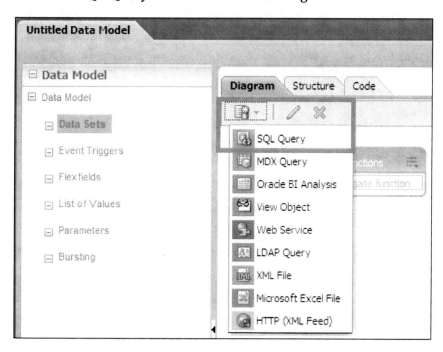

12. Enter the **Name** as Employee Query (this can be any name) and enter select * from oehr_employees where employee_id like nvl(:BIP_EMP_ID,'%') in **SQL Query** text box. Check the **Oracle Query Data Source** radio button as shown in the following screenshot. Click on the **OK** button:

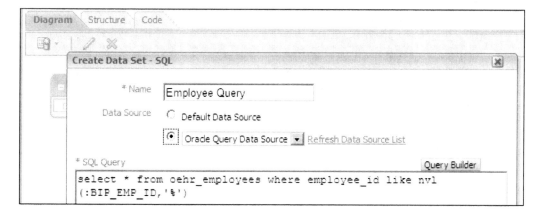

13. Click on the **Parameters** link and then click on the green colored plus sign (**+**) to add a parameter. Name it `BIP_EMP_ID` and give `Enter employee id:` as its label as shown in the following screenshot. Note that we are naming it BIP_EMP_ID because we had used `BIP_EMP_ID` in the query in step 12.

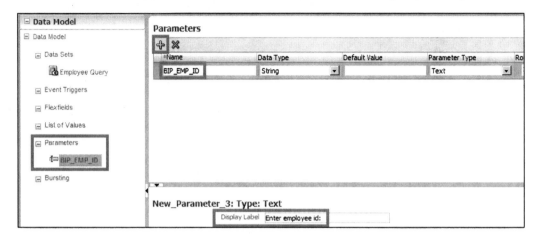

14. Click on the **Save** button (highlighted in the following screenshot). Create a new folder called `BIP Data Model` under **Shared Folders** in the catalog and save this data model in it.

15. Click on the **Get XML Output** (highlighted in the preceding screenshot) button. Enter `100` in the **Enter employee id:** textbox and click on the **Run** button as shown in the following screenshot. This XML will help us in the next step of making rtf templates. Save the part of this XML starting from `<DATA_DS>` and ending at `</DATA_DS>`. Also remove the (-) characters highlighted in the following screenshot:

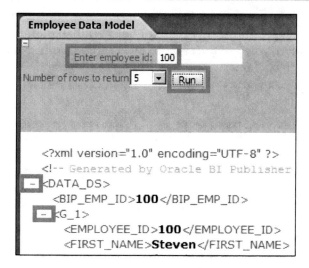

16. Upload this file in the **Data Model** link in the **Sample Data** link under the
    Attachment section as shown in the following screenshot. Save the data model.

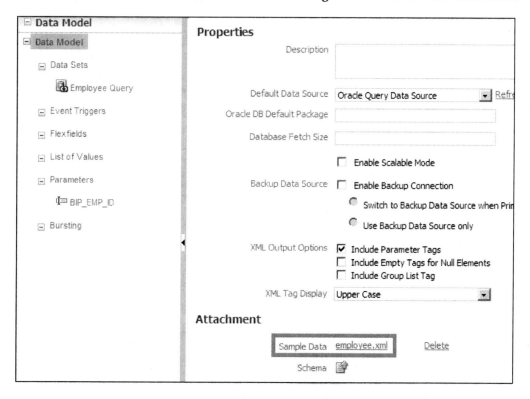

BI Publisher data model gives you a lot more options than the ones mentioned here. I believe you must have felt it by now. I cannot talk about all of those because it would require another book devoted to the subject, but I can certainly point you to the documentation which contains a good description of these options. Have a look at http://docs.oracle.com/cd/E23943_01/bi.1111/e22258/toc.htm.

Using the BI Publisher's MS Word plugin to make rtf templates

Let us now make a template for our data. We have chosen to make an rtf template and we will do this using BI Publisher's MS Word plugin. We can download this plugin from our BI Publisher application itself. Let's see the process now.

1. Click on the **Home** link in BI Publisher and then click on **Download BI Publisher Tools** in the **Getting Started** section in the left panel.

2. Download and install **BI Publisher desktop**. Choose 30 bit / 64 bit according to the machine on which you plan to create your templates. Install the same. This will help you see the **BI Publisher** tab in MS Word. This tab is highlighted in the following screenshot.

3. Open MS Word and click on the **BI Publisher** tab and then on the **Sample XML** button as shown in the following screenshot. Load the XML file which you got from step 15 of the *Creating data model in BI Publisher* section. You should get the **Data loaded successfully** message. Select **Table Wizard** (highlighted in the following screenshot).

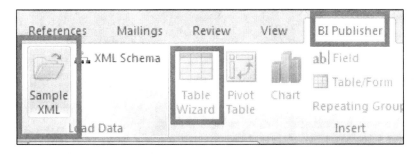

4. Select **First Name**, **Last Name**, **Email**, **Salary**, and **Employee id** from the shuttle, keep the defaults in the other steps, and click on **Finish**.

5. Save this file as employees.rtf on your local machine.

The template automatically gets a loop to iterate through the rows of the data set. Check the help texts of various form fields (grey boxes) in the rtf file and match the values with the tags in the screenshot under step 15.

You will find `<?for-each:G_1?>` in the help text of the form field with the label 'F'. `<?for-each:G_1?>` is basically a loop of G_1. Everything between `<?for-each:G_1?>` and `<?end for-each?>` is iterated for each value of G_1. You will find values such as `<?FIRST_NAME?>` between `<?for-each:G_1?>` and `<?end for-each?>`. This arrangement ensures that the value of `FIRST_NAME` of the datasource (SQL query in our case) is iterated for every value of G_1. There is a whole science behind template building and you can check out its documentation at `http://docs.oracle.com/cd/E23943_01/bi.1111/e22254/toc.htm`.

Assembling the rtf template and data model together

After creating the template, we have to create a BI Publisher report using the template and data model. Let's see the steps for it.

1. Log in to BI Publisher and click on the **Report** link (highlighted in step 9 of the *Creating data model in BI Publisher* section) to create a new BI Publisher report.

2. Click on **Use existing Data Model**. Select the data model which you had created and click on **Next**.

3. Select the **Use Report Editor** radio button and click on **Finish**.

4. Save this report in a new folder called `BIP reports`.

5. Click on the **Add New Layout** button as shown in the following screenshot:

6. Upload the created RTF file in the **Upload or Generate Layout** section and save the report.

7. Now click on the **View Report** tab(highlighted in the preceding screenshot) to see this report. The report will look like the following screenshot:

First Name	Last Name	Email
Steven	King	SKING
Neena	Kochhar	NKOCHHAR

This ends our discussion on creating a simple report in BI Publisher. We dedicated a substantial section to creating reports in BI Publisher because BI Publisher is often coupled with APEX for report printing.

Scheduling reports and e-mail delivery in BI Publisher

Let us now see the process of scheduling reports in BI Publisher. Scheduling reports in BI Publisher is a simple process. Here, we will have a look at the BI Publisher's system to schedule reports and will later look at a method to run the schedule from APEX using web services.

1. Log in to BI Publisher and click on the **Administration** link on the top-right corner.

2. Click on the **Email** link under the **Delivery** section. Note the other methods of report delivery. These methods include delivery to the **Printer, Fax, WebDAV, FTP, HTTP,** and **CUPS** servers.

3. Click on the **Add Server** button.

4. Enter **Host** as smtp.gmail.com and **Port** as 465. Enter your Gmail username and Gmail password. Enter Gmail in the **Server Name** field. Server Name can be any wild string. Click on the **Apply** button. The following screenshot should help you in the configuration:

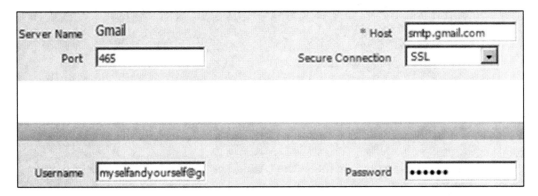

 We could also have used Stunnel as well for delivering mails.

5. Open the report again and click on the **Schedule** link as shown in the following screenshot:

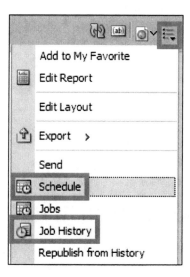

6. Click on the **Output** tab, select **Email** in the **Destination Type** button, and then click on the **Add Destination** button.

7. Enter a To address, the **Subject** and **Message** fields, and click on the **Submit** button.

8. Give a **Report Job Name** and click on the **OK** button. You should get an alert for the successful submission of the job.

9. Click on the **Return** button.

10. Click on the **Actions** button again and select the **Job History** link (highlighted in the preceding screenshot) this time.

11. You should be able to see your successfully executed report and the delivered report in your e-mail inbox.

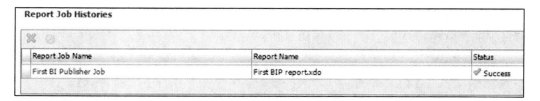

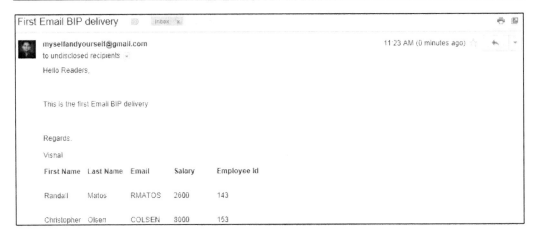

Creating barcode reports in BI Publisher

We are talking about creating barcode reports because these reports are not available in APEX. This is unique to BI Publisher and hence mandates a deeper look.

In BI Publisher 10*g*, we had to go through a long process of registering the barcode encoding class with BI Publisher, so that it can be instantiated at runtime to apply the formatting. However in 11*g*, some barcode fonts are shipped with BI Publisher and we don't need any registration, if we use these implemented barcode fonts.

The process to create a barcode report is not too different from the process to create any other BI Publisher report. All just have to copy `128R00.TTF` from `<BI_ Middleware_home>\Oracle_BI1\common\fonts` to `C:\WINDOWS\Fonts`. Note that other barcode fonts in BI Publisher are in the `B39R00.TTF` and `UPCR00.TTF` files. `128R00.TTF` supports the `code128a`, `code128b`, and `code128c` algorithms. `B39R00. TTF` supports the `code39` and `code39mod43` algorithms, while `UPCR00.TTF` supports the `upca` and `upce` algorithms.

I have created an rtf template (`Barcode.rtf`, shipped with the book) that uses the `code128a` algorithm. I have displayed the salaries of employees as barcodes. To do this, I have changed the font to `Code 128`. You should be able to see `Code 128` in the list of fonts in MS Word after you copy `128R00.TTF` to `C:\WINDOWS\Fonts`. I have also put `<?format-barcode:SALARY;'code128a'?>` in the help text of the **Salary** column form field. We can add the help text by clicking on the form field (the grey colored boxes) and then clicking on the **Add Help Text** button in MS Word.

If the barcodes do not display properly in the PDF format on the BI Publisher portal then perform the following steps:

1. Click on the **Home** link, and then click on the **Edit** link under the **Barcode report** tab.

2. Click on the **Properties** button on the top-right corner of the browser and then click on the **Font Mapping** tab.

3. Under **RTF Templates**, click on the green plus sign (+).

4. Enter Code 128 as **Font family**, Normal as **Style** and **Weight**, Truetype as **Target Font Type**, 128R00.TTF as **Target Font**, and leave **TTC Number** blank.

5. Click on the **OK** button.

The report should look like the following screenshot:

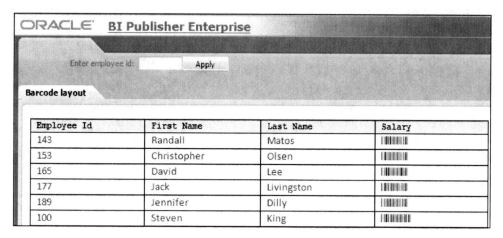

 We can also check the report in MS word itself by loading the employees.xml file (shipped with the book) and generating the sample report in the rtf/excel/html formats in MS Word. The method to use MS word to test templates has been shown in the following section.

Dynamic BI Publisher

Alright, till now we have been dealing with the basic functions of BI Publisher but I wanted to include this exotic section, so that the readers of this book could take their BI Publisher programming to a higher level.

Open the RTF file created in *Using the BI Publisher's MS Word plugin to make rtf templates* section to make more sense of this section. You can also open employee.rtf which has been shipped with the book. We have seen that RTF templates have form field which have place holders such as <?EMPLOYEE_ID?> to display the columns of the data source in the data model.

In our case, we have used SQL Query as the data source. We have also seen how we can use the form fields to iterate through the rows of a data source. The syntax used to iterate through the rows of our query on `oehr_employees` is `<?for-each:G_1?>`. Here `G_1` is the parent node that holds the columns of the query output. So `<?for-each:G_1?>` helps us to iterate through different rows of the `G_1` data group. We had a short discussion about `<?for-each:G_1?>` and other tags of the rtf file in step 15 of *Creating data model in BI Publisher* section as well. You can validate the presence of `G_1` in the data source by having a look at the screenshot under step 15 of *Creating data model in BI Publisher* section. We see here that the for loop and the `<?FIRST_NAME?>` place holder work on fixed tags, that is, `G_1` and `<?FIRST_NAME?>`.

What if we have a requirement of displaying different columns based on certain conditions in BI Publisher? This will mean that the column names to be displayed and to be used in for loops will not be known at the time of creation of the template. This section tries to address the question of dynamically displaying columns in BI Publisher.

A sample RTF (`Dynamic BIP using params.rtf`) and XML file (`Dynamic BIP using params.xml`) has been created so that you can test the working code on your local desktop without uploading the code on the BI Publisher's server. Perform the following steps to test this:

1. Open `Dynamic BIP using params.rtf` and load `Dynamic BIP using params.xml`.

2. Click on the **PDF** button as shown in the following screenshot:

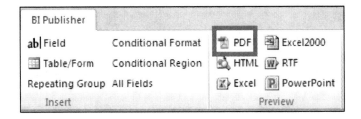

3. You will see the following output:

Name	PhoneNumber	DateOfBirth	Age
Vishal	(222) 122-8946	01-Mar-9999	99
Tom	(555) 789-9878	20-Mar-1111	89
Harry	(666) 678-2341	15-Apr-2222	79
Elena	(444) 242-5676	30-Aug-3333	69
Barry	(666) 123-3231	22-Sept-6666	59

Let us now see the code that helps us in making the template dynamic. The same is shared for your convenience as follows;

```
<?param@begin:Column1;'"Name"'?>
<?param@begin:Column2;'"PhoneNumber"'?>
<?param@begin:Column3;'"DateOfBirth"'?>
<?param@begin:Column4;'"Age"'?>
```

<?$Column1?>	<?$Column2?>	<?$Column3?>	<?$Column4?>
`<?for-each:Employee?>` `<?./*[name() = $Column1]?>`	`<?./*[name() = $Column2]?>`	`<?./*[name() = $Column3]?>`	`<?./*[name() = $Column4]?>` `<?end for-each?>`

We first declare a `param` parameter in the `begin` context using `<?param@begin:Column1;'"Name"'?>`. Note that `Column1` is the name of a `param` parameter. Params are the parameters which we declare in the data model. Templates can also have variables which can be used for certain calculations in the template and are local to the template. `Column1 param` here is set to have a default value of `Name` but the value of `Column1 param` can be passed while running a BI Publisher report as well. We can have a dropdown parameter type in BI Publisher. We can have a list of column names as different values in this list and we can let the user select the column that he wants to see in the report using the parameter. The column name value that the user selects, in the parameter, can be captured in the template using `<?param@begin:Column1;'"Name"'?>` where `Column1` is the name of the parameter. The next important thing is the use of this `param` to code dynamic columns in rtf template. This is done by `<?for-each:Employee?><?./*[name() = $Column1]?>`.

Note that you will have to open `Dynamic BIP using params.xml` to comprehend the code. We are dealing with the animal called the XPATH syntax here. It's an industry standard developed by **World Wide Web Consortium (W3C)**. It is a method to navigate in XML documents. The first `.` in `./*[name() = $Column1]` is for the current node. Since we are running the loop of `Employee`, the dot is for the `Employee` node. `/` is for the descendants of the current node(`Employee` in our case). `*` is a wild card character in the XPATH syntax. So this means that we are considering all the descendants of the `Employee` node. `[]` is for filtering, so we first consider all nodes and then put a filter that the node should be the one whose name matches with the value of `Column1 param`.

The BI Publisher syntax is simplified XSL instructions. You can also use native XSL commands in your templates. The code you put in your templates is converted to XSL-FO when you upload the template. Since we just saw that we can have dynamic columns using BI Publisher syntax so we should be able to make dynamic columns using XSL syntax as well. The syntax for the dynamic columns for loop in XSL syntax is `<xsl:for-each select=".//node()[local-name()=$P_LOOP]"><?sort:name;'ascending';data-type='text'?>`.

Similarly, syntax for dynamic display of column is `<xsl:value-of select=".//node()[local-name()=$P_SORT_BY]">`.

Consider `Dynamic Grouping Employees.xml` and `Dynamic Grouping Employees.rtf`. The only special thing in this template is the dynamic `for-each-group`, that is, `<?for-each-group:ROW;./*[name(.) = $group1]?>`.

Have a look at `Dynamic Sort.rtf` and `Dynamic Sort.xml` to get the code for dynamic sorting.

 I hope you remember our discussion on the Table functions from our discussion in *Chapter 3, In the APEX Mansion – Interactive Reports*. That table function can also be used in BI Publisher when we select SQL Query as the data source. This can enable us to materialize the thought of dynamic data source.

Integrating BI Publisher with APEX

We have seen various examples of creating reports in BI Publisher. I hope you understand that there is a lot more to BI Publisher than what I have written here. BI Publisher can be used for generating charts, matrix reports, republish the generated reports, and a lot more. There is tremendous flexibility in the security model as well. Again data model and templates can also be made in a number of other ways. BI Publisher also gives a utility called **Template Viewer** which can be used to see the reports generated by templates designed in other medium such as excel and PDF without having to upload the templates on the server. This saves time and helps to validate the templates offline. The BI Publisher desktop utility also installs a number of samples which can serve as good training material for BI Publisher.

Now that we have some idea about the enormous possibilities open to us using BI Publisher, the time is apt to check out the integration of this tool with APEX.

Using convert servlet in Instance Settings

Usually, integrations with other tools work with web services. This basically means that the code exists on the tool which is being integrated and is accessed by some other tool using web services. Although APEX and BI Publisher can be integrated using web services, and we will see this integration in a short while, the two tools can also be integrated using convert servlet. In this method, the data and the template are passed by APEX to convert servlet of BI Publisher which generates the report in the desired format and sends it back to APEX. So the code in this case exists in APEX and it just leverages the reporting engine of BI Publisher to generate high fidelity reports. This integration works in a similar way to the integration between APEX and Apache FOP or APEX and Apache Cocoon. The configuration is done in the **Report Printing** section of **Instance Settings**. Since we have been to this place while configuring Apache FOP and Apache Cocoon, let me just put the screenshot which shows the BI Publisher specific values to be put in this section.

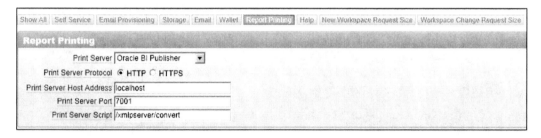

Page 4 of the reference application uses the APEX_UTIL package to transmit a **Report Layout** and **Report Query** stored in shared components to BI Publisher which finally returns the document. As pointed out in the Apache Cocoon and Apache FOP section, if you have an APEX report, then you can use this configuration to print that report in various formats by going to the **Print Attributes** page of the report.

Integrating APEX with BI Publisher using web services

BI Publisher can also be integrated using web services. We have already created a report in BI Publisher, we can pass parameters to BI Publisher from APEX and then direct BI Publisher to run the report using the values passed from APEX. The generated report can then be fetched from BI Publisher to APEX. Not just this, we can also get the status of the submitted jobs at APEX end to inform the user about the status of his submitted report. Using this mechanism, we can make sure that the user never leaves the APEX screen while BI Publisher does all the hard work at the backend.

An example of APEX using BI Publisher's web service has been coded for you in the page 2 of the reference application. Make sure that you change the ports and configure the ACL according to your environment. My APEX is working on the `8001` port and BI Publisher is working on the `7001` port.

I am using a PL/SQL process to parse calls and web services but we have already seen a number of other ways of doing this and I am sure you would explore other ways such as using APEX web service references.

A report has been created for you on page 5 of the reference application which demonstrates the process of passing APEX items to BI Publisher. The only trick in passing the parameters is to use the `#<APEX_ITEM_NAME_WITHOUT_ANGLE_BRACKETS>#` syntax in the web service reference. Check the code for more details.

The code for getting the response has been coded according to the web service responses which I am getting on my environment. You might have to tweak it according to the responses on your environment.

BI Publisher guest folder

Apart from the two techniques mentioned in the preceding section, BI Publisher also has a guest folder feature. We can specify one of the folders in the catalog as guest folder and reports placed in this folder will not require any access credentials. This is an insecure method but I thought you should know. The URL required to access the reports can be found in BI Publisher. To get the URL, click on the **Actions** button. The process to reach the **Actions** button of a report has already been shared with you in this chapter. Move your mouse over **Share Report link** and then click on **Document Only**. You would get an info dialogue box which will give you the link to the report. You can call this link from any place and the report will open for you. The only condition is that the report and the data model it references should be in the Shared Folder and the Shared Folder should be configured. Guest access will not work if we are sharing the catalog with OBIEE. Let us now see the process to configure the Shared Folder.

1. Click on the **Administration** link on the top-right corner, and then click on **Server Configuration** under **System Maintenance**.

2. Select **Oracle BI Publisher – File System** in the **Catalog Type** dropdown and enter a value in the **Path** textbox. For example, `C:\OracleProducts\BI_Middleware\instances\instance1\BIPCatalog`.

3. Go to the path folder and create a folder called `Reports` in it.

4. The changed configuration does not take effect till BI Publisher is restarted. For restarting BI Publisher, log in to console (`http://<obiee_presentation_server_ip>:<obiee_presentation_server_port>/console`) and click on **Deployments**. Use the **Next** link to go to **bipublisher (11.1.1)**. Select **bipublisher (11.1.1)** and then click on the **Stop** button. Select **Force Stop Now** from the list. Select **Yes** in the following step. We now start the server by selecting **bipublisher (11.1.1)** again and hitting the **Start** button this time. Select **Servicing all requests** from that. Select **Yes** in the step that follows.

5. Log in to BI Publisher again, click on the **Administration** link on the top-right corner, and then click on **Security Configuration** under **Security Center**.

6. Check the **Allow Guest Access** checkbox and enter the name of the guest folder in the **Guest Folder Name** textbox. For example, `Guest_folder`.

7. Click on the **Apply** button.

8. Click on the **Administration** link and then click on the **File** link under **Data Sources**.

9. Click on **demo files** and check the **Allow Guest Access** checkbox in the **Security** section.

 I am doing this because the report which I would create in the guest folder will use this data source. You have to do this with the data source which you would use in the report stored in the guest folder.

10. Click on the **Apply** button.

11. Create a `Guest_folder` folder in the `Reports` folder which you created in step 3.

12. Restart BI Publisher.

13. Create a report and its data model in the `Guest_folder` folder.

14. You can call this report from anyplace without any authentication. The link to call the report can be found from the **Share Report Link** in the **Actions** menu. The link looks similar to `http://<obiee_presentation_server_ip>:<obiee_presentation_server_port>/xmlpserver/Guest_folder/emp_report.xdo?_xpf=&_xpt=0&_xdo=%2FGuest_folder%2Femp_report.xdo&_xmode=4&_xt=emp_layout&_xf=html&_xautorun=true`.

Another famous way of integrating applications on an enterprise is to use **Single Sign On (SSO)**. SSO can be used to configure tools to share a single authenticating server and logins to individual tools is avoided. SSO can also be used to integrate APEX with OBIEE.

Summary

The goal of this chapter was to introduce you to OBIEE and to give you a good idea about the strengths of the tool, so that you are in a position to use it when the need be. The intent was also to introduce some of the major reporting mechanisms which are easily possible in OBIEE, but are a little difficult to achieve using traditional APEX programming. OBIEE has been the back bone of Oracle's Business Intelligence and reporting solution, so it mandated a chapter on it.

We will talk about integrating some other known technologies with APEX in the next chapter.

8
All About Web Services and Integrations

This chapter is entirely dedicated to web services and integrations. While we have been talking about web services all along, we haven't discussed the process to create web services. This chapter will talk about the creation of both RESTful and SOAP web services. We will talk using them as well. We will then discuss the creation of BPEL processes and a simple crystal report. We will then move on to read about migrating Microsoft Access reports to APEX. We will also learn about the migration of Oracle forms to APEX. Finally, we will have a short discussion about using Google web services and Oracle R enterprise in Oracle APEX. Enough talking, let's roll.

The following are the major learning outcomes of this chapter:

- Creating web services using native the XML DB web service
- Querying data using native web service
- Creating RESTful web service using Resource Templates
- Creating a simple synchronous **BPEL (Business Process Execution Language)** process
- Creating an asynchronous BPEL process with human workflows.
- Integration of SAP crystal reports with APEX
- Migrating MS Access application to APEX
- Migrating Oracle Forms and Reports to APEX
- APEX integration with Google web services
- Using Oracle R enterprise in APEX

Understanding reports on web services and collections

This section deals with the creation of a report on web services and collections. I have grouped these two topics together because the response of a web service can be stored in APEX collections, which can then be used in APEX reports. We will also see Resource Templates in this section. Resource Templates help us build RESTful web services and we will learn to create a report on that as well.

> Throughout the chapter, I have used my database credentials, ip address, WebLogic address and port numbers. You are expected to replace there your corresponding information.

We can store the response of web services in either page items or collections. Here, we are using web services to populate collections but the APEX_COLLECTION API can also be used to do all sorts of operations on collections. Some of the methods in this API are APEX_COLLECTION.ADD_MEMBER, APEX_COLLECTION.TRUNCATE_COLLECTION, and APEX_COLLECTION.SORT_MEMBERS. The information stored in the collections can be retrieved by either querying apex_collections or wwv_flow_collections.

Most of the web services discussed in this chapter are hosted on XML HTTP Server. We have to grant access to packt_schema to use XDB web services. We also have to create an Access Control List. Execute the following to do this:

```
SQL> @4-98-9_02_acl_for_web_services
```

You can find 4-98-9_02_acl_for_web_services.sql in the code pack for *Chapter 2, Conventional Reporting in APEX*. Put APEX_040200 in Enter the schema which will run the webservice: prompt.

Grant the following privileges to packt_schema:

```
GRANT XDB_WEBSERVICES TO packt_schema;
GRANT XDB_WEBSERVICES_OVER_HTTP TO packt_schema;
```

Execute the following statements from SQL*Plus using SYSDBA:

```
exec DBMS_NETWORK_ACL_ADMIN.ADD_PRIVILEGE('/sys/acls/apex_users.xml',
'PACKT_SCHEMA',TRUE, 'connect');
commit;
```

If the name of the ACL in your case is different then use the same in the above command.

Understanding native XML DB web services

We have learned a few things about XMLHTTP Protocol server in the first chapter. This chapter will introduce the configuration and use of XML HTTP Protocol server to expose stored PL/SQL functions and procedures as web services. The input and output **XML schema definition (XSD)** are governed by the arguments and the return values of stored procedures and functions.

Setting XML DB web services

The following are the steps to configure XML DB web services:

1. Execute the following code after connecting from command prompt as `sys` to enable XML HTTP Protocol server to work on port 8080:

   ```
   Begin
   DBMS_XDB.sethttpport(8080);
   End;
   ```

   If 8080 port is in use then configure some other port number.

2. Open command prompt and get into the directory that contains the following script. Execute the following command after connecting as `sysdba`. This step helps us to present stored functions and procedures as web services.

   SQL> @4-98-9_08_enableWebservice

   This script tweaks `xdbconfig.xml`, which is the configuration file for the XML HTTP Protocol server. `xdbconfig.xml` can be changed using the `DBMS_XDB` package. The preceding script does the necessary changes for us.

If you have executed the scripts under *Understanding reports on web services and collections* section and this section then, you should now be able to see the WSDL for the `Get_employee` function of `Chapter2` PL/SQL package when you fire the following URL:

`http://localhost:8080/orawsv/PACKT_SCHEMA/CHAPTER2/GET_EMPLOYEE?wsdl`

This URL will prompt you for credentials. Pass your `packt_schema` credentials to see the WSDL.

Creating a report on native XML DB web services

Let's now now see the process of creating reports on web service responses stored in collections/items associated with the APEX web service references/processes. Get employee manual and GET_EMPLOYEE_TABService web service references of *Chapter2, Conventional Reporting in APEX* reference application use native web services. We will talk about GET_EMPLOYEE_TABService in some time. Let's now talk about the Get employee manual web service reference.

The Get employee manual web service reference of *Chapter 2, Coventional Reporting in APEX* reference application has a manually written SOAP envelope. We know that our web service needs authentication. We can pass the credentials from the URL. If we pass the credentials from the URL then we have to mark that the web service does not need basic authentication. Enter http://packt_schema:packt_schema@localhost:8080/orawsv/PACKT_SCHEMA/CHAPTER2/GET_EMPLOYEE in the **URL** textbox of the Get employee manual web service reference of *Chapter 2, Conventional Reporting in APEX* reference application. Note that we are passing packt_schema credentials by using the @ symbol. Change the credentials according to your own environment. We'll see another method of authentication in the next section. Replace localhost with the ip address of your database server

The following is the code of a manually written SOAP envelope of the Get employee manual web service reference for your reference:

```
<?xml version='1.0' encoding='UTF-8'?><SOAP-ENV:Envelope xmlns:SOAP-
ENV="http://schemas.xmlsoap.org/soap/envelope/" xmlns:SOAP-
ENC="http://schemas.xmlsoap.org/soap/encoding/" xmlns:xsi="http://
www.w3.org/2001/XMLSchema-instance" xmlns:xsd="http://www.w3.org/2001/
XMLSchema">
  <SOAP-ENV:Body>
<ns1:CCHAP2_EMP_TYPE-GET_EMPLOYEEInput xmlns:ns1="http://xmlns.oracle.
com/orawsv/PACKT_SCHEMA/CHAPTER2/GET_EMPLOYEE">
<ns1:EMP_ID-NUMBER-IN>#P8_EMP_ID#</ns1:EMP_ID-NUMBER-IN>
</ns1:CCHAP2_EMP_TYPE-GET_EMPLOYEEInput>
</SOAP-ENV:Body>
</SOAP-ENV:Envelope>
```

The SOAP envelope in the Get employee manual web service reference is written according to my environment. If your environment needs a different envelope then use soapUI (http://www.soapui.org/Downloads/download-soapui-pro.html) to create a SOAP envelope that suits your environment. soapUI will expect the WSDL written at the end of the *Setting XML DB web services* section, to create a SOAP envelope.

Note that #P8_EMP_ID# is highlighted in the preceding code. The P8_EMP_ID item is on page 8 of the *Chapter2, Conventional Reporting in APEX* reference application and holds the value of employee ID selected by the user while using this page. The preceding SOAP envelope passes the employee ID selected by the user to the native web service using #P8_EMP_ID#. Now to get a response from this web service reference, we have to invoke it. Invocation is done by the Get employee page process. The Get employee page process invokes the Get employee manual web service reference, which in turn invokes the chapter2.get_employee function. The following is the code of chapter2.get_employee:

```
FUNCTION get_employee(emp_id NUMBER) RETURN chap2_emp_type
AS
  emp_object chap2_emp_type;
BEGIN
  SELECT chap2_emp_type(first_name, last_name, employee_id, email,
job_id)
  INTO emp_object
  FROM oehr_employees WHERE employee_id = emp_id;
  RETURN emp_object;
END;
```

The employee ID passed from the manually written SOAP envelope, that is, #P8_EMP_ID# is mapped to the emp_id argument of the chapter2.get_employee function. So the value passed from #P8_EMP_ID# is captured in the emp_id argument of the chapter 2.get_employee function. Note that the chapter2.get_employee function returns an object of the chap2_emp_type type. We created the chap2_emp_type type, because a function can return only one value and we wanted to get more than one attribute of the selected employee. The SELECT statement in the get_employee function uses emp_id, which was passed as an argument to fetch the details of the selected employee. We cast the details of the selected employee to the chap2_emp_type type in the SELECT clause and store it in emp_object. This object is finally returned by the chapter2.get_employee function. This returned object is a part of the web service response. The web service response is captured in APEX tables. The storing of response in APEX tables happens because we have GET_EMP_MANUAL in the **Store Response in Collection** textbox of the Get employee manual web service reference. GET_EMP_MANUAL is an APEX collection and we will soon use it in our report. APEX collections can be retrieved by using APEX_COLLECTIONS or wwv_flow_collections. We can put any name in the **Store Response in Collection** textbox, but we will have to use the same name while framing our report on the web service response.

Let us now look at a typical web service response returned by a call to the `Get employee manual` web service reference. Note that our report region will be heavily dependent on the structure of this XML:

```xml
<?xml version="1.0" ?>
<soap:Envelope xmlns:soap="http://schemas.xmlsoap.org/soap/envelope/">
  <soap:Body>
    <GET_EMPLOYEEOutput xmlns="http://xmlns.oracle.com/orawsv/PACKT_
SCHEMA/CHAPTER2/GET_EMPLOYEE">
      <RETURN>
        <CHAP2_EMP_TYPE>
          <FIRST_NAME>Neena</FIRST_NAME>
          <LAST_NAME>Kochhar</LAST_NAME>
          <EMPLOYEE_ID>101</EMPLOYEE_ID>
          <EMAIL>NKOCHHAR</EMAIL>
          <JOB_ID>AD_VP</JOB_ID>
        </CHAP2_EMP_TYPE>
      </RETURN>
    </GET_EMPLOYEEOutput>
  </soap:Body>
</soap:Envelope>
```

Note the structure of the nodes in the preceding XML. We will use this structure while framing our XPATH when we create a report based on the `Get employee manual` web service reference.

Let's now talk about creating a report on our web service response. We can either create a classic report and frame the query to fetch the data from `GET_EMP_MANUAL` APEX collection ourselves, or can follow the steps mentioned in the following paragraph to create a report.

To create a report on the `Get employee manual` web service reference, we have to create a **Report** region, and then select **Web Service Result**. We will have to select **Manually Created** as **Web Reference Type**, **Get employee manual** as **Web Service Reference**, enter `/GET_EMPLOYEEOutput/RETURN/CHAP2_EMP_TYPE` in **Result Node Path (XPath)**, `http://xmlns.oracle.com/orawsv/PACKT_SCHEMA/CHAPTER2/GET_EMPLOYEE` in **Message Namespace** and `FIRST_NAME, LAST_NAME, EMPLOYEE_ID, EMAIL`, and `JOB_ID` in **Parameter Names** textboxes. Following these steps will automatically create a **Report** region with the necessary query in it. It is easy to draw a relation between the value of **Result Node Path (XPath)** and the sample web service response shared previously.

Let's now look at the query of the **Get employee** region. This region is based on the **Get employee manual** web service reference, and hence it uses the `GET_EMP_MANUAL` collection (highlighted in the following code).

```
select extractValue(value(t),'/*/FIRST_NAME','xmlns="http://xmlns.
oracle.com/orawsv/PACKT_SCHEMA/CHAPTER2/GET_EMPLOYEE"') "FIRST_
NAME", extractValue(value(t),'/*/LAST_NAME','xmlns="http://xmlns.
oracle.com/orawsv/PACKT_SCHEMA/CHAPTER2/GET_EMPLOYEE"') "LAST_
NAME", extractValue(value(t),'/*/EMPLOYEE_ID','xmlns="http://
xmlns.oracle.com/orawsv/PACKT_SCHEMA/CHAPTER2/GET_EMPLOYEE"')
"EMPLOYEE_ID", extractValue(value(t),'/*/EMAIL','xmlns="http://xmlns.
oracle.com/orawsv/PACKT_SCHEMA/CHAPTER2/GET_EMPLOYEE"') "EMAIL",
extractValue(value(t),'/*/JOB_ID','xmlns="http://xmlns.oracle.com/
orawsv/PACKT_SCHEMA/CHAPTER2/GET_EMPLOYEE"') "JOB_ID"
  from wwv_flow_collections c,        table(xmlsequence(extract(c.
xmltype001,'//GET_EMPLOYEEOutput/RETURN/CHAP2_EMP_
TYPE','xmlns="http://xmlns.oracle.com/orawsv/PACKT_SCHEMA/CHAPTER2/
GET_EMPLOYEE"'))) t
```

where `c.collection_name = 'GET_EMP_MANUAL`

Let me now talk about the `extract` function (made bold in the preceding code). `extract` uses a `varchar2` string containing a XPATH, another string holding the namespace information, and an XMLTYPE value (this is our web service response) as arguments. It returns the part of the XMLTYPE value encapsulated by the XPATH passed to it as an argument. The XPATH (made bold in the preceding code) informs the `extract` function about the part of the XML (web service response) in which we are interested. It is easy to draw a relation between this XPATH and the structure of the sample web service response shared previously. `extract` returns this desired fragment as an XMLTYPE value. The output of the `extract` function is fed to `xmlsequence`. `xmlsequence` has two forms. One form accepts a XMLType and the other accepts a ref cursor. We will use the former. `xmlsequence` returns a varray of the top-level nodes in the XMLType value. This set of varrays is then fed to our old buddy, the `table` function.

If you observe the web service response shared in this section, you will find that the nodes encapsulated by `/GET_EMPLOYEEOutput/RETURN/CHAP2_EMP_TYPE` are `FIRST_NAME`, `LAST_NAME`, `EMPLOYEE_ID`, `EMAIL`, and `JOB_ID`. The `extract` function gives us the web service response fragment inside `/GET_EMPLOYEEOutput/RETURN/CHAP2_EMP_TYPE`, and we then get the values of `FIRST_NAME`, `LAST_NAME`, `EMPLOYEE_ID`, `EMAIL`, and `JOB_ID` using the `extractValue` function in the `select` clause. Now that we understand the query, we can change the way in which we retrieve the data. We can put `//GET_EMPLOYEEOutput/RETURN` instead of `//GET_EMPLOYEEOutput/RETURN/CHAP2_EMP_TYPE` as an argument to the `extract` function. If we do this, then the `extract` function will give us the XML fragment encapsulated by `//GET_EMPLOYEEOutput/RETURN`. We will then have to accordingly modify the `extractValue` function in the `select` clause. For example, we will have to change the expression for the `LAST_NAME` column to `/*/CHAP2_EMP_TYPE/LAST_NAME`. The `extractValue` function takes the XMLType and XPATH as the arguments and returns the scalar value of the XPATH node.

Since we have configured the native web service and have done environment specific changes, so your **Get employee** region, **Get employee using XMLTable** region, and **Get employees** region should work perfectly. But before we see them in action, we will have to make the following changes on page 8 of the *Chapter 2, Conventional Reporting in APEX* reference application:

1. Set the condition of the **getOrders** page process to **never**.
2. Enter your credentials of `packt_schema` in the **Get employees** page process.
3. Click on the **Items** radio button under the **Web Service Output Parameters** section of the **Get employees** page process. Remove `EMP_TAB_COLLECTION` from the **EMPLOYEE_ID** textbox and click on the **Apply Changes** button. Now select the **Collection** radio button under the **Web Service Output Parameters** section of the **Get employees** page process, and enter `EMP_TAB_COLLECTION` as the collection name in the text box next to **Entire Response Document** and click on the **Apply Changes** button again.

We have discussed the process of creating a native XMLDB web service and checked out a report region based on it. Let us now talk about the **Get employee using XMLTable** and **Get employees** regions. **Get employee using XMLTable** shows a newer and improved syntax of extracting values from an XML, while the **Get employees** regions is based on a native web service that returns a set of records unlike the **Get employee manual** web service reference which returned only a single record.

Using XMLTable to parse a web service response

Oracle has come up with a new method of parsing XML in SQL query. We can now use the more concise `XMLTable` method instead of the old mechanism of using table function with `xmlsequence`. The newer syntax offers significant performance improvement. However, the wizard that creates a report on web services in APEX 4.x still creates the report using `xmlsequence`. The **Get employee using XMLTable** region in page 8 of the reference application uses the newer syntax to display the same data as in the previous section. The following code of this region has been shared for your convenience:

```
select FIRST_NAME,LAST_NAME,EMPLOYEE_ID,EMAIL,JOB_ID FROM wwv_flow_
collections c,
XMLTABLE( XMLNAMESPACES ('http://schemas.xmlsoap.org/soap/envelope/'
as "soap", 'http://xmlns.oracle.com/orawsv/PACKT_SCHEMA/CHAPTER2/GET_
EMPLOYEE' as "EMP_NS")
,'/soap:Envelope/soap:Body/EMP_NS:GET_EMPLOYEEOutput/EMP_NS:RETURN/
EMP_NS:CHAP2_EMP_TYPE' PASSING c.xmltype001
COLUMNS "FIRST_NAME"  VARCHAR2(20 BYTE) PATH 'EMP_NS:FIRST_NAME',
"LAST_NAME"  VARCHAR2(25 BYTE) PATH 'EMP_NS:LAST_NAME',
```

```
"EMPLOYEE_ID"  NUMBER(6,0) PATH 'EMP_NS:EMPLOYEE_ID',
"EMAIL"  VARCHAR2(25 BYTE) PATH 'EMP_NS:EMAIL',
"JOB_ID"  VARCHAR2(10 BYTE) PATH 'EMP_NS:JOB_ID')
where c.collection_name = 'GET_EMP_MANUAL'
```

Using a native web service to return a collection of rows

Let's now discuss a method to get a bunch of records as a response from a native web service. The trick lies in the way we write our function which is finally invoked through a native web service. The web service behind the **Get employees** region returns a collection of records. Check out GET_EMPLOYEE_TABService web service reference. This is not a manually written web service. So it takes care of environment-related troubles for framing the SOAP envelope.

The web service reference says that it needs basic authentication. The authentication parameters are passed from the Get employees page process on page 8. Recollect that we passed the authentication credentials in the URL in the Get employee manual web service reference. Change the packt_schema credentials in the Get employees page process to your own schema credentials. Have a look at the WSDL of the GET_EMPLOYEE_TABService web service reference to see its structure. You can use the following URL, to check out the WSDL, which lets us get multiple rows:

```
http://localhost:8080/orawsv/PACKT_SCHEMA/CHAPTER2/GET_EMPLOYEE_
TAB?wsdl
```

The GET_EMPLOYEE_TABService web service reference calls the chapter2.get_employee_tab function. Let's have a look at this function now, which is as follows:

```
FUNCTION get_employee_tab RETURN chap2_emp_tab_typ_obj AS
   l_return chap2_emp_tab;    l_return2 chap2_emp_tab_typ_obj;
BEGIN
   SELECT chap2_emp_type(FIRST_NAME,LAST_NAME,EMPLOYEE_ID,EMAIL,JOB_ID)
BULK COLLECT INTO l_return
   FROM oehr_employees;
   l_Return2 := chap2_emp_tab_typ_obj(l_return);
   RETURN l_Return2;
END;
```

In the preceding function, we use BULK COLLECT to put the data in a collection. This is a performance booster and we will read about it in Chapter 9. chapter2.get_employee_tab returns an object of type chap2_emp_tab_typ_obj. chap2_emp_tab_typ_obj is an object which has an attribute of type chap2_emp_tab. chap2_emp_tab in turn is a table of type chap2_emp_type. This arrangement helps us return a bunch of rows from the native web service call to get_employee_tab function.

The `Get employees` page process invokes the `GET_EMPLOYEE_TAB`Service web service reference, which in turn invokes the `chapter2.get_employee_tab` function. The response of the web service is stored in `EMP_TAB_COLLECTION` APEX collection. This collection is declared in the `Get employees` page process.

Finally, the **Get employees** region is built on top of the `EMP_TAB_COLLECTION` collection. The query is similar to the query of the **Get employee** region discussed previously. The end structure of the web service might change in your environment. So take soapUI's help to understand the structure in your environment and change the **Region Source** of the **Get employees** region accordingly.

Querying XML DB using a web service

Till now, we have seen the process of calling a stored PL/SQL function using web services. This section will present a method of firing queries on tables using a native web service. The queries are sent in a standard XML syntax to the web service defined by the `http://localhost:8080/orawsv?wsdl` WSDL. Details of the query syntax can be found at `http://docs.oracle.com/cd/E11882_01/appdev.112/e10492/xdb_web_services.htm#CHDEGIEE`

`Chapter2.get_emp_frm_ws_query` is an example of firing queries on tables using a native web service. The following code of this function is shared for your convenience:

 Change the credentials and the WSDL in the following function according to your own environment.

```
FUNCTION get_emp_frm_ws_query(employee NUMBER) RETURN xmltype
AS
   request utl_http.req;       response utl_http.resp;
   envelope    VARCHAR2(3000) := '<packt:Envelope xmlns:packt="http://
schemas.xmlsoap.org/soap/envelope/">
<packt:Body>
<query xmlns="http://xmlns.oracle.com/orawsv">
<query_text type="SQL">
select * from oehr_employees where employee_id = :employee
</query_text>
<bind name="employee">'||employee||'</bind>
</query>
</packt:Body>
</packt:Envelope>';
   resp_store VARCHAR2(32767);
   xml_resp xmltype;
BEGIN
```

```
   request := utl_http.begin_request('http://packt_schema:packt_
password@localhost:8080/orawsv', 'POST', 'HTTP/1.1');
   utl_http.set_authentication(request, 'packt_schema', 'packt_
password');
   utl_http.set_header(request, 'Content-Type', 'text/xml');
   utl_http.set_header(request, 'Content-Length', LENGTH(envelope));
   utl_http.write_text(request, envelope);
   response := utl_http.get_response(request);
   utl_http.read_text(response, resp_store);
   xml_resp := xmltype(resp_store);
   utl_http.end_response(response);
   RETURN xml_resp;
END;
```

Note that authentication (the preceding second highlighted code) can be done by both the `utl_http.begin_request` and `utl_http.set_authentication` functions. Note the process of binding variables to filter records in the result set in the first highlighted piece of the preceding code. Note the namespace declarations as well.

The preceding function returns an XMLType object. We will soon see that we pass `:P8_EMP_ID` from the region source to `chapter2.get_emp_frm_ws_query` function. This value is collected in the `employee` argument in the `chapter2.get_emp_frm_ws_query` function. The `employee` argument is then used in the native query call to filter the records. This can be seen in the first highlighted piece of the preceding code.

Let us now go from top to bottom in the preceding `chapter2.get_emp_frm_ws_query` function.

The `envelope` variable holds the manually written SOAP envelope. `utl_http.set_header` is used to set the header of the request. `utl_http.write_text` writes the SOAP envelope in the `utl_http.req` variable. `utl_http.get_response` gets the response of this request. This response is of the `utl_http.resp` type. `utl_http.read_text` converts the response to the `varchar2` type. `XmlType()` is used to cast the `varchar2` response to XMLType, so that we can use the `extract` function to get the relevant parts of the response and parse it to generate our report.

We invoke `chapter2.get_emp_frm_ws_query` from the **Get employee from PLSQL web service query call** region. The following code of this region is shared for your convenience:

```
return 'SELECT extractValue(value(t),''/*/FIRST_
NAME'',''xmlns="http://xmlns.oracle.com/orawsv"'') FIRST_NAME,
extractValue(value(t),''/*/LAST_NAME'',''xmlns="http://xmlns.oracle.
com/orawsv"'') "LAST_NAME",
extractValue(value(t),''/*/EMPLOYEE_ID'',''xmlns="http://xmlns.oracle.
com/orawsv"'') "EMPLOYEE_ID",
```

```
extractValue(value(t),''/*/EMAIL'',''xmlns="http://xmlns.oracle.com/
orawsv"'') "EMAIL",
extractValue(value(t),''/*/JOB_ID'',''xmlns="http://xmlns.oracle.com/
orawsv"'') "JOB_ID",
extractValue(value(t),''/*/SALARY'',''xmlns="http://xmlns.oracle.com/
orawsv"'') "SALARY",
extractValue(value(t),''/*/HIRE_DATE'',''xmlns="http://xmlns.oracle.
com/orawsv"'') "HIRE_DATE",
extractValue(value(t),''/*/PHONE_NUMBER'',''xmlns="http://xmlns.
oracle.com/orawsv"'') "PHONE_NUMBER"
  FROM TABLE(xmlsequence(extract(chapter2.get_emp_frm_ws_query(:P8_
EMP_ID),''//queryOut/ROWSET/ROW'',''xmlns="http://xmlns.oracle.com/
orawsv"''))) t';
end;
```

Note the argument of the `extract` function (highlighted in the preceding code) in the `from` clause and compare it with the argument of the `extract` function in the previous regions. In the previous regions, APEX was storing the web service response in an `XMLType` column called `xmltype001` of an APEX collection. We are not using APEX collections here. `chapter2.get_emp_frm_ws_query` is returning an `XMLType` object that contains the web service response here. Also note that we are passing the value of `P8_EMP_ID` from the table function to `chapter2.get_emp_frm_ws_query` which captures this value in its employee argument and uses employee argument to filter the records.

> The **Get employees from PLSQL web service call** region uses PL/SQL to fire a SOAP request for a native XML DB web service. This region uses the `xmltype` value returned by `chapter2.get_emps_frm_ws` function to build a report. This function shows the process to return a bunch of records using native webservice query call. Replace the credentials in this function with your own credentials to see the code in action.

Implementing and using RESTful web services using Resource Templates

Resource Templates are a feature of APEX listener and they let us define handlers for the `HTTP GET`, `HTTP POST`, `HTTP DELETE`, and `HTTP PUT` methods. Resource Templates can be used to create RESTful web services.

> Note that Resource Templates work only with the APEX listener and not with `mod_plsql`.

Let's now enable RESTful web services. Perform the following steps to do this:

Configuring RESTful web services using Resource Templates

1. Run `<directory where apex is unzipped>\apex\apex_rest_config.sql` as `sysdba`. This script will help us to create the `APEX_LISTENER` and `APEX_REST_PUBLIC_USER` schemas.

2. Run the following command:

   ```
   java -jar <directory in that contains the currently hosted apex.
   war file>\apex.war setup
   ```

   We can find `<directory in that contains the currently hosted apex.war file>` by logging into the WebLogic console and navigating to **Deployments | apex**. The path will be visible next to the **Path:** label in the **Overview** tab. Running the preceding command will prompt you to enter your database configurations and passwords of the `APEX_LISTENER` and `APEX_REST_PUBLIC_USER` schemas. Fill in these details. This command will update your `apex.war` file. We should now replace the existing `apex.war` deployment on WebLogic with the new file.

3. Update the APEX listener installation by logging to the console, clicking on **Deployments**, selecting the **Apex** checkbox, and then clicking on the **Update** button. Keep the defaults in the wizard and finish the update process.

4. Execute the following statement as `sysdba`:

   ```
   alter user packt_schema grant connect through APEX_REST_PUBLIC_
   USER;
   ```

5. Login to the **INTERNAL** workspace and navigate to **Manage Instance | Feature Configuration**. Select **Yes** in the **Enable RESTful Services** dropdown present under the **SQL Workshop** tab and click on the **Apply Changes** button.

Creating RESTful web services using Resource Templates

Let us now create a Resource Template by performing the following steps:

1. Login to your workspace and navigate to **SQL Workshop | RESTful Services**.

2. Click on the **Create** button.

3. Enter any name in the **Name** textbox, and enter `packt/` as **URI Prefix**. `packt/` will be a part of the URL of RESTful service.

4. Enter `getAllDepartments` in the **URI Template** textbox.

5. Select **GET** in the **Method** dropdown.

6. Let **Source Type** be **Query** and **Format** be **JSON**.

7. Enter `select department_id, department_name, location_id, manager_id from oehr_departments` in the **Source** textbox, and then click on the **Create Module** button.

8. Click on the **GET** link (highlighted in the following screenshot):

9. Select **No** in the **Requires Secure Access** dropdown, if the server on which your listener is hosted does not accept https requests. Click on the **Apply Changes** button.

10. Click on the **TEST** button under the **Source** section. Your RESTful URL will look like the following:

```
http://localhost:7001/apex/packt_workspace/packt/
getAllDepartments
```

Change the preceding URL according to your environment.

11. You should be able to see the following output:

 Note that the response is a JSON object. We will see the parsing of a JSON object in a short while.

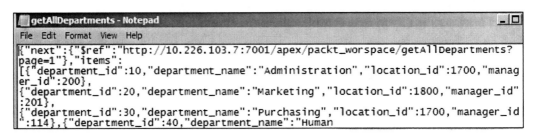

The newly created Resource Template does not accept any argument. We can however create a Resource Template that accepts arguments. Import `4-98-9_08_ packt_restful_service_module.sql` in your workspace. Open the `packt. RESTful.Service.Module` module, and then select the `getEmployee/{emp_id}` template. `getEmployee/{emp_id}` does a select on the `oehr_employees` table and returns the details of the employee whose ID is passed to it. The URL for accessing this Resource Template will be similar to `http://localhost:7001/apex/packt_ workspace/packt/getEmployee/100`. The initial part of the URL will depend on your environment, but `/packt/getEmployee/100` will remain the same. `100` in this example is used inside the handler as a bind variable.

> Commented code in the **Report on Resource template** region on page 8 of the reference application demonstrates the method to pass the employee ID to a resource template and get a response. To see the output of the commented code, replace the URL in the `UTL_HTTP.begin_request` function with your RESTful URL and execute it. The code posts the output using `DBMS_OUTPUT.put_line`.

The uncommented code in the **Report on Resource template** region uses the **getAllDepartments** Resource Template, and then parses it using regular expressions. Let's now understand the parsing of the JSON object.

Parsing JSON objects and using MAKE_REST_ REQUEST

Note that results from a RESTful service created using Resource Templates can be in either CSV or JSON form. We will see the process to parse a JSON object and frame a report on top of it.

Enter the URL of your `getAllDepartments` RESTful service as a value of the `p_url` argument of the `APEX_WEB_SERVICE.MAKE_REST_REQUEST` function in the region source of the **Report on Resource template** region on page 2 to make the region work. The query of this region source is also shared in the lower-half of this section.

The parsing of JSON objects can be tricky, because Oracle does not have functions to parse it like it has functions to parse XML data. The following is an example of one such JSON object generated for a few columns of two rows of the `oehr_ departments` table:

```
{"items":[{"department_id":10,"department_
name":"Administration","manager_id":200,"location_
id":1700},{"department_id":20,"department_name":"Marketing","manager_
id":201,"location_id":1800}]}
```

Now, if any of the column values has null in it, then that column does not feature in the JSON object at all. So this means that we cannot use the position of a column in JSON object to parse it, because if the value of this column for a particular row is null then the position of this column in the JSON object will be occupied by the column following it. However, the following packages published by a few private parties can be used to parse JSON objects:

- `http://sourceforge.net/projects/pljson/files/latest/download?source=files`

- `http://reseau.erasme.org/IMG/zip/JSON-1.1-2.zip`

I am using regular expressions to get the required string to be displayed in the report, because my requirement is very specific and I feel more comfortable with regular expressions. Run `http://localhost:7001/apex/packt_workspace/packt/getAllDepartments` to get a feel of the response from an RT. Replace `localhost:7001` according to the APEX Listener configuration of your environment

Note that this section also introduces `APEX_WEB_SERVICE.MAKE_REST_REQUEST` to you. We can also use the traditional PL/SQL method to call web services, but this method is more concise. The following code is provided for your convenience:

```
SELECT regexp_substr(regexp_substr(column_value,    '("department_
id":)+[[:digit:]]{1,},'),    '[[:digit:]]{1,}') "Department id",
  regexp_substr(regexp_substr(column_value,    '("department_
name":")+[[:alnum:] ]{0,}'),    '[[:upper:] ]+[A-Z,a-z]{0,}')
"Department name",
  regexp_substr(regexp_substr(column_value,    '("location_
id":)+[[:digit:]]{1,}'),    '[[:digit:]]{1,}') "Location id",
  regexp_substr(regexp_substr(column_value,    '("manager_
id":)+[[:digit:]]{1,}'),    '[[:digit:]]{1,}') "Manager id"
FROM TABLE(chapter2.chap2_srt_2_tab_4_query(SUBSTR(apex_web_service.
make_rest_request(p_url => 'http://localhost:7001/apex/packt_
workspace/packt/getAllDepartments',   p_http_method => 'GET'),    12),
'},{'))
```

The `substr` function in the FROM clause is used to remove the unnecessary parts from the JSON object string. `},{` is the separator based on which we will break the string into rows. This breaking of a string into rows is done by the `apex_util.string_to_table` function in `chapter2.chap2_srt_2_tab_4_query`. `chapter2.chap2_srt_2_tab_4_query` returns an `apex_application_global.vc_arr2`, which is passed to the `table` function.

The following code of `chapter2.chap2_srt_2_tab_4_query` is shared for your convenience:

```
FUNCTION chap2_srt_2_tab_4_query(
    p_clob CLOB,      p_seperator VARCHAR2 )
  RETURN chap2_srt_2_tab_4_query_typ PIPELINED
IS
  l_tab apex_application_global.vc_arr2;
BEGIN
  l_tab := apex_util.string_to_table(p_clob,p_seperator);
  FOR i IN 1 .. l_tab.count
  LOOP
    pipe row(l_tab(i));
  END LOOP;
END;
```

The next stage of parsing happens in the SELECT clause by regular expressions. This parsing finally gives us the required value. Note the use of the `column_value` pseudo column in the SELECT clause of the preceding shared query. Database returns a virtual table with a single column called `column_value` in the following two conditions:

- When we refer to an XMLTable construct without the `columns` clause
- When we use the `table` function to refer to a scalar, nested table type

RESTful web services have a number of other features. Check the following documentation to learn more about them:

```
http://docs.oracle.com/cd/E37097_01/doc/doc.42/e35128/restful_svc.htm
```

Creating and using RESTful PL/SQL web service

RESTful PL/SQL web services are a close kin of **Database Access Descriptors (DADs)**. DADs had been the backbone of Oracle APEX architecture until the advent of APEX Listener.

To see a working example of the RESTful PL/SQL web service we will have to execute the following steps:

1. Create `packt_dad` by executing the `4-98-9_Appendix_create_dad.sql` script of the Appendix code pack.

2. Ensure that the ANONYMOUS account is OPEN by executing the following query as sysdba:

   ```
   select account_status from dba_users where username = 'ANONYMOUS'
   ```

3. Execute the following to configure the attributes of `packt_dad`:

```
begin
  dbms_epg.set_dad_attribute (dad_name => 'packt_dad', attr_name
=> 'path-alias', attr_value => 'plsql_rest');
  dbms_epg.set_dad_attribute (dad_name => 'packt_dad', attr_name
=> 'path-alias-procedure', attr_value => 'chapter2.plsql_rest_
handler_proc');
end;
```

Our DAD configuration is now complete. Let's now understand the process of passing parameter values to a RESTful PL/SQL web service. There are two methods to pass the parameters to a PL/SQL RESTful web service and your attention is required, because both the methods appear to be similar. Before we talk about the method to pass the values, let us see the code of `chapter2.plsql_rest_handler_proc`. `chapter2.plsql_rest_handler_proc` is the final user of the passed argument. The following code is shared for your convenience:

```
PROCEDURE plsql_rest_handler_proc(p_path IN VARCHAR2) AS
  l_req_method VARCHAR2(20) := owa_util.get_cgi_env('REQUEST_METHOD');
  l_input      VARCHAR2(20) := owa_util.get_cgi_env('QUERY_STRING');
  l_response CLOB;
  l_number_of_rows NUMBER := 0;
BEGIN
  SELECT SUBSTR(l_input,13) INTO p_path FROM dual;
  IF l_req_method = 'GET' THEN
    SELECT COUNT(*)
    INTO l_number_of_rows
    FROM oehr_orders
    WHERE customer_id  =l_input;
    IF l_number_of_rows > 0 THEN
      SELECT dbms_xmlgen.getxml('select * from oehr_orders where
customer_id='
         || l_input) xml
      INTO l_response
      FROM dual;
    ELSE
      SELECT dbms_xmlgen.getxml('select ''No data found'' as Order_id
from dual') xml
      INTO l_response
      FROM dual;
    END IF;
    OWA_UTIL.mime_header('text/xml');
    HTP.print( l_response );
  END IF;
END;
```

`chapter2.plsql_rest_handler_proc` has an argument called `p_path`.Values can be fed to the `p_path` argument from the URL using the `http://localhost:8080/packt_dad/plsql_rest/145` URL. Replace localhost with the ip address of your database server. Here, `145` is accepted as the value of `p_path`. We can test the passing of values from URL by replacing `l_input` by `p_path` in the preceding two highlighted SELECT statements and then firing the preceding URL. You should get an XML as a response. `145`, passed from the URL, is compared inside the `plsql_rest_handler_proc` procedure with the `customer_id` column of the `oehr_orders` table to return the records.

However, as you notice, if we have to pass the value of `p_path` from the URL then the URL will have to be changed for every value. We don't want this because we have to mention the URL endpoint of the RESTful Web service in **Web service references** in **Shared Components** in APEX and hence the URL has to be static.

The process of passing argument values in the URL of a PL/SQL RESTful web service might work well if we invoke the RESTful web service URL in a procedure, and are hence able to change the value in the URL on the fly.

The second method to pass values is by configuring input parameters for the APEX RESTful web service reference. Notice that the `getOrdersREST` web service reference has `customer_id` configured for it. This `customer_id` is passed to the QUERY_STRING environment variable. The whole list of environment variables can be found by entering `http://localhost:8080/packt_dad/plsql_rest*/` in the browser. The * in the end makes the URL pattern incorrect, and hence you see the error message along with the list of environment variables. Replace `localhost` with the ip address of your database server.

It is important to note that configuring input parameters also changes the GET HTTP request, but then this change of URL happens internally. Let me explain it to you with an example. Consider the `getOrdersREST` web service reference. The endpoint of this reference is `http://localhost:8080/packt_dad/plsql_rest/dummy_text` and `customer_id` is configured to be an `input` parameter. Replace `localhost` with the ip address of your database server. `dummy_text` at the end of the URL can be any wild text. Let's say that a value of `145` is passed to `customer_id` input parameter. The final URL, which will be framed by APEX on passing `145` as the value of `customer_id`, will be `http://localhost:8080/packt_dad/plsql_rest/dummy_text?customer_id=145`. Replace `localhost` with the ip address of your database server. Now, the `customer_id=145` is passed to the QUERY_STRING environment variable. Check the code of `chapter2.plsql_rest_handler_proc` (shared previously) to understand the use of `owa_util.get_cgi_env` to capture the value. The whole advantage of using this parameter method is that we can have a static URL in the APEX web service reference endpoint and still pass the necessary parameters.

Revert the code in the two highlighted select statements, that is, replace p_path in the select statements with l_input. The getOrdersREST REST web service reference is called from the getOrders page process, and the values returned by this web service are stored in the ORDERS_COLLECTION collection. The ORDERS_COLLECTION collection is used to build the report in the **REST PLSQL webservice** region. The getOrders page process was made conditional in the *Creating a report on native XMLDB webservice* section and its condition was set to never. Remove this condition and run page 8 again.

Understanding and implementing BPEL

An understanding of developing BPEL processes is vital to an advanced APEX developer because APEX is often used as the front end to expose business process to the end user. We will dedicate the next few sections to understand BPEL (Business Process Execution Language), to install and configure it, to develop a simple composite using database adapter in it, to deploy and test the code, and to understand the process of developing and testing Human Workflows.

What is BPEL

BPEL is used to code business processes. Although BPEL is coded as a Java composite, JDeveloper provides a pretty user interface which transforms the development from a Java intensive programming to a Drag-and-Drop operation. We will certainly not be able to check out all the features of BPEL, but I will try to ensure that you get a good feel of the tool and are able to code business process in BPEL, whenever required. One of the most important features of SOA is the worklist and Human Workflows. Human Workflows are used in almost every place where BPEL is used. Human Workflows are useful in a number of ways and one of their important feature is to let you put a task from the work stack of one user to the work stack of another. So, if a junior officer has worked on a task, then Human Workflows can help you to move the task to the manager's worklist and can help you send it back to the junior officer's worklist, when the manager sends some comments on the task. This process of transferring a job helps us code most of the business processes.

The end result of coding a BPEL process will be the creation of a web service. The web service exposes the operations according to your needs. These operations can be accessed from APEX. We have seen a number of examples of using SOAP web service in APEX. Imagine BPEL to be the glue that can gel all your tools together. This is because BPEL can help us invoke web services of a number of tools on our enterprise, code some additional logic on top of these web service and present the whole solution as a new web service to the external world. Since it works on XML schemas, the configuration and interface can be configured very easily. The UI of JDeveloper further simplifies our life.

We will, however, limit ourselves to the essentials. This chapter will provide you with a good start on how you could use this technology in APEX, and will give you an idea on where you could use it.

Installing BPEL

The following steps will help us install SOA components and also help us to extend the domain upon which APEX is installed to handle SOA composites.

1. Download the SOA suite from Oracle's website.

2. Go to the following location: `<Directory in which the SOA suite is unzipped>\Disk1\install\win64` and execute `setup.exe`.

3. Enter your JDK path, for example `C:\Program Files\Java\jdk1.6.0_26`, when prompted for a JRE/JDK path.

4. Click on **Next**. I skipped the software updates. You can insert your credentials if you want updates.

5. Click on **Next** again after the wizard does its prerequisites check.

6. Enter the middleware home directory of the WebLogic on which your listener is hosted in the **Oracle Middleware Home** textbox. For example, `C:\OracleProducts\Middleware`. Enter `Oracle_SOA` in the **Oracle Home Directory** textbox.

7. Select **WebLogic** as **Application Server**.

8. Click on the **Install** button, and click on **Next** after the completion of installation.

9. Save the configuration details and click on **Finish**.

10. This completes the BPEL installation. We now have to link it to a WebLogic domain and a server.

11. Run the RCU which you had downloaded with OBIEE 11G's download page. You have to execute `rcu.bat` in the `rcuHome\BIN` directory to do this. Note that the RCU should be of 11.1.1.6 Version.

12. Enter your database details and set the schema prefix. Setting of schema prefix is done in step 3 of the RCU wizard. If you still have OBIEE 11G installed, then select the **Select an existing Prefix** radio button.

13. Check the **SOA and BPM Infrastructure** checkbox. Click on **Next**. Follow the wizard to finish the installation.

14. Go to **Oracle SOA 11g - Home1** program group in the **Start** menu and select **Configure Application Server**.

15. Select **Extend an existing weblogic domain** and click on **Next**.

16. Select the domain on which you had installed APEX. This is not a good practice, but then installing everything on one server of a domain will mean that we would only have to start a single server to get everything to work. This will save precious RAM. Note that this arrangement is suggested to create a testing environment only, not a production environment. Click on **Next**.

17. Select **Oracle SOA Suite for Developers – 11.1.1.0 [Oracle_SOA], Oracle Enterprise Manager – 11.1.1.0 [oracle_common],** and then click on **Next**.

18. Fill in the **Hostname, DBMS/Service,** and the **Port** fields for all the four schemas, enter the passwords for each of them and change the prefix from DEV to the one that you had set in step 12. Click on **Next**.

19. Enter the details of the schemas which had been created using RCU and click on **Next**. Test your credentials and click on **Next** again.

20. Check the **Deployments and Services** checkbox and click on **Next**.

21. Let all the checkboxes be checked in both **Target Deployments to Clusters and Servers** and **Target Services to Clusters and Servers** steps, and let the target be **AdminServer**. Click on **Next** for both these steps, then click on the **Extend** button, and finally click the **Done** button after the domain has been extended.

22. We should now install JDeveloper which will help us create our code. The wizard for JDeveloper is straightforward and does not warrant any discussion on it.

23. Download the Oracle SOA Composite Editor for JDeveloper from `http://www.oracle.com/ocom/groups/public/@otn/documents/webcontent/156082.xml`. I downloaded the 11.1.1.6.0.15.53 version.

24. Open JDeveloper Studio 11.1.1.6.0 and select **Default Role**.

25. Select **Check for Updates** from the **Help** menu.

26. Select **Install From Local File** in the **Source** section and browse for the downloaded file. Click on **Next >**, and then click on **Finish**.

27. This will restart JDeveloper after configuring it to develop SOA composites.

28. You can open the `packtApplication.jws` file from the code pack in JDeveloper. This will help you see the two projects in JDeveloper. Our discussion regarding BPEL in the rest of the chapter will revolve around these two projects.

Developing a BPEL Composite

Use **packtProject**, shipped with the book, for your reference while going through the following steps. You can open `packtApplication.jws` in JDeveloper to see the project. Perform the following steps to create a BPEL composite:

1. Compile the specification and body of `chapter08` package in `packt_schema`. `4-98-9_08_chapter08_pkg.sql` has the spec and the body and can be found in the code pack shipped with the book.

2. Open JDeveloper and click on the **New Application** button. Enter an application name and select **SOA Application**. Click on **Next >**.

3. Enter the name for the project, select **SOA** in the **Project Technologies** tab (as shown in the following screenshot), and click on **Next >**.

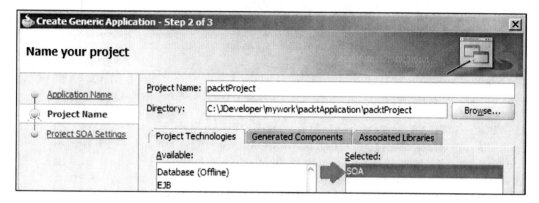

4. Select **Composite With BPEL Process** and click on **Finish**.

5. Select **BPEL 2.0 Specification** in the **Create BPEL Process** wizard, choose **Synchronous BPEL Process** as **Template**, and name your BPEL process. Keep the other defaults and click on **OK**.

6. Your JDeveloper window should now look like the following screenshot. Double-click on the BPEL process (highlighted in the following screenshot with an arrow):

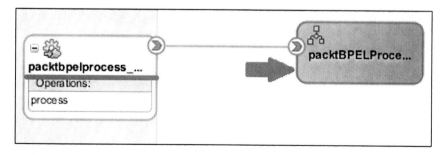

7. Double clicking on the BPEL process will open the following screenshot:

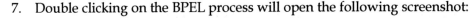

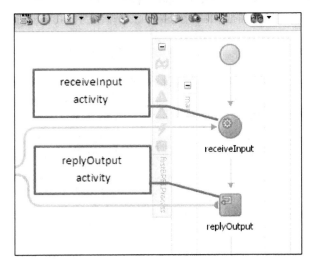

`recieveInput` and `replyOutput` (marked in the previous screenshot) are types of activities. Our BPEL code will be between these two activities. We will put more activities between these activity blocks and will connect adapters to the BPEL code so that the BPEL process can connect to external systems to create an enterprise business process. The `recieveInput` activity accepts input for our BPEL process and `replyOutput` sends the response to the client `packt bpelprocess_client` (underlined in the second screenshot of this section) is the interface for external application. Also note the **process** operation right under it. We will talk about **process** in a short while.

1. Double-click on the `recieveInput` activity.

Note that the name of the operation in the `recieveInput` activity is `process`. This basically means that or `receiveInput` activity will receive the input for `process` operation. Note that we had also noticed `process` operation while talking about `packtbpelprocess_client` as well. You would see `inputVariable` as the variable. This variable will be the input of your process operation. Similarly, you should see `outputVariable` in the `replyOutput` activity. This variable will be the response of your web service.

2. Expand **BPEL Services** in the **Component Palette** and drag **Database Adapter**. Put it on the grey area in the right-hand side as shown in the following screenshot:

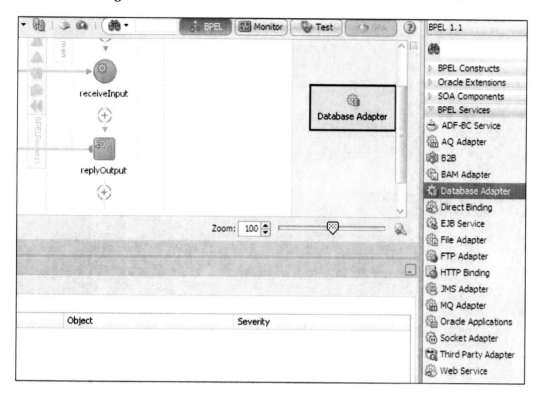

Adapters let us get information from different sources. A long list of adapters (refer to the preceding screenshot) in the **Component Palette** might have given you a good idea of the wide range of options to connect to external systems. The Database Adapter lets us perform an operation on a database from our BPEL code. Operations on the database are an external service to our BPEL process, just like our BPEL process is a service to any other system that wishes to use it.

Dragging the **Database Adapter** opens up the **Adapter Configuration Wizard**, which helps us set the specific function/procedure to be called by the adapter. The steps in the wizard are straightforward. The wizard initially expects us to create a database connection. This connection is required to fetch the input and output properties of the function/procedure and other database properties. Note that this connection is for JDeveloper, and you will have to configure a separate connection on your server so that your server can connect to the database when your code is executed on the web server. In the wizard, the JNDI name is automatically populated once you create a database connection. Note this JNDI name, as you will need it when you create a connection on the web server. I selected the **Call a Stored Procedure or Function** radio button in step 4 of the wizard and then selected CHAPTER08.DB_ADAPTER procedure in step 5. Select the defaults in all the other steps and click on the **Finish** button at the end. Click on the **OK** button.

I named my database adapter service as packtDBService and my application now looks like the following screenshot:

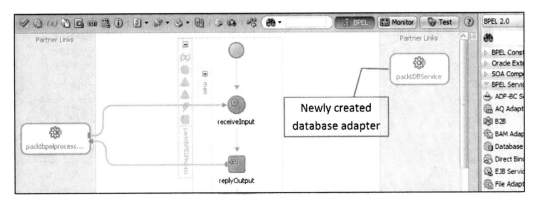

Invocation of the service exposed by the adapter happens by using an **Invoke** activity (You will see this activity under the **Web Service** section of **BPEL Constructs** in **Component Palette**). We will now see the steps to use the **Invoke** activity:

1. Drag the **Invoke** activity between the **reciveInput** and **replyOutput** activities as shown in the following screenshot:

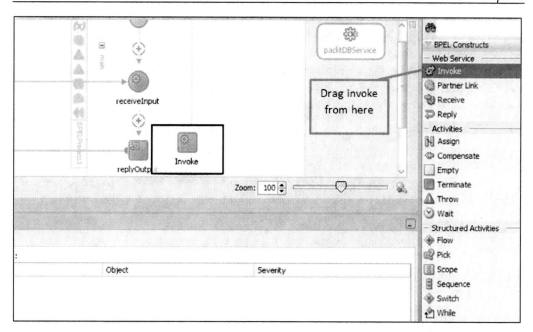

2. Use your mouse to drag a link from the right side of the **Invoke** activity to the DB Adapter service as shown in the following screenshot:

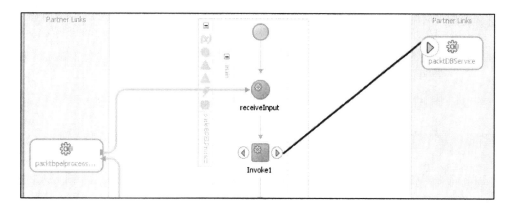

This will open a box that will let you edit the **Invoke** activity. We will now use this box to create an input and an output variable for this activity. We can then use the **Assign** activity to assign the inputVariable attribute seen in the **receiveInput** activity to the input variable of the **Invoke** activity. This will mean that the input of the user to the process operation will be passed to the DB adapter service using the **Invoke** activity by performing the following steps:

1. You would see a little green plus sign (highlighted in the following screenshot) on the box that lets you edit the properties of the **Invoke** activity. Click on that and create a variable. You would see an **Output** tab (highlighted in the following screenshot) that lets you create an output variable. Create an output variable as well. The response from your adapter is stored in the output variable created in this place. Click on **OK** after doing this.

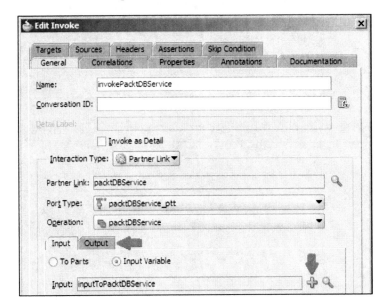

2. Drag the **Assign** activity (from **BPEL Constructs** in **Component Palette**) between the **reciveInput** and **invoke1** activities. You can rename the **invoke1** activity and the newly created **Assign** activity to a more meaningful name.

3. Double-click on the **Assign** activity, click on the **Copy Rules** tab and assign the input variable (discussed in step 1 of the previous series of steps) to the input of the **Invoke** activity as shown in the following screenshot. Assigning can be done by dragging your mouse pointer from the variable on the left to the variable on the right. A line should appear between the two variables once your operation is finished as shown in the following screenshot. Click on the **OK** button.

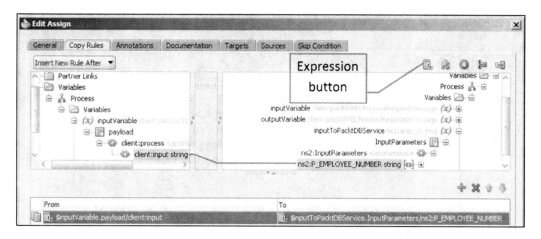

We will now put an **Assign** activity to assign the output of the **Invoke** activity to the **replyOutput** activity. We will use this **Assign** activity to concatenate `first_name` and `last_name` found in the output of the **Invoke** activity, and then assign it to the `outputVariable` variable (discussed in step 1 of the previous series of steps) of the **replyOutput** activity.

4. Drag an **Assign** activity between the **replyOutput** and the **Invoke** activity. Click on **Copy Rules** tab, and then click on the **Expression** button (Marked in the preceding screenshot).

5. Select **String Functions** from the **Functions** dropdown and double-click on **concat** present in the list under it.

6. Now, move your cursor inside the round brackets of the `concat` function in the **Expression** text area, and select both P_FIRST_NAME and P_LAST_NAME (highlighted in the following screenshot) from the output variable of the **Invoke** activity. My final expression looks as follows:

```
concat($outputFromPacktDBService.OutputParameters/ns2:P_FIRST_
NAME,$outputFromPacktDBService.OutputParameters/ns2:P_LAST_NAME)
```

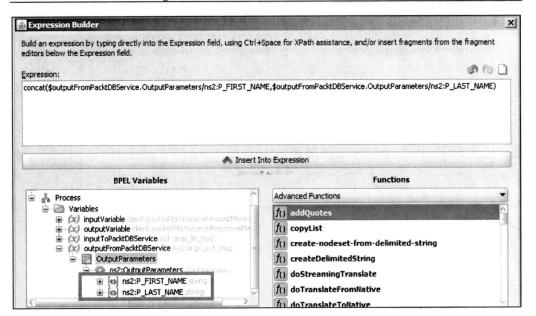

 Note how BPEL has created P_FIRSTNAME and P_LASTNAME inside the output variable of the **Invoke** activity that invokes the DB service. BPEL has fetched this information from the signature of the stored procedure, which is invoked by the DB service. P_FIRSTNAME and P_LASTNAME are the two out arguments in the signature of the chapter08.db_adapter procedure.

7. Click on **OK**.

8. Drag from the right side of the newly created expression to the output variable of **replyOutput** as shown in the following screenshot:

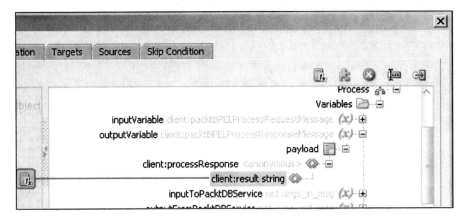

9. Click on the **OK** button after this.

 You could also change **replyOutput** such that it accepts P_FIRSTNAME and P_LASTNAME as separate values, and you can then concatenate the values in APEX.

10. Click on the **Save All** button in JDeveloper.

This brings us to the end of a simple BPEL implementation. We will now see the process of deploying the code on WebLogic.

Deploying BPEL code

Let's see the process to deploy our code. We will have to create a connection to the application server. Since we have installed SOA on the admin server of the same domain that hosts APEX, let us first start the admin server of APEX's domain. Once the server is started, we can then create a connection in JDeveloper to the server by performing the following steps:

1. Select **Application Server Navigator** from the **View** dropdown.
2. Right-click on **Application Server** and select **NewApplication Server...**.
3. Select **Standalone Server** and click on **Next >**.
4. Give a connection name and select **Weblogic 10.3** in the **Connection Type:** dropdown.
5. Enter your weblogic admin credentials and click on **Next >**.
6. Enter the other necessary parameters and test your connection. Click on **Next >** and finally on **Finish**.

Now that we have created an application server connection, we must deploy our code on the server. Perform the following steps for this:

1. Right click on **SOA Project** (your project) in Application Navigator, select **Deploy** and then **select SOA Project...**.
2. Select **Deploy to Application Server** and click on **Next >**.
3. Keep the defaults in click on the **Next >** button again.
4. Select the application server connection and click on **Next >**.
5. Select the admin server (the server on which the code will be deployed) of your domain and click on **Next >** again. Click on the **Finish** button at the end.

We must now create a database connection on the WebLogic server, so that our deployed composite is able to call the `chapter08.db_adapter` procedure from the web server. Perform the following steps to do this:

1. Log in to the console (`http://localhost:8001/console`) and click on **Data Sources** under the **Services** group. Replace `localhost:8001` with the ip address and port of your WebLogic

2. Click on **New**, select **Generic Data Source** and enter `jdbc/packtDBConn` in the **JNDI Name** textbox.

3. Click on the **Deployments** link under your domain in the **Domain Structure** panel.

4. Click on **DbAdapter**, then on the **Configuration** tab and finally on the **Outbound Connection Pools** tab.

5. Expand `javax.resource.cci.ConnectionFactory` and click on the **New** button.

6. Select `javax.resource.cci.ConnectionFactory` in the **Outbound Connection Group** list, and then click on the **Next** button.

7. You now have to put JNDI name. Note that this JNDI name should match with the JNDI name, which was automatically populated when you created the database connection in JDeveloper. My JNDI name is `eis/DB/packtDBConn`.

8. Go to the **Outbound Connection Group** list again. You would see a link on your JNDI name. Click on the same.

9. Click on the **Property Value** column of the **xADataSourceName** row. An editable textbox will appear on clicking. Enter `jdbc/packtDBConn` in the textbox and press the *Enter* key on your keyboard.

> Note that if you do not press the *Enter* key, then the value will not be saved.

10. We have entered `jdbc/packtDBConn` in the textbox, because we have created a data source with the same name in step two.

11. Click on the **Save** button and restart WebLogic.

Testing the BPEL code

We had checked **Oracle Enterprise Manager – 11.1.1.0 [oracle_common]** in step 17 of the *Installing BPEL* section. This extension can now help us to control and test our BPEL code. Let us see the steps for the same:

1. Log in to the enterprise manager (`http://localhost:8001/em`). Replace `localhost` with the ip address of your WebLogic server using your WebLogic admin credentials.

2. You should be able to see SOA group on the left side of the browser. Expand it, and then expand everything that comes under it until you see your deployed BPEL project.

3. Click on your project and then click on the **Test** button on the top.

4. This will take you to a page that shows the WSDL and the endpoint URL of the web service. You would need these while calling the web service from APEX.

5. Note that the operation is in process. You would see this process operation if you click on the **receiveInput** activity in JDeveloper. We had discussed process operation in the *Developing a BPEL Composite* section.

6. Enter `100` as the value in the input textbox and click on the **Test Web Service** button on the top.

7. You should see a result textbox with `StevenKing` in it as the response.

8. Click on the **Launch Flow Trace** button. You would see a link on your BPEL process. Click on the same.

9. This will show you a step-by-step execution of the activities. Click on the **Flow** tab to get a pictorial representation that mimics the activity icons in JDeveloper. I love this not just for the beautiful arrangement of the activities but also because debugging and error tracking is so easy this way. You can see one such flow in the first screenshot under *Understanding Human workflows and Worklist* section.

10. You can now create a web service reference in APEX using the endpoint URL and the WSDL, which you had captured in step four.

> The good thing about BPEL web service is that every execution is logged with an instance ID, and you can check your executions in the enterprise manager.

Implementing BPEL Human Workflows

Human Workflow is one of the most interesting features of BPEL that helps a developer to code business process in BPEL. As discussed in previous sections, workflows usually involve a task which is transferred from the work stack of one person to the work stack of another person in an organization. BPEL gives a readymade activity called Human Workflows. Human Workflows has an Invoke activity that connects as an out-of-the-box web service which maintains a task. This web service is called the Task service. Once a Human Workflow task is initiated, methods of the task service can be used to put the task from the work stack of one user to the work stack of another. Since we can call web services from PL/SQL and from APEX, we can trigger the shifting of a task based on the action of a user in APEX.

Let us now code a human workflow in BPEL by performing the following steps:

> Use the **humanTasksProject** project, shipped with the book, for your reference while going through the following steps. You can open **packtApplication.jws** in JDeveloper to see the project.

1. Execute the first five steps of the *Developing a BPEL composite* section with a difference of selecting **Asynchronous BPEL Process** as **Template** in step five. Drag a **Human Task** present under **SOA Components** between the **recieveInput** and **callbackClient** activities.

> Note that we are creating an asynchronous process here, because a synchronous process waits until the Human Workflow process completes. Human Workflow process might take a long time to finish and the time will depend upon the users who act on the process.

2. Double-click on the **Human task** and click on the green plus sign under the **General** tab. This will help us create a task definition. Have a look at the next screenshot to get a feel of the .task file. Task definition defines the behavior of our human task.

3. Give a name to the task definition and note that the possible **Outcomes** of the task are **APPROVE** and **REJECT**. We can add more possible outcomes, if required. Click on **OK**. This will create a new .task for you which can be edited to change task definition.

4. Click on **OK** again. This will open the .task file for you.

The following is a screenshot of one such .task file. Let us now talk about the various sections (tabs on the left hand side of the following screenshot) of this task file and their use.

The **General** section is for title, description, outcomes, and other such attributes of the task. The **Data** section is for defining the types of the messages which you might need in the task. The **Assignment** section lets you set the participants in the task and configure the routing policy. The **Presentation** section is for multilingual and other such settings. The **Deadlines** section lets you set the expiry date and the due dates of the task. **Notification** is for sending alerts for the various status changes of the task. **Access** section is more like authorization and it lets you specify access rules and assignment restrictions. The **Events** section is for BPEL Callback configuration for tasks and routing assignments:

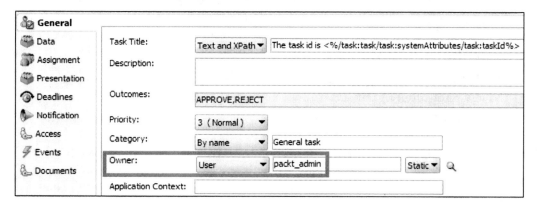

Note that in the next two sections, we will talk about the .task file of the humanTasksProject project. humanTasksProject is shipped with the book. You will have to make similar changes in the .task file of your project based on the understanding of this file.

Configuring the General section

Let us now try to dig deeper in the **General** section of the `.task` file. Keep an eye on the preceding screenshot to make more sense of the following talk:

1. Enter `The task id is <%/task:task/task:systemAttributes/ task:taskId%>` in the **Task Title** textbox. This will help us see the task id in the worklist and we will need this task id for transferring the tasks from the work stack of one user to the work stack of the other.

> Note that you can use the expression builder to frame the XPath by clicking on the **Build title from XPath...** button next to the **Task Title** textbox. The button is not visible in the preceding screenshot, but is present to the right of the **Task Title** textbox.

    All the tasks created by us appear in the BPM worklist. So, a worklist is the face of the tasks. It shows various properties associated with a task. Now, we might have a number of tasks for various purposes. These tasks might have the same task definition or might have different ones. The important point is that the value of the **Category** textbox of the tasks is displayed in the worklist. Hence the value of the **Category** textbox of the tasks can be used to inform the viewer about the broad categories of a task. We can give a dynamic XPath expression for the category or can put a static text.

2. Let's use static text for **Category**. Change the value in the dropdown to **By name**. Refer to the preceding screenshot.

    The task owner is a sort of an administrator of a task. He can perform operations on behalf of other participants because he owns the task. We can use the application server connection that was used to deploy the pervious project to fetch the users in the embedded LDAP server of WebLogic. A connection will be made to the identity store of the application server and you would get an option to select the owner of the task.

3. Click on the magnifying glass next to the **Owner** textbox, and then click on the **Lookup...** button. This will give you the list on users in the identity store of your application server. Select **packt_admin** from these and click on the **Select** button. Click on the **OK** button. Refer to the preceding screenshot.

Configuring the Assignment section

Open the **Assignment** section of the `.task` file (`humanTaskDefination.task`) of **humanTasksProject project**. The following screenshot of the Assignment section is shared for your convenience:

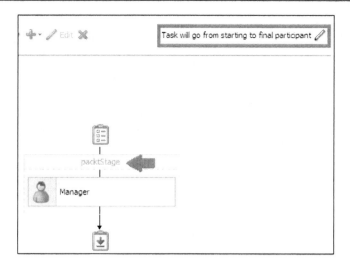

The **Assignment** section lets you set the participants in the task. Participants are grouped under stages which can be put in parallel or series to form a complex approval structure. We will keep things simple.

1. Double click on **State1** and put your own stage name I named it **packtStage** (highlighted in the preceding screenshot).

   We will now add participants for our task. Participants can also be of multiple types. The possible types of participants are Single, Parallel, Serial, and FYI. We will create a Single type participant.

   A Single participant type can have a list associated with it. One of the users from the list should acquire the task and act on it. Since the type is Single, the action of one user is enough to change the status of the task. I created a user (participant2) by navigating to **Home | Summary of Security Realms | myrealm | Users and Groups** in WebLogic server and added the user in this participant list.

2. Add the participant and click on **OK**.

   At this point, we will have packt_admin and participant2 in our participant list. Note that we have an **Advanced** section right under the participant list. This section lets us configure the time limit and other such properties for acting on the task. We can however configure the expiration in the **Deadlines** section. If the expiration configuration is done in the **Deadlines** section, then it is valid across all participants.

Although we will use Single participant type, let us talk about the other participant types as well. The parallel participant type is used where multiple people have to act in parallel to reach a decision. Any kind of voting can be an example of this type of decision making system. The FYI participant type is used when the business process does not have to wait for the action of the user.

Advanced configuration of the routing of the task can be done by clicking on the **Task will go from starting to final participant** button. This button is highlighted in the preceding screenshot. In our case we have a Single participant type with a participant list that consists of two users (`packt_admin` and `participant2`). Any of these two users can act on the task but from the perspective of the task, it just needs one user to act on it. If we had added more users (note that this is different from adding users to the participant list) then we could have used the **Task will go from starting to final participant** button for advanced configuration.

3. Save your `.task` file and open your `.bpel` file.

   You would see that an `If` activity has been placed under the human task which is followed by one branch each for the APPROVE and REJECT outcomes and an extra branch that caters to the `else` condition. You can replace the empty activities in each of the branch with an Assign activity or any other logic that suits you. An Assign activity has however been added for your reference in the **APPROVE** branch of the **humanTasksProject** project.

   It is important to note that the Human Task is itself composed of the basic activities, which we have seen while creating the previous composite. If you expand the plus sign next to the green colored Human Task, then you will find that a human task consists of an Assign activity, an Invoke activity, a receiveComplete activity, and a partner link of the Task service. The Invoke activity is used to invoke the Task service and the recieveComplete activity is used to get the response from the service.

   Read more details on creating the Task definition from the following:

   http://docs.oracle.com/cd/E14571_01/integration.1111/e10224/bp_hwfmodel.htm#SOASE007

   http://docs.oracle.com/cd/E14571_01/integration.1111/e10224/bp_introhwf.htm

4. Deploy the code on the application server. Refer to *Deploying BPEL code* section for steps to deploy the code.

Understanding Human workflows and Worklist

Let us now understand the execution flow of Human workflows and the use of Worklists.

Log in to the Enterprise Manager and run this BPEL process just the way you ran the previous one to see the execution of Human workflow.

You would find that the logic after the **receiveCompletedTask** of the Human Workflow has not been executed as shown in the following screenshot:

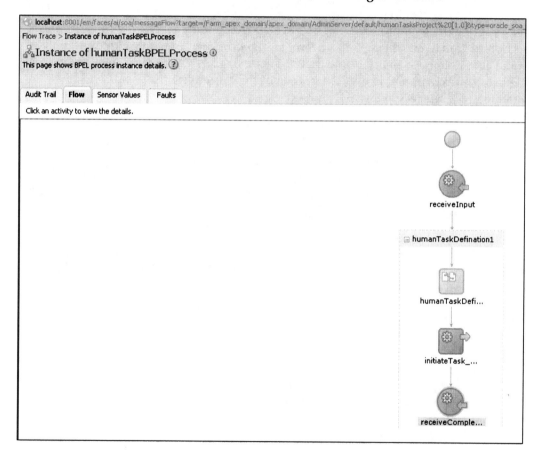

This is because the Human Workflow is not finished. It can finish only when it reaches an outcome, be it **APPROVE** or **REJECT**. We can use the methods defined in the Task service to change the state of the task created in the BPEL process. A typical URL of the WSDL of the task service is as follows:

```
http://host:port/integration/services/TaskService/TaskServicePort?WSDL
```

We will use the `reassignTask` and `updateTaskOutcome` methods of the Task service in our experiment. Note that we had made `packt_admin` as the owner of the task in step three of the *Configuring the General section* section. So PACKT_ADMIN can reassign the task to `participant2`. `participant2` is another user in the LDAP server. We had created `participant2` in step two of the *Configuring the Assignment section* section. Once the task has been reassigned, `participant2` can use the `updateTaskOutcome` method to either APPROVE or REJECT the task. In either case, the task will be completed and the branch of the `If` activity that deals with the outcome will be executed.

Let us now walk the talk. We will use soapUI to invoke the `reassignTask` and `updateTaskOutcome` methods of the Task service. We have seen enough examples of invoking a SOAP webservice method using PL/SQL and APEX. Invocation of the `reassignTask` and `updateTaskOutcome` methods of the Task service using PL/SQL or APEX is left to you as an exercise. Invocation of these methods will help us finish the execution of this business process.

Use soapUI to create a soapUI project using the WSDL of the task service. Note that the SOAP envelope of both the `reassignTask` and `updateTaskOutcome` methods are huge and have a number of optional tags. We will limit ourselves to the most important ones.

The following is my envelope of the `reassignTask` method. Have a good look at it. This soap envelope passes the credentials of the owner of the task. This part has been highlighted in the following code. Task ID (second highlighted piece of code) is a unique ID for the human task. We had configured the title to have the task ID in step one of the *Configuring the General Section section*. If you go to the flow of the BPEL process in the Enterprise Manager and then click on the **initiateTask** activity of the human workflow then you will find the task ID in the `title` tag. Use this task ID in the following SOAP envelope.

```
<soapenv:Envelope xmlns:soapenv="http://schemas.xmlsoap.org/soap/
envelope/" xmlns:tas="http://xmlns.oracle.com/bpel/workflow/
taskService" xmlns:com="http://xmlns.oracle.com/bpel/workflow/
common" xmlns:task="http://xmlns.oracle.com/bpel/workflow/
task" xmlns:tas1="http://xmlns.oracle.com/bpel/workflow/
TaskEvidenceService">
```

```
      <soapenv:Header/>
      <soapenv:Body>
         <tas:reassignTask>
            <com:workflowContext>
               <com:credential>
                  <com:login>PACKT_ADMIN</com:login>
                  <com:password>PACKT_ADMIN</com:password>
               </com:credential>
            </com:workflowContext>
            <tas:taskId>b418e5fe-8adf-45e8-b413-a17e48c6874a</tas:taskId>
            <tas:taskAssignees>
               <tas:taskAssignee isGroup="No">participant2</
tas:taskAssignee>
            </tas:taskAssignees>
         </tas:reassignTask>
      </soapenv:Body>
   </soapenv:Envelope>
```

Invoke the `reassignTask` method using soapUI. This invocation assigns the task to `participant2`. We can now use the credentials of participant2 to invoke `updateTaskOutcome` method of Task service. Below is my envelope to invoke the service.

```
<soapenv:Envelope xmlns:soapenv="http://schemas.xmlsoap.org/soap/
envelope/" xmlns:tas="http://xmlns.oracle.com/bpel/workflow/
taskService" xmlns:com="http://xmlns.oracle.com/bpel/workflow/
common" xmlns:task="http://xmlns.oracle.com/bpel/workflow/
task" xmlns:tas1="http://xmlns.oracle.com/bpel/workflow/
TaskEvidenceService">
   <soapenv:Header/>
   <soapenv:Body>
      <tas:updateTaskOutcome>
         <com:workflowContext>
            <com:credential>
               <com:login>participant2</com:login>
               <com:password>participant2</com:password>
            </com:credential>
         </com:workflowContext>
         <tas:taskId>b418e5fe-8adf-45e8-b413-a17e48c6874a</tas:taskId>
         <tas:outcome>REJECT</tas:outcome>
      </tas:updateTaskOutcome>
   </soapenv:Body>
</soapenv:Envelope>
```

Once we finish the task, the flow of the process in the Enterprise Manager should finish. Your flow should now look like the following screenshot:

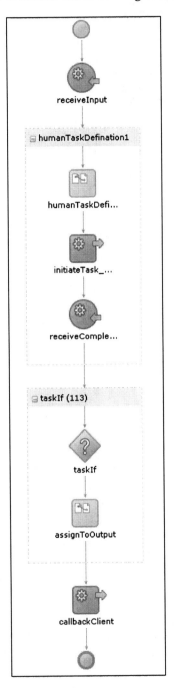

We can use Oracle BPM worklist to view the tasks. The URL of the worklist is `http://localhost:8001/integration/worklistapp/faces/login.jspx`.

Replace `localhost` with the ip address of your SOA server Log in to the worklist using the admin credentials of your domain and click on the **Administrative Tasks** tab.

You can use the **State** dropdown to filter the tasks based on their status. Let me show you a screenshot of the worklist:

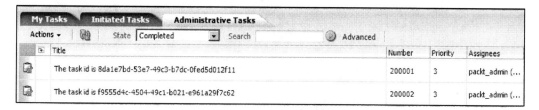

If you think that BPEL could be a technology which could help you meet your business ends then you should have a look at the Mediator and Business Rule. Mediator helps us transform and route requests to various services. Oracle BPEL Process manager provides a mechanism to code rules as a reusable service which can be used in multiple processes.

>
> Since BPEL processes can be invoked using SOAP requests and since we have learned a number of methods of invoking SOAP requests using APEX, using BPEL in APEX should be a cakewalk.

Integration with SAP crystal reports

SAP's crystal Reports shares the reporting market with Oracle products such as OBIEE and BI Publisher. Since Oracle APEX is a reporting and rapid application development tool, we should have a brief look at the way in which crystal reports can be integrated with APEX. Let's begin:

1. Download Crystal report designer (development tool for crystal reports) from the following link:

   `https://www.sap.com/campaign/ne/free_trial/crystal_reports_2011/index.epx?URL_ID=crcom&kNtBzmUK9zU=1`

2. Unzip `51043408.zip`, go to `51043408\DATA_UNITS\CrystalReports` and execute `setup.exe` to install the designer. You will get the Installation key code in the e-mail Id submitted while filling the form before downloading the installer. Use this code to install the product.

   If your system memory is a constraint then do a custom install, because the default installation installs the drivers for all kinds of data sources and makes arrangements for integration of Business Objects with tools such as SAP, Peoplesoft, JD Edwards, Siebel, and EBS.

3. Copy `ojdbc14.jar` from `<Oracle database home>\owb\wf\lib` to `C:\Program Files (x86)\SAP BusinessObjects\SAP BusinessObjects Enterprise XI 4.0\java\lib\external`.

4. Edit `C:\Program Files (x86)\SAP BusinessObjects\SAP BusinessObjects Enterprise XI 4.0\java\CRConfig.xml` and add `C:\Program Files (x86)\SAP BusinessObjects\SAP BusinessObjects Enterprise XI 4.0\java\lib\external\ojdbc14.jar` to the `Classpath` tag. `ojdbc14.jar` holds the driver which will help us connect to Oracle database so we are putting it in right places for Crystal Reports to use it.

5. Open crystal reports 2011 and click on the **Blank report** link under the **Start A New Report** section.

6. Expand **Create New Connection** and select **JDBC(JNDI)** from it.

7. Select the **JDBC Connection** radio button, enter `oracle.jdbc.driver.OracleDriver` as **Database ClassName**, and `jdbc:oracle:thin:@localhost:1521:ORCL` (change this according to your database server) in the **Connection URL** textbox. Give a name to the connection and click on **Next >**.

8. Enter your schema name and password and click on the **Finish** button.

9. Select the `OEHR_EMPLOYEES` table and click on the **OK** button.

   Designing the report after this point is similar to designing the report on iReport for Jasper or on Eclipse for BIRT. Open `firstCrystalReport.rpt` in the code pack for reference. `firstCrystalReport.rpt` has been built by following the nine steps mentioned previously.

10. We can now deploy this report on a crystal server. We can download and install the crystal server from `http://www54.sap.com/solutions/sme/software/analytics/crystal-server/index.html`.

11. `firstCrystalReport.rpt` can then be deployed on your crystal server and integration with APEX works by the URL mechanism. SAP publishes an entire guide that can be used for URL integration. You can find this guide at `http://help.sap.com/businessobject/product_guides/boexir4/en/xi4_cr_url_reporting_en.pdf`.

We can reference a crystal report of **Central Management Server (CMS)** using a URL similar to `http://<servername>:<port>/BOE/CrystalReports/viewrpt.cwr?id=1783`.

Here `1783` is the unique ID of the report. The invocation of these URLs from APEX can happen from any of the standard ways of URL invocation such as buttons.

Migrating from MS Access to APEX

Let us now look at migration of code from MS Access to APEX. The code pack has the `sampleDB.mdb` file which contains an `employee` table. `mdb` is an MS Access database file format. Let us now see the process of converting the `sampleDB.mdb` file to an APEX application. Let us see the process of migration now:

1. Log in to the APEX workspace, click on the arrow next to **Application Builder** and select **Migrate** (as shown in the following screenshot) from it.

2. Click on **Download Exporter for the Microsoft Access** link in the **Tasks** panel.
3. Download `omwb2007.zip` and unzip it.

   `omwb2007.zip` contains `omwb.chm` which gives all the details about the migration.

4. Open MS Access and open `omwb2007.mde` in it.

This will open Oracle Migration Workbench Exporter for Microsoft Access 2007. We can either get an export for Oracle Application Express or can get an export for Oracle SQL Developer. The export for Application Express is a .sql file. We will, however, see the process to export for SQL Developer, which is as follows:

1. Select **Export for Oracle SQL Developer** and click on **Next >**.

2. Choose the sampleDB.mdb file, select an output directory to store the exported XML file, check the **Export Table Data** checkbox and click on the **Export** button.

3. Exit the wizard.

4. Open SQL Developer and navigate to **Migration | Migrate** from the **Tools** menu.

5. Select the packt_schema connection for the Migration repository in step 2 of the wizard and click on **Next >**.

6. Give a name to the project and choose **Output Directory** and click on **Next >**.

7. Select **Offline Mode** in step 4 of the wizard and choose the exported XML file of step 6. Click on the **Next >** button.

8. Click on the **Next >** button. Choose packt_schema as the target connection is step 7, and let the **Mode** be **Online** and click on the **Finish** button.

9. You will now be able to see your Migration Project in the **Migration Projects** window. You would also be able to see a bunch of Captured and Converted objects as shown in the following screenshot:

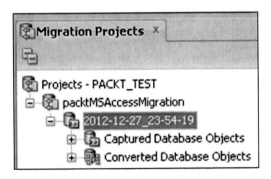

10. Right-click on **Converted Database Objects** and click on **Generate Target**.

11. Click on **Next >** and you will be prompted to select a schema for target objects. Select packt_schema for this purpose and let the **Mode** be **Online** and click on **Finish**.

This will generate a `.sql` and executing that `.sql` file is the final step in the migration from MS Access to Oracle. You can now customize the `.sql` file in your own way.

> If you want to create your own MS Access application then you can download the product from `http://www1.buyoffice.microsoft.com/usa/product.aspx?family=o14_officepro_try&country_id=US&WT.mc_id=ODC_enUS_Pro_Try`.

Migrating from Oracle Forms and Reports

We will now look at the process of converting Oracle Forms and Reports to Oracle APEX. Fortunately, Oracle APEX is shipped with a set of four files to test the migration of Oracle Forms and Reports to APEX. We can find the sample XML files when you log in to the APEX workspace, by performing the following steps:

1. Click on the arrow next to **Application Builder**.
2. Select **Migrate** from the list.
3. Click on the **Sample Files** link in the **Tasks** panel on the right-hand side of the page.

Have a look at the XML files. These XML files contain all kinds of information such as the names of the parent modules from which the file was generated. These files also contain the names of the APEX items which will be created using the file, the SQL queries, the fonts, and other properties required for creating APEX regions and pages. So, the XML file basically contains all the required metadata for generating an APEX application.

The objects are converted to APEX using the process described here, but we have to be careful with the business logic. Once the conversion is complete, we should check the newly generated application and tweak it, wherever required.

> In the following steps, you could also use the files (`forms_conversion_ddl.sql`, `forms_conversion_data_insert.sql`, `customers_fmb.xml` and `orders_fmb.xml`) of the code stack shipped with the book. The files will ensure hassle free execution.

Let us now see the process of conversion:

1. Execute `forms_conversion_ddl.sql` followed by `forms_conversion_data_insert.sql` in `packt_schema` to ensure that the objects referred to in the XML files are available in the database.

2. Create a migration project by clicking on the arrow next to **Application Builder**, selecting **Migrate** in the list and, then clicking on the **Create Project** button.

3. Select **Forms** in the **Type** dropdown, and select a schema (`packt_schema` in our example) that holds the Oracle Form's objects.

4. Select **customers_fmb.xml** in the **Forms Module XML File** browse item and click **Next >**. Click on the **Upload Another File >** button.

5. Select **Forms Module (_fmb.XML)** in the **File Type** dropdown, select **orders_fmb.xml** file and click on the **Upload >** button.

6. Click on the **Create** button and follow the wizard to create your migrated application.

Integration with Google API

Proximity analysis and location intelligence are the need of the day. This kind of analysis require data about all landmarks across the globe so that the distances can be calculated and co relation with landmarks can be discovered. For example, a retail store chain might be interested to know about the influence of the proximity of a cinema hall to their store. For getting a good understanding of this, one would need the data on the existing store's location (this we would have because it is business data) and we will need the location of cinema halls in that area. If the retail chain is spread across the globe then we will need information about all the cinema halls spread across the globe. Certainly we cannot have cinema hall's data in our database as many more different kinds of land marks are possible and the data volume of all of these will be huge. This is where Google's Places API becomes handy. It is a means of getting all location data from Google which can then be combined with our business data and used to create reports in APEX.

 Note that we are using Google's Places API here. The same process can be used for any of the other APIs of Google.

Let us first have a look at various services given by Google. We will be using the Places API but there are many more services which can be put to good use. Have a look at the following link to check out the various APIs, developer tools and announcements from Google:

```
https://developers.google.com/
```

The link for the Places API can be found in the following location:

```
https://developers.google.com/places/?hl=en
```

Detailed documentation on the Places API can be found at
```
https://developers.google.com/places/documentation/.
```

Let me first explain the process:

We have to use our Gmail account to get a key which will help us to use the API. We then have to create a wallet so that we are able to send https requests from our PL/SQL program. We will also have to create an ACL to enable our schema to make network requests and finally we have to code to invoke the API and parse the response. Let us begin:

1. Log in to the following URL using your Gmail ID and click on the **Create project** button:

   ```
   https://code.google.com/apis/console
   ```

2. Activate **Places API**. You will be prompted for your organization's name and URL. Provide the same and click on **Submit**.

3. You will have to **Accept** an agreement document by Google. You will then see that the **Places API** has been switched **ON** for your use as highlighted in the following screenshot:

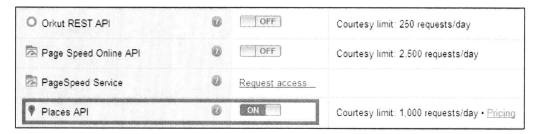

4. Click on the **API Access** tab (highlighted in the following screenshot) under API Project and note your API key (highlighted in the following screenshot). We will need this key to make requests to Places API:

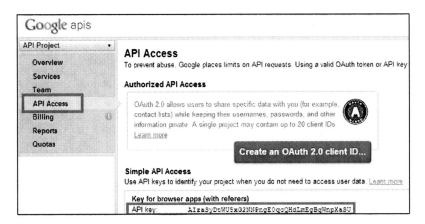

5. Right click on your Internet Explorer in the **Program Group** and select **Run** as administrator. This is necessary for downloading the certificates in the next step. Use your API key as shown in the following URL to test whether you are able to access the API or not:

```
https://maps.googleapis.com/maps/api/place/textsearch/
xml?query=Restaurants+in+London&sensor=true&key=AIzaSyDtWU5
xG2NNPngE0qcQHdLmEgBqWnpXaSU.
```

Have a good look at the structure of the XML returned by the above URL. The structure will be used to parse the XML and get the required values. Note that we are trying to get the locations of Restaurants in London using the preceding call. In our code we will pass these two values, that is, landmark and city as arguments to our PL/SQL function. Let us now see the steps to use the Places API.

1. Let us create a wallet to make calls to Places API. Click on the little lock icon (highlighted in the following screenshot) next to the address bar, and then click on **View certificates** (highlighted in the following screenshot):

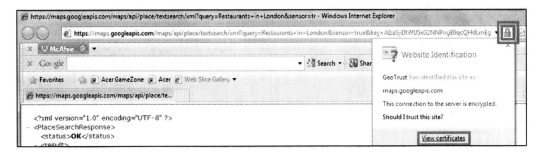

2. Click on the **Certification Path** tab (highlighted in the following screenshot) and download all certificates in the chain in the `Base-64 encoded X.509` `(.CER)` format. The following screenshot shows three certificates in the chain. Downloading can be done by double-clicking a certificate in the chain, clicking on the **Details** tab of that certificate, and then clicking on the **Copy to File...** button, and then using the wizard to download the certificate in the `.CER` format:

3. Once the certificates are downloaded, we can create a wallet and import the certificates in it. Import the certificate at the lowest level in the chain first and then follow a bottom-up approach. For example, I executed the following commands to create my wallet. The first command creates a wallet and the rest three statements import the certificate in it. In the following example, my wallet is created in `C:\Users\vishal\Desktop\wallet` as follows:

```
orapki wallet create -wallet C:\Users\vishal\Desktop\wallet  -pwd
packt_password -auto_login

orapki wallet add -wallet C:\Users\vishal\Desktop\wallet -trusted_
cert -cert C:\Users\vishal\Desktop\Certs\googleapis.cer -pwd
packt_password

orapki wallet add -wallet C:\Users\vishal\Desktop\wallet -trusted_
cert -cert C:\Users\vishal\Desktop\Certs\GoogleInternetAuthority.
cer -pwd packt_password

orapki wallet add -wallet C:\Users\vishal\Desktop\wallet -trusted_
cert -cert C:\Users\vishal\Desktop\Certs\GeoTrust.cer -pwd packt_
password
```

4. Let us now create an ACL to enable network calls from our schema. Execute the following statements for this:

```
BEGIN
  DBMS_NETWORK_ACL_ADMIN.CREATE_ACL('google_usrs.xml','ACL for
google users','PACKT_SCHEMA', TRUE, 'connect');
  DBMS_NETWORK_ACL_ADMIN.ASSIGN_ACL('google_usrs.xml','*');
END;


commit;
```

5. We will now create the types which can hold the parsed response of our Places API in the following way:

```
CREATE OR REPLACE type google_type AS
object(l_name VARCHAR2(100),    l_address VARCHAR2(300),    l_
latitude NUMBER,    l_longitude NUMBER)


CREATE OR REPLACE type google_typ_tab AS
TABLE OF google_type
```

6. Let us now see the code that can help us fire the Places API on the fly based on certain parameters and can parse the response and present it as a table using the following code:

```
create or replace
FUNCTION google_rpt(p_city VARCHAR2,    p_category VARCHAR2) RETURN
google_typ_tab pipelined AS
type rc IS ref CURSOR;
l_rc rc;
-----------------------------------------
l_clob CLOB := NULL;
l_eob boolean := FALSE;
l_http_req utl_http.req;
l_http_resp utl_http.resp;
l_buff VARCHAR2(32767);
l_google_type google_type := NULL;
l_query VARCHAR2(5000) := 'select name,address,latitude,longitude
     from xmltable(''//PlaceSearchResponse//result'' passing
xmltype(:l_clob)
                   columns name varchar2(100) path ''//name'',
                   address varchar2(300) path ''//formatted_
address'',
                   latitude number path ''//geometry//location//
lat'',
```

```
                      longitude number path ''//geometry//location//
lng'') xml_tab';
----------------------------------------------

l_name VARCHAR2(100);
l_address VARCHAR2(300);
l_latitude NUMBER;
l_longitude NUMBER;

BEGIN

  dbms_lob.createtemporary(l_clob,    TRUE);
  --utl_http.set_proxy('<proxy server user id>:<proxy server
password>@<proxy server>:<proxy server port>');
  utl_http.set_wallet('file:C:\Users\vishal\Desktop\wallet',
'packt_password');
  l_http_req := utl_http.begin_request('https://maps.googleapis.
com/maps/api/place/textsearch/xml?query=' || p_category || '+in+'
|| p_city || '&sensor=true&key=AIzaSyDtWU5xG2NNPngE0qcQHdLmEgBqWnp
XaSU',    'GET',    'HTTP/1.1');
  l_http_resp := utl_http.get_response(l_http_req);

  WHILE NOT(l_eob)
  LOOP
    BEGIN
      utl_http.read_text(l_http_resp,    l_buff,    32767);
      -- buffer = VARCHAR2(32767)

      IF l_buff IS NOT NULL
       AND LENGTH(l_buff) > 0 THEN
         dbms_lob.writeappend(l_clob,    LENGTH(l_buff),
TRANSLATE(TRANSLATE(l_buff,    '&',    ';'),    '''',    ' '));
      END IF;

    EXCEPTION
    WHEN utl_http.end_of_body THEN
      l_eob := TRUE;
    END;
  END LOOP;

  utl_http.end_response(l_http_resp);
  --------------------------------------------------------
  OPEN l_rc FOR l_query USING l_clob;
  LOOP
    FETCH l_rc
    INTO l_name,
      l_address,
      l_latitude,
```

```
        l_longitude;
      l_google_type := google_type(l_name,   l_address,   l_
latitude,   l_longitude);
      EXIT
    WHEN l_rc % NOTFOUND;
    pipe ROW(l_google_type);
END LOOP;

CLOSE l_rc;
dbms_lob.freetemporary(l_clob);
RETURN;

EXCEPTION
WHEN others THEN
DBMS_OUTPUT.PUT_LINE(l_query);
DBMS_OUTPUT.PUT_LINE(utl_http.get_detailed_sqlerrm);
DBMS_OUTPUT.PUT_LINE(sqlerrm);
CLOSE l_rc;
dbms_lob.freetemporary(l_clob);
utl_http.end_response(l_http_resp);
END;
```

Please execute the set define off command before executing the preceding code, otherwise &sensor and &key in the preceding utl_http.begin_request procedure call will be considered as substitution variables, and the compiled function will not have the right string to make the request to Places API.

Let us now try to understand the preceding code. We had seen the response XML of the Places API in step five of the previous series of steps, so we use it to frame our query to parse the response. This query is assigned to the l_query variable in the first highlighted part of the code. We see that l_clob is passed to this query. We will talk about l_clob and the process of filling values in this variable in a short while. I have commented the utl_http.set_proxy code, but utl_http.set_proxy can be used if your network calls have to pass through a proxy. utl_http.set_wallet is then used to set the wallet, so that we can make https requests. utl_http.begin_request then makes the request and we convert the response to a clob. This converted response is stored in l_clob. We then open a cursor for the query stored in l_query and pass l_clob to it. We then run a loop to store the parsed values and pipe the output. Note the use of utl_http.get_detailed_sqlerrm and sqlerrm to print runtime exceptions.

7. Execute the following statement to test the code. The following statement can be used as a region source in APEX and the arguments passed to the query can be APEX items::

```
select * from table(google_rpt('Restaurants','London'))
```

Your output will look like the following screenshot:

Enter SQL Statement:

```
select * from table(google_rpt('Restaurants','London'))
```

Results | Script Output | Explain | Autotrace | DBMS Output | OWA Output

Results:

	L_NAME	L_ADDRESS	L_LATI...	L_LONGI...
1	Terroirs	5 William IV Street, London, United Kingdom	51.509411	-0.125261
2	Ambassadors Bloom...	12 Upper Woburn Place, London, United Kingdom	51.526615	-0.129766
3	Asia de Cuba	45 Saint Martin s Lane, London, United Kingdom	51.510461	-0.126504
4	St. John	26 Saint John Street, London, United Kingdom	51.520494	-0.101437
5	Inamo	134-136 Wardour Street, London, United Kingdom	51.514401	-0.134595
6	Goodman	24-26 Maddox Street, London, United Kingdom	51.513131	-0.142224
7	Tom Aikens Restaur...	43 Elystan Street, London, United Kingdom	51.491542	-0.167686
8	Veeraswamy	99-101 Regent Street, London, United Kingdom	51.509977	-0.137747
9	Galvin @ Windows Bar	London Hilton Park Lane, 22 Park Lane, London, United Kingdom	51.505551	-0.150412
10	Le Gavroche	43 Upper Brook Street, London, United Kingdom	51.511206	-0.155147
11	Rowley s	113 Jermyn Street, London, United Kingdom	51.509006	-0.134979
12	Circus	27-29 Endell Street, London, United Kingdom	51.514442	-0.12458
13	Bavarian Beerhous...	190 City Road, London, United Kingdom	51.527867	-0.090614
14	Carluccio s - Coven...	Garrick Street, London, United Kingdom	51.511486	-0.12545
15	Galvin La Chapelle	35 Spital Square, London, United Kingdom	51.52008	-0.078368
16	Masala Zone Coven...	48 Floral Street, London, United Kingdom	51.513385	-0.122883
17	Hibiscus	29 Maddox Street, London, United Kingdom	51.512737	-0.142108
18	Villandry	170 Great Portland Street, London, United Kingdom	51.521454	-0.143156
19	Bella Vista Cucina It...	3-5 Montpelier Vale, London, United Kingdom	51.466627	0.008436
20	Imperial China	25 Lisle Street, London, United Kingdom	51.511683	-0.130031

Apart from restaurants, we can search for a number of other landmarks. A complete list of landmarks can be found in the following link.

```
https://developers.google.com/places/documentation/supported_types
```

 If you get an `ORA-28759: failure to open file error`, then you have an issue with OS level permissions on your wallet. Copy the directory (`C:\Users\vishal\Desktop\wallet`) in this example to some other directory, for example, `C:\packt_wallet`. Put this new directory path in the `utl_http.set_wallet` procedure of the `google_rpt` function and compile the function again to fix the problem.

The `SDO_GEOM.SDO_DISTANCE` in the `MDSYS` schema can be used for distance calculations. So we can combine the `google_rpt` function with the latitude/longitude information of our data to find the distance of our data from major landmarks in a city. The `MDSYS` schema holds spatial data and methods which can be helpful in location related business queries.

Integration with Oracle R Enterprise

Oracle R is a statistical tool and can be used for data mining and predictive analysis. We haven't showcased this capability yet and predictive analysis is an important part of intelligent reporting. More information on Oracle R Enterprise can be found at `http://www.oracle.com/technetwork/database/options/advanced-analytics/r-enterprise/index.html`.

We can check the process of configuring and installing Oracle R by going through the following guide:

```
http://docs.oracle.com/cd/E36939_01/doc/doc.13/e36763.pdf
```

We can find out about the new features in 1.3 release of Oracle R in the following documentation:

```
http://www.oracle.com/technetwork/database/options/advanced-analytics/r-enterprise/ore-new-features-1882823.pdf
```

The user guide for Oracle R Enterprise 1.3 can be found at `http://docs.oracle.com/cd/E36939_01/doc/doc.13/e36761.pdf` and you can refer to the following blog to get an introduction of the product:

```
https://blogs.oracle.com/R/entry/introduction_to_the_ore_statistics
```

In this section, we will try to implement the use case of identifying the best locations for putting ATMs in an area of interest depending on customer density spread across the area of interest. Let us first create the data for our analysis.

We will consider that our area of interest, where we want to plant our ATM machines, lies between 36 and 37 degree latitude and -122 and -123 degree longitude.

Let us say that we have data of all 100,000 people living in our area of interest. We can use the following query to create this data for us. Execute this in the RQUSER schema. RQUSER schema is an integral part of Oracle R.

```
CREATE TABLE customer_locations AS
SELECT dbms_random.VALUE(36,    37) latitude,
   dbms_random.VALUE(-123,    -122) longitude
FROM dual CONNECT BY rownum <= 100000
```

Now let me explain our objective here. We will use the K-Means clustering algorithm to find the centroids in the data set created by the above query. Check the user guide above to know more about the K-Means clustering algorithm. These centroids will be the centers of densest locations in our area of interest. These centroids can hence be the potential locations for placing our ATM machines. We will first see the code to get the centroids as an output of a SQL query and will then get these points plotted and get the plot as a PNG image. We will also understand the process of passing arguments to Oracle R script. Let us begin.

sys.rqscriptcreate can be used to create Oracle R scripts and sys.rqScriptDrop can be used to drop them.

Log in to the RQUSER schema and execute the following script. Replace the values in ore.connect command with your environment values:

```
BEGIN
   sys.rqscriptcreate('find_centers',    'function() {
   library(ORE)
ore.connect("rquser","<database_SID>","<database_host_name>","<RQUSER_
password>",<database_port_number>)
ore.sync()
ore.attach()
var_cust_locs <- ore.pull(CUSTOMER_LOCATIONS)
ret_centroids <- kmeans(var_cust_locs,4,3)
df <- data.frame(ret_centroids$centers)
df}');
END;
```

The preceding anonymous PL/SQL block uses `sys.rqscriptcreate` to create the Oracle R `find_centers` script. The `library(ORE)` command loads the Oracle R libraries. We then connect to the RQUSER schema using `ore.connect`, so that we can access the data of CUSTOMER_LOCATIONS table inside the R script. `ore.sync()` is used to sync the metadata of the database with Oracle R. We then use `ore.attach()` to attach the schema so that we can use its objects in our R script. We use `ore.pull` to pull the data from the CUSTOMER_LOCATIONS table and create the `var_cust_locs` data frame. We pass `var_cust_locs` as an argument to `kmeans`. The second argument, that is, 4 tells the `kmeans` function that we wish to get 4 centroids for our data set and the last argument, that is, 3 tells the `kmeans` function that it can run 3 iterations to get the centroids. After the algorithm has executed, we use `ret_centroids$centers` to get our centroids and then assign it to the `df` data frame using the `data.frame` method. We finally have `df` in the end, so that the data frame can be used by the calling query.

Run the following query to see the 4 centroids.

```
select *
  from table(rquser.rqEval(NULL,
                   'select 1 latitude, 1 longitude from dual',
                   'find_centers'));
```

The first argument of the `rquser.rqEval` function, that is, NULL is for any input that we wish to give to the R script. The `select` statement defines the output table definition and the third argument, that is, `find_centers` is the name of our R script.

The output of this looks like the following screenshot:

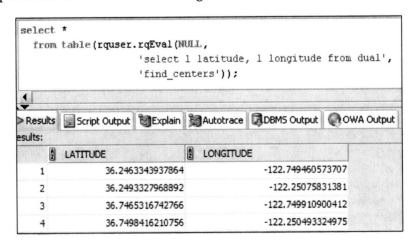

Once the right grants have been provided, we can use the above query in our APEX application.

Let us now see the code that can help us get the centroids plotted on a chart and get the chart as a PNG image (This image can then be downloaded from APEX):

```
begin
sys.rqScriptCreate('display_chart',
'function(x) {
ore.connect("rquser","<database_SID>","<database_host_name>","<RQUSER_
password>",<database_port_number>)
ore.attach()
 ore.sync()
ret_centroids <- kmeans(x,12,20)
plot(ret_centroids$centers)
}');end;
```

The code is more or less similar to the previous code. The only major difference is that we are using the `plot` method to plot the centroids and the fact that this script accepts an argument, that is, x. We will talk about x in a short while from now. We can use the following query to get an XML that contains our desired PNG image. We have seen enough examples of extracting information from XML documents and downloading files, so this one is left to you as an exercise. Note that ORE 1.3 supports PNG output as well, so you can get your data directly as a `.png` file in ORE 1.3:

```
select value
from table(rqTableEval( cursor(select * from customer_locations),
NULL,'XML','display_chart'))
```

We are using `rqTableEval` here instead of `rqEval`. The first cursor is passed as an input to the `display_chart` script. This is captured in the script using the x variable. The second `NULL` is for the parameter cursor. The third argument, that is, `XML` tells the R script that we need an XML output, and the fourth argument is the name of the R script.

We can drop the above script, if required, using the following code:

```
begin
   sys.rqScriptDrop('display_chart');
end;
```

The definitions of the scripts created using `sys.rqScriptCreate` can be found using the following query:

```
select * from sys.rq_scripts
```

We can get more information about `rq*Eval` functions from `http://docs.oracle.com/cd/E36939_01/doc/doc.13/e36761/scripts.htm#autoId18`.

The select statements that use `rqEval` and `rqTableEval` can be used as region source in APEX after assigning necessary privileges. Note that the above scripts help us run our algorithms (kmeans) online. However, if the data volume for analysis is huge and if the algorithm is talking a lot of time to execute, then we can put the R script in a `bat/sh` file. This R script can execute and store the results in a table. The table can them be used for our reporting. The following code is an example of storing the output of the `kmeans` algorithm in a database table:

```
library(ORE)
ore.connect("rquser","<database_SID>","<database_host_name>","<RQUSER_
password>",<database_port_number)
ore.sync()
ore.attach()
var_cust_locs <- ore.pull(CUSTOMER_LOCATIONS)
ret_centroids <- kmeans(var_cust_locs,4,3)
df <- data.frame(ret_centroids$centers)
ore.create(df,table="STORE_CENTROIDS")
```

Summary

This chapter was dedicated to web services, business processes and integrations with some of the well-known tools. We started with understanding native XMLDB web services and then moved on to look at the method to create RESTful web services using Resource Templates. We learned about BPEL, which is Oracle strategic tool to code business processes. We then focused on understanding the conversion of applications from other commonly used technologies. We also saw the process of integrating SAP Crystal Reports, Oracle R Enterprise, and Google API with APEX.

This brings us to the end of our discussion on using foreign tools in/for APEX. Tuning is one of the most interesting activities in APEX development and involves a lot of techniques. We will see some of the most interesting tuning procedures in the next chapter.

Performance Analysis

9

This chapter brings us to the end of our discussion on Oracle APEX, and the tools that can help us in the process of report development using APEX. We discussed the core and advanced features of APEX in the initial chapters, then moved on to know about other technologies which can be used for reporting with APEX, and we are now at a point, where we can now sink a little deeper to understand the ways and means to tune our APEX application. Since the APEX application is stored on the database, and talks to the user through a web server, the tuning exercise will largely focus on knowing about ways to tune the database and will have a few headings that will talk about the web server and the APEX Listener. The Listener, a JEE application living on the web server, also has a few parameters which can be tuned for better performance.

Let us now discuss a few best practices that can help us write efficient code.

Tuning pointers for development

We will now look at a few pointers for developers that can help us improve the performance of our APEX applications. Let us start with the use of v().

Using v()

Using APEX items as bind variables instead of v() in the SQL queries is advisable. This is because constant switches between the SQL and the PL/SQL engines can result in poor performance. For example, if we wish to call a stored procedure from an APEX page process, and we wish to pass an APEX page item to it, and if this procedure uses the page item in a SQL query, then it is far better to pass the value of the page item as bind variables to the stored procedure, against fetching the value of the page item using v() inside the SQL query of the stored procedure. This will avoid unnecessary switches between the SQL and the PL/SQL engines. These switches will happen if v() is used in a SQL query. An example of passing values as bind variables can be seen in AD_PRES authorization scheme of the reference application of Chapter 3.

Using the page and region caching

Page and region caching should be used wherever possible to reduce load on the server. We can set these in the **Edit Page** or the **Edit Region** pages of APEX. Administrators can login to the Admin console and purge these caches. The settings of the cache lets us set the time out for the cache. We can also set conditional caches. In other words, the data from the cache is fetched only if the condition set by us returns true. If the condition returns false, then the data is fetched according to the coded logic, and the cache is bypassed. Again, we can cache the page/region for every user. Setting the cache for every user can be achieved by selecting **Yes** in the **Cache By User** dropdown present in the **Server Cache** section of the page definition. Caching a region for every user can be achieved by selecting **Cached by User** in the **Caching** dropdown of the **Caching** section in the region definition page.

Understanding the weighted page performance of APEX

Log in to your APEX workspace and click on the arrow next to **Administration** on the top. Click on **Monitor Activity**, go to the **Page View Analysis** section, and then click on **By Weighted Page Performance**. You will get a report that will list the APEX application pages with **Median Elapsed**, **Weighted Average**, and **Page Events**. We can find the worst performing pages by considering **Weighted Average** and **Median Elapsed**. **Page Events** include page rendering and page processing events.

Using the #TIMING# substitution string

We can put the #TIMING# substitution string in an APEX region footer to display the time taken to load the region. This can help us show the contribution of each region to the total time taken to load the page. This can help us decide on the primary target for tuning the performance of a page.

Choosing a pagination scheme

Choosing a pagination scheme such as **Page X to Y of Z**, needs extra processing to calculate Z. So such pagination schemes should only be used when the user absolutely has to know the count of the total number of pages. Again, **Partial Page Refresh** (PPR) for pagination should be used so that time is not wasted in loading the unchanged parts of the page.

Tuning the like comparisons

We often have to use the `like` keyword for wildcard searches. This section shows a method to optimize such queries.

Let us first create a table with 100,000 rows in it.

```
CREATE TABLE "PACKT_SCHEMA"."PERFORMANCE_TEST"
   (
      "EMPLOYEE_NAME"   VARCHAR2(4000 BYTE),
      "DEPT_NUMBER"     NUMBER,
      "SHIRT_COLOR"     VARCHAR2(6 BYTE),
      "EMPLOYEE_NAME2"  VARCHAR2(4000 BYTE)
   );

INSERT INTO performance_test
SELECT DBMS_RANDOM.STRING ('u', 10) AS employee_name,
CEIL (DBMS_RANDOM.VALUE (1, 10)) * 10 AS dept_number,
DECODE (FLOOR (DBMS_RANDOM.VALUE (1, 5)), 1, 'Blue', 2, 'Green',
   3, 'Purple', 4, 'Red' ) AS shirt_color,
   DBMS_RANDOM.STRING ('u', 10)
AS employee_name2
FROM DUAL
   CONNECT BY ROWNUM <= 100000;

CREATE BITMAP INDEX "PACKT_SCHEMA"."PERF_TEST_COLOR_BTMP_IDX" ON
   "PACKT_SCHEMA"."PERFORMANCE_TEST" ( "SHIRT_COLOR" );

CREATE INDEX "PACKT_SCHEMA"."PERF_TEST_NAME_BTRE_IDX" ON
   "PACKT_SCHEMA"."PERFORMANCE_TEST" ( "EMPLOYEE_NAME" );

CREATE INDEX "PACKT_SCHEMA"."PERF_TEST_NAME_CTX_IDX" ON
   "PACKT_SCHEMA"."PERFORMANCE_TEST" ( "EMPLOYEE_NAME2" )
   INDEXTYPE IS "CTXSYS"."CONTEXT";

EXEC DBMS_STATS.GATHER_TABLE_STATS ('packt_schema',
   'performance_test');
```

Execute the following statement and check the plan:

```
explain plan for
select shirt_color from performance_test where
   contains(employee_name2,'%ASDFRED%') > 0;

@C:\Oracle11GDB\product\11.2.0\dbhome_1\RDBMS\ADMIN\utlxpls.sql
```

Replace the path in the preceding code with the path of your `utlxpls.sql` file. Execute the following statement and check the plan again:

```
explain plan for
select shirt_color from performance_test where employee_name like
  '%ASDFRED%';

@C:\Oracle11GDB\product\11.2.0\dbhome_1\RDBMS\ADMIN\utlxpls.sql
```

You will see that the context index is used in the query with the `contains` clause and the cost of the query is reduced. The following is a screenshot showing the plans of the two queries on my system:

Read more about Oracle text indexing at `http:/docs.oracle.com/cd/E11882_01/text.112/e24436.pdf`.

Using the bind variables

If the bind variables are used, then the query is parsed on first execution, and every subsequent execution of the query only results in a soft parse of the query.

Till Oracle10*g*, cursor sharing was not adaptive. So the use of bind variables in skewed column data was troublesome. Let me explain this with an example. Let's say that we have a table with a year column, and that we have 100,000 records for the year 2010 and 5,000 records for the year 2011. The queries to filter the records for a year would differ only in constant for the year. Till Oracle10*g*, the use of bind variables in such cases would use the same plan to fetch the data for both years. But, the data volumes in the two years might differ a lot. In such a case, using the same plan to fetch the records might be incorrect. To solve this problem, Oracle11*g* has Adaptive Cursor Sharing functionality. Adaptive Cursor Sharing uses the same plan only if it is appropriate. Read about adaptive cursors at http://www.oracle.com/technetwork/articles/sql/11g-sqlplanmanagement-101938.html.

The cursor_sharing parameter is another important thing to consider, while formulating a strategy for bind variables. It determines what kind of queries can share the cursors. The possible values include EXACT, SIMILAR, and FORCE. We can set the cursor_sharing parameter using Alter session or alter system statements. The EXACT value only allows the queries with exactly same text to share the cursor. The SIMILAR value lets the similar queries that differ only in literals to share the cursor, unless the literals affect either the meaning of the statement, or the degree to which the plan is optimized. The FORCE value lets similar queries that differ only in literals to share the cursor, unless the literals affect the meaning of the statement.

Cursor sharing also reduces latch contention, and hence improves concurrency. If bind variables are not used, then the library cache will be flushed with a number of queries, which will try to acquire the latches on resources such as the shared SQL area, and hence result in poor performance.

The use of bind variables also reduces the SQL Injection attacks. We have a discussion on this in the *SQL Injection* section of the *Appendix*.

Using materialized views

Materialized views or M-views are used to pre-calculate the aggregations and calculations used in a report. Pre-calculation results in lesser time to display a report, and hence better user experience. Views have a SQL query associated with them, which is executed when we select from the view. So views do not have data of their own. However, materialized views have their own data, hence the name materialized. Materialized views have a query and a refresh frequency associated with them. The associated query is executed at a set frequency, and the data returned by the query is stored.

If Oracle feels that a query request, built on relational tables, can also be fulfilled using M-views, then Oracle uses M-views to fulfill the request. Oracle does this favor without any change from the developer. This is called the query rewrite feature of Oracle. Oracle takes the rewrite decision based on a SQL text of the query and the one associated with the M-view, or it takes the decision based on the joins, selected columns, grouped columns, and other such properties of the query and the M-view. Creating dimensions (using the `create dimension` statement), constraints, and maintaining referential integrity also improves the optimizer's intelligence of rewriting the query. The `DBMS_MVIEW.EXPLAIN_REWRITE` method can tell you the possibilities of rewrite of a query. The `DBMS_ADVISOR.TUNE_MVIEW` method can be used to get a query of the M-view that is more suited for enabling the use of the M-view for query rewrite.

Read more at `http://docs.oracle.com/cd/E11882_01/server.112/e10706/repmview.htm`.

Using bulk operations

The use of statements such as `FORALL` and `BULK COLLECT` can improve the performance when dealing with large volumes. These help in reducing context switches between a SQL and the PL/SQL engines, and hence improve performance. The higher the number of rows involved, greater will be the benefit of using them. You can find examples and more information on bulk operations at `http://www.oracle.com/technetwork/issue-archive/2012/12-sep/o52plsql-1709862.html`.

Read the *Using native web service to return a collection of rows* section of *Chapter 8, All About Web Services and Integrations*, to see an example of `BULK COLLECT`.

Using sequences

We can also use the cache setting to enhance the performance of sequences. The `cache` clause of the `create sequence` statement can be used for better performance. If this is used, then the database preallocates a bunch of sequence numbers and keeps them in memory for faster access.

Understanding indexes

Index compression is usually used for better data storage and for the fact that Oracle will have to scan lesser data blocks for fulfilling the query. This will result in lesser I/O and hence improved performance. So, index compression is the trade-off between lesser data blocks versus more work by CPU to decompress. Compressing unique indexes might not be helpful because every entry is unique, so we have nothing to compress.

 We can enable index monitoring by using the `ALTER INDEX MONITORING USAGE` statement, and then query the `V$OBJECT_USAGE` view to get usage information.

Understanding the bitmap index

The bitmap index works extremely well for low cardinality columns, which are not updated frequently. They not only improve the data retrieval process, but also save space. Unlike the B-tree index, the bitmap indexes store null values, and hence can be used even if the queries have an `is null` comparison.

The bitmap join index takes the advantage of the bitmap indexes a step further. It stores the result of a join, and can completely prevent a join from happening on the tables, resulting in improved performance. The bitmap join index can be used to improve the performance of the queries involving inner joins in a data warehouse. Again, the bitmap join indexes compress better than the regular bitmap index on a join column, so it improves data storage as well.

However, the bitmap indexes can cause sufficient problems, if the table having a bitmap index is frequently updated. During **DML** when the index is updated, all bitmap segments are locked. This can result in a lot of locking on the database. Since the bitmap index is smaller as compared to a B-tree index on the same column, an index fast full scan is faster. Read more about the bitmap indexes at `http://docs.oracle.com/cd/E11882_01/server.112/e25554/indexes.htm#CIHGAFFF`.

Understanding the reverse key index

In a reverse key index, index entries are spread across multiple data blocks and hence the contention for a single hot block is reduced. If values are stored in a key using a sequence, then consecutive increasing values from the sequence are stored in the rightmost leaf block of a B-tree index. So if multiple sessions are inserting, then an index block can become a hot block. To avoid this situation, we can use the reverse key indexes. The values of the reverse key indexes are stored in reverse order, and hence the data values no longer seek the rightmost leaf block, and get scattered in multiple blocks, which reduces contention. For example, if the values from a sequence are 123, 124, and 125, and if these values are stored as the primary key of a table, then each of these would seek the rightmost leaf block because the rightmost block is for the largest value. If a reverse key index is used, then the values would be reversed to 321, 421, and 521 before inserting. This will result in scattering of the values, and hence will reduce the contention.

However, the reverse key index can result in full table scan, where a B-tree index would use an index range scan. This is because the values in the index of a reverse key index are not adjacent. Range scans usually happen when we have range predicates in the `where` clause.

Ordering columns in an index

The ordering of columns in an index depends on our requirements. The order of columns in an index can dictate whether the index will be used to fulfill a query, or not.

For very selective range scans, the column which is fetched most frequently (most selective), should be the first column in the index.

If the range scan is huge, then I/Os can usually be reduced by ordering the columns in the least selective order or in a manner that sorts the data in the way it should be retrieved.

Using the with clause

If a sub query is used in multiple places in our query, then we can give a name to that subquery using the `WITH` clause, and reference it in all the places where the subquery is written. Oracle stores this subquery in the `temp` tablespace, and then uses the result wherever the `WITH` clause is referenced in the query. This not only helps to reduce the complexity of the query, but also improves performance, since the sub query in the `WITH` clause would have executed at all referenced places, if it was not in the `WITH` clause.

Have a look at the *Understanding the WITH clause* section and the *Creating a hierarchical report using the recursive WITH clause* section of *Chapter 2, Conventional Reporting in APEX*, to see the examples of WITH clause.

Understanding partitioning strategies

Partitioning a huge table helps in managing the table, and can also help in a quicker response time due to partition pruning and partition-wise joins. Partition pruning is the process by which the query accesses only the necessary partitions to retrieve the data rather than accessing the whole table. Partition-wise joins are used only if at least one of the tables is joined on the join key. This technique breaks the bigger join into many smaller joins that fastens the data fetching process. Partition-wise joins can either be Full Partition-Wise Joins or can be Partial Partition-Wise Joins. Each of these has its own requirements. Read about these at http://docs.oracle.com/cd/E11882_01/server.112/e16541/part_warehouse.htm.

Partitioning can be a good strategy for DML operations as well because it allows the degree of parallelism equal to the number of partitions. If one partition of a table is unavailable, other partitions can remain online. Partitions can be configured such that each partition is stored in a separate tablespace. This can enable DBAs to do backup and recovery on individual partitions.

We can partition the data based on the data in a column. For example, we can have partitions based on a date column. In other words, we can have a partition for every month. This kind of partitioning is called range partitioning. We can also have a list that defines the data distribution and group multiple values of a column under a single value of the list. Such type of partitioning is called list partitioning. Hash partitioning allows the partitioning of data based on the hash algorithm.

These distribution methods can be applied at a single level or two levels. We can have one level of partition using one method, and then these partitions can again be partitioned using another method. This is called composite partitioning. However, we can also have single partitioning. In composite partitioning, we cannot use the hash-range and the hash-list partitioning methods. Some newer forms of partitioning such as interval partitioning, REF partitioning and virtual column based partitioning have been introduced in Oracle11g.

Read more about partitioning at http://www.oracle.com/technetwork/database/options/partitioning/index.html.

Understanding anonymous blocks versus stored procedures

Stored PL/SQL procedures are better than anonymous PL/SQL blocks. When a procedure/function/package is in the shared pool of the SGA, retrieving from disk is not required and the execution can begin immediately. Anonymous PL/SQL blocks in APEX are stored in the APEX metadata tables. This code has to be fetched and parsed on every execution. Packing similar procedures in a package is better as it will result in the loading of the entire package in the memory after the call to any procedure/function of the package. So, no disk I/O will be required for any procedure/function of the package after the call to any one procedure/function of the package.

Using star transformation

Star transformations are little more than just a joining strategy. The idea is to fetch only those rows from the huge fact table that satisfy the filters on the smaller dimension tables that join with the facts. If star transformation is used in the execution of a query, then oracle does not even refrain from using temporary tables and rewriting of the query in order to speed up the data retrieval process. Rewriting of the query involves the creation of subquery predicates which join to the fact. These subquery predicates are referred to as bitmap semi-join predicates. Star transformation works only if we have the bitmap indexes on the join columns of the fact table. The transformation first filters the relevant rows from dimensions, and then uses the bitmap indexes of the fact to get relevant fact rows. These fact rows are joined back to the dimensions to get the selected columns of the dimension tables. Note that we had to join the fact rows back to the dimensions because there might be some columns of the dimensions, which might be selected, but might not appear in the WHERE clause. The initial filter on the dimensions only deals with the conditions in the WHERE clause. Star transformation can be enabled using the star_transformation_enabled parameter.

Read more about star transformation at http://docs.oracle.com/cd/B28359_01/server.111/b28313/schemas.htm#i1006335.

Understanding clustering of tables

The single big purpose of clustering is to reduce the amount of I/O because disk operations are slower than data buffer operations. Clustering basically involves the storage of similar data together. So the number of data blocks to be read to fulfill a query is significantly reduced.

This improves query performance. Using clusters for single table improves the performance of range scans. Similarly, we can store the rows of multiple tables together, if they share a common key. This can be done using the multi table index clusters or the multi table hash clusters. The index clusters give good performance, if the query involves the join, on the column in the index. In the hash clusters, the index is replaced by a hash function. We can use the sorted hash clusters to improve the performance of queries involving sorting.

Clustering also has side effects. If we query only a single table from a multi table cluster, then the performance might be poor because we would be reading a larger record since the data of both the tables is stored together. Again, DML on clusters is slower.

Queries on the index clusters have to access the index segments, and also the table segments, so the performance of the hash clusters is known to be better than the index clusters in most cases. The hash clusters work with a hash function, and hence do not need an index, although hash clusters can have an index. The hash clusters require less storage because they do not need the index segment. However, the hash clusters should be used only in a situation, where the table is static because if the tables of a hash cluster require more space than initial allocation, then overflow blocks are required, which degrades performance. If most queries, on the hash clusters, retrieve a range of values based on the cluster key, then the hash function cannot be used. This will result in a full table scan which is costly in clusters. Equality operation on the cluster key can use the hash clusters, and hence are better to be used with hash clustering. Again, we have to tactically set the HASHKEYS parameter because if the cardinality grows over the specified value, then we will have to rebuild the cluster, and setting an oversized value will result in wastage.

Understanding parallelism

We can use parallel hints for queries that involve large table scans, joins, or partitioned index scans. However, it must be pointed out that parallelism might spoil performance on over utilized systems or systems with small I/O bandwidth. Parallelism involves breaking a huge task into a number of smaller tasks, which are executed in parallel.

We can use the DBMS_PARALLEL_EXECUTE package to update large amount of data as it improves performance, reduces rollback space consumption, and we do not lose all our work if something fails in the process of updating.

Using code inlining

Code inlining results in faster execution, but is certainly not the best method to write the code as it harms readability. Oracle11*g* gives us a solution to this problem by giving us `plsql_optimize_level`. If the value of `plsql_optimize_level` is set to 3, then the PL/SQL compiler is directed to find the prospects to inline the code. So, our readability is not hampered, and our code works faster. Code inlining shows better result when used with native compilation.

Understanding short circuit evaluation

If any of the expressions joined together by logical `OR` operators are true, then the result of the entire expression is true. So if we have a lot of `OR` conditions, then oracle does not execute other `OR` conditions, if the first one returns true. This is called short circuiting. So, in a series of expressions joined by the `OR` operator, make sure that you order the expressions such that the least expensive expressions are in the beginning.

Understanding PLSQL_CODE_TYPE

We can use `PLSQL_CODE_TYPE` to define the method used to compile our code. If the value is set to `INTERPRETED`, then the code is compiled to the PL/SQL byte code, which is used by the PL/SQL Interpreter engine. If the value is set to `NATIVE`, then the PL/SQL code will be compiled to the native machine code. Using `NATIVE` or `INTERPRETED` does not affect the speed of execution of the SQL, but using `NATIVE` compilation increases the speed of execution of PL/SQL code. Compiling code in the `NATIVE` mode is a lot easier in Oracle11*g* than in the previous versions, and Oracle calls it Real Native Compilation. Datatypes such as `simple_integer`, `SIMPLE_FLOAT`, and `SIMPLE_DOUBLE` when used in combination with native compilation show significant performance benefits. The `simple_integer` datatype is a subtype of the `pls_integer` datatype.

Using PL/SQL datatypes

Choosing the correct datatype can be vital for performance. If we know that our variables will never have null values, then using `SIMPLE_INTEGER`, `SIMPLE_FLOAT`, or `SIMPLE_DOUBLE`, rather than `BINARY_FLOAT` or `BINARY_DOUBLE` will result in better performance. The benefit is greater with native compilation. Operations on datatypes such as `PLS_INTEGER`, `BINARY_FLOAT`, and `BINARY_DOUBLE` use hardware arithmetic, so use them instead of using `NUMBER` because the `NUMBER` operations use library arithmetic.

The use of constrained datatypes involves an additional check during each assignment. One should make sure that one uses the same datatype for similar operations, so that implicit conversion of the datatypes is minimized. Read more about the datatypes at `http://docs.oracle.com/cd/E11882_01/appdev.112/e10472/datatypes.htm`.

Using HTML in SQL

Coding HTML in SQL hampers the reusability of the code. APEX has other, better ways such as templates and item formatting to code HTML.

Implementing XML PIVOT queries

We have seen the pivot clause in the *Implementing matrix report* section in *Chapter 2, Conventional Reporting in APEX*. We had used substitution variables to make the IN clause dynamic. But, such queries are prone to SQL Injection attacks. We have a discussion on this in the *SQL Injection* section of the *Appendix*. The solution is to use the PIVOT XML clause. If the PIVOT XML clause is used, then we can have a subquery in the IN clause, and hence it makes the IN clause, dynamic. The PIVOT XML clause returns an XMLTYPE datatype, which can be easily converted to more meaningful information by using the extract and the extractvalue functions. Have a look at the following query:

```
SELECT *
    FROM   oehr_employees
    PIVOT  XML
            (SUM(salary) FOR department_id IN
(select department_id from oehr_departments)
    )
```

This query uses a nested query in the in clause, and hence we can eliminate the need of substitution variable.

Understanding denormalization

Normalization is the organization of data in such a way that data redundancy is minimized, and updates in data result in minimum changes in the database. Normalization primarily has three forms, namely, 1NF, 2NF, and 3NF. These days, memory is becoming cheaper, which has resulted in the focus shift from reducing redundancy to improving performance. Since joining one table to the other is a costly affair, data warehousing environments are usually modeled as the star schema, which is highly denormalized.

Understanding secure files, deduplication, and large object storage

The default storage method of LOBs is BASICFILE, but Oracle11*g* has a better storage method called SECUREFILE. This method provides better security and space utilization by encryption, compression, and deduplication. Deduplication is the process by which Oracle stores only one copy of the **LOB**, even if it is associated with multiple rows. The DB_SECUREFILE parameter is the governing initialization parameter that decides which LOB will be created as a SECUREFILE LOB, and which one will be created as BASICFILE.

Both BASICFILE and SECUREFILE have some caching options too. These options lets us cache the LOB for both read and read/write operations. Deduplication option of SECUREFILE prevents the duplication of LOB at table or partition level. Similarly, the COMPRESS option of SECUREFILE lets us compress the LOB to the LOW, MEDIUM, and HIGH level. The LOW compression level in Oracle11*g* Release 2 involves minimum CPU overhead. The SECUREFILE LOBs can also be encrypted, and we can choose from a variety of encryption algorithms.

The DBMS_LOB API can be used for managing the BASICFILE and the SECUREFILE LOBs.

The DBMS_SPACE.SPACE_USAGE procedure is an overloaded procedure, which returns information about the LOB space usage in blocks, but it only works with tablespaces created with Auto Segment Space Management. The use of the NOLOGGING option is faster because changes are not logged in the redo log. However, the use of the LOGGING option ensures that data is recoverable, if the face of some database problems during the DML operation. The FILESYSTEM_LIKE_LOGGING logging option is available only for the SECUREFILE LOBs. It logs the metadata, but doesn't log the data itself. The FILESYSTEM_LIKE_LOGGING logging option also ensures that the data is completely recoverable after server failure.

Read more about SECUREFILE at http://docs.oracle.com/cd/E11882_01/appdev.112/e18294/adlob_smart.htm.

Discussions on HTML, JavaScript, and client-side tools

We will dedicate the next few sections to understanding the ways in which HTML, JavaScript, and client-side tools can be used to improve performance.

Let us start with looking at a better way of storing static images.

Understanding image storage

Static image stored in file system are better than images stored as blobs in tables because images stored in the file system can be cached by the browser, and will result in quicker load of the page in subsequent runs. So, it is better to store images such as logo in the files, since logos are present on every page, and the caching by the browser will improve the performance. The APEX Listener provides `cache.procedureNameList` in `defaults.xml` to cache the files based on database procedures.

Using browser-specific tools

Firefox has lead from the front in developing add-ons that can help a developer play with the HTML and JavaScript code at his end. These tools not only help a developer debug JavaScript and jQuery code, but also enable him to understand scripting security threats in the code. Some of the major add-ons which can be used with Firefox are Firebug, YSlow, Web developer, and Greasemonkey. You can read more about these at `https://addons.mozilla.org/en-us/firefox/collections/mozilla/webdeveloper/`. Similarly, IE has Microsoft script debugger, which can be enabled by clicking on the **Advanced** tab in **Internet Options**, and then unchecking the **Disable script debugging (Internet Explorer)** and the **Disable script debugging (Other)** checkboxes. IE 8 also has a whole bunch of developer tools, which can be accessed by pressing the *F12* key. These tools also include a profiler, which can be used to give us timing information about the load of various components of a web page. Similarly, Chrome has tools such as the speed tracer. Read more about speed tracer at `https://developers.google.com/web-toolkit/speedtracer/`. These tools not only help us debug our problematic code, but also help us know the response time. This information can not only be used for tuning the application, but also for tuning the network.

Using minified JavaScript

Minified JavaScript files should be used since JavaScript files are cached in the browser at first execution. Minified JavaScript files are the ones, which do not have any unwanted characters and comments. Again inline JavaScript code is loaded every time the page is executed, and it increases the HTML page size. This affects the performance. So, we should always put our JavaScript in separate files. The loading of these files can be done strategically. We should not load all our JavaScript files at login time as it can harm the user's experience. It is important to understand that JavaScript code compressors are available.

Compressing HTML for better performance

If you are using the Apache based web servers, then you can use the `mod_deflate` module to compress the data sent to the client browser. To use `mod_deflate`, we first have to register it in the `httpd.conf` file, and then configure it to accept response from the server, so that the uncompressed data is not sent directly to the client browser. We can also use `mod_gzip` to compress files, if using any Apache based server. In WebLogic, we can use the `compress-html-template` element to compress HTML in JSP template blocks. Tuning a web server is a whole different subject, and different web servers can be tuned in different ways. Some of the other things which we can do with WebLogic include turning off the logging and precompiling JSP. Read more about these at `http://docs.oracle.com/cd/E14571_01/web.1111/e13814/webapptune.htm`.

Learn more about tuning WebLogic at `http://docs.oracle.com/cd/E14571_01/web.1111/e13814/wls_tuning.htm`.

> Scaling of images using HTML consumes memory of the client-side computer. Hence, it is best to avoid this wherever possible. Use the file format that results in smallest file size. Image size is usually smaller if the image quality is lower.

APEX Listener parameters

APEX Listener lets us cache file content fetched through database procedures. We can edit the `defaults.xml` file of the Listener configuration for this purpose, or can use SQL Developer for the configuration. The `jdbc.InitialLimit` method of the `defaults.xml` file lets us set the initial number of connections that should be made to the database. This value should be carefully selected according to your user base in order to ensure that the wait time is minimized.

The `defaults.xml` file also has many more properties related to connection pooling. These properties can have significant impact on user experience. Learn more about APEX Listener at `http://docs.oracle.com/cd/E37099_01/doc/doc.20/e25066.pdf`.

Also, have a look at the `defaults.xml` file of your listener installation. The names of most of the parameters are self-explanatory.

Discussions on database tools for performance tuning

We will now have a look at a few database tools that can help us understand the performance bottlenecks, and can help us tune our APEX applications. An understanding of these tools can change our development perspective, and help us code better APEX applications.

Using PL/SQL hierarchical profiler and DBMS_PROFILER

PL/SQL hierarchical profiler is new to Oracle11g, and can help us find the execution time taken by individual subprograms called from a function. It also gives the time taken by the SQL and the PL/SQL engines to fulfill a call to a function. We can create the necessary tables for hierarchical profiler by executing the `dbmshptab.sql` script. The raw data collector component of the profiler collects the data of execution, while the Analyzer component then puts it in a format which can be more easily understood. The data of the profiler is stored in tables such as DBMSHP_RUNS, DBMSHP_FUNCTION_INFO, and DBMSHP_PARENT_CHILD_INFO. The profiler also has the `plshprof` command-line utility which can be used to get the information gathered by the profiler in HTML. We can use the information collected by the profiler to find the problematic parts of our code.

We can start the collection of profiling statistics by using DBMS_HPROF.START_PROFILING, and can stop the collection by using DBMS_HPROF.STOP_PROFILING. The DBMS_HPROF.ANALYZE function analyzes the raw profiler output and stores them in tables. Read more about hierarchical profiler at `http://docs.oracle.com/cd/E11882_01/appdev.112/e25518/adfns_profiler.htm`.

Both hierarchical profiler (DBMS_HPROF) and traditional profiler (DBMS_PROFILER) serve similar purpose, but have a very important distinction. The DBMS_HPROF method clearly shows the hierarchical call stack of execution, while DBMS_PROFILER shows line-by-line details. So, if function A calls function B, which in turn calls function C, then hierarchical profiler can clearly show the hierarchical chained execution and the time taken by each module for executing. We will learn more about DBMS_PROFILER in a short while.

The DBMS_PROFILER method works like a charm to collect statistics of PL/SQL code. The package helps us pinpoint the part of code, which is contributing maximally in performance degradation. Execute proftab.sql and profload.sql in sequence to configure the profiler. Profiler information is stored in the plsql_profiler_units, the plsql_profiler_data, and the plsql_profiler_runs tables. These tables can be joined on the runid column to know about the start of the run, stop of the run, line number, and the duration of the run. We can also join the line# column of plsql_profiler_data with line column of the user_source view to get the text of each line of the executed code. Read more about the columns of the user_source view at http://docs.oracle.com/cd/E18283_01/server.112/e17110/statviews_5437.htm. The dbms_profiler.start_profiler method can be used to direct the profiler to start collecting the statistics and dbms_profiler.stop_profiler can be used to stop the collection of the statistics. Read more about the DBMS_PROFILER package at http://docs.oracle.com/cd/E11882_01/appdev.112/e16760/d_profil.htm.

Understanding Data Guard

If you need to run your analytical queries on huge set of data, and you cannot afford to run ETL processes on your primary OLTP database, then you could use Data Guard to create a replica of your primary database, and do the necessary operation on the replica. Whenever a commit happens in the primary database, the Data Guard transport services read the redo logs of the primary database and write in the redo log of the replica. This process is highly efficient as it does not involve any disk I/O during the process. Synchronous redo transport ensures that the commit in the primary database happens only after it receives an acknowledgement from the replica of receiving the information. This ensures that the data loss is reduced to zero, but also introduces latency in the primary database. However, Data Guard Oracle11*g* Release 2 has a number of new things that helps to reduce the impact of synchronous redo transport. Asynchronous redo transport may result in some data loss, but unlike synchronous redo transport, it does not impact the primary database.

The replica can also be used for testing, backup, and failover. Active Data Guard is an option that requires a separate license. Active Data Guard enables read-only access to a physical standby database for queries, sorting, and reporting. Active Data Guard can also auto repair corrupt blocks. Data Guard can be managed from enterprise manager.

GoldenGate is another Oracle product that performs similar functions. GoldenGate is however loaded with cross platform migrations, two way and multi master replication.

Understanding SGA result cache

The shared pool of the SGA has a new component in Oracle11*g* called the result cache, which can further be subdivided into the SQL Query result cache and the PL/SQL function result cache. The DBMS_RESULT_CACHE package lets us do the administration of the result cache, and we can see and monitor the impact of our changes using the V$RESULT_CACHE_* views. These views show the objects that have been cached, the memory and cache settings, dependencies, and other such information. In case of the query result cache, the results of a query are cached, and on subsequent execution, the result of the query is fetched from the cache. In case of the function result cache, the output of the function is stored for a set of inputs, and the value is fetched from the cache, when the same values of arguments are passed. The database invalidates the query result cache, when the underlying objects are changed by DML operations. The RESULT_CACHE_MODE initialization parameter can be used to control the queries which can be cached. You will have to use the /*+ result_cache */ hint, if RESULT_CACHE_MODE is set to MANUAL. If RESULT_CACHE_ MODE is set to FORCE, then you can use the /*+ no_result_cache */ hint to prevent the result of a query from being cached. The result cache is disabled if RESULT_ CACHE_MAX_SIZE is set to 0 on startup. The RESULT_CACHE_MAX_SIZE parameter can be used to set the max size of the result cache. The result_cache_max_result parameter specifies the percentage of result_cache_max_size that a single result can use.

Understanding SQL work areas

Properly-sized work areas can significantly improve the performance of the queries. Examples of work areas are sort area and hash area. Ideally, operations such as sorting should happen in the RAM, but then if the sort area is not sized properly, then spillover can happen to the temp tablespace. This basically means that a part of the sorting would be done in the temp tablespace. Sorting in the temp tablespace will increase I/Os, and hence degrade performance.

The same principle can also be applied to hash area. Oracle can automatically manage the memory allocated to different work areas. The memory management is done with a goal of maximizing the performance of the memory intensive SQL operations. The total amount of memory that can be used for all work areas is governed by the `PGA_AGGREGATE_TARGET` parameter which is set by the **DBA**. On an instance that runs huge amount of memory intensive queries, the distribution of RAM between SGA and PGA can be as high as 70 percent to PGA, and 30 percent to SGA. However, the actual distribution depends on your own requirements. The DBA should run a representative workload on a new instance to estimate the size of `PGA_AGGREGATE_TARGET` in this environment. The `PGA_AGGREGATE_TARGET` parameter can also be tuned using PGA advice statistics. Views such as `V$PGASTAT`, `V$PROCESS`, `V$PROCESS_MEMORY`, `V$SQL_WORKAREA_HISTOGRAM`, `V$SQL_WORKAREA_ACTIVE`, and `V$SQL_WORKAREA` can helps us monitor our memory settings. The Automatic PGA memory management is disabled, if `PGA_AGGREGATE_TARGET` is set to 0. The `V$PGA_TARGET_ADVICE` and the `V$PGA_TARGET_ADVICE_HISTOGRAM` parameters can be used to understand the impact on key PGA statistics on changing `PGA_AGGREGATE_TARGET`. The `STATISTICS_LEVEL` parameter should be set to `TYPICAL` or `ALL`, and `PGA_AGGREGATE_TARGET` should be set, if you wish to use the `V$PGA_TARGET_ADVICE` and the `V$PGA_TARGET_ADVICE_HISTOGRAM` views.

Read more about memory configuration at `http://docs.oracle.com/cd/E11882_01/server.112/e16638/memory.htm`.

Using data compression

We can compress both table and index data, if we find from the trace that high I/O has been the reason for slow performance. Compressions are helpful in queries that do a full table scan. Oracle Advanced Compression Advisor has been implemented through the `DBMS_COMPRESSION` package. The advisor gives the estimated benefit of using the table compression feature.

Also, see `http://docs.oracle.com/cd/E11882_01/appdev.112/e25788/d_compress.htm` for more info on the `DBMS_COMPRESSION` package.

Understanding segment space problems

Frequent DML operations on a table can result in fragmentation of the data storage. We can use the Segment Advisor to find the objects, which can be tweaked for better data storage and faster retrieval. The Segment Advisor can be used either with Enterprise Manager or in PL/SQL by using the `DBMS_ADVISOR` package.

We can view the results of Segment Advisor by querying the DBA_ADVISOR_* views, viewing the results in Enterprise Manager, or calling the DBMS_SPACE.ASA_RECOMMENDATIONS procedure. We have the freedom of configuring Automatic Segment Advisor. We can also use the ALTER TABLE, ALTER VIEW, ALTER MATERIALIZED VIEW, and ALTER MATERIALIZED VIEW LOG statements with SHRINK SPACE clause to reclaim wasted space and rest the **High Water Mark**. This will help in improving the performance of queries, which involve full table scans.

Understanding the Database Resource Manager

The Database Resource Manager can be used for prioritizing jobs so that the response time of high priority jobs is minimized. So, we can prioritize jobs such that the jobs of online users always get a higher priority, and some other jobs such as the ETL might get a lower priority. Database Resource Manager can also queue all subsequent requests, if the specified maximum number of concurrently active sessions is reached.

Understanding the SQL Access Advisor and SQL Tuning Advisor

The SQL Tuning Advisor issues advisories such as reorganizing SQL for improved performance. The SQL Access Advisor suggests partitioning strategies, creation and dropping of indexes, and materialized views. The SQL Access Advisor can use the methods defined in DBMS_ADVISOR package to perform its operations. Have a look at the following list of subprograms of DBMS_ADVISOR. It shows which subprograms can be used for the SQL Access Advisor. Read about it at http://docs.oracle.com/cd/E18283_01/appdev.112/e16760/d_advis.htm#CHDEGCBJ. The recommendations will be more accurate if the advisor is executed against a workload that mimics your live environment. We can also schedule the advisories of SQL Access Advisor and SQL Tuning Advisor. The SQL Access Advisor is primarily for making schema modifications and the SQL Tuning Advisor is for making SQL related changes such as creation of SQL profiles. We will again talk about the SQL Tuning Advisor in a short while again.

Understanding temporary tablespace

Proper configuration of the temporary tablespace can help to optimize disk sort performance. Oracle recommends that we use locally managed temporary tablespaces with a uniform extent size of 1 MB, although dictionary managed tablespaces are also possible.

Dictionary managed tablespaces store the extent allocation information in Oracle dictionary. Locally managed tablespaces on the other hand maintain a bitmap that is modified when an extent is freed or allocated for use. If the number of users in an application is huge, then the extent size should be reduced. Every usage requires at least one extent, so the reduction in extent size ensures that extents are available for every user session.

If temporary tablespace has been increased due to some one-off database operation, then we can shrink the size of temp table space to the original by using the alter tablespace shrink space statement. Similarly, we can also shrink a tempfile using the alter tablespace shrink tempfile statement. The DBA_TEMP_FREE_SPACE view can be used to see temporary tablespace usage information.

Understanding SQL monitoring

Oracle11g has two new views, which can be used to get performance metrics of queries that consume for more than 5 seconds of CPU or I/O time, and the queries running in parallel mode. Based on this information, the DBA can take a call to let the query execute or terminate it. We can get the SQL monitoring active report in HTML format using the DBMS_SQLTUNE package, or can get the report from Enterprise Manager. The V$SQL_MONITOR and V$SQL_PLAN_MONITOR views have been introduced in Oracle11g to support SQL monitoring. Real time SQL monitoring also helps us to understand what part of the execution plan corresponds to most utilization of resources.

Views such as V$ACTIVE_SESSION_HISTORY, V$SESSION_LONGOPS, V$SQL_PLAN, and V$SQL can be used for monitoring queries.

Understanding DB_FILE_MULTIBLOCK_ READ_COUNT

The DB_FILE_MULTIBLOCK_READ_COUNT parameter is the number of blocks, which are read in a single I/O during a full table scan or index fast full scan. If the value of this parameter is large, then full table scans become cheaper resulting in the optimizer going for a full table scan, rather than an index scan. Optimizer also uses it to cost index fast full scans. Larger DB_FILE_MULTIBLOCK_READ_COUNT would mean that Oracle will be able to read a larger number of blocks in a single I/O. Hence, sort merge joins might become less costly in comparison to nested loop joins. Hence, this parameter should be set according to your query workload. The default value of DB_FILE_MULTIBLOCK_READ_COUNT corresponds to the maximum I/O size that can be efficiently performed on a platform.

Understanding extended statistics

In Oracle11g, we can collect the statistics of multiple columns together. If we have a table with two columns such that the combination of the two columns becomes very selective, but individually the columns are not selective, then collecting the statistics together makes sense because it will help the optimizer to understand the structure of the data, and hence frame better plans. The DBMS_STATS.CREATE_EXTENDED_STATS parameter can be used to create such statistics. Extended statistics can also be used when the data in the columns is skewed. Basically, extended statistics is a method to inform the optimizer about the correlations among the data of various columns. Histograms were used in Oracle10g to inform the optimizer about the skewness of data, but gathering extended statistics is a more direct way of handling the situation. Once the extended statistics are created, we would see a system generated name in the USER_TAB_COL_STATISTICS view, which stands for the newly connected statistics of the column group. We can view extended stats in the DBA_STAT_EXTENSIONS view.

Understanding SQL Performance Analyzer

The SQL Performance Analyzer enables us to forecast the impact of system changes on SQL performance by testing these changes using a SQL workload on a test system. SPA is used to understand the effect on the system by doing a certain change to the database. The process is to first create a SQL tuning set, which is a combination of the SQL statements with execution context, plans, statistics, and other such information. Tuning set can be created using the DBMS_SQLTUNE package or from the enterprise manager. This tuning set can then be exported to a testing system, where we can do the proposed change. SPA gives us the freedom to order the SQL statements in a tuning set. The process is to first invoke the SPA, which executes the SQL statements, make the change, and then invoke the SPA again after the change. SPA then gives the verdict on the improvements after considering before and after change performance. After the verdict, we can use the SQL Tuning Advisor and SQL plan baselines to tune the SQL statements further. SPA tasks can be created using the DBMS_SQLPA package.

Understanding SQL Tuning Advisor

Oracle database can be configured for automatic SQL tuning. If configured, Oracle optionally implements recommendations for high impact SQLs. These high impact SQLs are picked from the **AWR** report and the task is done in maintenance time slots. Before the implementation, only those recommendations are accepted that result in three times performance improvement.

The suggestions include collection of statistics, building of indexes, restructuring query, and setting a profile for the query. Automatic tuning configuration can be done using the DBMS_AUTO_TASK_ADMIN package. We can use the SQL Tuning Advisor from SQL Developer as well. The report can be generated using DBMS_AUTO_SQLTUNE.REPORT_AUTO_TUNING_TASK. Input to manually execute tuning advisor can come from any source including **ADDM**, AWR, tuning sets, and shared SQL area. The report can be seen using DBMS_SQLTUNE.REPORT_TUNING_TASK. The status of a tuning task can be seen in USER_ADVISOR_TASKS, and the process of execution can be seen in V$ADVISOR_PROGRESS. Many more views are associated with SQL tuning activity, and you can find more information about these and the tuning advisor at http://docs.oracle.com/cd/E11882_01/server.112/e16638/sql_tune.htm.

Understanding pinning in keep pool

Any small table which has full table scans and is used frequently can be pinned to the keep pool. We can monitor the DBA_HIST_SNAPSHOT, DBA_HIST_OPTIMIZER_ENV, DBA_HIST_SQLTEXT, and DBA_HIST_SQL_PLAN views to find possible candidates for pinning. We could also collect information from the AWR report. We can use the DB_KEEP_CACHE_SIZE parameter to assign RAM memory to the keep pool. Oracle has given the following query to find out the objects whose data blocks reside in buffer cache:

```
SELECT o.OBJECT_NAME, COUNT(*) NUMBER_OF_BLOCKS
    FROM DBA_OBJECTS o, V$BH bh
  WHERE o.DATA_OBJECT_ID = bh.OBJD
    AND o.OWNER          != 'SYS'
  GROUP BY o.OBJECT_NAME
  ORDER BY COUNT(*);
```

Again, the contents of the buffer cache change frequently, so a constant monitoring will be required. We can pin tables to the keep pool by using the following statement:

```
ALTER TABLE kp_test STORAGE (buffer_pool KEEP)
```

We can also configure other pools. Read the following for more information:

http://docs.oracle.com/cd/E28271_01/server.1111/e16638/memory.htm

Understanding Automatic Database Diagnostic Monitor (ADDM)

ADDM is one of the most important reports in Oracle. Its advisory includes changes in initialization parameter settings, partitioning advice, hardware changes, use of bind variables, and many more. ADDM report not only lists problem, but also gives solutions to fix it. An ADDM analysis is done between a pair of snapshots and we can either get the report from Enterprise Manager or by using the addmrpt.sql script. We can also do our operations using the DBMS_ADDM package. If we wish to analyze all instances of a database, then we can run the ADDM in database mode, If information about a single instance is required, then we can execute it in instance mode, and if information about a group of instances is required, then we can run it in partial mode. The findings of the ADDM can also be seen in the DBA_ADDM_FINDINGS view. The DBA_ADVISOR_RECOMMENDATIONS view can be seen to know more about the recommendations.

Understanding Automatic Workload Repository (AWR)

AWR report is by far the most import report in Oracle. The data in the workload repository is used by ADDM report, SQL Tuning Advisor, undo advisor, and segment advisor. It contains usage and access information of objects, **Active Session History (ASH)** statistics, statistics about SQLs that are burdening the system, and system and session statistics. Actions for the AWR report can either be performed using Enterprise Manager or by using the DBMS_WORKLOAD_REPOSITORY package. We can generate AWR reports using the awrrpt.sql, awrrpti.sql, awrsqrpt.sql, and awrsqrpi.sql scripts as well.

We can also generate an AWR compare report that generates a report comparing two snapshot intervals. We can use the awrddrpt.sql and the awrddrpi.sql scripts to generate this report.

The USER_ADVISOR_FINDINGS view lists the findings of all advisors.

Understanding index-organized tables

Index-organized tables is a specialized storage method that stores the data in the form of a B-tree index structure in a primary key sorted manner. If queries on a heap table use an index, then the necessary records are first searched in the index, and the data is then fetched from the tables. In IOTs, the data itself is available in sorted form in a B-tree data structure, and can hence be fetched very quickly. This not only quickens the process, but also saves space, since the information is not stored in two places (index and table). We can create an IOT by using the ORGANIZATION INDEX clause at the end of the CREATE TABLE statement. Just like B-tree indexes, IOTs can also be fragmented due to incremental updates. We can rebuild an IOT using the ALTER TABLE...MOVE statement. Small lookup tables are usually good candidates for IOT.

Understanding row chaining and row migration

Before we try to understand row chaining and row migration, let us first understand the organization of our data in Oracle. Data of Oracle objects is stored in segments. Segments are a collection of extents, and extents are a collection of data blocks. Extents of a segment can be spread in many datafiles. However, a single extent can only belong to a single datafile only. All extents of a segment are always stored in one tablespace, but can belong to multiple datafiles. Every operating system has its block size, and Oracle's block size is a multiple of the operating system block size. Every data block has some memory dedicated to overhead. Overhead is a collection of information about the block, memory addresses, and the information about the object to which the block belongs. The overhead is followed by a bunch of rows. Now, when we insert a row, the row can be too big to fit in a single data block. In such cases, oracle stores a part of the row in one block and other part in some other data block. Oracle then chains the two data blocks. This is called row chaining.

Let's say that we had a row that was stored in a data block, but after updating, the data block became too small to store the row. In such a case, Oracle can move the whole row to a new data block, and the current data block then contains a reference to the new block. This is called row migration. In either case, the amount of I/O required to fetch the entire record is higher as compared to a row that is stored in a single block. Execute the utlchain.sql script, and then execute the analyze table statement with the with chained rows clause to find the changed rows in the table. After this, the information of the chained rows can be fetched from the chained_ rows table. The Chained_rows table is created by the utlchain.sql script. If you wish to know the count of chained rows, then you could gather the stats, and then type select chain_cnt from user_tables where TABLE_NAME=<table_name>.

While row chaining is unavoidable, we can fix row migrations. If there are a huge number of chained rows, then questions should be raised about the design, and we should consider changing the block size. Again, it is important to understand that multiple tablespaces of different block sizes can be a trouble for the DBAs, since the DBA will have to reserve space in the buffer cache for a different DB block size, and the buffer cache memory of one block size cannot be used for different size. This results in memory wastage. Bigger blocks size also results in contention for blocks. Row migration can either be fixed by table reorganization, or by reinserting the rowids of problematic rows. We can get these rowids from the `chained_rows` table. We can reinsert the rows, and then delete the problematic rows.

Row migration can also be minimized by setting a bigger value of `PCTFREE`. The `PCTFREE` parameter decides the amount of free space that is left in a block to handle future updates. If this value is too low, then bigger updates will not be able to fit in the same data block, and will hence result in row migration. So Oracle always reserves `PCTFREE` percentage of space for future use, and if the rest of the space is utilized, then the data is inserted in a new block. Oracle considers a block unfit for insertion until the percentage of free space falls less than the value of `PCTUSED`. We can approximate the size of a table using different values for the `PCTFREE` parameter in the `DBMS_SPACE.CREATE_TABLE_COST` procedure.

Statements, for example, `Alter table move` statement and export/import can also help to fix the row migration problem.

Understanding the clustering factor

Clustering factor is the ordering of the rows of a table with respect to a particular index. Every index on a table has a clustering factor of its own. We can ensure that the clustering factor of one index is minimized, but the rows of a table cannot be ordered according to all the indexes, so the clustering factor of all indexes cannot be reduced. The lowest clustering factor is equal to number of data blocks that hold the table data, and the highest clustering factor is equal to the number of rows of the table. Higher clustering factor can result in huge I/Os, and in certain situations, the optimizer might opt for not using the index because of high cost. Again, higher clustering factor can result in higher number of blocks in the buffer cache, and hence undue wastage of space in the cache. If the first index entry corresponds to a row is in one block, and if the next index entry corresponds to a row in another block, then the clustering factor is incremented by one. So, if the clustering factor is equal to the number of rows, then this means that every next reference of the index is to a row in a different block.

Clustering factor equal to the number of data blocks of the table means that the rows are perfectly ordered, and the clustering factor increments because one data block is full and next row has to be stored in a new data block. Clustering factor is important in case of index range scans and index full scans. If the stats are gathered, then we can find the clustering factor using the following query:

```
select clustering_factor from user_indexes where
    index_name='<index_name>';
```

We can improve the clustering factor by **CTAS (CREATE TABLE AS SELECT)** with an `order by` clause, or can use the `DBMS_REDEFINITION` package to rebuild table and order rows. Read about `DBMS_REDEFINITION` at `http://docs.oracle.com/cd/E11882_01/appdev.112/e25788/d_redefi.htm`.

Understanding the Active Session History report

Active Session History (ASH) reports are used to find transient problems that last for a few minutes in the database. We can get the ASH report from the Enterprise Manager or by running the `ashrpt.sql` or the `ashrpti.sql` script. The report helps us find the blocker and waiter queries. It also gathers information such as `SQL_ID`, SID, module, action, and block. Two important views related to ASH reports are `DBA_HIST_ACTIVE_SESS_HISTORY` and `V$ACTIVE_SESSION_HISTORY`. The `DBA_HIST_ACTIVE_SESS_HISTORY` view displays the history of the contents of the in-memory active session history of recent system activity. This view contains snapshots of `V$ACTIVE_SESSION_HISTORY`. The ASH report gives us the execution plan, which can help us find which part of the SQL made the maximum contribution to the SQL elapsed time.

Summary

This chapter was dedicated to the ways and means of tuning the APEX application and the database on which it lives. The end of this chapter brings us to the end of our journey. This book was dedicated to present Oracle APEX as a reporting solution. We started with understanding APEX architecture, and created a variety of reports using APEX features. We customized our reports using jQuery and CSS. We also looked at a number of other technologies, which can be coupled with APEX, and finally ended our discussion with tuning techniques. The objective was to introduce the reporting features of Oracle APEX, to empower you to use Oracle APEX with any existing reporting solution in your organization, and to help you understand and evaluate the integrations of Oracle APEX with any proposed reporting solution that you might want to use for your organization.

Appendix

The topics contained in this section are not vital to understanding the concepts but can boost the understanding of the way APEX functions. Before we get into the specific sections in this appendix, it is important that we compile the `Appendix` package. Use the steps described in the *Steps to create PACKT_SCHEMA* section to create the `PACKT_SCHEMA.Appendix` package. The `PACKT_SCHEMA.Appendix` package is dependent on a number of objects. The installation of these objects is carried out in *Creating database objects and installing the reference application* section of *Chapter 2, Conventional Reporting in APEX*. Once this is done, execute `4-98-9_Appendix_appendix.sql` from SQLPLUS after logging in as `sydba`:

```
SQL> @4-98-9_Appendix_appendix
```

Steps to create PACKT_SCHEMA

We will now see the steps to create PACKT_SCHEMA. This schema will hold all our APEX applications and the supporting code used in this book. Open SQLPLUS using `sysdba`. Enter the following command in the SQL prompt to create a new tablespace called `packt_tablespace` and a new schema called `packt_schema`. Note that, in the command prompt, you should get into the directory that contains `4-98-9_Appendix_create_ts_and_user.sql` before executing the following command. This caution applies for all the files executed from SQL Prompt:

```
SQL> @4-98-9_Appendix_create_ts_and_user
```

Now, perform the following steps:

1. Enter `packt_tablespace` in the `Enter tablespace name:` prompt.
2. Enter the location in which you will want the `.dbf` file to be created in the `Enter dbf file location [For example:C:\Oracle11GDB\oradata\ orcl\oracle_apex_packt_datafile.dbf]` : prompt.

3. Enter `packt_schema` in the `Enter user name:` prompt.

4. The previous steps will create the `packt_schema` along with all the necessary privileges. Enter `packt_password` in the `Enter user passowrd:` prompt.

SQL Injection

This section talks about various ways in which SQL Injection can happen. It also discusses some steps that can help us avoid it. This exercise uses the `OEHR_EMPLOYEES` table. You will have to execute `4-98-9_02_install_schema.sql` using `SYS` to install the schema before doing this exercise.

Execute the following statement from `sysdba` to check whether the installation is successful or not. This statement should not return any records:

```
Select * from all_objects where owner='PACKT_SCHEMA' and status =
'INVALID';
```

Dynamic SQL with concatenated variables

In the SQL Injection attacks that happen because of Dynamic SQL with concatenated variables, the input value, put by the hacker, to a PL/SQL function is such that a part of the dynamic SQL code gets commented.

Let us understand this with an example. Let us say you have two conditions in a `where` clause and have a concatenated variable in the first condition. If the hacker puts `--` (PL/SQL comment) in the variable, then our string will be generated with `--`. The parser will consider anything after `--` as a comment and since the placement of `--` is in the first condition, anything following it, including your second condition, will not be executed.

Let's see this in action!

Compile the `APPENDIX` package contained in the `4-98-9_Appendix_appendix.sql` file. Package can be compiled after logging in as `sysdba`. The `APPENDIX` package contains a procedure called `sql_injection`. This procedure is prone to SQL Injection. Check out the code of this procedure. It shows the count of employees whose salary is greater than 2000 and who work in the department whose ID is passed to this procedure.

Run the following in SQLPLUS:

```
SQL> set serveroutput on
SQL> exec packt_schema.appendix.sql_injection(10);
```

You will get the following output:

```
SQL> set serveroutput on
SQL> exec appendix.sql_injection(10);
Query:select count(employee_id) from oehr_employees where department_id=10 and salary > 2000
Count:1

PL/SQL procedure successfully completed.
```

Now check out the query executed by this procedure:

```
select count(employee_id) from oehr_employees where department_id=10
and salary > 2000
```

If a hacker wants to get the count of all the records in the oehr_employees table, then he will need a query that looks like the following:

```
select count(employee_id) from oehr_employees where department_id =
department_id -- and salary > 2000
```

He can get this query by passing department_id -- as an argument in the procedure call as shown in the following screenshot:

```
SQL> exec appendix.sql_injection('department_id -- ');
Query:select count(employee_id) from oehr_employees where department_id=department_id --  and salary > 2000
Count:106

PL/SQL procedure successfully completed.
```

So we see that a hacker can get a count of all the rows in the table when the procedure was developed to return the count of employees of a specific department whose salaries are greater than 2000. Now the attack can be more severe and a hacker can can get a lot of information. If the variable is concatenated in the select list then a hacker can comment the FROM clause and select from some data dictionary view and expose the entire database's security.

The solution is three fold:

1. Grant the access to sensitive tables very carefully.
2. Use bind variables instead of string concatenation. It will prevent you from SQL Injection attacks and reduce parse time.

   The Appendix.sql_injection_using_bind procedure uses bind variables to achieve the same result as appendix.sql_injection but it is more secure and returns an error when the user tries to pass department_id -- to it as shown in the following screenshots:.

```
SQL> exec appendix.sql_injection_using_bind(10);
Query:select count(employee_id) from oehr_employees where department_id= :pos_1 and salary > 2000
Count:1

PL/SQL procedure successfully completed.
```

```
SQL> exec appendix.sql_injection_using_bind('department_id -- ');
BEGIN appendix.sql_injection_using_bind('department_id -- '); END;

*
ERROR at line 1:
ORA-01722: invalid number
ORA-06512: at "PACKT_SCHEMA.APPENDIX", line 17
ORA-06512: at line 1
```

So, we see that it is not possible to manipulate the query string if we use bind variables.

3. Use `DBMS_ASSERT` package to validate the user input.

Assumption of formats and implicit conversions

The second type of SQL injection is when you assume certain formats and rely on implicit conversions. Please check the following link for information on this kind of SQL injection:

`http://tkyte.blogspot.in/2012/02/all-about-security-sql-injection.html`

Cross-site scripting

The following is a brief code to demonstrate the use same origin policy to call web services of a resource hosted in the same domain. The code requires some knowledge of OBIEE, but the intent is to show the same origin policy in action. OBIEE is discussed in detail in *Chapter 7, Integrating APEX with OBIEE*.

Have a look at the following screenshot. Note that the web server host is `localhost`, the server is operating on port `9704`, and the resource is `analytics`:

I have put the following JavaScript in the **Text Properties** textbox. Let me briefly describe the function of this code. Have a look at the highlighted line of code. An HTTP post call is made to a resource called `xmlpserver` which is hosted on the same server as the caller itself, that is, `localhost:9704`. Since the domain is the same, the call falls under the same domain policy. This policy is letting us access the web service of some other resource in the same domain using a client-side scripting language.

A hacker makes a similar request to access web resources from a different domain using similar client-side scripting as shown in the screenshot shared after the code.

```javascript
<script language="Javascript">
function XMLPWebserviceFunction ()
{
var xmlhttp = new XMLHttpRequest();
xmlhttp.open("POST", "http://localhost:9704/xmlpserver/services/
PublicReportService_v11",true);
xmlhttp.setRequestHeader("Content-Type","text/xml; charset=utf-8");
xmlhttp.setRequestHeader("SOAPAction","getFolderContents");
xmlhttp.onreadystatechange=function (){
        if (xmlhttp.readyState ==4 && xmlhttp.status == 200){
                var xmlDoc=xmlhttp.responseXML ;
                var Xml2String;
                if (xmlDoc.xml) {
                    Xml2String=xmlDoc.xml
                }else{
                    Xml2String= new XMLSerializer().
serializeToString(xmlDoc);
                }
                var msg= "RESPONSE HEADERS ********\n";
                msg+=xmlhttp.getAllResponseHeaders();
                msg+="Response here ******************\n";
                msg+= Xml2String;
                msg+="\nResponse ends here ***************";
                alert( msg );
        }
    }
var xml = '<soapenv:Envelope xmlns:soapenv="http://schemas.xmlsoap.
org/soap/envelope/" '
 + ' xmlns:pub="http://xmlns.oracle.com/oxp/service/v11/
PublicReportService" '
+ 'xmlns:pub1="http://xmlns.oracle.com/oxp/service/
PublicReportService"> <soapenv:Header/> '
+ ' <soapenv:Body> <pub:getFolderContents> '
```

```
+ ' <pub:folderAbsolutePath>/Marketing</pub:folderAbsolutePath> '
+ ' <pub:userID>Administrator</pub:userID>
<pub:password>Administrator</pub:password> '
+ '</pub:getFolderContents> </soapenv:Body> </soapenv:Envelope> ' ;
xmlhttp.send(xml);
}
</script>
<html>
  <head>
    <title>Web services</title>
  </head>
<form>
 <table>
    <tr>
      <td> <input value="Click for response" type="button" onclick=
"Javascript:XMLPWebserviceFunction();"></td>
    </tr>
 </table>
</form>
</body>
</html>
```

Let me share the result after the invocation of the previous client-side code. The screenshot shows the data returned by the WebService accessed using JavaScript. Note that this attack is done through scripting language and hits the web server unlike SQL Injection, which attacks the database directly.

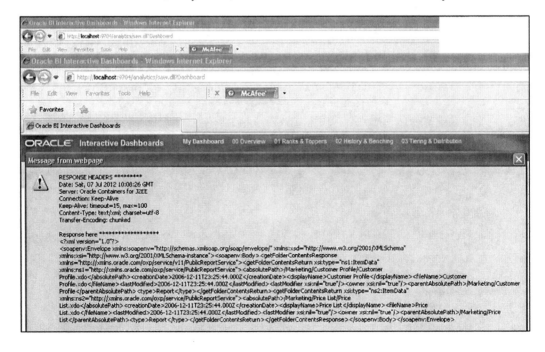

Database and web interaction in DAD and Listener configurations

This section is dedicated to the process of invocation of a stored PL/SQL function using DAD and APEX Listener. Let us first see the DAD configuration.

The DAD configuration

Let us try to recreate the fun of crafting APEX by making our own DAD and doing a few things with it. This will help us boost our understanding of the ins and outs of APEX. Make sure that you have set your XMLDB HTTP server to work on the port of your choice using `DBMS_XDB.sethttpport`. You will have to use this port and the IP address of your database server in all the URLs of this section. `<your_database_ip:<your_db_http_port>` will replace `localhost:8080` in the URLs of this section.

The code in `4-98-9_Appendix_create_dad.sql` creates and configures a DAD for you. The DAD you create is authorized to execute the procedures in the schema you mention in the `Enter the name of the schema with which you want to associate this DAD:` prompt. Execute the following using `sysdba`.

```
SQL> @4-98-9_Appendix_create_dad
```

I believe that you have compiled the `appendix` package in your schema. If not, then check the beginning of the *Appendix* to find to command to do this. Open the `Appendix` package and have a look at the `appendix.dad_proc` procedure.

Invoke the following URL. Here `packt_dad` is the name of the DAD which we just created:

```
http://localhost:8080/packt_dad/APPENDIX.DAD_PROC?val=Hello%20
World&redirect_url_var=http://www.google.com
```

We can also use the following URL:

```
http://localhost:8080/packt_dad/PACKT_SCHEMA.APPENDIX.DAD_
PROC?val=Hello%20World&redirect_url_var=http://www.google.com
```

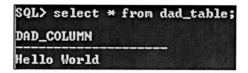

Invoking the previous URL opens the Google home page and inserts `Hello World` into the `dad_table`. The insertion is shown in the previous screenshot.

In this example, we saw the use of OWA package to do web interaction. We also saw insertions in the database. The best part was that both the web interaction and the database insertion were done by the same URL. This is pretty much what APEX does but it does it on a lot bigger scale.

The Listener configuration

We can call the same function in the Listener configuration by giving execute rights on this function to `APEX_PUBLIC_USER` and listing the function in the `defaults.xml` file of the Listener configuration. `Defaults.xml` can be found in the Listener's configuration directory. We can find the location of the Listener configuration directory by executing the following command:

```
C:\ >java -jar <Directory holding apex.war>\apex.war configdir
```

Add the following tag in the `defaults.xml` file and restart WebLogic:

```
<entry key="security.inclusionList"> apex, p, v, f, wwv_*,y*, c*,
PACKT_SCHEMA.*,packt_schema.*, apex_util.*</entry>
```

This will ensure that the procedures defined in `PACKT_SCHEMA` are directly accessible from the browser. If your schema name is different, then put the same instead of PACKT_SCHEMA in the previous code.

Execute the following using `sysdba`. This will ensure that `APEX_PUBLIC_USER` has execution rights on the `APPENDIX` package in `packt_schema`:

```
grant execute on packt_schema.appendix to apex_public_user;
```

The following link will open the Google home page and insert `Hello World` into `dad_table`:

```
http://<apex_listener_webserver>:<apex_listener_webserver_port>/
apex/PACKT_SCHEMA.APPENDIX.DAD_PROC?val=Hello%20World&redirect_url_
var=http://www.google.com
```

APEX behind the scenes

This section will help us see the entire flow of commands which are responsible for the generation of all pages in APEX. These commands flow from the Listener to the database.

Enabling auditing on the APEX_PUBLIC_USER schema

Perform the following for Enabling auditing on the APEX_PUBLIC_USER schema:

1. Log in to the database using sys and execute the following:

   ```
   SQL> @4-98-9_Appendix_enable_auditing
   ```

   The previous script enables the auditing and restarts the database, so you will have to restart WebLogic as well because the connection pool is destroyed by db restart.

2. Execute the following script now:

   ```
   SQL> @4-98-9_Appendix_check_calls_by_lsnr_2_web_toolkit
   ```

   This script contains a simple query on dba_audit_trial and it contains some SQLPLUS commands to format the output. The query shows the objects owned by sys which have been invoked in the last five minutes.

3. Now open your APEX workspace console.

   Since the console is also an APEX application, you will be able to see a lot of calls to HTP.P and OWA functions when you run the 4-98-9_Appendix_check_calls_by_lsnr_2_web_toolkit script again.

   In the output of the previous script, the client_id value in the output shown by the 4-98-9_Appendix_check_calls_by_lsnr_2_web_toolkit script is a combination of the user ID and the session ID of APEX.

Switching off the auditing

The following script should be executed using sydba to switch off the auditing:

```
SQL> @4-98-9_Appendix_disable_auditing
```

Index

Symbols

S

SAP crystal reports
  about 337
  integrating, with APEX 337-339
save report feature, IR actions menu 117
scan context 149
scatter chart 174
SDO_GEOM.SDO_DISTANCE
    function 350
search bar section, report attributes
    page 120
searched text
  highlighting, in report 59, 60
search functionality, IR 111
SECUREFILE LOB 368
segment space problems 374
select clause 51, 58
select columns feature, IR actions menu 112
select statement 76, 77
self-generated HTML charts 166, 167
sentry function 49
sequences
  using 361
server side image maps 186
session management, APEX URL
  about 31-33
  zero session ID 33, 34
Session State process 40
setFileName function 78, 83
SET_PARAMETER function 221
SGA result cache 373
short circuit evaluation 366
Single Sign On (SSO) 294
slider
  report, creating with 162, 163
  URL 163
Slider function 164
soft deletion
  implementing, with AJAX templates 88-91
  implementing, with APEX templates 88-91
sort
  enabling 53
sparkline reports
  creating 160, 161
sparklines class 160
sparkType attribute 162

SQL Access Advisor 375
SQL Injection
  about 45, 384
  dynamic SQL, with concatenated
    variables 384, 385
  formats assumptions 386
  implicit conversions 386
SQL monitoring 376
SQL Performance Analyzer 377
SQL Tuning Advisor 377, 378
SQL work areas 373
star transformation
  reference link 364
  using 364
stored function
  used, for downloading reports 85-87
strategy management, OBIEE 264
style attribute 178
subscription feature, IR actions menu 119
substitution variables
  used, for creating dynamic messages 71
  used, for labels 83
sum function 102
SYS_CONNECT_BY_PATH function 74
sys_context function 49
System Components 254

T

table authentication
  implementing 48, 49
table function 100
tables
  clustering 364, 365
table tag 57, 169
tabular form
  creating 95
  implementing 95
  item type, changing on user event 96-98
tag cloud
  about 193
  creating 193
TCPS dispatcher 15
td elements 57
td tags 57
template
  editing, for additional formatting 60, 61

Thank you for buying
Oracle APEX 4.2 Reporting

About Packt Publishing

Packt, pronounced 'packed', published its first book "Mastering phpMyAdmin for Effective MySQL Management" in April 2004 and subsequently continued to specialize in publishing highly focused books on specific technologies and solutions.

Our books and publications share the experiences of your fellow IT professionals in adapting and customizing today's systems, applications, and frameworks. Our solution based books give you the knowledge and power to customize the software and technologies you're using to get the job done. Packt books are more specific and less general than the IT books you have seen in the past. Our unique business model allows us to bring you more focused information, giving you more of what you need to know, and less of what you don't.

Packt is a modern, yet unique publishing company, which focuses on producing quality, cutting-edge books for communities of developers, administrators, and newbies alike. For more information, please visit our website: www.packtpub.com.

About Packt Enterprise

In 2010, Packt launched two new brands, Packt Enterprise and Packt Open Source, in order to continue its focus on specialization. This book is part of the Packt Enterprise brand, home to books published on enterprise software – software created by major vendors, including (but not limited to) IBM, Microsoft and Oracle, often for use in other corporations. Its titles will offer information relevant to a range of users of this software, including administrators, developers, architects, and end users.

Writing for Packt

We welcome all inquiries from people who are interested in authoring. Book proposals should be sent to author@packtpub.com. If your book idea is still at an early stage and you would like to discuss it first before writing a formal book proposal, contact us; one of our commissioning editors will get in touch with you.

We're not just looking for published authors; if you have strong technical skills but no writing experience, our experienced editors can help you develop a writing career, or simply get some additional reward for your expertise.

Oracle APEX Best Practices

ISBN: 978-1-849684-00-2   Paperback: 298 pages

Accentuate Oracle APEX development with proven best practices

1. Oracle APEX Best Practices will get you started with Oracle APEX for developing real-world applications that perform and maximize the full potential of Oracle APEX

2. You will also learn to take advantage of advanced SQL and PL/SQL along the way

3. Combines the knowledge of Oracle Apex Experts -- Alex Nuijten, Iloon Ellen-Wollf, and Learco Brizzi

4. Setting up your environment and getting ready for developing applications

Oracle Database XE 11gR2 Jump Start Guide

ISBN: 978-1-849686-74-7   Paperback: 146 pages

Build and manage your Oracle Database 11g XE environment with this fast paced, practical guide

1. Install and configure Oracle Database XE on Windows and Linux

2. Develop database applications using Oracle Application Express

3. Back up, restore, and tune your database

4. Includes clear step-by-step instructions and examples

Please check **www.PacktPub.com** for information on our titles

Oracle Application Integration Architecture (AIA) Foundation Pack 11gR1: Essentials

ISBN: 978-1-849684-80-4   Paperback: 274 pages

Develop and deploy your Enterprise Integration Solutions using Oracle AIA

Oracle Application Integration Architecture (AIA) Foundation Pack 11gR1: Essentials

Develop and deploy your Enterprise Integration Solutions using Oracle AIA

Hariharan V. Ganesarethinam

[PACKT] enterprise

1. Full of illustrations, diagrams, and tips with clear step-by-step instructions and real time examples to develop full-fledged integration processes.

2. Each chapter drives the reader right from architecture to implementation.

3. Understand the important concept of Enterprise Business Objects that play a crucial role in AIA installation and models.

Governance, Risk, and Compliance Handbook for Oracle Applications

ISBN: 978-1-849681-70-4   Paperback: 488 pages

Written by industry experts with more than 30 years combined experience, this handbook covers all the major aspects of Governance, Risk, and Compliance management in your organization

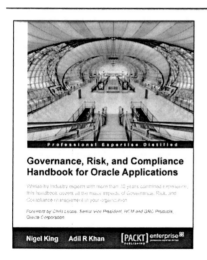

Governance, Risk, and Compliance Handbook for Oracle Applications

Written by industry experts with more than 30 years combined experience, this handbook covers all the major aspects of Governance, Risk, and Compliance management at your organization.

Foreword by Chris Leone, Senior Vice President, HCM and GRC Products, Oracle Corporation

Nigel King   Adil R Khan

[PACKT] enterprise

1. Risk Management: Creating a risk management program, performing risk assessment and control verification, and more

2. To maximize real world learning, the book is built around a fictional company establishing its governance processes

3. Written by industry experts with more than 30 years combined experience

Please check **www.PacktPub.com** for information on our titles

CPSIA information can be obtained at www.ICGtesting.com
Printed in the USA
LVOW09s2353010416

481869LV00019B/235/P

9 781849 684989